PUBLIC SPECTACLES OF VIOLENCE

PUBLIC

SENSATIONAL CINEMA and JOURNALISM

SPECTACLES

in EARLY TWENTIETH-CENTURY

OF VIOLENCE

MEXICO and BRAZIL

Rielle Navitski

Duke University Press

Durham and London   2017

© 2017 Duke University Press
All rights reserved
Printed in the United States of America on acid-free paper ∞
Designed by Heather Hensley
Typeset in Garamond Premier Pro by Westchester Publishing Services

Library of Congress Cataloging-in-Publication Data
Names: Navitski, Rielle, author.
Title: Public spectacles of violence : sensational cinema and journalism
in early twentieth-century Mexico and Brazil / Rielle Navitski.
Description: Durham : Duke University Press, 2017. | Includes bibliographical
references and index.
Identifiers: LCCN 2016054235 (print)
LCCN 2017001028 (ebook)
ISBN 9780822369639 (hardcover : alk. paper)
ISBN 9780822369752 (pbk. : alk. paper)
ISBN 9780822372899 (e-book)
Subjects: LCSH: Motion pictures—Mexico—History—20th century. |
Motion pictures—Brazil—History—20th century. | Sensationalism in
motion pictures. | Violence in motion pictures.
Classification: LCC PN1993.5.M6 N385 2017 (print) | LCC PN1993.5.M6
(ebook) | DDC 791.43097209/04—dc23
LC record available at https://lccn.loc.gov/2016054235

Cover art: Execution scene from *El automóvil gris*.

For my family

CONTENTS

A NOTE ON USAGE

All translations from Spanish and Portuguese, except where otherwise noted, are my own. For purposes of consistency, Portuguese spellings have been modernized in conformity with the Portuguese Language Orthographic Agreement of 1990, enacted in 2009.

Films mentioned in the text have been attributed to individuals rather than production companies. Although the figure of the film director did not exist as such in many of the contexts analyzed herein, production companies were highly precarious, so I have preferred to cite the individuals involved and clarify their roles, where possible, in the body of the text.

ACKNOWLEDGMENTS

The research and writing of this book were made possible by generous support from the Institute for International Education, the Graduate Division of the University of California, Berkeley, and the Willson Center for Humanities and Arts at the University of Georgia.

I am deeply indebted to archivists and librarians in Mexico and Brazil for facilitating access to materials and permissions to reproduce images. I would like to express my gratitude to the staffs of the following archives and libraries: the Archivo General de la Nación, Biblioteca Miguel Lerdo de Tejada, Biblioteca Nacional and Hemeroteca Nacional, Cineteca Nacional, and Filmoteca de la Universidad Nacional Autónoma de México (special thanks to Antonia Rojas Ávila, Nahún Calleros Carriles, and Víctor Manuel Romero Cervantes) in Mexico City; the Arquivo Geral da Cidade do Rio de Janeiro, Arquivo Nacional, Biblioteca Nacional (special thanks to Bruno Brasil for assistance with copyright matters), and Museu da Imagem e do Som in Rio de Janeiro; the Cinemateca Brasileira in São Paulo; and the Fundação Joaquim Nabuco in Recife. For assistance with and permission to reproduce images, I thank the staffs of the New York Public Library and the Nettie Lee Benson Latin American Collection at the University of Texas at Austin. (special thanks to Michael O. Hironymous, Juan Felipe Leal, and Blanca Sánchez of Juan Pablos Editor.) Thanks are also due to the efficient staff of the Interlibrary Loan Department at the University of Georgia.

This book began its life as a Ph.D. dissertation completed in the Department of Film and Media at the University of California, Berkeley. I am deeply grateful to my dissertation chair, Kristen Whissel, for her intellectual sharpness, generosity, and unwavering support in all areas of my professional development, as well as to my committee members Natalia Brizuela (who first encouraged me to study Brazil), Mary Ann Doane, and Mark Sandberg for their invaluable guidance and insightful feedback. I was fortunate to study with many other distinguished thinkers at Berkeley beyond my committee; among them, the scholarship and pedagogy of Jennifer M. Bean, Anton Kaes, Francine Masiello, Candace Slater, and Linda Williams played an especially significant role in the development of this project. I would also like to express my thanks to the Society of Cinema and Media Studies Dissertation Award committee and the participants in the Visual Cultures Working Group at Berkeley.

Portions of chapter 1 were published in an earlier form as "Spectacles of Violence and Politics: *El automóvil gris* (1919) and Revolutionary Mexico's Sensational Visual Culture," *Journal of Latin American Cultural Studies* 23, no. 2 (2014): 133–52.

Earlier versions of parts of this work were presented at the Society for Cinema and Media Studies conference, the Latin American Studies Association International Congress, the Seminar on the Origins and History of Cinema at the Museu del Cinema in Girona, Spain, Domitor, the Jornada Brasileira de Cinema Silencioso, the International Berkeley Conference on Silent Cinema, the Cinematic Times Symposium at the University of California, Berkeley, and the Congreso del Instituto Internacional de Literatura Iberoamericana. I am grateful to audience members and fellow panelists for their feedback.

I am truly fortunate to be working with Duke University Press and with senior editor Courtney Berger. Her guidance, enthusiasm, and faith in this project have been transformative. I am deeply grateful to the manuscript's two anonymous readers for their thoughtful, detailed, and extremely useful comments. I would also like to thank editorial assistant Sandra Korn and project manager Danielle Houtz for their dedication.

Archival research abroad involves considerable logistical, intellectual, and emotional challenges, and I am deeply appreciative of the researchers based in Brazil and Mexico who helped guide me through these challenges. I thank Misha Maclaird for helping launch me on my first research trip to Mexico City, in 2008, and for her hospitality on recent visits. David M. J. Wood, Itzia Fernández, and Adilson Mendes were instrumental in helping me build connections with other researchers and institutions in Mexico City and São Paulo. Fabiana Díaz, Hernani Heffner, Pedro Lapera, Sheila Schvarzman, Carlos Roberto de Souza, and Esperanza Vázquez Bernal generously took time to share their knowledge and expertise, and Paulo Carneiro da Cunha

Filho made me the kind gift of a copy of his recently published book. Ronaldo Correia de Brito enlisted members of Recife's intellectual and artistic circles on behalf of my research, and he, Avelina Brandão, and Isabel Correia Brandão welcomed me into their home at a moment when I felt lost. I will always remember their kindness. Luciana Corrêa de Araújo and Rafael de Luna Freire shaped this book by sharing their own meticulous historical research, reading work in progress, and providing enormously helpful suggestions and sources, and have become valued friends. I am grateful for the camaraderie of fellow researchers Katherine Brodbeck, Leonardo Cardoso, Anne Megan Daniels, Evan Farr, Danny Gough, Aialä Levy, Sara Anne Potter, and Lena Suk during my time abroad (and beyond), as well as to Claudia Paz, Vanya Tsutsui, Oswaldo Mejía Mendiola, Patricia Méndez Obregón, Sonia de Otto, and Diana Restrepo Restrepo for their friendship.

This book took on its current form in the Department of Theatre and Film Studies at the University of Georgia. Fellow writing-group members Jonathan Baillehache, Shira Chess, Emily Sahakian, and Frans Weiser provided invaluable feedback and motivation that helped move this project forward. I also want to thank Antje Ascheid, Marla Carlson, Amma Y. Ghartey-Tagoe Kootin, Richard Neupert, David Saltz, and Christopher Sieving for their encouragement and support; I am particularly indebted to Richard for his extensive help with illustrations. I am also grateful for the work of the Latin American and Caribbean Studies Institute and its director, Richard Gordon. The friendship of Mark Anderson, María-Alejandra Calva, Khédija Gadhoum, Miriam Jacobson, Pablo Lapegna, Ari Lieberman, Cecilia Rodrigues, Roberta Salmi, Paola de Santo, Alberto Villate Isaza, and Ilya Winham has greatly enriched life in Athens.

I was fortunate to encounter a supportive intellectual community in graduate school, including Robert Alford, Juan Caballero, Emily Carpenter, Alenda Chang, Paul Dobryden, Robin Ellis, Patrick Ellis, Kris Fallon, Muna Güvenç, Laura Horak, Jen Malkowski, Dolores McElroy, Simon Porzak, Jennifer Pranolo, Alisa Sánchez, Maria Vendetti, and Damon Young. Juan Sebastián Ospina León's dedication to the study of Latin American silent film has made him an especially valued interlocutor, as well as a dear friend. I am grateful to a broader community of scholars, including Jerónimo Arellano, Luisela Alvaray, Gilberto Blasini, Giorgio Bertellini, Jason Borge, Andrea Cuarterolo, Maria Chiara D'Argenio, Aurelio de los Reyes, Tamara Falicov, Annie Fee, Allyson Nadia Field, Colin Gunckel, Tom Gunning, Margaret Hennefeld, Brian R. Jacobson, Anupama Kapse, Dona Kercher, Ana M. López, Leslie

Marsh, Nicolas Poppe, Yeidy Rivero, Irene Rozsa, Ignacio Sánchez Prado, Laura Isabel Serna, Kim Tomadjoglou, Sarah J. Townsend, João Luiz Vieira, Sarah Ann Wells, and Tami Williams, for encouragement, suggestions, and stimulating exchanges. Xiaojue Hu, Emily Stoddard, and Daniela Tijerina Benner have been treasured friends for more than a decade now, and I continue to rely on their support.

My family has made my intellectual pursuits possible and kept me afloat during trying times. My sister, Alanna Navitski, has given me a more inclusive and humane understanding of what it means to be an educator. My father, Al Navitski, helped instill a passion for the past and for reading with his devotion to breathing life into forgotten books by uniting them with new audiences. My mother, Regina Edmonds, embodies the model of a scholar deeply committed to bettering the lives of those around her through empathy and compassion; her influence is felt on each page of this book.

My life took a turn I never expected the day I met José Guadalupe Vázquez Zavala. His presence has opened up worlds previously unknown to me, and his energy, generous spirit, and support have kept me moving *puro pa' delante*.

INTRODUCTION

Films that restaged public spectacles of real-life violence became the first popular successes of both Mexican and Brazilian cinema. In 1908, *Os estranguladores* (*The Stranglers*), a filmed reenactment of a robbery and murder in Rio de Janeiro's Italian immigrant community that is considered Brazil's first feature, was advertised as screening more than 830 times over three months.[1] Produced by the exhibitor and cameraman Antônio Leal to capitalize on sensational newspaper coverage and theatrical productions based on the case, *Os estranguladores* triggered a local craze for screen adaptations of real-life crimes. These early experiments with narrative films based on topical events exemplified the significant if short-lived success of local film production in Rio de Janeiro and São Paulo between 1908 and 1911. Through the teens and twenties, sensational subjects ranging from infamous criminal cases to railway accidents figured prominently in efforts to establish film production in Brazil's fastest-growing cities, as well as in regional capitals and even small towns, where the effects of modernization were slow to materialize.

More than a decade after the premiere of *Os estranguladores*, veteran Mexican cameraman Enrique Rosas produced *El automóvil gris* (*The Grey Automobile*, 1919), a multi-episode serial film that became one of Mexican cinema's earliest box-office hits. *El automóvil gris*, like *Os estranguladores*, was an early experiment with narrative film in its country of production, as Mexican cinema was dominated by nonfiction films that documented the events of the Revolution between 1910 and 1917. Building on investigative newspaper reports,

El automóvil gris made use of real-life locations and participants in its re-construction of acts of robbery, kidnapping, and murder attributed to "The Grey Automobile Gang," a criminal group with murky links to high-ranking military officers. Skillfully adapting the conventions of popular French and American serial films, *El automóvil gris* reportedly attracted 40,233 spectators in Mexico City in a single day and went on to break box-office records outside the capital.[2] Whereas *El automóvil gris* highlighted a revolutionary-era crisis of state authority that blurred the distinction between military and criminal violence, by the early 1920s, the production of adventure films in rural settings intersected with emerging currents of postrevolutionary nationalism. Fram-ing film production as a sign of national progress, early film critics fostered ambitions for a uniquely Mexican cinema that nevertheless drew heavily on the codes of imported film genres (such as crime films and westerns) and formats (particularly sensational serial films).

The enthusiastic reception of *Os estranguladores* and *El automóvil gris* sig-nals the pivotal role of sensational subjects in the development of film pro-duction and the expansion of mass culture in Mexico and Brazil between 1900 and 1930, a moment of accelerated industrialization and urbanization. Through an examination of the sensational visual cultures of early twentieth-century Mexico and Brazil, I contend in this volume that the sensational mode is uniquely revealing of the transformation of quotidian experience and pub-lic life under capitalist modernity, particularly in Latin American contexts, where modernization has often accentuated profound social divides. Popular sensationalism—which I define as cultural forms that elicit powerful sensu-ous, emotional, and moral responses, that provoke intense public interest by referencing topical events and pressing social problems, and that are dis-seminated on a wide scale—is a product of the modern era. Like the distinct but often overlapping mode of melodrama, it dramatizes dominant moral values and their transgression in a post-sacred era, resonating with the social and perceptual transformations accompanying modernization.[3] Mexico and Brazil both experienced rapid change in the late nineteenth and early twen-tieth centuries, as their economies were increasingly integrated into global circuits of trade and finance capital, railway networks spread across national territory, and the population of major cities expanded. Yet popular sensa-tionalism gave expression not to a wholesale liquidation of premodern social organization and experiences of time and space, but rather to a "multitem-poral heterogeneity" marked by the coexistence of modernity and tradition and the persistence of profound social inequality alongside liberal ideals and democratizing impulses.[4]

In the first three decades of the twentieth century, both countries faced low literacy rates (22 percent in Mexico and 31 percent in Brazil in 1900), high urban crime rates, and outbreaks of internal armed conflict.[5] In these social conditions, visual depictions of violence became the focus of intense public interest, contributing to the expansion of mass culture. Although there was very little direct contact between the two nations' film cultures in the first three decades of the twentieth century, Mexico and Brazil shared complex experiences of modernization as triumphant in some geographic locations and elusive in others, and as both accelerated and delayed relative to the trajectories of development that had made nations like the United States and Great Britain industrial powers.

At the end of the nineteenth century, Mexico and Brazil possessed Latin America's two most highly industrialized economies.[6] By the late 1930s, they boasted two of the region's most robust culture industries. Following the transition to sound cinema at the end of the 1920s, Mexico and Brazil, together with Argentina, became the region's most prolific film-producing countries, as popular films capitalized on the musical genres of the Brazilian samba and Mexican *ranchera*. Together with the Argentine tango, these popular rhythms were increasingly viewed as sonic expressions of national cultures imagined as unified.[7] In Argentina, silent films had enjoyed some success in forging cinematic icons of the nation that conquered domestic and even some international markets, most notably the heroic gaucho of *Nobleza gaucha* (*Gaucho Nobility*, Humberto Cairo, Ernesto Gunche, and Eduardo Martínez de la Pera), which screened not only in Buenos Aires, but also in Barcelona, Lima, Rio de Janeiro, and Santiago.[8] *Nobleza gaucha* juxtaposed scenes of rural life with images of a modernizing Buenos Aires, whose urban spaces were reimagined as territories defined by immigrant and class identities in the silent films of José Agustín "El Negro" Ferreyra and others.[9] In Mexico and Brazil, by contrast, silent-era "foundational fictions" and other overtly nationalistic narratives found comparatively little commercial success. The two nations' early film cultures thus cannot be fully explained using the framework of the national cinema, which has been critiqued in recent decades.[10] Although domestic productions were often called "national films" in both countries during the period under study, they must be interpreted in the light of the global circulation and local reception of forms of mass culture produced in highly industrialized countries. In particular, I trace sensational cinema's dialogues with French and American sensational journalism, popular detective fiction, and suspenseful serial films, as well as melodramatic forms (particularly serial literature and popular theater) specific to local and national contexts.

In *Public Spectacles of Violence* I read Mexico and Brazil's sensational silent-era cinema through its close relationship with print culture—graphically illustrated police reportage, serial literature, and fan magazines—in order to demonstrate how early twentieth-century visual culture in the two nations addressed experiences of modernization and novel forms of public life that were shaped by pervasive violence. To use Guy Debord's terms, public spectacles of violence constituted "a social relation among people, mediated by images."[11] I develop my analysis through close readings of surviving films, partial reconstructions of lost works from press accounts and archival sources, and attention to the reception of sensational genres, which influenced film production as well as debates about cinema's social effects and unique qualities as a medium. My analysis at once builds on and shifts direction from previous critical studies of the impact of cinema and photography in Mexico and Brazil, which tend to place literary production, and modernist writing in particular, at the center of their inquiry.[12] Instead, I recuperate the ephemeral artifacts of popular visual culture.

Exploring cinema's role in the emergence of mass media in two rapidly modernizing and highly stratified societies, I chart intersections between local experiences of modernization and emerging configurations of "international-popular culture." (These intersections, of course, are not limited to sensational cinema, but encompass a wide range of films that addressed local, regional, and national experiences of modernization, from actualities, travelogues, and promotional films, to narrative films that adapted literary classics or events from national history.) Formulated by Monica Dall'Asta to address the "repetitions, imitations, and cross-breedings" between U.S. film producers and their European rivals in the 1910s, the term "international-popular culture" refers specifically to the capacity of serial cinema to perpetuate itself across national borders.[13] As in the case of the Italian serials analyzed by Dall'Asta, the forms of international-popular culture that emerged from encounters between Mexican and Brazilian publics and imported films were marked by clear power differentials. Film exports from Mexico and Brazil to the United States were rare in the period, although they did exist. The exchanges that defined international-popular culture were often indirect, mediated by a process that Paul Schroeder-Rodríguez calls "triangulation." He notes that Latin American silent-film producers navigated between multiple reference points—the cinemas of major film-exporting nations (particularly the United States, France, and Italy) and emerging conceptions of national culture marked by exclusionary notions of citizenship.[14] Informed by these dynamics, the cinemas of early twentieth-century Mexico and Brazil gave expression to accelerated modernization in societies marked by regional, ethnic, and class divides.

Tracing parallel trajectories in the visual cultures of Mexico and Brazil, I develop a comparative analysis across its two national case studies. I begin with the Mexican case, which to some extent rewards analysis through a conventional national cinema framework. As I detail below, the Mexican Revolution (1910–1920) fostered the development of a sensational visual culture, and postrevolutionary nationalism actively shaped film production of the 1920s. In the book's second half, I turn to the Brazilian context, which demands close attention to the local and regional scales. Whereas in Mexico filmmaking was concentrated in the capital—though there was significant regional production as well, notably in the states of Yucatán and Veracruz—in Brazil filmmaking activities emerged in multiple cities and towns, none of which managed to dominate or centralize the nation's production during the first three decades of the twentieth century.[15]

In part I, I trace the reception and production of sensational film genres and their print intertexts in early twentieth-century Mexico, reading narrative films made between 1919 and 1927 alongside forms of visual culture that date from the turn of the century, while in part II, I chart parallel developments in Brazilian film production between 1906 and 1930. The differences in these chronologies signal the impact of historical events on the development of narrative film language in the two countries. Sensational subjects loomed large in local efforts to win popular success for Mexican productions following a turn to narrative film in the wake of the Revolution. In particular, they intersected with a vogue for serial films that was closely linked with Hollywood studios' aggressive expansion into Mexico in the late teens, extending the dominance of foreign markets achieved during the First World War, which hampered the production and export of European cinemas.[16] Conversely, reconstructions of real-life crimes played a key role in the development of complex narrative films in Brazil beginning in the first decade of the twentieth century, prior to abortive experiments with the production of serials in the late teens. By the 1920s, fictional spectacles of violence—ranging from physical combat to technological disaster—were cultivated widely in both Mexican and Brazilian cinemas.

Across the book's two parts, I identify two principal modes of staging cinematic spectacles of violence. Beginning in the first decade of the twentieth century and continuing through the late 1920s, what I call "violent actualities" both recorded and reconstructed real-life incidents of violence. Incorporating production practices like location shooting, reenactment, and onscreen appearances by participants in the events, these films adopted an ambiguous relationship to topical happenings that recalls the mode of actuality filmmaking prevalent in cinema's earliest years, which encompassed both unstaged and staged footage. Testifying to cinema's unique ability to capture—or to convincingly fake—acts of violence, violent actualities reenacted unpredictable events that escaped the camera's lens. As I explore in chapters 1 and 3, films produced in Mexico City, Rio de Janeiro, and São Paulo between 1906 and 1922 framed real-life criminal acts as signs of the industrial modernity embodied by metropolises like Paris, London, and New York.

Beginning in the late teens and early twenties, the production of what I refer to as "sensational fictions" in Mexico and Brazil offered film audiences wholly fictional spectacles of death, bodily peril, and technological catastrophe. As I show in the study of the reception and production of crime films in Rio de Janeiro in chapter 4, sensational fictions initially capitalized on the popularity of imported serials and their novelizations, published in installments in local newspapers. Sensational adventure melodramas—an expansive term I use to refer to crime and adventure serials and westerns of varying lengths and formats, which were often grouped together by local critics and fans—were considered outdated in Brazil's major cities by the early 1920s. Yet they continued to be exhibited widely in second-run neighborhood movie theaters and more remote locations. Their conventions proved particularly fruitful for filmmakers working outside metropolitan areas in both Mexico and Brazil, where the hyperkinetic physical action and special effects of westerns and crime and adventure serials were perceived as uniquely cinematic. Adventure melodramas offered models of cost-effective forms of film production that allowed filmmakers to showcase local landscapes.

As I argue in chapters 2 and 5, in both Mexico and Brazil sensational fictions played a prominent role in films made outside major cities, which framed their sites of production as modern communities and offered film enthusiasts the thrill of an encounter with modern visual technologies. Referring to Colombian cinema of the 1920s, Juana Suárez observes that being captured by the camera was part of the appeal for participants in regional production: "Film, in this sense, was not used only to record modernity but to produce it."[17] Drawing on narrative models from imported cinema to (re)stage topical events and display local spaces, violent actualities and sensational fictions were seen as quintessentially modern and cinematic, and figured prominently in early efforts at narrative filmmaking across Latin America and beyond.[18]

Although distinctions between fiction and nonfiction remained somewhat fluid even after the consolidation of continuity editing codes in Hollywood cinema around 1915, unusual combinations of narrative film language with elements of documentation appear in the silent cinemas of Mexico and Brazil. Repurposed actuality footage and images of local landscapes cultivated a "view aesthetic," "capturing and preserving a look or vantage point" on a locale or event not specifically prepared for filming.[19] Although they often fulfilled narrative functions, these elements also held the potential to function as semiautonomous attractions for spectators.[20] Elements of visual documentation—including location shooting and reenactment—were highlighted in publicity discourses, suggesting their special appeal for spectators. Articulations of fictional and nonfictional conventions thus register the process by which internationally dominant cinematic codes were reformulated in the staging of local modernities. Conceptions of genres developed in major film-exporting countries were reconfigured through their audience and critical reception and in the production of films that drew selectively on their semantic and syntactic elements (that is, aspects of plot, setting, and costuming associated with a particular genre, and underlying narrative structures and thematic oppositions).[21] In Mexico and Brazil, sensational cinema emerged in dialogue with understandings of film genres developed elsewhere and reflected locally specific conceptions of the ontology of the moving image, its relationship to the real, and its ability to capture the present.

The extant and lost films I analyze in this book share their drive to document and display local spaces, and to create a sense of timeliness and eventfulness, with an expanding illustrated press. Throughout the book, I examine the intersection between sensational cinema and print culture, tracing a shift from cinema's position as an element of highly intermedial visual and entertainment cultures, to the popularization of serial films in close connection with serial literature, to the emergence of specialized discourses on cinema in newspapers and magazines as the fiction feature became increasingly dominant.[22] In chapters 1 and 3, I analyze the print intertexts of violent actualities, particularly the illustrated police blotter, whose narrative uses of photography overlapped with early cinema in Mexico, Brazil, and elsewhere, as Andrea Cuarterolo has shown in the case of Argentina.[23] Even as major film-exporting countries shifted from the presentational thrills of a "cinema of attractions" toward "classical" forms of narrative illusionism, spectacles of physical violence and peril continued to offer pleasurable forms of thrilling realism.[24] By the mid-1910s, as imported serial films gained popularity with audiences, the practice of publishing tie-in novelizations in local newspapers in Brazil gave rise to forms of fan consumption across media that fueled the production of locally made serial films and fictional narratives, practices that reconfigured elements of international-popular culture produced abroad for local uses. While tie-in novelizations never became widely popular in Mexico, critics interpreted serial films through the lens of the serial novel (*folletín*). Close connections between cinema and the popular press emerged partly in response to the obstacles facing film production: producers evoked existing forms of sensational print culture to appeal to local audiences, and critics presented filmmaking itself as a newsworthy public spectacle. In chapters 2, 4, and 5, I examine how the reception and production of sensational fictions shaped early film criticism, discussions of cinema's specificity as a medium, and debates about the genres and strategies that should be adopted in national film production.

By the early 1920s, emerging forms of film criticism and fan culture in Mexico and Brazil increasingly framed film production as an indicator of modernity (whether national, regional, or local). Press discourses arguably had a greater public impact than the films themselves, which often received a lukewarm reception from spectators, and in the case of regional productions in particular, had difficulties reaching a wide audience. Laura Isabel Serna argues that in the Mexican case, the novel social practices surrounding the local reception of Hollywood films, including moviegoing, fan culture, and criticism, had a potentially greater impact than the small number of domestically produced films.[25] By contrast, I emphasize the discursive—if not the economic—significance of Mexican film production as mediated by the illustrated press.

The rationale for employing an intermedial approach in this book is twofold, responding both to these intimate links between cinema and the illustrated press, and to the dismal survival rate of silent films from Mexico and Brazil.[26] While the scope of this study is shaped by a desire to address those films that have survived, it also responds to a growing body of scholarship that takes the absence of film texts as potentially generative, building on the influential work of Giuliana Bruno.[27] In her recent study of "uplift cinema" at the Hampton and Tuskegee Institutes, Allyson Nadia Field emphasizes "the presence of absence," stressing the need to grapple with both gaps and significant traces in the archive.[28] Writing in the context of early twentieth-century Japan, Aaron Gerow affirms the value of a "discursive history" of cinema's cultural field of reception. He argues that the loss of nearly all pre-1925 Japanese films prompts a productive break with textual and auteurist approaches, focusing attention on the constitutive force of discourse in contexts of cultural exchange.[29] Rather than recuperating lost films as evidence of a national cinema that asserts itself against the dominance of imported film (particularly Hollywood), this study reads the sensational cinemas of early twentieth-century Mexico and Brazil through their intertexts in print culture and popular entertainment, examining local horizons of film reception and production alongside region-wide affinities and international exchanges.

National Modernities, International-Popular Culture

The parallel trajectories of silent film cultures in Mexico and Brazil are particularly striking if we consider the two nations' divergent paths of historical development. Mexico, like most present-day Latin American nations, is a product of an independence movement triggered by the Napoleonic invasion of Spain. The forced abdication of the Bourbon monarch Carlos IV and the installation of Joseph Bonaparte on the Spanish throne in 1808 weakened the legitimacy of the colonial government, favoring a shift towards greater local autonomy that culminated in the declaration of Mexico's independence in 1810, achieved in 1821 after more than a decade of conflict. Internal conflicts between liberals and conservatives (The War of the Reform, 1858–1861) and foreign wars and interventions (including the Mexican-American War of 1846–1848 that resulted in the loss of over half of Mexico's territory and the French Intervention of 1862–1867) hampered the development of a strong nation-state prior to the regime of Porfirio Díaz (1876–1911).[30] Seizing power in the Tuxtepec Rebellion, Díaz went on to serve as president for over three decades, enacting an aggressive program of political centralization alongside industrialization and modernization projects fueled largely by foreign capital.

Brazil's historical trajectory is more unusual within the Latin American context. A monarchy for much of the nineteenth century, Brazil became the seat of the Portuguese empire when the royal family fled from an invasion by Napoleonic forces in 1807 to establish its court in the New World. In 1820, liberals in favor of a limited monarchy triumphed in Portugal, demanded the return of João VI and later his son Pedro I, and moved to restore Brazil to its status as a colony. Instead, Pedro I declared Brazil an independent empire in 1822. By the final quarter of the nineteenth century, internal political divisions linked to the abolitionist movement had weakened the empire. Shortly after the 1888 "Golden Law" emancipated enslaved Brazilians, a largely bloodless 1889 coup against the aging Pedro II, led by Manuel Deodoro da Fonseca, resulted in the proclamation of the First Republic. Although the coming of the republic held out the promise of increased political power for social sectors outside the traditional agrarian elite (access to the vote had been progressively restricted under the empire), in practice the full exercise of citizenship in Republican Brazil was sharply limited along racial, class, and regional lines.

In Mexico, social unrest generated by economic inequality and labor repression, among other factors, erupted into civil war in 1910. Campaigns against the reelection of Díaz, who triumphed over Francisco I. Madero with obviously fraudulent poll results, tapped into discontent fueled by the regime's anti-democratic methods and the destabilizing effects of its programs of capitalist modernization. Díaz's policies had heavily favored foreign interests (while also benefiting Mexican industry) and contributed to the widespread dismantling of communal forms of social organization and economic production. Military victories by revolutionary forces under Pascual Orozco helped ensure the elections that brought Madero to power in 1911, but he failed to deliver sweeping social reforms. Madero was overthrown and then assassinated on the orders of his former military commander Victoriano Huerta during the 1913 counterrevolution known as the Decena Trágica (Tragic Ten Days). After Huerta was deposed, bitter rivalries between military factions persisted, with the moderate Constitutionalists, including Venustiano Carranza and Álvaro Obregón, ultimately prevailing over Emiliano Zapata and Pancho Villa, who advocated more radical agrarian and social reform.[31]

Although Brazil did not experience military conflict approaching the scale of the Mexican Revolution in the early twentieth century, the First Republic witnessed a series of revolts that "brought into sharp relief the latent violence in defining state authority, citizenship, and racial power under republicanism."[32] In the Canudos War of 1896–1897, the government waged a bloody military campaign against a millenarian religious community led by Antônio Conselheiro in the interior of the state of Bahía, viewed as a threat to the state's authority. In the 1904 Revolt of the Vaccine, Rio de Janeiro's working classes violently protested obligatory public health measures and, implicitly, the modernization programs that increasingly pushed them to the margins of the capital city. In the wake of rebellions against the government led by army lieutenants (*tenentes*) in Rio de Janeiro in 1922 and in São Paulo in 1924, and at a moment of economic crisis, the republic fell in a military coup that brought the populist leader Getúlio Vargas to power in 1930.

In the first three decades of the twentieth century, modernity's promised benefits failed to materialize for most of Mexico's and Brazil's citizens, as traditional landowning elites continued to enjoy disproportionate wealth and influence. The embrace of liberalism in both nations was belied by a political culture that favored loyalty less to state institutions than to charismatic leaders who often relied on physical force. Referred to as *caudillos* or *caciques* in Mexico and *coronéis* in Brazil, these figures were linked to clientelistic political networks that spanned the municipal, regional, and national levels.[33] As modernization outpaced democratization, elites initiated programs of social reform designed to institute "order and progress" by aggressively combating alcoholism, criminality, and disease. Emerging state institutions exercised expanded forms of social control without addressing the profound social inequalities that contributed to these ills.

Economic disparities frequently took on spatial dimensions in Mexico and Brazil's rapidly modernizing metropolises. Early twentieth-century urban reforms intended to beautify Mexico City, Rio de Janeiro, and São Paulo, among other cities, worked to widen divides between social classes and city neighborhoods.[34] At the same time, economic growth, driven by the export of mineral resources from Mexico and agricultural products from both nations, tended to increase disparities between geographic regions. In particular, northern Mexico (with its close connections to the U.S. economy) and southeastern Brazil (where the then capital Rio de Janeiro and the industrial powerhouse São Paulo were located) prospered, while economic growth stagnated in other regions, most notably Brazil's northeast.

In early twentieth-century Mexico and Brazil, sensational cinema and journalism at once highlighted and tentatively bridged these social and spatial divides, working to forge a mass public through the use of novel visual and print technologies. With the introduction of the rotary press and the halftone printing process that permitted the direct reproduction of photographs, illustrated newspapers like Mexico City's state-subsidized *El Imparcial* and Rio de Janeiro's *Gazeta de Notícias* achieved unprecedented circulation levels in the late nineteenth and early twentieth century.[35] Working to extend the reach of an emergent mass culture to illiterate consumers, sensational cinema and journalism forged public spheres premised on the collective consumption of spectacles of violence. In his discussion of public spheres in Latin

America—which he argues must be understood through reference to Gramscian notions of hegemony as well as Habermas's model of the bourgeois public sphere—Pablo Piccato argues for "the central role of violence in the construction of Latin American polities," observing "the expressive function of violence [as] part of discursive public exchanges."[36]

Graphic and thrilling depictions of death, injury, and bodily peril in narrative films, illustrated newspapers and magazines, and popular theater spectacularized the social ills accompanying modernization, from industrial and railway accidents to the perceived rise in crime that accompanied the rapid growth of major cities.[37] Imported forms of yellow journalism, literature, and film forged strong associations between criminality and industrialized metropolises, and local journalists paradoxically hailed violent incidents as markers of modernity. In this manner, the sensational visual culture of early twentieth-century Mexico and Brazil voiced profound desires for economic and technological development and an implicit acceptance of modernization's costs. Real-life narratives and fictional depictions of modernization's social toll ironically became a profitable and pleasurable means of affirming the modernity of one's city, region, and nation.

In giving expression to local desires for modernity, sensational visual cultures capitalized on the unique capacities of visual technologies and on international forms of popular culture that resonated with new forms of subjective experience. Miriam Hansen's concept of "vernacular modernism" has proved highly influential in efforts to conceptualize the relationship between mass culture and the senses and to chart global processes of cultural exchange. Hansen advocates a conception of modernism more expansive than high-modernist canons, a conception that encompasses "a whole range of cultural practices that register, respond to, and reflect upon processes of modernization and the experience of modernity" and that "situates artistic practices within a larger history and economy of sensory perception."[38] (It should be noted that the sensational visual cultures analyzed herein were contemporary with vibrant literary and artistic avant-gardes like *estridentismo* in Mexico and *modernismo* in Brazil, but rarely intersected with them directly.)[39] Resonating with industrialization, urbanization, shifting social relations, and the emergence of mass consumer culture, cinema "engaged the contradictions of modernity at the level of the senses, the level at which the impact of modern technology on human experience was most palpable and irreversible."[40] According to Hansen, in light of differential experiences of modernization across the globe, the affective resonances of classical Hollywood cinema allowed it to function as "something like the first global vernacular."[41]

Yet Hansen's account of vernacular modernism threatens to reduce processes of cultural exchange with a high degree of complexity to "a dyadic pattern involving Hollywood with each of innumerable peripheral cinemas."[42] In centering the role of U.S. cinema, the concept of vernacular modernism tends to gloss over the heterogeneity of cultural products available in a given local market (in terms of both their national origin and their cultural register) and the manner in which power differentials within the "host" society define the terms of cultural exchange and conceptions of media themselves. Beyond Hansen's implication that "Hollywood occupies the center, and is the one to be translated," Gerow critiques models of transculturation in which "the ability to appropriate is taken as a given, is seen as inherent in the semiotic process; a notion such as this elides the often-contentious history of conflict over the extent and possession of this ability."[43] Although Hansen does stress that classical Hollywood's global reach can be attributed to its "key role in mediating competing cultural discourses on modernity and modernization," she does not consider the role of local conceptions of cinema's medium specificity in this process.[44]

In this study, I focus not only on intermedial horizons of reception, but also on historically and spatially situated understandings of the ontology of photographic and cinematic images. In early twentieth-century Mexico and Brazil, mechanically reproduced depictions of violence attested to the ability of novel visual technologies to capture—or to convincingly stage—the rapid flow of events viewed as defining modern experience. Vanessa Schwartz has shown that in fin-de-siècle Paris, the emergence of mass entertainments was premised on the "visual representation of reality as spectacle."[45] Illustrated newspapers, early cinema, and other emerging forms of popular culture simultaneously documented and dramatized quotidian experience, presenting it as thrilling and extraordinary. Irreversible and often unpredictable events like deaths, injuries, and accidents were perceived as having a special affinity with the quintessentially modern technologies of cinema and photography, with their unique ability to register and preserve photochemical impressions of fleeting moments.[46]

Yet violent acts also pushed this capacity to record the ephemeral to its limits. Beyond social and legal restrictions on the direct recording of violence, its visual capture also presents practical and ethical obstacles. Real-life acts of violence frequently eluded the camera's lens, could be dangerous to record, and could not be precisely recreated without causing physical harm. For this reason, depictions of violence were bound up with fictionalization and special effects from cinema's earliest days. A fascination with portraying real-life bodily violence gave rise to filmed reenactments—like the Edison Manufacturing Company's *Execution of Czolgosz, with Panorama of Auburn Prison* (Edwin S. Porter, 1901), which combined a staged version of the electrocution of President William McKinley's assassin with exterior shots of the prison on the day of the execution—as well as visual effects like the camera stoppage used in the 1895 Edison film *Execution of Mary, Queen of Scots* (William Heise) to substitute a live actress with a dummy just before the moment of beheading.[47] At the same time, the socially disruptive force of violent happenings demanded containment within melodramatic narrative structures that offered moral legibility.[48] In the sensational visual cultures of early twentieth-century Mexico and Brazil, elements of melodrama imbued violent acts with clear moral meanings, framing them within dominant discourses of modernization and political authority. Observing the radical uses of sensational visual culture in early twentieth-century anarchist and socialist movements spanning the U.S.-Mexico border, Shelley Streeby emphasizes its potential to "incite strong feelings, sentiments, and sensations that might lead to the overturning of existing hierarchies."[49] Yet in the contexts under study, public spectacles of violence and crime often served to reinforce social and spatial divisions.

Sensational cinema and journalism in early twentieth-century Mexico and Brazil sought to make sense of the profound social costs of industrialization and urbanization by framing violence through a melodramatic cultural repertoire that was at once national and international in scope. Through a comparative analysis of the two nations' visual cultures, I explore how the global circulation of sensational cinema and print culture intersected with local responses to modernization, giving rise to distinct but parallel developments in silent-era film production that would later be overshadowed by the rise of national film industries. Highlighting the role of spectacles of violence in forging public spheres in early twentieth-century Latin America, these case studies also shed light on broader questions regarding three distinctly modern, and often interconnected, modes of cultural production—sensationalism, melodrama, and seriality—that resonate with profound transformations of daily experience and public life under industrial capitalism.

Sensationalism, Mass Culture, and Modern Public Spheres

In the past two decades, scholars of visual culture have posited popular sensationalism as a key category for charting the intersections between mass culture and sensuous experience in the wake of the Second Industrial Revolution. Ben Singer demonstrates how sensational journalism, stage melodrama, and cinema capitalized on the overwhelming sensory shocks of modern urban life, while Schwartz contends that "sensationalizing and literally spectacularizing became the means through which reality was commodified."[50] These scholars draw on an intellectual tradition that emerges from the work of cultural critics like Georg Simmel and Walter Benjamin, who claimed that industrial-capitalist modernity radically transformed not only daily life, but also the capacities of the senses. In their accounts, human perception itself was altered by the unprecedented growth of cities, which transformed metropolitan life into a series of anonymous encounters and fleeting impressions, and by new communication and transportation technologies like the railway, the automobile, the airplane, the telegraph, and the telephone, which transformed subjective experiences of time and space, giving rise to a sense of unprecedented speed and simultaneity.[51] Adherents to "the modernity thesis" (to use Singer's term) contend that the cinema in general, and sensational films like serials in particular, both mirrored and actively shaped these sweeping transformations of social life and perception.[52]

In *Public Spectacles of Violence*, I argue that in the early mass cultures of Mexico and Brazil, cinematic and photographic depictions of death, violence, and physical peril did not simply constitute mimetic responses to the experience of modernization. In contexts where industrial modernity had yet to be fully achieved, sensational cinema and journalism worked to actively construct experiences of time as distinctly modern, in that it was characterized by a rapid flow of unpredictable, contingent, and disruptive events. The visual cultures of early twentieth-century Mexico and Brazil thus prompt a reevaluation of key components of the "modernity thesis," particularly the notion of "cinema as a *consequence* of modernity"—that is, an organic outgrowth of technological advances and the transformation of social life—and the "key formal and spectatorial resemblances between cinema . . . and the nature of metropolitan experience."[53] As Ana M. López observes, "in reference to Latin America, it is difficult to speak of the cinema and modernity as 'points of reflection and convergence,' as is the presumption in U.S. and European early cinema scholarship," given that "the development of early cinema in Latin

America was not directly linked to previous large-scale transformations of daily life resulting from industrialization, rationality, and the technological transformation of modern life."[54] Building on López's corrective, I investigate how sensational forms of mass culture took on a special resonance in locations where modernization was perceived as delayed, stagnant, or incomplete.

A quintessentially modern mode, sensationalism was pivotal in mediating the affective and moral dimensions of Latin American modernities. While the term was coined in the nineteenth century, sensationalism's roots can be traced to the early modern era, when sixteenth- and seventeenth-century pamphlets and ballads narrated real-life accounts of shocking crimes.[55] Joy Wiltenburg argues that these lurid texts solicited "both a visceral response to violence itself and the quasi-religious dilemma posed by transgression of core values," taking on the "ability to mold common responses to extreme violations of social norms" in an increasingly secular order, analogous to the social function of melodrama as "the principal mode for uncovering, demonstrating, and making operative the essential moral universe in a post-sacred era" outlined by Peter Brooks.[56] In his discussion of the police blotter (*nota roja*), the Mexican cultural critic Carlos Monsiváis emphasizes the sensational mode's moral complexity, observing how the nota roja works "to simultaneously condemn and exalt 'the forbidden,'" functioning as "a (negotiable) manual of social mores."[57]

Through graphic depictions of violence and melodramatic moral polarities, sensationalism links individual sensuous and affective reactions to the enforcement of collective values in a public sphere shaped by mass culture. Monsiváis suggests the expiation of moral transgressions in the police blotter enacts a collapse between private and public, constituting a "conversion of intimacy into scandal, and of scandal into an intimacy shared by readers and listeners."[58] This description recalls Mark Seltzer's contention that modern mass media have forged a "pathological public sphere" through the dissemination of "shared and reproducible spectacles of pathological public violence."[59] While provocative in his claims that in late capitalism, networks of transportation and communication technologies produce subjective experience on a mass scale, Seltzer's mode of reading deliberately collapses national, racial, class, and gender differences, and thus proves of limited usefulness for making sense of differential experiences of modernization in Latin America. By contrast, I explore sensationalism as a structuring category of public discourse in modernizing, stratified societies, making my analysis adjacent to the "affective turn" in studies of film and visual culture. In particular, I build on historically grounded works such as Weihong Bao's *Fiery Cinema: The Emergence of an Affective Medium in China, 1915–1945* and Laura Podalsky's *The Politics of Affect and Emotion in Contemporary Latin American Cinema*, which conceive of affect as an intersubjective and intermedial category that defines the terms of public engagement.

In staging an encounter between public and private spheres, popular sensationalism relies on media technologies—particularly mass-circulation newspapers and cinema—that have played a pivotal role in shaping collective forms of social life in the wake of the Second Industrial Revolution. As Benedict Anderson has influentially argued, the widespread practice of newspaper reading and the closely linked form of the novel worked to create a collective experience of temporal simultaneity that was pivotal in forging the "imagined communities" of emerging nineteenth-century nation-states.[60] In early twentieth-century Mexico and Brazil, the reading public was sharply limited, and citizens' interaction with print culture was often limited to its visual content.[61] Publishing graphic, sensationalized news reportage became a key strategy for expanding the audience for newspapers and magazines, particularly as the printing of halftone photographs bolstered these periodicals' claims to quickly and accurately render topical events.

If the forms of nineteenth-century "print-capitalism" examined by Anderson tended to reinforce dominant forms of nationalism and normative understandings of the national community, the register of the visual holds the potential to construct a more inclusive, "broad-based nationality" beyond the lettered elites.[62] Hansen argues that early experiences of moviegoing in the United States helped forge an "alternative public sphere" within emerging institutions of mass culture that were not yet fully commodified, where both traditional and emerging social hierarchies and moral codes were provisionally suspended.[63] Spectatorship takes a divergent path in Mexico and Brazil, where early elite embrace of the cinema and the medium's close links to dominant discourses of national progress limited its potential as an alternative public sphere.[64] Yet sensational and melodramatic cultural forms nonetheless straddled stark class divides, preserving popular elements within expanding mass cultures. Signaling the pivotal role of melodrama in mediating cultural hegemonies in Latin America, Jesús Martín Barbero defines the mode as the "cultural matrix that feeds the popular [classes'] recognition of themselves within mass culture" by working to reconcile the lived time of experience with industrial-capitalist forms of production and social organization.[65]

Throughout the region, the sensational and melodramatic modes have often overlapped and are closely (though not exclusively) associated with serial formats, signaling the historically and geographically specific relationships between these three uniquely modern modes. In Latin American contexts, popular forms characterized by sensation, sentiment, and episodic structure work to negotiate heterogeneous configurations of modernity and tradition across multiple media. The "intermedial character of melodrama," Hermann Herlinghaus argues, "its versatility in traversing various genres and media of communication," allows it to stage encounters between erudite and popular cultural registers, and, I would add, between national imaginaries and imported cultural products.[66]

In Latin American nations, serial forms of melodrama proved particularly significant in mediating forms of popular culture that circulated on an international scale. In nineteenth-century Latin American newspapers, the space at the foot of the page reserved for the serial novel (*folletín* in Spanish, *folhetim* in Portuguese) would play host both to "foundational fictions"—sentimental narratives that allegorized nineteenth-century nation-building projects—and to translations of Italian and French serial novels characterized by narrative twists and turns.[67] Martín Barbero observes that across the region, "the newspaper serial brought the melodrama from the theater to the press. There, it expanded the reading public and inaugurated a new relationship between popular readers and writing. . . . The 'open structure' of a tale written day-by-day, carried out according to plan, but open to the influence of its readers' reactions, propitiated the (con)fusion of fiction and life."[68] In contexts where literacy was low, serial narratives were often consumed collectively through reading aloud.[69] The narrative conventions of serial literature and stage melodrama were successively transformed throughout the twentieth century by new media technologies that disseminated them on a mass scale. A precursor to hugely popular serial radio dramas and television soap operas (*radionovelas* and *telenovelas*), serial literature became a key point of reference for the popular reception and critical understandings of cinema in early twentieth-century Latin America.

Fueled by competition between established and emerging media, serial cinema and literature encouraged ongoing consumption, and recognizable characters like the detective Nick Carter and the French archvillain Fantômas gave rise to narratives that could be extended almost indefinitely across media.[70] Building on the popularity of serial literature and attaining a regularized and industrialized mode of production and global distribution, the serial films of the 1910s arguably became "the most powerful vehicle in the emergence of a globalised, transnational culture."[71] Yet although serial narratives are heavily conditioned by the market demands and industrial scale of mass media, their unfolding in regular installments invites intense reader engagement, as the consumption of serial narrative becomes closely entangled with the rhythms of everyday life.[72] In early twentieth-century Mexico and Brazil, sensational films and serial formats were read through the lens of preexisting melodramatic cultural repertoires.

The folhetim/folletín acted as a pivotal "trope of film reception" in the region, shaping early film critics' attempts to make sense of cinema's specific qualities and cross-class appeal.[73] References to the folletín often had a pejorative tone; a 1914 article in the Argentine magazine *El Hogar* defined cinema's cultural standing through reference to the prolific authors of French *feuilletons*, expressing concern that film would "extend the genre cultivated by the gentlemen [Xavier de] Montepin, [Pierre Alexis] Ponson du Terrail, and Maurice Leblanc, threatening morals and good taste."[74] Beyond the perceived challenge to aesthetic hierarchies and public morality posed by film and the folletín, critics noted their shared reliance on melodramatic situations and series of peripeties. In Mexico and Brazil, adventure melodramas—particularly crime films—were often viewed as the genres "most full of cinematic visuality," in the words of one Mexican critic, due to their emphasis on dynamic physical action over psychological interiority.[75] Drawing on their viewing of U.S. serial films like *The Million Dollar Mystery* (Howell Hansel, 1914), the Mexican intellectuals Alfonso Reyes and Martín Luis Guzmán noted serial literature and cinema's shared capacity to create "collective emotional states" through "the aesthetic inherent to action."[76] The critics nevertheless signaled a key distinction between the two that speaks to cinema's specificity: "In the folletín, action is accompanied by bad literature; whereas in the cinema, with the disappearance of the word, one gains distance from the problem of style and only the action remains."[77] Reyes and Guzmán imply that the cinema is an essentially visual medium, capable of offering the vertiginous action of the folletín while eliminating the clichéd verbal register associated with it. In their account, cinema has a unique capacity to reconfigure preexisting forms of popular melodrama, shedding their class associations in the process.

As late as 1931, Chilean literary critic Raúl Silva Castro compared Charlie Chaplin's *City Lights*, a sentimental tale of a tramp who helps a blind shopgirl regain her sight, to the melodramatic repertoire of the folletín, arguing that the film, "if translated into words, into a novel, could perfectly well occupy a place beside the fantastic narrations of [Émile] Richebourg, [Paul] Féval, and Ponson du Terrail."[78] Arguing, in terms similar to Guzmán and Reyes, that cinema was an essentially visual medium that could redeem highly melodramatic content, Silva Castro suggests that when popular literature is adapted to the screen, "it is the cinema itself that manages to cleanse the most truculent plots of their folletín-esque content so that, once the film is made, it turns out to be tolerable or even worthy of admiration."[79] For Silva Castro, this transmutation signals a clear distinction between literary qualities and what he calls "cinematic values" (*valores cinescos*).[80] Significantly, the critic claims that cinema's audience goes beyond the "vehement reader of [Enrique] Pérez Escrich, of [Torcuato] Tárrago y Mateos, of M. Delly and Edgar Wallace," encompassing "demanding readers" as well as those "who are not readers of literature of any kind."[81] The critic implies that cinema's specific characteristics allow it to address an audience comprising both "lettered" intellectuals and illiterate or semi-literate spectators, suggesting how visual forms of mass culture might unsettle hierarchies premised on the written word, a point Ángel Rama leaves unaddressed in his influential *The Lettered City*.[82]

Addressing an emerging mass public through reference to familiar forms of popular melodrama, sensational cinema and journalism in Mexico and Brazil also highlighted social divides. In Mexico and Brazil, liberal principles of individual rights and the rule of law have long coexisted with forms of power based on networks of favor and patron-client relationships, and with the exercise of state violence heavily conditioned by class and race. While elites often enjoy impunity from criminal justice, police and judicial authority is disproportionately and often arbitrarily directed toward working-class, indigenous, and African-descended populations. As Josefina Ludmer asserts, crime functions as a "*cultural frontier* that separates culture from nonculture, which founds cultures, and which also separates lines in the interior of a culture. It serves to draw limits, to differentiate and exclude."[83] In early twentieth-century Mexico and Brazil, elite anxieties about the incidence of crime and violence were invoked to police the racial and class boundaries of national citizenship and to exert control over urban spaces undergoing rapid transformation.[84]

Narratives of sensational crime simultaneously reflected and fostered anxieties about criminal acts and moral transgressions among the working classes, as major cities in Mexico and Brazil were reshaped by waves of internal migrants and, in the case of Rio de Janeiro and São Paulo, large numbers of European immigrants. As historians Pablo Piccato and Teresa A. Meade have argued, respectively, elite-driven urban reforms in Mexico City and Rio de Janeiro constituted a struggle for control over public space.[85] Influenced by Baron Georges-Eugène Haussmann's transformation of Paris through the construction of broad boulevards, reforms in both cities aimed to eliminate spatial configurations dating from the colonial period and to discourage "disorderly" uses of the city. Working-class modes of sociability and even mere presence in public were criminalized; being recognized as a "known thief" or "vagrant" (anyone lacking an obvious occupation) became grounds for arrest.[86] Ongoing attempts to professionalize the police forces of Mexico City, Rio de Janeiro, and other major cities failed to stem complaints about the arbitrary use of force and the lack of due process.[87]

Narratives of crime, both fictional and factual, served to draw social distinctions in national contexts where modernization has often been framed as a struggle between "civilization and barbarism," a discourse that has helped legitimize pervasive public violence. Jean Franco observes that in twentieth-century Latin America, "the anxiety of modernity defined and represented by North America and Europe all too often set governments on the fast track that bypassed the arduous paths of democratic decision making while marginalizing indigenous and black peoples," enabling the exercise of state violence against "groups deemed subversive or alien to modernity."[88] At the same time, in much of the region, the state's monopoly on violence has historically been precarious, rendering clear-cut distinctions between "legitimate" and "illegitimate" uses of force difficult to sustain. Robert H. Holden argues that the concept of "public violence," which refers to violence exercised by various actors in the "social field" defined by the state (military and paramilitary forces, guerilla groups, participants in popular rebellions), most accurately captures the exercise of lethal force in Latin American nations since independence. Holden stresses that in "Latin America, public violence is dispersed, multidimensional, and subject to constant public observation; it is, above all, highly visible, habitually crossing the porous frontier between state and civil society."[89] Sensational forms of mass culture responded to and shaped experiences of public life marked by highly visible acts of violence.

Across the region, political instability and public violence actively shaped socially acceptable limits on the depiction of death in the first decades of the twentieth century, as violent actualities and sensational fictions played a key role in early efforts at film production through the end of the silent era. In Colombia, Vicenzo and Francesco di Domenico, members of an Italian immigrant family who controlled a thriving distribution and exhibition business, produced *El drama del 15 de octubre* (*The Drama of October 15th*, 1915). The film depicted events surrounding the assassination of politician Rafael Uribe Uribe in October 1914 by the tradesmen Leovigildo Galarza and Jesús Carvajal. According to Francesco di Domenico's memoirs, he shot "the funeral of General Uribe Uribe, his autopsy, and the accused, hiding ourselves in all the corners of the Panopticon [prison] to take them in flagrante and not in a forced pose."[90] Newspaper accounts from the period claim that the filmmakers also resolved "to bring to the screen a reconstruction, however imperfect, of the crime. . . . In effect, they filmed the principal sites of the bloody drama, and gained the consent of some persons, doctors, etc., to take part in the plot," paying the two perpetrators the sum of fifty dollars to play themselves.[91] The film ended with an apotheosis (allegorical tableau) showing a female figure representing Liberty posing at Uribe Uribe's tomb.[92] This device, rooted in popular theater, offered narrative and ideological closure to a film that blurred the boundaries between fiction and actuality. While the apotheosis's highly legible meaning could help circumscribe audience interpretations of public violence, spectators' reactions to the film signal its failure to contain the disruptive force of this violence.

El drama del 15 de octubre's politically charged subject matter and the participation of the alleged perpetrators in the reconstruction of the killing sparked a public outcry led by the politician's family and the Bogotá newspaper *El Liberal*, fanning tensions between liberal and conservative factions that had given rise to the Thousand Days' War (1899–1902). A moviegoer in Girardot (a town roughly 150 kilometers from Bogotá) even reported that a shot was fired through the screen when Uribe Uribe's image appeared early in the film.[93] Although *El drama del 15 de octubre* was exhibited in some cities without objection, negative publicity apparently prevented it from reaching a wide release.[94] By contrast with the profitable packaging of criminal violence in *Os estranguladores* and *El automóvil gris*, the cinematic restaging of politicized violence proved too inflammatory for most Colombian audiences, and the di Domenicos' efforts at film production were temporarily frustrated.[95]

As in Mexico and Brazil, sensational adventure melodramas proved influential in Colombian fiction filmmaking of the 1920s, including production outside the capital, Bogotá. In 1926, the adventure film *Garras de oro: Alborada de justicia* (*Golden Claws: The Dawn of Justice*) was produced in Cali (or possibly shot abroad) by Alfonso Martínez Velasco in collaboration with a group of intellectuals and entrepreneurs.[96] *Garras de oro* lambasted the United States' 1902 declaration that the Isthmus of Panama (site of the planned canal) was independent from Colombia in violation of an 1885 treaty between the countries. The film frames this conflict through a fictionalized version of a public feud about the matter between Theodore Roosevelt and Joseph Pulitzer, editor of the sensationalistic *New York World* (who is replaced with a character named James Moore in the film). To defend himself from a libel suit, Moore sends a detective to Colombia in search of documents that prove wrongdoing on the part of the U.S. government, resulting in a series of daring exploits that end with the vindication of Moore and Colombia's violated sovereignty. Along with features like *Garras de oro* that adapted serial conventions of fast-and-furious action, a handful of serials were produced in Latin America in the silent era, including, beyond those analyzed herein, the Cuban film pioneer Enrique Díaz Quesada's ten-episode *El genio del mal* (*The Spirit of Evil*, 1920), believed to be lost.

Filmmakers in the region continued to capitalize on acts of public violence into the late 1920s. In Uruguay, newspaper accounts of a shocking crime and an act of heroism—after being attacked by his stepfather, a young boy carried his younger sister several miles to safety before collapsing and dying—became the basis for Carlos Alonso's *El pequeño héroe del Arroyo de Oro* (*The Little Hero of Arroyo de Oro*). Produced between 1929 and 1933, the film reconstructed the events in real-life locations.[97] In Bolivia, violent actualities that combined unstaged footage with reenactment were produced as late as 1928. In 1927, Alfredo Jáuregui was executed for the suspected assassination of the former president José Manuel Pando (who may have died of natural causes), after a judicial process that lasted a decade. Two competing films based on the events shot by Luis del Castillo and Arturo Posnansky were released shortly after. Castillo filmed Jáuregui's final moments and his execution by firing squad, incorporating them into *El fusilamiento de Jáuregui* (*The Execution of Jáuregui by Firing Squad*), also known as *El bolillo fatal o el emblema de la muerte* (*The Fatal Lot or the Emblem of Death*). These sequences were edited together with reconstructions of the alleged crime and of the trial, with some participants, including a judge, playing themselves.[98] For his part, Arturo Posnansky "reconstructed all of the scenes of the trial" for his film *La sombría tragedia de Kenko* (*The Dark Tragedy of Kenko*).[99] (Kenko, a small town outside La Paz, was the site where the former president's body was found.) Castillo's version, a great success with audiences, was banned by La Paz's mayor. It later became the object of a presidential decree that allowed it to be shown in the country but not abroad, due to concerns about its unflattering portrayal of criminal justice in Bolivia.[100] As in the case of *El drama del 15 de octubre*, the two films depicting Jáuregui's trial and execution sparked debates regarding the political and ethical limits on the depiction of public violence that resonated across early twentieth-century Latin America.

In my analysis of the violent actualities and sensational fictions of silent-era cinema in Mexico and Brazil, I first turn to the Mexican case and the intersection of sensational visual culture with national modernization and international-popular culture. Tracing shifts and continuities in Mexican visual culture from the final years of the Díaz regime through the most active phase of the revolutionary conflict, I focus on depictions of public violence, which, following Holden, I define as acts of aggression that blurred the distinction between criminal and political uses of force. In early twentieth-century Mexico, mechanically reproduced images of crime, punishment, and military conflict both asserted state power (defined by the legitimate exercise of physical force) and demonstrated its crisis. As the illustrated press expanded in the final years of the nineteenth century, photographic images that captured or reconstructed assaults, murders, and executions fueled anxieties about criminality while also rendering the Díaz regime's expanded methods of social control spectacularly visible. After the outbreak of revolution in 1910, illustrated journalism and nonfiction films about the conflict worked to capture—and to ideologically manage—sabotage, combat, and murder. As nonfiction filmmaking declined after 1916, fictionalized narratives of public violence would play a pivotal role in efforts to establish profitable film production in Mexico City. Analyzing the surviving film *El automóvil gris* and traces of the lost films *La banda del automóvil* (*The Automobile Gang*, Ernesto Vollrath, 1919), based on the same events, and *Fanny o el robo de los veinte millones* (*Fanny or the Theft of the Twenty Millions*, Manuel Sánchez Valtierra, 1922), which referenced other military and political scandals, I contend that these productions framed public violence as popular entertainment, linking them to a cosmopolitan imaginary of crime that drew on imported literature and cinema. Mixing fictional strategies with reenactments and visual documents—most strikingly, seemingly unstaged images from the criminals' execution in *El automóvil gris*—these productions drew on the conventions of imported serials to frame criminality as a sign of Mexico City's burgeoning modernity.

The following chapter turns to the period of national reconstruction in the 1920s, when modernization programs promoting education, hygiene, and the expansion of transportation networks intersected with efforts to construct and disseminate a unified national culture in the visual arts and popular press by showcasing rural customs and landscapes. Adventure melo-dramas filmed outside Mexico City emphasized scenic views while drawing on the kineticism of North American serials and westerns. Incorporating thrilling scenes of violence while attempting to skirt the racist images of Mex-icans as "bad men" and bandits in Hollywood productions, adventure films shot on location figured prominently in emerging discourses of film criticism in the Mexico City press. Journalists framed film production as a sign of na-tional progress and a newsworthy spectacle in itself by emphasizing physical exploits and dangerous stunts. Examining press discourses surrounding a se-ries of lost adventure films by the director and actor Miguel Contreras Tor-res, including *El Zarco* (1920) and *El caporal* (*The Foreman*, 1921), I observe how they articulated the codes of imported adventure film with emerging national icons, particularly the figure of the *charro* (cattle wrangler). While the production of rural adventure melodramas had declined sharply by the mid-twenties, regional productions made later in the decade drew on the con-ventions of serial films to highlight the dark underside of modernization. In the city of Orizaba in the state of Veracruz, Gabriel García Moreno directed *El tren fantasma* (*The Ghost Train*, 1926) and *El puño de hierro* (*The Iron Fist*, 1927), which display the ambivalent effects of urbanization and expanding transportation networks. Incorporating elements of imported adventure melodramas in their display of local landscapes, García Moreno's adventure films signal the tensions and contradictions of postrevolutionary modern-izing projects.

Part II develops local and regional approaches to sensational cinema in early twentieth-century Brazil. In chapter 3, I analyze the spectacles of real-life crime that unfolded across illustrated journalism, popular theater, and early narrative film in Brazil's burgeoning cities at the turn of the twentieth century. As elites sought to transform Rio de Janeiro and São Paulo by encour-aging European immigration and implementing reforms that pushed poor and working-class residents out of city centers, the journalistic genres of the police blotter and the essayistic *crônica* charted the spatial and social divides of an urbanizing Brazil. Police reportage and early narrative films framed real-life acts of violence involving newly visible social actors, especially immigrants and young women, as thrilling signs of local modernity. Drawing explicit par-allels with "grand crimes" committed in Paris, London, and New York, these sensational narratives acknowledged the human costs of rapid urbanization, even as they transformed criminality into a public spectacle with a power-ful cross-class appeal. Building on this culture of popular sensationalism, film producer-exhibitors in Rio de Janeiro and São Paulo adapted real-life cases to the screen, resulting in a vogue for filmed reenactments of sensational crimes that included significant early experiments with narrative form. After production in Rio and São Paulo declined after 1911, as importers of foreign films increasingly cornered local exhibition markets, *O caso dos caixotes* (*The Case of the Strongboxes*, 1912) and *Um crime sensacional* (*A Sensational Crime*, 1913), adapted from criminal cases by the brothers Alberto and Paulino Botelho, sought to recapture audiences for locally made films. Reconstructing these lost works of early Brazilian cinema, I trace how violent topical events shaped emerging conceptions of filmic narrative, as filmed reenactments sensationalized the present and framed acts of violence in melodramatic and moralistic terms.

Turning to the film culture of Rio de Janeiro in the late 1910s, in chapter 4 I explore a local craze for French, Italian, and American serial films, analyzing how these cultural products fostered new practices of film consumption, novel conceptions of cinema's defining characteristics, and fresh ambitions for local film production. The popularity of the genre inspired a series of local productions that staged narratives of crime and adventure in iconic Rio locations, including *Os mistérios do Rio de Janeiro* (*The Mysteries of Rio de Janeiro*, Coelho Neto and Alfredo Musso, 1917) and *A quadrilha do esqueleto* (*The Skeleton Gang*, Eduardo Arouca and Carlos Comelli, 1917). While the latter film focused on the local criminal underworld, *Os mistérios do Rio de Janeiro* and *Le film du diable* (*The Devil's Film* [released with a French title], Louis Monfits and [first name unknown] Dillac, 1917), evoked an international imaginary of military conflict as Brazil's government contemplated entering the First World War. The reception and production of serials fostered new understandings of the links between cinema and other melodramatic forms, giving rise to the locally specific concept of the *truc*, a French loanword used interchangeably in Brazilian film criticism to refer to daring physical feats, cinematic special effects, and the *coups-de-théâtre* characteristic of serial literature. Emerging at the intersection between national literary traditions and imported cinema, the appeal of the cinematic truc was highlighted in later films that drew on the conventions of imported adventure films.

Tracing the persistence of sensational film genres in Brazil through the 1920s, in Chapter 5 I examine the production of adventure melodramas outside Rio and São Paulo at a moment when the dynamics of the Brazilian economy, particularly the coffee boom, fueled growing disparities between the urban southeast and other regions of the country. Patterns of film exhibition in the period also show a marked geographic unevenness that shaped film production and fan discourse. Elegant venues in Rio de Janeiro and São Paulo screened lavish Hollywood "superproductions," while crime and adventure serials and westerns continued to dominate movie screens outside the southeast and in smaller towns long after they were considered outdated in major cities. Semi-amateur filmmakers in regional capitals and small towns sought to appeal to local audiences through strategic use of these action-oriented genres' conventions, especially location shooting and daring stunts. The display of local landscapes, actors' physical virtuosity, and cinematographers' technical capacities became key audience attractions in serial-influenced films like *Tesouro perdido* (*Lost Treasure*, Humberto Mauro, 1927), made in the town of Cataguases in the state of Minas Gerais, and in productions that drew on the western, such as *Jurando vingar* (*Swearing Revenge*, Ary Severo, 1925), shot in the northeastern city of Recife. Regional productions sparked debate in Rio de Janeiro film magazines like *Cinearte*, *Selecta*, and *Para Todos...*, which called for the modernization of film exhibition and the creation of a national film industry on the model of Hollywood, often dismissing regional films as unmodern and uncinematic. Analyzing critical debates on film production in the 1920s, correspondence between journalists and filmmakers, and several lost films, as well as surviving films and fragments, I examine the pivotal role of sensational genres in forging cinematic visions of regional modernity that contested the privileged place of Rio de Janeiro and São Paulo in a modernizing Brazil.

The case studies that follow demonstrate how early mass culture in Mexico and Brazil combined a fascination with visual documentation with a tendency to frame everyday life in melodramatic terms, mixed moralistic discourses with sensational violence, and reinforced class and racial divisions while working to construct mass audiences. Emerging at the intersections of cinema and print culture, of melodramatic repertoires and serial forms, of national modernization and globalized forms of mass culture, sensational cinema and visual culture capitalized on new visual technologies' unique capacity to render spectacular the conflicts of modernization in early twentieth-century Mexico and Brazil.

PART I

SENSATIONALIZING
VIOLENCE IN MEXICO

Chapter 1

STAGING PUBLIC VIOLENCE IN PORFIRIAN AND REVOLUTIONARY MEXICO, 1896-1922

Often considered the first major commercial success of Mexico's cinema, the 1919 film *El automóvil gris* (*The Grey Automobile*, Enrique Rosas) is a curious hybrid of fictional and nonfictional conventions that contains a deeply unsettling sequence: a series of seemingly unstaged images showing the execution of several members of the "Grey Automobile Gang," who were accused of committing a series of violent robberies while disguised as soldiers during the military occupations of Mexico City (1914–1915). Building on press discourses that framed the Grey Automobile Gang's crimes as both a distinctly national problem and as a sign of local modernity, since they recalled infamous cases that scandalized Paris, New York, and other industrialized capitals, *El automóvil gris* capitalized both on public curiosity and a local craze for imported serial films. Evoking serials' criminal themes, daring stunts, and episodic structure, most of the film's sequences make skillful use of the continuity editing codes dominant in most imported fiction films by the late 1910s. Yet the visual conventions of the execution scene strongly evoke the early genre of the actuality, which blurred the distinction between the spontaneous recording and the reenactment of topical events.

Composition, camera movement, and movement within the frame evoke the fortuitous capture of an event unfolding in real time.[1] As the sequence opens, a rapid pan left, then right, shows a group of soldiers in medium shot, apparently posing with one of the accused. Following a brief shot of the soldiers milling about as they prepare for the execution, a slower pan along an exterior wall displays

FIG 1.1 The execution scene of *El automóvil gris* uses the conventions of the actuality film, including moving figures that pass in close proximity to the camera. Video still.

the line of the criminals facing the firing squad. A wide shot of an expectant crowd is followed by a reverse shot of the criminals; suddenly, we see puffs of gunsmoke and a line of falling bodies. Soldiers approach the prone figures to give each the coup de grâce, onlookers stream past the lens, and the scene abruptly ends. In this sequence, the execution is staged as a ritualized public event: the bodies of the accused are held up for display to spectators both inside and outside the film by means of the panning camera movements. These pans, like the wide-shot scale and the chaotic flow of figures past the camera, avoid a close focus on individual criminals. Instead, the execution scene orchestrates a mass spectacle of violence and politics, a tendency that pervaded Mexico's sensational visual culture during and after the militarized phase of the Mexican Revolution (1910–1920).

While this scene's visual language evokes a real-life event recorded on the fly, it is impossible to verify whether these images captured an actual instance of capital punishment.[2] It is known that the film's director, Enrique Rosas, had close business ties to Pablo González, a general in Venustiano Carranza's forces and later a presidential hopeful, who ordered the execution. (González is perhaps best known for orchestrating the assassination of Emiliano Zapata in April 1919.) A veteran cameraman of the revolutionary conflict, Rosas had advertised images of the Grey Automobile Gang's execution as part of his compilation film *Documentación nacional histórica 1915–1916* (*National Historic Documentation, 1915–1916*), which reviewed recent events of the revolutionary conflict.[3] This footage took on renewed commercial value in 1919 after developments in the case of the Grey Automobile Gang, including the deaths of two suspected members in prison, sparked a series of exposés in Mexico City newspapers. The press coverage seems to have inspired the production of *El automóvil gris*, as well as a competing film financed by the exhibitor Germán Camus, *La banda del automóvil* (*The Automobile Gang*, Ernesto Vollrath, 1919). Even as it capitalized on the scandal, Rosas's film appears to have been designed to repair González's public reputation in the face of rumors that he and other high-ranking military officials were complicit in the gang's crimes: González announced his candidacy on the day of its premiere in December 1919.[4]

El automóvil gris's execution scene evokes the intimate connections between political power, military force, and visual technologies in Mexico during and after the Revolution. Most immediately, the inclusion of the footage signals a collective fascination with real-life spectacles of violence during the extended hostilities, which resulted in a death toll estimated at over a million in a country of 12 million. Over the course of a civil war marked by fleeting alliances, betrayals, and conflicting claims to political authority, the militarization of public life further destabilized the government's historically precarious "monopoly of legitimate physical violence."[5] As Paul Vanderwood has argued in his study of bandits and *rurales* (mounted police), in Mexico "brigands and lawmen" have frequently swapped roles, functioning "as double agents of order and disorder."[6] The events of the Revolution spilled across the pages of the illustrated press, which had expanded considerably in the latter years of Porfirio Díaz's regime (a period referred to as the Porfiriato), and became the principal subject of Mexican films produced between 1911 and 1916. Visual records of death and injury—irreversible, unrepeatable happenings—attested to mechanical reproduction technologies' unique capacity to capture the ephemeral. At the same time, unpredictable and disruptive events like combat and murder stretched this capacity to its limit. Olivier Debroise argues in his history of Mexican photography that the chaotic conditions of the Revolution's documentation highlight dilemmas specific to the medium of photography (and by extension, film): "To anticipate and understand and then halt the destruction for a given moment, just before its irrevocable disappearance, is a special kind of photographic exercise—an exercise in limits."[7]

Public interest in the events of the conflict, combined with the inherent challenges of documenting them, prompted photographers and camera operators to stage and reenact violent events and to impose a narrative organization on topical happenings. This impulse is already evident during the Porfiriato, when the illustrated press cultivated a public fascination with images of revolts, executions, and murder victims. As early as 1907, police and journalists staged and photographed reconstructions of crimes and accidents, producing visual documents with both forensic and commercial uses.[8] *El automóvil gris* extended these practices by reenacting criminal violence on location and featuring real-life participants in the events. According to advertisements, the lead detective in the case, Juan Manuel Cabrera, appeared as himself, and the serial featured "scenes filmed in the precise places where the events took place."[9] Press coverage also noted that journalist Miguel Necoechea, who worked extensively on the police beat, had collaborated on the script.[10]

By combining narrative sequences with images that purport to show real death, *El automóvil gris* recalls the representational strategies of early actualities, which created a sense of topicality by capturing current events as they unfolded, restaging them, or combining both approaches in a single film. The actuality's ambiguous relationship to topical events is exemplified by the early subgenre of the execution film; Miriam Hansen argues that execution films' "sensationalist appeal . . . cuts across documentary and fictional modes of representation and overtly caters to sadistic impulses; later films could do this only in the guise of narrative motivation and moral truth."[11] If narrative helped curtail the disruptive force of violent images by attributing them with clear moral meanings, the shift to the production of narrative film in the United States and Europe around 1903 also helped limit moving images' privileged, yet ultimately ambiguous relationship to historical time. Mary Ann Doane argues that even as reenactments capitalized on a sense of timeliness and topicality, "the very acceptability of the reconstruction of an event constituted the acknowledgment of the atemporality of the image, the fact that it did not speak its own relationship to time. . . . What came to be known eventually as 'deception' in the reenactment was made harmless as 'illusion' in the narrative film."[12] She contends that the shift from the dominance of "the actuality, with its allegiance to the ephemeral and the contingent, to narrative as a tightly structured web of manufactured temporalities" worked to domesticate moving images' inherent indeterminacy.[13]

The unique trajectories of Mexican cinema's development shaped historically specific understandings of the ontology of the moving image, leading to unique configurations of documentation and fictionalization. Nonfiction compilation films dominated domestic production through 1917, when the first feature films were produced in Mexico City.[14] *El automóvil gris*'s juxtaposition of apparently unstaged footage, reenactments, and fictionalized scenes that deviated from the facts of the case as reported in the press marks it as a transitional text in this shift. In its selective use of ostensibly authentic and overtly fictional elements, *El automóvil gris* highlights the political uses of cinema's and photography's privileged yet uncertain relationship to topical events in light of an acute crisis of political legitimacy during the Revolution. The film's narrative sequences elaborate a convenient political fiction, working to deflect suspicion about the complicity of high-ranking officials in the Grey Automobile Gang's crimes. By contrast, the execution scene's demonstration of the military's repressive power is framed as authentic and thus irrefutable. *El automóvil gris* demonstrates how images of a violent present could be strategically framed to reinforce or critique the exercise of physical force, presenting it as either criminal or legitimate (state) violence.

El automóvil gris's visual codes and production history suggest how the conventions of popular crime narratives, both literary and cinematic, could be used to package violence for public consumption, rendering it pleasurable and profitable. By drawing on a cosmopolitan imaginary of crime cultivated by French and North American crime serials, popular literature, and scientific and journalistic discourses, *El automóvil gris* recasts violence as a threatening yet thrilling sign of local modernity. The film exemplifies the visual culture of violence that flourished in early twentieth-century Mexico, at once intensely national in its preoccupations and conditioned by foreign journalism and cinema, a visual culture that marshaled the "reality effects" of mechanically reproduced images in the service of both popular entertainment and social control.[15]

El automóvil gris holds both an exemplary and exceptional status within histories of Mexican cinema. The serial is one of the only silent-era Mexican films from which considerable portions have been preserved, albeit in an altered form; it owes its survival to its re-release in 1933 in a shortened version with an added soundtrack.[16] Few fiction features from the era have survived, and the structure of nonfiction compilation films has been lost as they were cannibalized for use in later films. As Rosas's repurposing of the execution footage in *El automóvil gris* suggests, during and after the Revolution actuality footage was frequently bought, sold, and reused in other works, such as the multiple versions of *Historia completa de la Revolución* (*Complete His-*

tory of the Revolution) assembled by the cameraman Salvador Toscano beginning in 1912.[17] In later decades, these images were reworked in documentaries like *Memorias de un mexicano* (*Memories of a Mexican*, Carmen Toscano, 1950) and *Epopeyas de la Revolución* (*Epics of the Revolution*, Gustavo Carrero, 1961/1963).[18] Although its survival makes it unique, *El automóvil gris*'s strategy of framing violent events through a popular imaginary of criminality exemplifies a broader tendency in Mexican cinema of the period: to narrate and dramatize public violence.

Between 1919 and 1922, a number of early features and serials, most notably *La banda del automóvil* and the 1922 feature *Fanny o el robo de los veinte millones* (*Fanny or the Theft of the Twenty Millions*, Manuel Sánchez Valtierra), fictionalized real-life crime and military misconduct. Whereas *El automóvil gris* capitalized on the very criminal and political scandal it attempted to defuse, press accounts suggest that *La banda del automóvil* focused less on real-life crime than on a thrilling brand of urban modernity embodied by the circulation of motorized bandits on broad avenues lit by electric light, emblems of ongoing urban reforms. The presence of a female villain—a mysterious "woman in mourning" who carries out criminal acts in the defense of her son—added an additional frisson. Similarly drawing on the titillating potential of female criminality, *Fanny* took a more critical approach in its appropriation of the narrative and visual conventions of imported serial films. Like *El automóvil gris*, *Fanny* was produced with the help of a military patron and put a flattering spin on scandals involving the armed forces. The film's plot centered on the struggle for possession of a map belonging to the military, which would have reminded spectators of government documents compromised in a recent security breach. The twenty millions of the title referenced the amount stolen by Carranza from the national treasury when he fled Mexico City in 1920, following a contested presidential succession that resulted in his assassination.[19] According to *Fanny*'s surviving script, the film at once mimicked and critiqued the figure of the American "serial queen" embodied by daredevil actresses like Pearl White, Helen Holmes, and Ruth Roland.[20] In her pursuit of the map, the eponymous villain carries out death-defying stunts. Yet she also seduces the hero out of the arms of his long-suffering wife, suggesting the pernicious effects of a sexually adventurous model of womanhood closely linked with Hollywood cinema and U.S. consumer culture.

Whereas *Fanny* implied that the presence of North American cinema could erode conventional ideals of feminine behavior, topical films depicting women accused of real-life "crimes of passion" played on anxieties linked to women's expanded—and contentious—presence in the public sphere in the wake of the Revolution. In a span of two years, three films sought to capitalize on high-profile trials of women in which the lawyer Querido Moheno argued for the defense: the nonfiction film *El proceso de Magdalena Jurado* (*The Trial of Magdalena Jurado*, producer not identified, 1922), the dramatic reconstruction *Redención* (*Redemption*, producer not identified, 1924), based on the case of Luz González, and *El drama de Alicia Olvera* (*The Drama of Alicia Olvera*), which was planned but never produced.[21] Encouraging his clients to cultivate sympathy by appearing in mourning dress, Moheno also challenged the notion that the right to use physical violence in the defense of personal honor (that is, in an illegal but legitimate fashion) was an exclusively male privilege. The media spectacles surrounding these cases in the cinema and the illustrated press renegotiated the socially acceptable exercise of violence in Mexican public life, even as they tried to contain the disruptive potential of this shift by dramatizing feminine suffering and vulnerability.

At a moment when public violence pervaded everyday life, melodramatic rhetoric aided audiences in making sense of violent events, which they were encouraged to interpret through a matrix of popular narrative conventions with both thrilling and reassuring effects. Newspapers and magazines sensationalized criminality and violence by adopting narrative tropes familiar from serial literature, detective stories, and serial films. At the same time, public officials and journalists weighed whether crime films were a threat to public order. Debates surrounding the social effects of cinema in general, and crime films in particular, shaped notions of its medium specificity on a global scale, as Aaron Gerow demonstrates in his account of the reception of the French crime series *Zigomar* in Japan.[22] The perceived two-way traffic between criminal acts and criminal fictions indicates how early twentieth-century urban experience in Mexico City was interpreted through the lens of popular crime narratives. Robbery and murder were simultaneously condemned as breakdowns in public order and ironically celebrated as quintessentially cosmopolitan problems that attested to Mexico City's modernity. Highlighting and discursively managing threats to the social order, popular sensationalism capitalized on the privileged abilities of newspapers, photography, and cinema to stage an eventful—and thus quintessentially modern—experience of the present.

In this chapter, I reconstruct the production and reception histories of *El automóvil gris* and contemporaneous crime films that are believed lost, positioning them within a broader panorama of visual and print cultures that mediated violence through modern visual and print technologies. By adopting this strategy, I shift emphasis from previous approaches to early twentieth-century Mexican visual culture, which tend to emphasize photography and cinema directly linked to the Revolution.[23] Where other scholars have focused on images of military conflict, my focus is on public violence, in which the boundaries between state and criminal aggression are blurred. Furthermore, while many studies of Mexican visual culture present the Revolution as a point of rupture with the visual conventions and epistemological models of the regime of Porfirio Díaz, I examine continuities in what Claudio Lomnitz calls "the management and representation of death . . . keys to the implantation of the modern state."[24] Tracing the construction of a public culture of violence in Porfirian and revolutionary Mexico across media whose histories are often traced separately—film, photography, and illustrated journalism—I examine the pivotal role of mechanically reproduced images and sensational and melodramatic narratives in mediating a violent present.

Managing Power and Conflict:
Visual Culture in Porfirian Mexico, 1896–1910

During the Porfiriato (1876–1911), photography and cinema played a pivotal role in the public staging of political power and national progress.[25] In August 1896, Díaz and his entourage became the first Mexican spectators to view the Lumière Cinématographe; shortly thereafter, Lumière agent Gabriel Veyre trained his camera on the president.[26] Díaz was also a favored subject for pioneering cameramen like Toscano and Guillermo, Eduardo, Salvador, and Carlos Alva, who documented official junkets, the inauguration of public works, and the festivities organized for the 1910 centennial of Mexico's declaration of independence.[27] Ruthless in his military suppression of political dissent, Díaz did not balk at committing electoral fraud in order to hold power for three decades. Yet he also sought to more subtly shape public opinion by giving generous subsidies to print publications sympathetic to the regime, most notably the newspapers and magazines owned by Rafael Reyes Spíndola, whose novel use of lithography and halftone photographic reproductions helped inaugurate a new model of mass-circulation journalism in Mexico.

Bringing political stability to the nation after the decades of conflict that followed Mexico's wars of independence, Díaz pushed an aggressive program of capitalist development oriented by positivist notions of social progress and largely bankrolled by North American, British, and French investors. The increasing integration of Mexico's economy into global markets, especially through the development of railroads, the cultivation of cash crops for export, and the accelerating extraction of mineral resources, entailed profound social costs. By facilitating the sale and expropriation of communal land for private development, Díaz's policies removed a key means of self-sufficiency for many rural populations, fueling internal migration and generating profound social unrest. When Díaz hinted he might be prepared to step down in a 1908 interview with the American journalist James Creelman, Francisco I. Madero mounted a presidential challenge that concluded with an obviously fraudulent victory for Díaz, sparking widespread uprisings. In May 1911, the forces of Pascual Orozco (who aligned himself with Madero despite their differences regarding military strategy) crippled a federal battalion in Ciudad Juárez, leading Díaz to renounce the presidency and install an interim government pending new elections, in which Madero triumphed by a wide margin. Yet Madero failed to deliver substantial reforms and to neutralize pro-Díaz forces. In 1912 and 1913, counterrevolutions broke out in the port of Veracruz and then in the capital, where the Decena Trágica (Tragic Ten Days) ended in the assassination of Madero and his vice president, José María Pino Suárez, on the orders of Madero's former military commander Victoriano Huerta. After troops under Francisco "Pancho" Villa ousted Huerta, the Revolution devolved into an extended series of power struggles between military forces led by charismatic leaders (*caudillos*), with the reformist Constitutionalists, including Venustiano Carranza and Álvaro Obregón, ultimately triumphing over the more radical factions of Villa and Emiliano Zapata.

As Lomnitz observes, the Revolution entailed an unprecedented "deployment of efficient mechanized killing, with its infrastructure of machine guns, modern artillery, and troop transportation by rail."[28] Yet violence on a mass scale had clear precedents in the previous regime: "Porfirian industry, peace, and progress brought mechanized killings to Mexico: railroad accidents, mass deportations to labor camps, ethnocidal campaigns in areas that underwent rapid incorporation into capitalist export production, violent suppression of labor strikes." Lomnitz argues that this "massification of death" was inextricable from the restructuring of Mexico's economy and the emergence of new institutions of health, education, and punishment during the Porfiriato.[29] As Shelley Streeby demonstrates, socialist and anarchist movements spanning the U.S.–Mexico border sought to generate powerful sensations and sentiments by graphically depicting the abuses committed under the Díaz regime with the complicity of U.S. economic interests.[30] Yet while the contradictions of modernization under Díaz found vibrant expression in the celebrated broadsheets of the printmaker José Guadalupe Posada and in the satirical penny press targeted to working-class consumers, visual evidence of these abuses was largely suppressed from mass-circulation newspapers and magazines as the press began to develop on an industrial scale.[31]

In the final decade of the nineteenth century, developments in print technology, including the introduction of linotype and rotary presses, facilitated new economies of scale. Government subsidies allowed for investments in new equipment for publications favorably disposed toward the regime, and the small-scale, independent press was increasingly marginalized, as the market favored periodicals with larger circulations and a cheaper cover price.[32] Rafael Reyes Spíndola adopted this model with great success in his newspaper *El Imparcial*, founded in 1896 and considered the emblematic newspaper of the late Porfiriato. The growth of mass-circulation dailies—in spite of low literacy rates, especially outside the capital—displaced an earlier model of politically oriented journalism, instead focusing on informing readers about current events.[33] Illustrations contributed to this sense of topicality, adding graphic impact to the sensationalistic news that was central to the appeal of the emerging mass press. In 1892, Reyes Spíndola introduced lithographs in his newspaper *El Universal*; by 1896, halftones were introduced in *El Imparcial* and the magazine *El Mundo Ilustrado*, rapidly circulating photographs of current events.

The illustrated press disseminated a selective and at times contradictory vision of a modernizing Mexico. In both subsidized and independent publications, photographs of urban reforms and public works offered visual evidence of national progress. Similarly, coverage of the leisure activities and charitable efforts of the upper classes projected an impression of social stability and elite benevolence, reinforcing the notion of Díaz's regime as a prosperous "Pax Porfiriana."[34] Yet the vision of turn-of-the-century Mexico that emerges in the pages of the illustrated press is far from an exclusively tranquil one.[35] Alberto del Castillo Troncoso observes that *El Universal* cultivated a fascination with political and criminal violence from the publication of its very first lithographs.[36] John Mraz notes illustrated periodicals' obsessive focus on the polarized social categories of elites and offenders during the Porfiriato: "the Mexican masses were excluded from the nation of order and progress constructed by the illustrated press, which reduced the panorama of ethnic and social variety in Mexican society to the successful and the criminal."[37]

The fascination with crime and violence apparent in the illustrated press of the late Porfiriato signals a deep ambivalence about criminality's role in Mexico's incipient modernity. Criminological science, which flourished under the Díaz administration, tended to associate crime with degeneracy and backwardness. In 1893, *El Universal* declared, "In Mexico, criminality has not advanced sufficiently to penetrate into certain superior classes: crime has all the brutal simplicity of a group of humans in the first stages of civilization."[38] This set of associations began to shift as new conceptions of criminality, including the French sociologist Émile Durkheim's insistence on the normality of crime, gave rise to discourses that "linked the nation's social and economic modernization with a refinement of crime."[39] In 1897, *El Imparcial* described an "Evolution of Robbery" in which brutal physical aggression was replaced by cunning and careful planning on the part of criminals.[40] During the Revolution, Jesse Lerner argues, "crime acquired a new signification—no longer as a symptom of the inferiority and backwardness of the population as a whole, but on the contrary, as proof of a new emergent modernity."[41]

Photography played a pivotal role in journalistic and criminological texts that drew on the positivist principles of the *científicos*, a coterie of advisors to Díaz who sought to overcome obstacles to national modernization by making empirical observations of social conditions and developing compensatory measures. Mexican criminologists warned of the dangers posed to social hygiene and national progress by racial characteristics considered inherently inferior—particularly indigenous ancestry—as well as by preventable ills, like poverty, alcoholism, disease. Drawing on varied and often conflicting strains of juridical thought, including the Italian criminologist Cesare Lombroso's notion of the "born criminal" who could be visually identified by "abnormal" physical features, scientific and journalistic texts on criminality developed systems of visual classification to draw distinctions between criminals and law-abiding citizens.[42]

The visual taxonomies developed by criminological texts and the popular press were incorporated into public discourses and policing practices that invoked criminality in order to reinforce divisions between races and classes in a rapidly expanding Mexico City. As Robert M. Buffington has argued, juridical, scientific, and popular discourses on criminality defined the racial and class boundaries that delimited the exercise of full citizenship in late nineteenth and early twentieth-century Mexico, working to "disguise the exclusions of modern Mexican society behind a veil of criminality—to proscribe as criminal certain activities that were clearly linked to marginalized groups."[43]

In Mexico City, Pablo Piccato has shown, the criminalization of working-class uses of public space was a tool used to police the boundaries of the "ideal city" that elites sought to construct in the city center and the upper-middle class neighborhoods being built along the Paseo de la Reforma in the capital's western districts.[44] Yet in practice these divisions proved impossible to maintain, in part because affluent households relied on the domestic labor of working-class populations who were increasingly able to traverse the city cheaply and efficiently on new trolley lines. Furthermore, elite criticisms of the immorality and criminality of the poor often concealed a reluctance to invest in the improvement of living conditions or the expansion of city services like sanitation and policing to working-class neighborhoods.[45] Piccato argues that attempts to divide the city and its populace proved counterproductive; for example, the classification of individuals as "known criminals" made citizens subject to arbitrary arrest, which in turn encouraged contact with more hardened offenders and increased recidivism.[46]

An important tool in producing (pseudo-)scientific knowledge about criminality, photography had been used by Mexican law enforcement since the 1850s, when police began photographing prisoners in the notoriously insecure Belém jail in Mexico City in order to facilitate their recapture in case of escape.[47] The medium occupied an increasingly important role as Díaz's regime strove to professionalize Mexico City's police force and refine its methods of juridical punishment.[48] In 1895, the police force in Mexico's capital adopted the Bertillon method for identifying and cataloging repeat offenders, creating an archive that combined photographic portraits of criminals with precise bodily measurements.[49] The construction of the Lecumberri prison on the model of Jeremy Bentham's Panopticon, completed in 1900, was perhaps the most emblematic sign of these efforts to exercise visual surveillance over the criminal.[50]

Dovetailing with these trends in criminology and policing, popular and official publications worked to classify and display the offender, capitalizing on photography's capacities to render criminality a public spectacle. Reyes Spíndola's *El Universal* published a "Galería de Rateros" (Thieves' Gallery), while the official publication *Gaceta de Policía* maintained a similar section, entitled the "Página Negra" (Black Page). Both drew on the conventions of the physiognomic portrait and the mug shot used in scientific and juridical contexts. Featuring both frontal and profile images, the "Galería de Rateros" closely resembles the images in Carlos Roumagnac's later work of criminal anthropology, *Los criminales en México* (Criminals in Mexico, 1904). Similarly,

PAGINA NEGRA.

RATEROS

Agustín Montaño (6) Maestro.—Antonio de P. Narvais.—José Suárez.—Julián Chavira.

Agustín Montaño (a) «El Maestro.» Es cruzador y carterista de fama. Entre las hazañas de este individuo, hace algunos años se verificó un baile en el edificio de Minería, donde logró entrar, robándole al Sr. Pombo una magnífica repetición de oro; ha extinguido varias condenas por robo y lesiones, tanto en la capital como en Querétaro, Guadalajara, Monterrey y otros Estados. Actualmente se encuentra en esta capital, libre.

Antonio de P. Narviz ó Antonio Pérez (a) «El Mexicano.» Este individuo es cruzador, timador y carterista sumamente hábil; son sus compañeros José Suárez ó Manuel Marcot y Freire (a) «El Galleguito» y Julián Chavira, con quienes tima y anda por los ferrocarriles robando carteras. Actualmente se encuentra preso en Guadalajara en unión de Suárez.

José Suárez ó Manuel Macot Freire (a) «El Galleguito.» Es timador y carterista de fama. En 1902 estuvo preso en Monterrey, donde fué sentenciado á dos años por el conocido timo del testamento, sentencia que cumplió en 1904. Actualmente se encuentra preso en Guadalajara en unión de Antonio de P. Narviz ó Antonio Pérez (a) «El Mexicano,» donde han cometido varios timos y robos de carteras en los ferrocarriles.

Julián Chavira y Torres. Compañero de los dos anteriores. Ha tenido varios ingresos á la Cárcel por ebrio pendenciero y robo. Actualmente se encuentra libre.

CRUZADORAS.

Ausencia Morales.—Ricarda Gutiérrez.—Petra Basurto.—Magdalena Campos.

Ausencia Morales. Esta mujer es cruzadora, circuladora de moneda falsa y pendenciera; ha tenido como seis ingresos á la Cárcel por estos delitos.

Ricarda Gutiérrez. Cruzadora; ha tenido varios ingresos á la Cárcel por robo.

Petra Basurto. Cruzadora, querida de José Galindo (a) «El Marqués de las Arañas,» ratero. Se dedica á robar en las casas de comercio.

Magdalena Campos. Cruzadora; ha tenido varias entradas á la Cárcel por robo.

FIG 1.2 The *Gaceta de Policía* featured a "Black Page" that resembles the taxonomies of criminal "types" that appeared in works of criminology. *Gaceta de Policía*, 21 January 1906. Nettie Lee Benson Latin American Collection, University of Texas Libraries, University of Texas, Austin.

the grid layout of the "Página Negra" recalls the taxonomic studies of criminals in Francisco Martínez Baca and Manuel Vergara's 1892 *Estudios de antropología criminal* (Studies in Criminal Anthropology). If works like Roumagnac's were intended, as Buffington suggests, for a popular as well as a specialist audience, the incorporation of criminal photography in the pages of the mass press disseminated racialized visions of criminality even more widely.[51] Intended to help law enforcement identify and apprehend offenders, the sections also encouraged readers to scan their environment for potential threats and to develop a racially coded notion of what criminals looked like, simultaneously fostering and managing anxieties about rising crime.

The *Gaceta de Policía* constitutes one of the most suggestive intersections between policing, criminology, and illustrated journalism during the late Porfiriato. Printed between 1905 and 1908, the magazine combined discussions of forensic science with thrilling images of physical violence. In the inaugural issue, an editorial declared, "In addition to its obvious utility, we can assure you that our publication will also be of thrilling interest, given that, to the extent possible and without compromising our service, one will be able to read in our newspaper the story of each crime that makes Mexican Society tremble."[52] Openly acknowledging a tension between fighting crime and sensationalizing it, the magazine published articles on forensic procedure and profiles of exemplary officers alongside illustrated accounts of murders and gruesome accidents. The *Gaceta de Policía* emphasized the progress of criminology and the professionalization of the police alongside violent incidents that remained uncontained by "improved" methods of social control.[53] In this context, photography was attributed with both a forensic value and an ability to dramatize an eventful and contingent present.

The *Gaceta de Policía*'s coverage of the shooting of the married actress María Reig by her lover Manuel Algara y Terreros in the city of Chihuahua exemplifies the visual and verbal strategies used by the publication to dramatize crime, as well as the class bias that permeated the popular press of the period. Official and commercial publications alike framed violence among the working classes as at once more threatening and more banal than violence among the middle and upper classes.[54] The *Gaceta de Policía* acknowledges that if Reig's murder "had taken place in the slums of the capital, and if its protagonists had been degenerated people without principles of education, [it] would only have given material for an insignificant paragraph in the *faits divers* [*gacetilla*]."[55] The article draws on both moralistic and criminological discourses to account for the attack, suggesting that the illicit couple's "shameful love" was responsible for the fact that "jealousy caused the idea of committing a horrifying crime to be born in his unbalanced brain."

Dramatizing the crime while emphasizing the individuality of the perpetrator and victim, the article utilized diverse modes of visual representation with varying degrees of proximity to real-life events. The article's layout combines a drawing showing Algara y Terreros's attempt to kill himself after mortally wounding Reig with halftone portraits of the victim and perpetrator, which add a kind of surplus authenticity to the speculative reconstruction of the crime. Visual reconstructions of real-life crimes took on similarly complex forms in other publications that developed "graphic reportage with a certain independence from the text, which presented complete stories with a narrative unity expressed in different frames or vignettes," a technique that del Castillo Troncoso first observes in *El Imparcial* in 1903.[56] These sequences of images possess a protocinematic quality that highlights photography's limits—its

ASESINATO Y SUICIDIO (¿)

CRIMEN SENSACIONAL.

Actriz muerta á manos de un desequilibrado.

Gran sensación causó entre los corrillos de lagartijos la noticia de un acontecimiento que, de haberse desarrollado en uno de los barrios bajos de la capital, y habiendo sido sus protagonistas gente degenerada y sin principios de educación, sólo hubiera dado tema para una insignificante párrafo de gacetilla; pero que por haber tenido lugar entre personas conocidas, ha sido y es comentado de mil maneras.

Nos referimos al asesinato proditorio perpetrado por Manuel Algara y Terreros en la persona de María Reig, en el hotel Palacio, de Chihuahua.

María Reig era una actriz que vino al país con la Compañía dramática de María Guerrero, y que más tarde ingresó á la de Virginia Fábregas. Era una mujer hermosa, y su labor artística fué recibida con agrado por el público. Casada con un artista de apellido Herrero, que actualmente trabaja en el Teatro Principal, hubo de separarse de él debido á algunos serios disgustos surgidos entre ellos.

Manuel Algara era uno de tantos desocupados que pasan la vida sin provecho, estorbando las aceras del *boulevard* y haciendo conquistas entre los bastidores de los teatros, oficio que les conquista el nombre de *sportman*, que bien puede traducirse por el de *vagos edinerados*. Aprovechando las desavenencias que existían entre el matrimonio, se dedicó á enamorar á María, logrando ser correspondido por ella, y entablando unas relaciones íntimas entre ambos, que parecían hacer ostentación de sus vergonzosos amores. En los primeros tiempos parecían ser felices; pero bien pronto, tal vez por la desilusión causada por la posesión, Algara sintió el hastío, y comenzó para los amantes una vida de disgustos y reyertas, en que siempre tocaba la peor parte á la infeliz adúltera.

En tal situación se ofreció el viaje de la Compañía Fábregas para Chihuahua, y María salió con ella, haciendo lo mismo Algara algunos días más tarde.

Allá obtuvo la actriz algunos triunfos escénicos,

MARÍA REIG

MANUEL ALGARA Y TERREROS
Asesino de María Reig.

MANUEL ALGARA en los momentos de intentar suicidarse (¿), después de herir mortalmente á María Reig.

FIG 1.3 An illustrated account of the shooting of María Reig combined portrait photographs with a drawn reconstruction of the crime. *Gaceta de Policía*, 28 January 1906. Nettie Lee Benson Latin American Collection, University of Texas Libraries, University of Texas, Austin.

inability to capture and render the unfolding of an event in a fluid, continuous manner—even as it attempts to compensate for them.

While the *Gaceta de Policía* and *El Imparcial* spectacularized violence by combining preexisting photographs and drawings, law enforcement and illustrated publications used photography to reconstruct and analyze violent events, restaging accidents, suicides, and crimes for both juridical and journalistic ends.[57] Rather than merely recording the aftermath of a crime for evidentiary purposes, these reconstructions promised to clarify the sequence of the events and to help attribute guilt and innocence. Photographic reconstructions became public spectacles in their own right, drawing crowds of curious onlookers and coverage in the illustrated press.[58] These images were reproduced in newspapers and magazines through the Revolution and beyond, adding visual drama to coverage of infamous cases like the death of the Grey Automobile Gang member Francisco Oviedo in prison in 1918 and

EL JUEZ VARELA HIZO RECONSTRUIR AYER, EL ASESINATO DE FCO. OVIEDO

Brown explicó cómo sostuvo la lucha con su contrario y pudo aclararse que al ser herido Oviedo se encontraba en posición "algo encogido"

DECLARACIONES DE MARIA CONESA

Primer caso de Aplicación Concreta de los Decretos Sobre el Petróleo

FIG 1.4 A reconstruction of the murder of Francisco Oviedo provides graphic visual material for ongoing coverage of the case. *El Universal*, 22 January 1919. Biblioteca Miguel Lerdo de Tejada, Secretaría de la Hacienda y Crédito Público.

Alicia Olvera's alleged murder of her husband in 1920.[59] Occasionally, newspapers and magazines photographed their own reconstructions, generating exciting visual material that was almost impossible to gather spontaneously. Overlapping with policing practices, photography and illustrated journalism worked to commodify violence in turn-of-the-century Mexico City.

Scholars of Porfirian visual culture have emphasized how sensational police reportage deliberately fostered fears about criminality, bolstering support for authoritarian rule and enhanced mechanisms of social control.[60] Yet photographic images of violence also signal the ways in which sensational visual culture exceeded this authoritarian agenda. As the case of the *Gaceta de Policía* indicates, working to suppress crime through modern scientific

methods and staging it as a thrilling spectacle for readers were acknowle
as conflicting goals that were nevertheless closely entwined in the pages
popular press. Criminality, along with forms of bodily violence ranging from
accidents to murders, was framed not as inimical to modernity but as its dark
underside. Unpredictable and violent events could not be fully contained
within official discourses of order and progress. Beginning in 1910, the mass
violence unleashed by the Revolution began to generate novel modes of capturing current events and new strategies for visually and discursively managing a violent present.

Mediating the Revolution, 1910–1920

As the Revolution fostered new modes of documenting current events, illustrated journalism faced new challenges and opportunities. As the direct links
between the press and state power were eroded, Díaz's intermittent repression of independent periodicals was replaced by the threat of military repri-
sals in a rapidly shifting political landscape. Many Porfirian-era publications
languished in the absence of government subsidies, with most disappear-
ing by 1914 to be replaced by new modern-format newspapers. Prominent
among these was a new incarnation of *El Universal*, founded in 1916 by the
revolutionary activist Félix Palavicini, and *Excélsior*, whose layout was closely
modeled on the *New York Times*.[61] Photojournalism took on new significance
with the emergence of photographic exchanges, most notably the Agencia
Fotográfica Mexicana, founded in 1911 by Agustín Víctor Casasola, who
purchased and resold images from photographers working across the country.[62] Feeding the public's desire for up-to-date information on the conflict,
photojournalism bolstered the claims of the illustrated press to timeliness
and topicality.

As evolving forms of Mexican visual culture capitalized on the conflict,
they were shaped by both practical and ideological limits on depictions of
combat and its aftermath. In addition to a paper shortage linked to the outbreak of the First World War, editors had to navigate a complex and highly
unstable political environment in which revolutionary factions gained and
lost military and political control in quick succession.[63] (Most photographers
and filmmakers were closely aligned with individual caudillos, giving them
fuller access to troop movements and combat.[64]) In many cases, visual documents were framed by verbal discourses that attributed moral meanings to
violent happenings, suggesting a desire to make sense of public violence by

legitimizing (precarious) state power and criminalizing the more radical currents of revolutionary movements. Tending to support the faction currently in power, illustrated magazines catering to a bourgeois readership reserved their most strident rhetoric for the Zapatistas, who were equated with bandits and criminals. Magazines often published graphic images of the corpses of Zapatista soldiers, while avoiding photographs that showed dead or dying federal soldiers.[65]

Whereas illustrated magazines observed selective prohibitions on graphic images of violence, other forms of visual culture circumvented the financial and editorial restrictions on print publications. Inexpensive cameras and printing equipment allowed picture postcards to be produced cheaply in large quantities by photographers on both sides of the U.S.–Mexico border. Postcards could circulate quickly among a much broader audience than magazines or newspapers, and they often depicted executions, combat, and slain soldiers in an unrestrained fashion.[66] The work of the American photographer Walter H. Horne, one of the most prolific postcard photographers working on the border, exemplifies the fortuitous capture and rapid dissemination of images. Horne managed to photograph the ruins of Columbus, New Mexico, after Villa's infamous raid on the town, and market his images before they appeared in newspapers. His most profitable series of postcards showed a triple execution carried out by Carranza's troops; his exposures even managed to capture the clouds of dust that formed after the bullets passed through the victims' bodies, impacting the wall at their backs.[67] Emphasizing the capture of contingent moments on the level of their content, and taking advantage of new means of rapidly disseminating images on a mass scale, revolutionary-era photography staked a claim to timeliness that made it profitable with consumers.

Despite shifts in the mass circulation of photography, there are clear continuities between the photojournalism of the Díaz regime and the revolutionary period. Many prominent photographers of the Revolution learned their trade at the mass-circulation newspapers of the Porfiriato; Casasola, for example, worked extensively for *El Imparcial*. Mraz notes that the emerging codes of modern photojournalism, which give the impression of an action caught in medias res, are already evident before 1910, and that "codes of realism varied greatly" in revolutionary-era photography. Some images made use of carefully staged compositions characteristic of pictorialism, while others strived to convey a sense of unfolding action.[68] Due to the inherent danger and unpredictability of combat, and to the variety of photographic equipment used during the period (including unwieldy tripod-mounted cameras), photographs that ostensibly showed battle were frequently posed, and military exercises passed off as actual combat. Elaborate narratives about the fortuitous capture of an image might supply a sense of topicality felt to be lacking in the image itself.[69] Mraz's observations about revolutionary-era photography indicate a tension between the fortuitous capture of contingent events and their careful staging.

Histories of filmmaking during the Mexican Revolution also stress the technical and practical challenges of depicting war, which encouraged the staging of topical events. In memoirs and press reports from the period, U.S. and European cameramen who documented the Mexican Revolution emphasize the challenges of successfully recording combat, which was both dangerous to life and limb, and often difficult to track down.[70] Constraints on image-making encouraged the tailoring of events to the needs of the camera: a contract between Pancho Villa and U.S. Mutual Film supposedly stipulated that battles be fought during the day to allow for clearer exposures. While in fact the agreement contains no such language, this clause was widely reported in both the Mexican and the American press, constituting a powerful myth that highlights how visual technologies did not simply capture, but actively manipulated, the revolutionary conflict.[71] Significantly, the Mutual feature film *The Life of General Villa* (Christy Cabanne, 1914) combined real-life scenes of combat featuring Villa with fictional sequences where Raoul Walsh played the general. The use of multiple representational modes may have maximized the film's appeal to U.S. audiences accustomed to sensational newspaper coverage of the conflict.[72]

Mexican camera operators documenting the Revolution faced similar challenges, and the publicity discourses surrounding their films signal the value placed on "authentic" images of combat and the physical peril involved in obtaining them. While some films only claimed to document the aftermath of battle, most advertisements trumpeted the camera's ability to register inherently dangerous, unpredictable happenings. Descriptions of the peril involved in capturing the images, bolstered by claims of wounded camera operators and destroyed equipment, were almost obligatory. An ad for *Sangre hermana (Fraternal Blood, 1914)* stressed that "its authenticity has been confirmed by certificates from the Military Authorities. . . . [T]he audience will remain absorbed at every instant when it considers that the lives of our valiant [camera] Operators have been in imminent danger."[73] Some films claimed to offer an almost unbelievable proximity to violent events; publicity for Enrique Rosas's

Revolución en Veracruz (*Revolution in Veracruz*, 1912), which documented Félix Díaz's first uprising against the Madero government, claims that "this film was shot with great courage on the part of the operator, because without fear of bullets he ventured right up to the firing line."[74] *Revolución zapatista* (*Zapatista Revolution, 1914*), the sole film of the period favorable to the faction, was billed as including images of "hand-to-hand combat between Federal troops and Zapatistas" and of "the explosion of trains," a common means of sabotaging enemy troop movements during the conflict.[75] Stretching the limits of credulity, these advertisements situate the camera in a seemingly impossible (or at least an impossibly dangerous) position. These publicity discourses frame the threat of injury to the camera operator's body as the guarantor of the images' authenticity, at once highlighting and defying practical limits on the filming of violent events.

Whereas publicity discourses stressed the spontaneous capture of images of combat, the narrative structure of revolutionary-era nonfiction films served to dramatize real-life events, extending developments during the Porfiriato. According to Aurelio de los Reyes, nonfiction films of the era adopted the strategies of the illustrated press, often hewing closely to the sequence of events as reported in newspapers.[76] For example, Salvador Toscano's 1906 *Viaje a Yucatán* (*Trip to the Yucatán*), which documented Díaz's official junket to the Yucatán Peninsula, appears to have been composed of a series of scenes documenting the president's arrival in the towns along the route, arranged precisely in the order reported by the press. By contrast, *Viaje a Yucatán*'s print intertexts—photo essays documenting the trip published in illustrated magazines—took more liberties with the spatial relationships between geographic locations in their layouts.[77] In 1909, *Entrevista Díaz-Taft* (*Díaz-Taft Interview*), a film by the Alva Brothers depicting meetings between Díaz and the U.S. president William Howard Taft, slightly altered the order of the real-life events in editing so that the film would culminate with the encounter between the two presidents. According to de los Reyes, this strategy indicates an increasing willingness to impose a narrative structure on topical happenings.[78]

Extending this tendency, revolutionary-era nonfiction films often incorporated an "apotheosis"—in this context, a sequence glorifying a military or political leader—to provide narrative and ideological closure. In 1911, *Asalto y toma de Ciudad Juárez* (*Attack and Capture of Ciudad Juárez*, Alva Brothers) concluded with a scene in which impassioned crowds hailed the victorious

Pascual Orozco.[79] The film prominently featured images of Madero and his wife, reducing the complex dynamics of a mass uprising in favor of a focus on the charismatic leader.[80] The inclusion of an apotheosis quickly became standard, to the extent that Victoriano Huerta reportedly threatened Toscano with violence when he refused to include an apotheosis hailing his victory in *Las 10 jornadas trágicas de México* (*The Tragic Ten Days in Mexico City*).[81] Beyond culminating scenes celebrating caudillos, revolutionary-era nonfiction films may have also included apotheoses in the form of staged allegorical tableaux, a convention that would have been familiar to audiences from topical musical revues (including productions like José F. Elizondo's 1913 *El país de la metralla* [*The Land of the Machine Gun*]) and imported French *féerie* films. A hand-colored frame from Toscano's archive shows an allegorical tableau: a white-clad female figure representing Mexico appears alongside two soldiers shaking hands in front of a bust of Madero, suggesting a reconciliation between military factions.[82] Whether affirming an individual leader's rise to power or evoking more generalized patriotic sentiments, the apotheosis would have worked to lend moral legibility to images of real-life violence.

In a similar vein, publicity for compilation films invoked melodramatic oppositions of good and evil in order to attribute unequivocal meanings to topical events. In particular, advertisements for the film *Sangre hermana*, considered lost to the historical record, are highly suggestive: assertions of the images' authenticity are intertwined with language that suggests their theatricalization and their emotional impact on audiences. One advertisement stressed, "This film is exciting and has the fine quality of being an exact copy from reality, without fictions, without deceptive scenery, the sets were provided by Mother Nature and the characters are those who act in the grand tragedy that currently moves us and produces our fatherland's anguish."[83] In a somewhat contradictory fashion, these images are valorized for faithfully reproducing the Revolution as real-life drama. Another advertisement describes the suspense generated by the film in moralistic terms: "This film will have the audience in constant tension as it reproduces scenes of both the heroism and valor of our courageous Army and the audacity of the Zapatistas . . . until the supreme moment when justice vindicates society."[84] The advertisement promises that the film's narrative tension will be resolved in the depiction of a real-life military victory described in moral and juridical terms. While it is impossible to know how *Sangre hermana*'s structure presented military conflict, its publicity campaign suggests how morally charged rhetoric was marshaled to discursively contain cinematic images of chaos and violence.

As in the case of the illustrated press, the treatment of the Zapatista faction in revolutionary-era nonfiction films acts as a limit case. The tendency to frame Zapatista aggression as illegitimate (criminal) violence seems to have permitted the loosening of prohibitions on the cinematic depiction of death—in particular, the filming of executions, which were photographed so often they became an emblematic trope of the Revolution so much so that this image obscured the strategies of modern mass warfare utilized during the conflict.[85] While Everard Meade argues that the proliferation and visual similarity of mass-mediated images of executions tended to gloss over the victims' political affiliations, the filming of executions seems to have been limited to Zapatistas and accused criminals.[86] *Revolución zapatista*, a film that was favorable to the faction, was billed as containing the "execution by firing squad of a Zapatista captain. We advise the public that this is the only film that has a real firing squad victim."[87] According to filmographies, the only other filmed execution scene advertised in the period is Rosas's footage of the Grey Automobile Gang, suggesting how limits on the display of real-life violence were shaped by the victims' perceived status as criminals or legitimate combatants, even as the revolutionary conflict blurred any clear distinction between the two.[88]

As Rosas's career suggests, the impulse to openly dramatize public violence, while imposing narrative structure and moral legibility on topical events, spans the transition from the revolutionary-era nonfiction films to fictional productions. By 1917, when the signing of a new constitution marked a turning point in the Revolution, nonfiction films had all but disappeared due to politically motivated film censorship, growing public opposition to the prolonged conflict, and ambitions for a domestic film industry.[89] By contrast with de los Reyes, who argues that the shift away from the nonfiction film after 1916 represents an abandonment of a uniquely national mode of filmmaking marked by fidelity to the real, I maintain that revolutionary-era visual culture was as invested in sensationalism and theatricality as in the truth-value attributed to cinema, which was often stretched to its limit by the circumstances of the conflict.[90] Violence persisted as a theme in fiction films whose proximity to topical events was attenuated. By linking everyday life in Mexico City to a cosmopolitan imaginary of crime, narrative films of the late teens and early twenties worked to commodify and ideologically manage public violence.

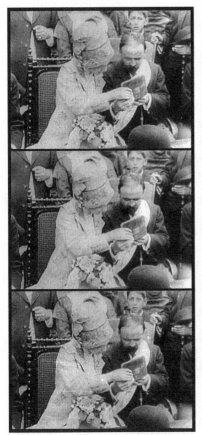

FIG 1.5 "Apotheosis: Mr. Francisco I. Madero and Mrs. Madero in front of the film cameras." The concluding scene in *Los últimos sucesos sangrientos de Puebla y la llegada de Francisco I. Madero a esa ciudad* (*The Latest Bloody Events in Puebla and the Arrival of Francisco I. Madero to that City*, Guillermo Becerril, 1911). Reprinted with permission from Juan Felipe Leal, *El documental nacional de la Revolución mexicana: Filmografía 1910–1914* (Mexico City: Juan Pablos Editor/Voyeur, 2012). Original source: Colección Filmoteca de la Universidad Nacional Autónoma de México.

FIG 1.6 Military action in *Revolución en Veracruz* (*Revolution in Veracruz*, Enrique Rosas, 1912). Publicity for the film promised that it "was shot with great courage on the part of the operator, because without fear of bullets he ventured right up to the firing line." Reprinted with permission from Juan Felipe Leal, *El documental nacional de la Revolución mexicana: Filmografía 1910–1914* (Mexico City: Juan Pablos Editor/Voyeur, 2012). Original source: Colección Filmoteca de la Universidad Nacional Autónoma de México.

Screening and Staging Crime in Revolutionary Mexico City

As Mexico City emerged from the violence and privation that had accompanied the military occupations of 1914–1915, forms of violence and disorder stemming from the conflict persisted alongside efforts to construct a postrevolutionary order. Expanding on imaginaries forged during the Porfiriato, the popular press framed criminality using tropes from cinema and serial literature, even as these cultural products were blamed for an increase in—and the increasing sophistication of—crime. At the same time, perceived links between criminality and cinema shaped debates regarding legal limits on film exhibition, cinema's social effects, and emerging conceptions of the medium's unique qualities.

In the late teens and early twenties, robbery and murder in Mexico City were envisioned both as a national problem and as a uniquely urban malady that was compounded by the blurring of the distinction between military and criminal violence. A suggestive October 1919 editorial in *El Universal* comments,

> For nine years, on this soil we have fought for all the ideals of free and civilized nations; blood has amply reddened the earth; but, sad to say, the greater part of those who have lost their lives, did not fall in combat; they fell in an immense series of murders that have unfolded like a great chain. . . .
>
> Enough! we say. Save something that is above the Revolution; save the Fatherland, which is drowning in a sea of blood. It is necessary, because, looking from above, as far as the eye can see, in long stretches, one can distinguish only victims and executioners, murderers and murdered.[91]

In the opinion of the editorialist, the Revolution had devolved into a bloodbath in which political violence could not be easily distinguished from criminal violence. In a series of articles in a similarly bombastic tone published throughout the late teens and early twenties, *El Universal* protested outbreaks of political conflict and waged a campaign against thieves (*rateros*), continually drawing attention to the unregulated exercise of public violence as a marker of social disintegration and insecurity.[92]

Criminal and political violence alike were interpreted through an existing cultural repertoire of melodramatic tropes, as becomes evident in another 1919 editorial, entitled "Baptism in Blood." The article begins, "Given this title appropriate to a sword-and-sandal novel, an exciting film, or an act of extreme banditry, our readers will think that we are going to comment in the lines of this severe and indignant editorial, the truculent episodes of the latest hold-up or train robbery."[93] Declaring that such crimes are now "everyday incidents" not worthy of sustained attention, the editorialist turns to a potentially graver matter: the conflict accompanying the early stages of the 1920 presidential campaign.

In a context of pervasive public violence, the media spectacles surrounding the Grey Automobile Gang case exemplify how sensationalistic narratives addressed nationally specific anxieties by referencing cosmopolitan tropes of criminality. Thanks to "an aura of technical prowess that resembled images imported in the form of movies and literature from Europe and the United States," the Grey Automobile Gang became "a symbol of modernization and danger in the capital; in the eyes of the population, it was clear evidence of the connivance between government officials and criminals that would distinguish the postrevolutionary era."[94] The issue of political corruption was thrown into relief by military misconduct during the occupations of Mexico City, and the increased presence of firearms and automobiles led to shifts in the character of violent crime.[95] Yet the popular press tended to present these transformations as markers of local modernity, more than as signs of the revolutionary conflict's disruptive effects.

Press discourses highlighting the costs of progress in industrialized nations affirmed Mexico City as a modern metropolis because of, rather than in spite of, its social problems. A 1916 chronicle entitled "Urban Maladies," which appeared in the magazine *Revista de Revistas*, linked the spread of typhus and the prevalence of armed robbery in Mexico City to the ills evident in highly industrialized cities in Europe and the United States.

> Not all is light in the great capitals: these have their zones of shadow, their dark stains, which not even the brilliance of their most positive acts of progress can dissipate; they suffer from ills that not even the most indisputable scientific progress can extirpate. These ills are epidemics and crime, and it is precisely in great capitals that they find an ample field to develop. There, the venomous flowers of civilization unfold, and articles from London, Paris, Berlin and New York inform us amply about the subject.

Presenting progress and decadence as interlinked, the editorialist presents Mexico City's social problems not as signs of backwardness, but rather as ills that flourish alongside and are effectively inseparable from modernization, and which are themselves highly mediated by the press. The journalist notes, "The events recorded by the informational press [*prensa de información*] have sowed panic, and although the public has added a good dose of imaginative fantasy, even inventing ones that never occurred, those that have been confirmed are sufficient to explain the current disquiet and alarm."[96] Noting the role of a journalistic model oriented toward topical events in creating a climate of public anxiety, the writer frames the problem of criminality within cosmopolitan rather than national horizons. In a similar fashion, the press often made ironic allusions to the growing "refinement" of crime, marked by increasing efficiency and even aesthetic sophistication, as signaled by frequent references to Thomas de Quincey's essay "On Murder Considered as One of the Fine Arts."[97] Journalists compared the misdeeds of con men and thieves to the exploits of Rocambole, the protagonist of a popular series of novels by Ponson du Terrail and of several Pathé film adaptations, which were released in Mexico City beginning in July 1914.[98] In particular, journalistic discourses on criminality were shaped by the local presence of French crime films—notably, those produced by Pathé and Éclair beginning in 1911—and a flood of Hollywood serials with criminal themes that accompanied the expansion of U.S. production companies into Mexican markets.[99]

An illustrated article entitled "The Modernization of our Thieves," published in *Excélsior* in October 1919, exemplifies how intersecting imaginaries of cinema and illustrated journalism equated cosmopolitan criminality with modernity in revolutionary Mexico City.[100] The article frames the activities of the Grey Automobile Gang and other recent cases as evidence of quintessentially modern forms of criminality, from robberies committed by "gentlemen in tails" who masquerade as members of the upper classes to the exploits of "moto-ladrones" (motorized thieves) who commit robberies and kidnappings with the help of automobiles. Adding sensational visual appeal, the article includes an assemblage of images that draw on tropes for representing criminality forged during the Porfiriato—the physiognomic portrait and the photographic reconstruction—with a knife dripping blood splashed across the page for good measure. Directly below the headline, heavily shaded drawings of "El Chato Bernabé," a member of the Grey Automobile Gang, and another infamous thief, "El Gurrumino," emphasize their menacing features. Below the portraits, a halftone with the caption "A Robbery in the Roma Neighborhood: Reconstruction by Our Photographer" shows two men perching on an automobile in order to climb through a second-story window. The use of a photographic reconstruction to illustrate the crime—which took

FIG 1.7 "The Modernization of Our Thieves." Physiognomic drawings and a photographic reconstruction sensationalize criminality. *Excélsior*, 26 October 1919. Biblioteca Miguel Lerdo de Tejada, Secretaría de la Hacienda y Crédito Público.

place in a wealthy *colonia* in the western zone of the city—dramatizes the event for the camera, offering a sense of journalistic exclusivity. The slippage between criminal acts and their restaging for the camera is emphasized by an anecdote (probably apocryphal): a pedestrian, attacked by automobile bandits, manages to flag down a passing car and pursue his attackers with the help of other passersby and a policeman. Unable to catch them, he learns the next day from the police that they were in fact actors who were filming a scene for Rosas's *El automóvil gris*.

Fact and fantasy mingled in the imaginary of modern criminality forged by the popular press, and, as in many national contexts, moving pictures were attributed with a unique power to foster crime. While the urbane journalist Francisco Zamora declared, referring to the eponymous villain of the 1913 French serial, "My concept of morality is not disturbed by the admirable efficiency with which Fantômas commits crimes," public officials were less sanguine.[101] In 1920, references to imported crime serials figured prominently in local debates regarding film censorship—sparked in part, de los Reyes speculates, by the legally problematic exhibition of *El automóvil gris*.[102] Defending government oversight in the service of public safety, Interior Minister Aguirre Berlanga claimed that the pernicious effects of imported crime films were already being felt: "Everyone will recall that in the past our thieves did not sedate their victims, nor were there masked robbers, nor high-class robberies. For this to occur, it was necessary that models come from abroad. And thus, due to the exhibition of 'The Mysteries of New York' with copious attendance by thieves, they modernized their strategies and were more easily able to elude the police."[103]

Whatever its concrete effects on the "progress" of crime in Mexico City, the exhibition of *Los misterios de Nueva York* (The Mysteries of New York), a reedited version of three Pathé Exchange serials starring Pearl White, became a key point of reference for early film critics.[104] The film pitted the wealthy heiress Elaine (Pearl White) and her champion, the "scientific detective" Justin Clarel (Craig Kennedy in the American version), against the formidable "Clutching Hand," with both sides taking advantage of fantastical technologies to defeat their enemies. According to "Nemo," a critic in the magazine *Don Quijote*, "In light of the great triumph achieved" by the film, "serials [*películas en episodios*] began to rain down." By 1919, he noted, serial "advertisements alone were sufficient to fill a movie theater."[105] First shown in Mexico City in May 1916, episodes from *Los misterios de Nueva York* were still being exhibited in late August, and it was reprised at least twice in Mexico City in the following two years.[106] This commercial success was followed by the release of a number of serials, including several starring White, who quickly became a local favorite. In *La casa del odio* (The House of Hate, George B. Seitz, 1918), White appeared alongside the Spanish actor Antonio Moreno. Moreno also enjoyed great local popularity (perhaps because he was sometimes misidentified as Mexican), as is suggested by the local release of the serial *Perils of Thunder Mountain* (Robert N. Bradbury and William J. Bauman, 1919) as *Aventuras de Moreno*.[107]

At the center of local debates regarding film's social effects, serial films and their dynamic kineticism also shaped emerging conceptions of cinema's specific qualities as a medium. As Jennifer M. Bean argues in the case of serial stars of the teens more broadly, the feats performed by Moreno's "extraordinary body" were linked to claims of verisimilitude.[108] A journalist notes in the magazine *Arte y Sport* in 1920, "In these films there is less margin for *trucos* [special effects]" than in comedy: "The proof is that Moreno has a broken arm and an infinity of scars from accidents in his work."[109] Whereas publicity for revolutionary-era nonfiction films invoked the imperiled body of the cameraman in the line of fire as the guarantor of their claims to authenticity, the daring feats performed by the serial star's "extraordinary body" offered a new standard of realism, even as special effects were openly acknowledged as part of cinema's repertoire.

Local critics linked the physical virtuosity displayed by serial films to what they perceived as a longer tradition of action-oriented films produced in the United States, encompassing a range of melodramas and westerns. According to "Nemo," before serials' arrival in Mexico City in the late teens, U.S. films had been considered "serious monstrosities. . . . Never were there seen more pursuits, more shootouts, more corpses, than in the films produced at that time by American companies."[110] Other journalists also equated North American films with a brand of adventure melodrama that encompassed "semantic elements" of the western.[111] Referring to the serial *The Adventures of Peg O' the Ring* (Francis Ford and Jacques Jaccard, 1916), the critic Rafael Pérez Taylor declared, "The American film is a synonym of a vulgar movie in which railroads, cowboys, assaults, beasts, struggles, leaps and crudely painted eyebrows are the indispensable corollaries of every plot."[112] Commenting dismissively on the appeal of serials, in an article on *The Iron Claw* (Edward José, 1916), starring Pearl White, Pérez Taylor describes their audience as comprising mostly "foreigners and children who in a continuous uproar celebrate the punishment of the villain and the triumph of the good man."[113] He was somewhat more favorably disposed toward French crime serials, describing the episodes of Louis Feuillade's *Les vampires* (1915) as "so interesting that the audience who sees the first, will have to undertake continuous trips to all the theaters where they are unfolding" (a comment that alludes to the irregular exhibition of serial episodes in Mexico City and elsewhere, noted by Laura Isabel Serna).[114] In 1921, after the popularity of imported serials had largely waned, the film critic Marco-Aurelio Galindo noted that criminal themes had been over-exploited in the cinema precisely because "crime plots [*asuntos policíacos*] are those that are most full of cinematic visuality," a quality that Galindo believed U.S. cinema had exploited from its earliest years.[115]

The perceived affinity between crime films and "cinematic visuality" was conditioned by a locally specific point of reference: the serial novel, or folletín. Although the tie-in novelizations used to promote serials in the United States and elsewhere never became popular in Mexico, many early critics referred to the folletín, which was associated both with sentimentality and with fast-and-furious narrative action, in an attempt to articulate cinema's specific characteristics.[116] In the article "La cinematografía en Estados Unidos," "Nemo" describes the serial film as "a work whose genuine representative in literature is the *novela por entregas* [novel in installments]," given that each episode "always ends with a greatly exciting scene with no conclusion, interesting the spectator enough to oblige him to return to the cinema the next day." The journalist noted that when movie theaters began offering programs that combined several episodes, a common practice in Mexico City—both *La banda del automóvil* and *El automóvil gris* were screened in multi-episode blocks over consecutive nights—the suspense provided by cliffhangers waned and, with it, serials' audience appeal.[117]

Beyond references to the episodic structure shared by the folletín and the serial film, critics invoked the literary form as part of a preexisting melodramatic repertoire articulated between Europe and Latin America. In 1920, an article signed by the writer Martín Luis Guzmán (originally published in Spain under a pseudonym shared with critic Alfonso Reyes) initially compares the cross-class appeal of cinema to that of the violent sport of bullfighting. Yet the article concludes that, "If we wish to find something whose function approaches that of the cinema, which, like it, has the virtue of producing collective emotional states, we must search for it in the literary field and especially toward its most humble regions: we will find it in the folletín."[118] As noted above, Guzmán argues that both forms exemplify "the aesthetic inherent in action," with a key difference: "In the folletín, action is accompanied by bad literature; while in the cinema, with the disappearance of the word, one gains distance from the problem of style and only the action remains."[119] Because it can directly render rather than describe action, cinema is purified of the ills of verbose, sentimental description. At the same time, it maintains its ability to provoke powerful emotions and sensations.

Press discourses on serial films emphasized their visceral impact on spectators. In an article about *Los misterios de Nueva York*, the critic and poet Rafael López observes

> the appeal held for the majority by the crime film, the ever-present crime film, which no program can do without. The producers, for their part, wisely take advantage of this morbid curiosity, and embolden it by serving up, in small doses, the truculent episodes and unprecedented exploits, alternately shared between detectives and bandits. . . . As for the public, day by day they lose their sensitivity and watch, unperturbed, the most blood-

curdling spectacles. They are like those "gourmets" with exhausted palates who need ever-stronger liquors in order to taste them.[120]

This description of crime films and other forms of popular sensationalism as a therapeutic shock for human senses ennervated by urban life is familiar from U.S. and European discourses on urban modernity, both popular and erudite, perceptively analyzed by Ben Singer.[121] Yet in a metropolitan area that was approaching one million inhabitants in 1919, where a lack of sanitation, streetlights, and effective policing were often more pressing threats to life and limb than the sensory overload of the urban environment, these notions of sensational film as a therapeutic shock to jaded senses must be reevaluated. As I demonstrate through closer attention to the production and reception of *El automóvil gris* and *La banda del automóvil*, in Mexico City in the late teens sensational subjects were viewed as inextricable from the spectacles of public violence that characterized revolutionary and postrevolutionary politics.

Sensational Authenticity and Urban Modernity:
El automóvil gris and *La banda del automóvil*

In January 1919, the popular magazine *El Universal Ilustrado* directly compared the Grey Automobile Gang case to a suspenseful film that unfolded over a series of distinct "episodes," linking it to a culture of sensationalism with an international scope. Noting the public rumours surrounding "the scandalous matter of the 'Grey Automobile,'" the journalist notes,

> The anticipation of the public, now very difficult to disturb, given the sensationalism to which it has become accustomed due to the rapid succession of surprising spectacles the world over, has followed with renewed avidity the most minor episodes of this tragic film in which those involved lose their lives in circumstances that are unclear to the authorities, the threads of the plot slip from one's hands, and the physiognomies of the true criminals are hidden behind a veil of mystery.[122]

Between late December 1918 and late January 1919, the popular Mexico City newspapers *El Universal, El Pueblo,* and *El Demócrata* published lengthy exposés about the case on an almost daily basis. Often, journalists dramatized these developments in the case by framing them in explicitly cinematic terms. *El Universal* described the escape of Grey Automobile Gang member Francisco Oviedo as having been achieved "with an audacity only imaginable in films."[123] Oviedo was later recaptured, and when he and fellow gang member Rafael Mercadante were murdered in prison only a few days apart in December 1918, the same newspaper stated, "It is indispensable that a film be released. Inevitably, we all must remember, as a comparison, the exciting and at times unbelievable episodes of *The House of Hate*, still fresh in the mind."[124]

Responding to the perceived affinities between current events and popular crime narratives, exhibitors and filmmakers rushed to capitalize on these apparent connections between sensational fact and serial fiction. Shortly after Rosas announced his intent to adapt the case to the screen, the distributor Martínez y Cia exhibited the Vitagraph serial *The Scarlet Runner* (Wally Van and William P. S. Earle, 1916) under the title *El automóvil gris*.[125] This marketing strategy prompted legal action from Rosas, who had copyrighted the title, as well as a publicity campaign that asserted the "thrilling topicality" (*palpitante actualidad*) of his own film.[126] Rosas also protested the production of *La banda del automóvil*, but to no avail. As the film's financier, the exhibitor Germán Camus was thus able to claim the distinction of having produced the "first Mexican serial film [*película en episodios*]."[127] (In fact, the nation's first serial film was *Xandaroff o Venganza de bestia* [*Xandaroff or the Beast's Vengeance*], produced by the wealthy film enthusiast Carlos Martínez de Arredondo in Mérida, Yucatán, and released in June 1919.)[128] Articles (likely promotional texts inserted by request) stressed the great length (10,000 meters) and expense (60,000 pesos) of *La banda del automóvil*, linking its grand scale to new ambitions for a film industry in Mexico City.[129]

To make matters worse for Rosas, his film's premiere was delayed by a plethora of legal problems, including libel suits lodged by two of the alleged gang members and the threat of censorship by local authorities, since the inquiry into the case was still pending.[130] Delaying the film's release, these legal battles resulted in ongoing newspaper publicity that may have ultimately supplemented its box office receipts. The writer and film critic Carlos Noriega Hope noted, "The red flags of scandal gave [the film] luster and splendor and all of the questions of judicial boards and watermarked paper served to stimulate the curiosity of our public on a daily basis."[131] A public debate about the legality of representing real-life crime, staged in the pages of the popular press, itself became spectacular entertainment.

While Rosas stressed the greater authenticity of his version, he sought, like his rivals Martínez and Camus, to profitably position his film within an imaginary of modern criminality circulating between Mexico, France, and the United States. Tellingly, both *El automóvil gris* and *La banda del automóvil* were interpreted through the lens of serial literature, with a reviewer asserting that *"El automóvil gris* is, considering that it is folletín-esque, a magnificent film" and observed that *La banda del automóvil,* "despite being folletín-esque, having a criminal air, and being of the episodic genre, is sensible, reasonable, sane, and sober." In fact, according to the same reviewer, *La banda del automóvil* failed to satisfy spectators who "enjoy that which is cliché, distorted, truculent, and even absurd, in order to experience those favorable violent emotions, those sudden shocks that this reasonable film does not provoke."[132] (Noriega Hope, by contrast, declared that *La banda del automóvil* "carries out propaganda in favor of death, illogical coincidences, and the five senses, with the exception of common sense.")[133] Ultimately, Rosas was able to release his film in nineteen movie theaters (later expanded to twenty-three), in comparison with ten for Vollrath's version; an advertisement claimed that 40,233 spectators had seen *El automóvil gris* in a single day.[134]

Upon the film's long-awaited release, Rosas launched an advertising campaign that included melodramatic descriptions of the events depicted in each of its three *jornadas* (evenings) of screenings. These descriptions stressed the film's close proximity to real-life events and its claims to topicality and authenticity:

> This film is not a fiction. Traced [*calcada*] from real events, it is an exact transcription of the truth, selected from the incongruent details of a mystery. Plotted around the crimes of the Grey Automobile Gang, it has exciting and dramatic details, terrible scenes and poetic renderings [*pinceladas*] which are rays, pious lightning bolts of virtue that from time to time break the shadow of the fearful den where evil and crime seek refuge.

Recalling the rhetoric of the newspaper exposés surrounding the case, the advertisement echoes their drive to investigate topical events, shedding light on murky happenings. These events, in turn, are imbued with a moral legibility characteristic of melodrama through the polar opposition of piety and "virtue" to "evil and crime." The advertisement emphasizes *El automóvil gris*'s narrativization of violent events, the manner in which it assembles a plot from a profusion of "incongruent details." At the same time, the rhetoric of illumination alludes to the role of light in creating a photochemical impression of the real, highlighting the indexical character of photochemical media that function as "traces" of contingent events. Claiming both to directly document real-life events and to narrate them through melodramatic tropes, *El automóvil gris* lent moral legibility to a real-life spectacle of public violence.

FIG 1.8 Advertisements for *El automóvil gris* incorporated a synopsis reminiscent of a folletín. *Excélsior*, 11 December 1919. Biblioteca Miguel Lerdo de Tejada, Secretaría de la Hacienda y Crédito Público.

Whereas reviews of *El automóvil gris* praised its suspenseful narrative structure and skillful cinematography, Rosas's advertising campaign emphasized not its effectiveness as a fiction but its elements of visual documentation and reenactment, especially the use of location shooting and the involvement of professionals with direct connections to the case. Yet although one of the film's reviewers claimed that the film was produced "without more changes to its scenes, than those indispensable to give theatricality to the subject," film historians have contested its account of real-life events in a number of ways.[135] In the anarchic atmosphere of occupied Mexico City, marked by violence, food shortages, and the proliferation of counterfeit currency, soldiers' indiscriminate looting undermined police authority.[136] Yet in *El automóvil gris* the police work efficiently and effectively to capture the gang; González himself appears in a scene where he urges the detectives to redouble their efforts. Other historical events are clearly distorted: while the search warrants used in the historical robberies bore the authentic signatures of military officers, in contrast to those used in similar crimes, in the film they are depicted as having been stolen by the gang's leader, Higinio Granda, with the complicity of a low-ranking colleague on the police force.[137] Official involvement in the robberies is further disavowed by means of a curious narrative device. Roughly midway through the film, Granda pretends to respond to the summons of a higher-up in a private room for the benefit of an accomplice; during a police raid later in the film, the supposed crime boss is revealed to be a mannequin dressed in a Carrancista uniform. De los Reyes notes that this strange scene deviates both from plausible historical fact and from preexisting legends about the gang, playing on and then refuting popular suspicion about military officers' complicity in the crimes.[138]

Despite apparent efforts to absolve González of any wrongdoing, the plot of *El automóvil gris* does make reference to the slippage between criminal, police, and military activity that marked the occupations of Mexico City. The historical Granda served as a Zapatista captain concurrently with his participation in the robberies, and as a court clerk after his imprisonment.[139] In *El automóvil gris*, his character infiltrates the ranks of both the police (to steal the search warrants used in the robberies) and the military (to escape prison through conscription into the army). In a parallel development, an elderly victim of one of the robberies receives police permission to dispense vigilante justice. Like the criminals, the authorities adopt disguises in the film, dressing as telephone company employees to gain entry to a rooming house where one of the bandits and his lover are in hiding. Rosas's original script even includes a scene, not present in the surviving version of the film, in which the police fight their own agents in disguise, having mistaken them for the bandits.[140] The blurring between military and criminal, judicial and extrajudicial, violence exemplifies the ambiguities of public violence in revolutionary Mexico.

While addressing locally specific conditions, this fluidity of authority and identity would also have recalled imported crime serials like Louis Feuillade's *Fantômas* and *Les vampires*, whose plots turn on disguise, impersonation, and criminals' infiltration of high society and the police. The visual and narrative conventions of *El automóvil gris* also have clear affinities to the Feuillade's serials, particularly the use of deep-focus compositions, location shooting, and stunts that capitalize on a thrilling verticality (including a spectacular leap from a high wall in the scene showing Francisco Oviedo's prison break). The costuming of the Grey Automobile Gang members, who wear caps, ascots, and suits that recall the clothing of the *apache* when not dressed in their military disguises, also evokes a distinctly French criminal underworld.

Some critics found these elements of the film to be uncomfortably incongruous, perhaps in part because they failed to conform with the racialized vision of criminality developed by scientific and journalistic discourses. Noriega Hope noted that the figure of Granda in Rosas's film possessed "distinction, elegance, gallantry and good manners which I fear do not conform closely to the historical truth." Evoking criminological discourses that equated certain physical characteristics with an innate propensity toward violence, Noriega Hope pictures the "real" Granda as a hirsute, menacing bandit, primitive in appearance and manners.

> I always thought that the fearful gang's leader was sturdy in appearance; I imagined that this offspring of evil would be a blood-soaked bandit, whose pupils would flash while his thick, hairy eyebrows underlined all of the horror of his look.... [But] in the film the leader of the Grey Automobile Gang shocks us with his broad gestures that have the air of the boulevard, with his graceful component of *sportman* [*sic*] dressed, for dilettantism, as a Parisian *apache*.[141]

While Granda was in fact a Spanish immigrant with light skin and delicate features, as readers of the illustrated press would have been aware, Noriega Hope's review suggests a dissonance between a local and a French iconography of crime, a precarious balance between national content and cosmopolitan imagery and style.

The physical appearance of the real-life bandits, who do not closely resemble the actors who play them in the fictional portions of the film, becomes a point at which the tension between the cosmopolitan and the national, and between documentation and dramatization, becomes strikingly evident. Reading the execution sequence as an attempt to quell Europe-oriented, bourgeois Mexicans' anxieties about shifting class and race hierarchies in the wake of the Revolution, Paul Schroeder-Rodríguez focuses on the film's inconsistent portrayal of the Grey Automobile Gang's members, noting that the "real-life bandits do not look anything like the ones played by actors. Rather, they look like indigenous-mestizo Zapatistas with their wide-brim hats and their tight pants."[142] In a recently restored version of the film, it is evident that the

FIG 1.9 The moving automobile emphasizes deep-focus shooting, while careful framing—including house numbers—calls attention to location. Video still.

FIG 1.10 Stunts in *El automóvil gris* incorporated a thrilling verticality. Video still.

criminals do not resemble the iconic image of the rural Zapatista; rather, they wear shapeless coats and nondescript fedoras that look distinctly urban.

Schroeder-Rodríguez also critiques the sequence's framing in long shot, suggesting that "what we see are not individuals, but a faceless, indistinct pattern of falling bodies. The effect of this closing montage is that the viewer's previous identification with the bandits is severed, criollo fears of losing their privileges and properties are effectively allayed, and revolutionary activity is equated with banditry."[143] Schroeder-Rodríguez helpfully calls attention to the intersection of local politics with the adaptation of imported film genres and conventions. However, what he interprets as a strategic dehumanization of the bandits can be more adequately explained as a strategic use of the reality effects produced by cinematic conventions, a shift from the codes of fiction to those of the actuality, which work to document—and construct—a mass spectacle of public violence. Rosas's film does not, as Schroeder-Rodríguez suggests, propose a conservative equation of revolution with banditry; rather, it makes a reactionary attempt to reimpose the distinction between legitimate and illegitimate violence and appropriations of private property that had effectively disappeared during the occupation of Mexico City.

Staging Urban Modernity in *El automóvil gris* and *La banda del automóvil*

Even as the problem of distinguishing between legitimate and illegitimate violence is navigated by *El automóvil gris*'s strategic use of fictional and nonfictional codes, urban space—devastated by conflict and modernized by recent reforms—takes center stage in the film. The bulk of *El automóvil gris* unfolds in the streets, police stations, and upper-class homes of Mexico City, although it also includes scenes where detectives track the criminals to Puebla and the town of Apam, motivating the display of "typical" rural customs (in the form of a cockfight). If journalistic discourses on criminality sought to reinforce spatial divisions between elites and working classes in a modernizing city, *El automóvil gris* emphasizes the permeability of urban space to criminal mobility. At key moments throughout the film, the appearance of large-scale maps signals the penetration of illicit activities into wealthy zones of the modernized capital. In the first sequence of the film, Granda indicates to his conspirators the route they will to take to reach their target on a map of the metropolis. In a later scene, Granda discusses another heist with an accomplice at the police station, using a wall-mounted map to explain the plan of attack. This second map clearly shows the city's broad avenues and the concentration of robbery sites in the affluent new *colonias* in the western sector of the city. These scenes subtly signal both exclusionary programs of urban reform in Mexico City and the capacity for illicit traffic along its modern thoroughfares.[144] The film's use of editing and sweeping tracking shots also reinforces the criminals' mastery of the cityscape, linked to their use of the eponymous automobile. When the first robbery is depicted in flashback, shortly after the opening scene described above, we see the automobile pause to pick up the individual robbers, now dressed in military uniforms, on various street corners. The sequence highlights the bandits' capacity for coordinated action across several urban locations. Tracking shots that follow the automobile in motion, which have been compared to Italian historical epics of the same period, harness the camera lens to the moving vehicle, foregrounding their joint role in traversing and mapping urban space.[145]

Presenting the refashioned cityscape, the automobile, and criminal activity as interlinked emblems of modernization, *El automóvil gris* showcased cinematic technique while refusing a cosmetic vision of the capital. In a review of Rosas's film in *Cine-Mundial*, the Spanish-language counterpart of *Moving Picture World* printed in New York City, the critic Epifanio Soto Jr. noted, "Strangely, the streets have not been scoured [for locations] to make Mexico City seem prodigiously beautiful, a mania of producers around here; almost everything was filmed in ugly, deserted alleyways, which give realism to the chases in other incredible locations, and the formidable combats, proper to the anarchic age in which they took place."[146] As this review suggests, *El automóvil gris* traded heavily on the sense of authenticity offered by filming on location. In sequences depicting the robberies, establishing shots are carefully framed to include specific house numbers. Deep-focus shots, many of which showcase the criminals' vehicle moving toward the foreground, simultaneously capture the urban backdrop and display a mastery of photographic technique.

The skillful photographic rendering of urban space also took center stage in *La banda del automóvil* which, while billing itself as a "film of actuality and sensation," focused less on the events of the Grey Automobile Gang case than on the display of local spaces, including the "authentic and luxurious interiors of lavish residences."[147] The same article notes that to faithfully capture such spaces, artificial lights and reflectors were used, a novel practice for local productions.[148] These techniques effectively created "a play of light which we frequently encounter in European and North American films, and which it was believed impossible to attain in Mexican productions."[149] Artificial lighting made possible dramatic chiaroscuro effects that approximated the film to its foreign competitors.

The display of photographic technique in *La banda del automóvil* may have reached its most spectacular point in the vista of Mexico City by night that opened the film, showcasing electric lighting as a marker of local modernity and demonstrating the cinematographer's capacity to capture a clear image under low-light conditions.[150] According to one reviewer, this sequence caused a stir among the attendees at an advance screening for the press: "An admiring exclamation escaped the spectators when the surprising effect of the Avenida del 5 de Mayo [a thoroughfare in the city center] at midnight appeared on the screen."[151] Referring to still photographs of buildings illuminated for the celebration of Mexico's centennial in 1910, Mraz writes, "Photographing the luminous city must have offered a double certification of the up-to-date: the images not only testified to Mexico's electrical capacity, but also demonstrated the technological capabilities of the photographers."[152] In a similar fashion, the opening scene of *La banda del automóvil* would have showcased the local cityscape through the interconnected technologies of electric light and cinema. Electrical illumination also figured prominently in *La banda del automóvil*'s publicity campaign, which stressed connections between criminal activity, the automobile, and modern urban space. An advertisement shows an automobile in the foreground, the beams of its headlights cutting across the pictorial space, with a line of lamps marking the vanishing point of the broad avenue. The image lacks any clear markers of the Mexico City setting; the imaginary of motorized crime evoked here is more cosmopolitan than local.

Accordingly, many reviewers suggested that *La banda del automóvil* was uncomfortably close to imported cinema. In *Cine-Mundial*, Soto criticized *La banda del automóvil*'s director for his adoption of a markedly foreign style, linking these traits to apparent export ambitions for the film. He writes, "To the excessive exoticism of the plot, he adds his own and makes a picture completely in the French style, which is Mexican only in name. . . . It is a film that could be exhibited abroad without diminishing us; but also without giving an idea of us, because, as I have said, it is completely exotic. It seems that an American business is in negotiations with the producers."[153] *La banda del automóvil* was later advertised to foreign distributors in *Cine-Mundial*, and its producer, director, and cinematographer traveled to New York to facilitate its sale in the United States, although I am unaware of any U.S. screenings.[154]

FIG I.II A publicity image for *La banda del automóvil* frames crime and electrified avenues as modern attractions. *Don Quijote*, 10 September 1919. Biblioteca Miguel Lerdo de Tejada, Secretaría de la Hacienda y Crédito Público.

Distancing itself from current events and adopting visual and narrative conventions that local critics viewed as Frenchified, *La banda del automóvil* highlighted an aspect of imported serial films with transgressive potential: the active participation of women in criminal activities. While *El automóvil gris* featured characters corresponding to the real-life Elvira Ortiz, a young woman who had been involved with Francisco Oviedo, and Carmen, a widow seduced by the criminal Ángel Chao, they play only a tangential role in the unfolding of events in the surviving version of the film. By contrast, both *La banda del automóvil* and the later film *Fanny o el robo de los veinte millones* capitalized on fears and fantasies about female criminality that resonated with imported crime narratives as well as with the renegotiation of women's place in public life in the wake of the Revolution.

Gendering Crime in Revolutionary Mexico City:
Women in Mourning and Serial Queens

In September 1916, the Mexico City newspaper *El Pueblo* reported on an attempted bank robbery with an unusual twist: the culprit was a woman in mourning dress who tried to conceal her identity behind a black veil. Echoing the press discourses linking cinema to criminality, the writer comments, "There is no doubt that refined criminal education, of a distinctly European stamp, which has been imported in recent years by means of the cinema, increases each day."[155] This news item prefigures the emergence of the *dama enlutada* (woman in mourning) as a recurring trope in the public spectacles of violence staged by the illustrated press and the cinema in the late teens and early twenties.

Suggesting the anxieties generated by acts of public violence committed by women in the wake of armed conflict, in *La banda del automóvil*, as well as the media spectacles surrounding real-life "crimes of passion" committed by women, the "lady in mourning" is associated with an overt performance of traditional femininity that tempers female criminality. By contrast, in *Fanny o el robo de los veinte millones*, the female criminal is clearly split from conventional models of Mexican womanhood. A blonde daredevil, seductress, and spy (presumably for the United States, although this is not specified in the film's script or publicity), Fanny acts as a counterpoint to the hero's virtuous wife. Resembling an American "serial queen" in her physical exploits—though not her overt sexuality—the figure of Fanny both capitalizes on and critiques the local popularity of Hollywood serials and their dynamic heroines.

The female villains of *Fanny* and *La banda del automóvil* indicate a dialogue with French and U.S. serials, which pleasurably distanced the films from the topical events on which they capitalized. A reviewer stressed that the plot of *La banda del automóvil* was "not at all related with the series of robberies and crimes committed by evildoers who seeded panic amongst neighbors in the 'City of Palaces.'" In fact, the reviewer continues, "it is not gold that impels the outlaws to commit kidnappings and other crimes, but rather the love of an anguished mother who watches over her son at a distance, that motivates the principal events."[156] Although very little information about the film's plot has been preserved, this emphasis on maternal love sentimentalizes crime in a manner that recalls the folletín's frequent pairing of sensationalism with sentimentality.

Although the character of the "woman in mourning" in *La banda del automóvil* may have been copied from Rosas's film—de los Reyes notes a suspicious parallel with one of *El automóvil gris*'s episodes, which referenced the attractive widow Carmen—traces in the illustrated press suggest that mourning dress took on complex connotations in the film, as both a means of concealing identity and a sign of feminine suffering.[157] Judging from surviving stills from *La banda del automóvil*, the black-clad, acrobatic villains of imported (particularly French) serials were likely a point of reference. In a photo spread devoted to the film in the newspaper *Excélsior*, a woman in mourning dress is shown ambushing a pedestrian with the help of a pistol and a masked accomplice. Another image, of a woman fleeing a room via a balcony as she points a pistol toward the camera, seems to show the same character.[158] This active, aggressive female figure is especially notable in its contrast with other images from the film that depict men as physically weak (the banker targeted by the criminals, played by Antonio Galé, is shown as an invalid) or comically ineffectual (the detective Maclovio, played by Ricardo Soto, appears romancing a lady rather than solving the mystery).[159] Yet the "lady in mourning" apparently failed to rival the seductive menace of Feuillade's Irma Vep or the athleticism of American serial queens. In *Cine-Mundial*, Soto describes the theater actress Matilde Cires Sánchez, who played the role, as "a lady in mourning who weighs a few more kilos than she ought and delays too long when acting or fleeing."[160] Soto's comments on her somewhat matronly figure and limited athletic abilities suggest a disconnect between the models of kinetic femininity showcased in French and U.S. cinema, and the distinct configurations of criminality and femininity that arose in the local context.

Beginning in 1920, the figure of the "woman in mourning" became central to the series of films (produced or planned) designed to capitalize on the sensational public trials of Magdalena Jurado, Alicia Olvera, and Luz González. These cases reversed the gender dynamics of the customary "crime of passion" in which husbands killed their wives or lovers. In his high-profile defenses of the women, the lawyer Querido Moheno apparently recommended several strategies that allowed the women to lessen the sense of gender transgression produced by their alleged crimes, thereby garnering the sympathy of the popular juries that had recently replaced military tribunals. Olvera, who was accused of shooting her husband, wept throughout her trial,

FIG 1.12 The "woman in mourning" in action in *La banda del automóvil*. *Excélsior*, 7 September 1919. Biblioteca Miguel Lerdo de Tejada, Secretaría de la Hacienda y Crédito Público.

while González, held responsible for the death of her lover at the hands of a romantic rival, frequently fainted in court. Suggesting the effectiveness of these performances of intense emotion and physical fragility, both Olvera and Jurado were acquitted, though González went through multiple trials before finally being freed.[161]

Like the Grey Automobile case, these trials were explicitly understood within the melodramatic, sensationalized imaginary of serial literature and cinema. Zamora noted that Olvera's trial won her "a disproportionate fame, which made the sensitive soul of every reader of truculent novels in this city moan with desire." Perhaps more troublingly, he also suggested that women who consumed sensational narratives were potential criminals themselves: "Tremble, oh husbands whose wives frequent the cinematograph and read folletín-esque literature! Alicia was like your wives. . . . She had a secret longing for adventure. . . . Alicia Olvera felt herself to be, at one moment, in the middle of a novel, and killed, to give a tinge of red to the grey opacity of her bourgeois existence."[162] Framed as a sensation-seeking behavior, the consumption of serial literature and cinema is presented (with a dose of irony) as a response to domestic monotony that might trigger real-life violence.

The fascination generated by accused female criminals in revolutionary Mexico City may be rooted in their transgression of the ideology of separate public and private spheres segregated along gender lines, with women's entry into public life marked by their exercise of violence. A high-profile case from 1920 exemplified this dynamic: the trial of fourteen-year-old María del Pilar Moreno, who shot Senator Francisco Tejeda Llorca after he killed her father, Senator Jesús Moreno, in a political dispute. Since Tejeda Llorca enjoyed judicial immunity due to his political office, María del Pilar took matters into her own hands. Killing in defense of family honor, like the commission of a "crime of passion" against an adulterous wife, was often judged legitimate if not legal when perpetrated by a man, serving as a mitigating factor in criminal prosecution.[163] Yet this case generated a firestorm of controversy because of Moreno's sex and age. Piccato argues that Moreno's case not only displayed the "masculine ferocity of politics" in the wake of the revolution, but also an "uncertainty about the role women would play in a new era expected to increase political liberties but also increasingly dominated by images of male heroism."[164] The media spectacles surrounding the case of Moreno and other alleged female criminals suggest the degree to which women's participation in public life in the years following the revolution was conditioned by highly public acts of violence.

Despite the extensive press coverage of these sensational cases, neither the actuality film shot during Magdalena Jurado's trial nor the dramatic reconstruction *Redención*, in which Luz González played herself, achieved anything approaching the box-office success of *El automóvil gris* or *La banda del automóvil*. If they were effective with juries, these women's self-consciously feminine performances apparently failed to impress onscreen. Cube Bonifant, one of Mexico's first female film critics, reviewed *Redención* with heavy irony. Aside from the "reconstruction of the crime," which Bonifant admired, she observes an overall lack of verisimilitude, noting that the "plot, in spite of supposedly being a copy of something real, is quite ludicrous."[165] This lack of believability was compounded by the artificiality attributed to González's performance, both in court and onscreen. Bonifant observes, "We already knew she was no measly theater actress. Luz González is truly sincere in her fakery." The paradoxical definition of her acting as "sincere fakery" highlights gender's performative aspects. At a historical juncture when models of womanhood were being contested and the public visibility of women recon-figured, González's strategic embodiment of femininity called attention to its historically and socially contingent character.

As female participation in public life was being renegotiated through media spectacles of violence, local filmmakers' attempts to emulate North American serials generated controversy about the strategies that should be adopted to stimulate domestic film production. In November 1919, the newspaper *Ex-célsior* announced the production of a serial based on the exploits of real-life nineteenth-century bandit Chucho el Roto. Echoing other hopeful reports of Hollywood stars' plans to film in Mexico, the articles featured stills of a blond American actress named Hilda North, whose participation was framed as a coup for local film production. (North had supposedly appeared in films with Mary Pickford.)[166] Yet a journalist in *Don Quijote* was less than enthusiastic, commenting, "It occurs to us to ask why one would import from Yankeeland [*Yanquilandia*], with an exorbitant salary, a 'miss' who will not fit as well in the role of this national film as a number of Mexican film artists would. . . . [I]t will not be much of a stimulus [to national production] to bring in a blond 'miss' for a role more suited to a lovely *criolla*."[167] For the plan's detractors, this casting choice threatened to Americanize Mexico's nascent cinema from within.

While the serial itself seems not to have materialized, responses to Hilda North's threatened incursion into Mexican film production signaled the am-bivalent role of the American serial queen in Mexico City's film culture. Of-fering new models of active, dynamic femininity, the serial queen's popularity suggested not only a perceived Americanization of Mexican film markets, but also the potential of American cinema and associated forms of consumer culture to transform models of Mexican womanhood. These anxieties were exemplified by public debates surrounding the *pelona*, a "modern girl" fig-ure analogous to the American flapper.[168] Yet because of its unsympathetic portrayal of a white woman implied to be American, *Fanny* was viewed as a potential blow against the negative effects of U.S. cinema. Critics grouped the film with productions like Miguel Contreras Torres's *El hombre sin patria* (*The Man Without a Country*, 1922), which included unsympathetic portray-als of Americans in an effort to strike back against "denigrating films" (*pelícu-las denigrantes*) that stereotyped Mexicans, leading to a national boycott of all films made by several U.S. studios that same year.[169] For this reason, *Fanny's* reviewers carefully distinguished between the title character and the Mexican actress who played her, claiming her physical feats as an achievement for local film production.

Fanny's critique of U.S. productions hinges on its sexualization of an anti-heroine who closely resembles a serial queen. According to an advertisement, Fanny rivals stars like Pearl White and Helen Holmes as she "carries out daring exploits that make her the equal of the most famous female stars of adventure films."[170] Yet unlike the serial queen, who tends to reject romance in favor of adventure, Fanny is presented as an agent of moral corruption.[171] She achieves her ends through the seduction of a military officer, Arturo Aguirre (Eduardo Urriola), rather than solely through physical prowess and daring. Surviving publicity images from the film show that her costumes varied accordingly, alternating between the jodhpurs and jaunty cap of the action heroine and the glamorous gowns of the vamp.[172] Furthermore, the film's surviving script indicates that parallel editing was to have been used throughout to contrast Fanny's unscrupulous behavior with the suffering of Arturo's long-suffering wife, Alma. Significantly, the two women were played, respectively, by the sisters María and Anita Cozzi. This extratextual information would have complicated the binary opposition between American and Mexican womanhood that the film establishes.

Evoking both imported serials such as *The Million Dollar Mystery* (Howell Hansel, 1914) and public scandals (the theft of sensitive military plans and Carranza's misappropriation of funds from the national treasury), *Fanny* draws on the structure of serial film plots, which often pivoted on a struggle for possession of a valuable object (here, the missing half of a map indicating the location of the stolen millions).[173] As in the case of *El automóvil gris*, military officials sponsored the reframing of public scandal as popular entertainment. According to one of the film's principal actors, Ángel Álvarez, General Rafael Cal y Mayor agreed to finance the film with the goal of repairing the reputations damaged by the scandal of the stolen plans.[174] The general also furnished troops to appear as extras in the scene of Fanny's capture at the end of the film, and used his personal influence to obtain favorable exhibition terms, although this did not translate into substantial profits for the filmmakers.[175] While *Fanny* was released in ten movie theaters, it was exhibited for only three days; it is unclear whether the film was pulled from exhibition in Mexico City by a newly established municipal censorship authority, as de los Reyes suggests, or merely failed to attract substantial audiences.[176]

According to *Fanny's* script, a flashback established its tenuous connection to real-life events and provided a pretext for a series of risky stunts, narrating the theft by two treasury employees, Fanny's lover Roberto Rufiar (Ángel Álvarez) and his accomplice Ruíz de Velasco (Néstor Vargas). Velasco then betrays his partner, hurling himself from a train to escape with the treasure, then burying it, hastily drawing a map to recall its location. Rufiar attacks him and in the following struggle, which nearly kills both, the map is torn in two. The half found on Velasco's corpse is turned over to the military authorities.[177] In collusion with Rufiar, Fanny resolves to obtain the missing half of the map through any means necessary.

Fanny's script suggests it incorporated a number of dynamic stunts involving transportation technologies. The hero's profession as a pilot motivates multiple scenes at an airfield, displaying the Mexican government's efforts to develop an air force during the period and tapping into public fascination with flight evident in the pages of illustrated magazines like *Revista de Revistas*, which chronicled aviation feats all over the world.[178] Pleasurable and threatening forms of urban circulation linked with the automobile also figure prominently in *Fanny*; early in the film, Captain Aguirre hires a car to take his family on an outing in the Alameda, an elegant park near the city center pivotal to bourgeois rituals of circulation in public space.[179] As the film progresses, the figure of Fanny takes on a potentially menacing mobility as she travels through the city by car in the search for the map. After meeting Aguirre, she arranges a "chance" meeting in another elegant public park, the Bosques de Chapultepec. Her seduction culminates in an invitation to visit her hotel room with the map in tow. According to the script, the encounter acted as a pretext for morally loaded parallel editing between Fanny, who is plying Arturo with champagne, and Alma, who is tearfully waiting for her husband, and led into one of the film's riskiest stunt sequences. Once Arturo falls asleep from overindulgence, Fanny and Rufiar lock him in one of the suite's rooms, but he awakens before they can carry out their objective of copying the map. Discovered, Fanny and Rufiar are forced to make their escape by means of an electric wire suspended high above the street.[180]

The filming of this sequence, as recounted by the actor Eduardo Urriola, turned film production itself into a sensational public spectacle. In an interview conducted in the 1950s, Urriola describes a near-fatal accident that occurred when he took the place of his co-star Álvarez, in order to demonstrate that the stunt was safe:

> As it had been announced in the press that the sequence would be shot with total realism (seeking publicity), starting in the early morning hours a multitude of curious onlookers had gathered, and not wanting to look ridiculous in front of them, seeing that Álvarez resisted, to encourage him,

FIG 1.13 Staging cinematic stunts as a public spectacle in *Fanny o el robo de los veinte millones. Cinema Repórter,* 18 August 1954. Colección Filmoteca de la Universidad Nacional Autónoma de México.

I tried to show him it was easy, and putting my money where my mouth was, I leapt off the balcony and threw myself into the void, confident of myself.[181]

According to Urriola's account, this boldness was nearly fatal; the wire he was holding snapped immediately, and he would have fallen if he had not become tangled in the electrical, telephone, and telegraph cables. After he was rescued by firefighters, a second, similarly ill-fated crossing was attempted: María Cozzi became tired and almost plunged to her death before Álvarez managed to pull the two of them across the wire.

This anecdote, quite possibly apocryphal, invokes the rhetoric of "real" physical danger integral to the star texts of serial actors. The promise of "total realism" invoked by Urriola signals what Bean has called "the lure of [a] referentiality" premised on "catastrophe, disorder, and disaster," in which the virtuosic body of the serial star, subjected to constant danger, became the site where the verisimilitude attributed to the filmic medium was invested.[182] In the production of *Fanny*, the display of bodily peril, linked to the conventions of imported films, demonstrated actors' physical capacities and filmmakers' technical prowess. The public display of risky stunts, framed as newsworthy in themselves, would become a key element in press coverage of domestic film production during the early twenties.

Although the high-wire sequence may have proved the most dangerous to shoot, the script calls for virtuoso stunts to rise to delirious heights in *Fanny*'s final scenes, which stage a chase involving two cars, two airplanes, and a moving train. Once they escape with the map, Fanny and Rufiar steal a Ford and set off, with Aguirre in hot pursuit in a police car. Upping the ante, the two criminals arrive at the airfield and trick Aguirre's colleague Luis into preparing the plane for a pleasure flight. Rufiar knocks Luis unconscious and leaves him on the ground, while Fanny pilots the plane. After Luis and Arturo launch a second airplane in pursuit, yet another vehicle comes into play, as Rufiar and Fanny jump from the plane onto a passing train. Arturo's plane then overtakes the train and he boards, struggling with Rufiar atop the vehicle. The two villains escape, only to come to the edge of a steep canyon in their flight. The two throw a cord across the void, but Rufiar falls to his death—to have been depicted in a suspense-creating series of close-ups on the fraying rope—and Fanny is forced to surrender to the authorities.[183]

According to the script, the chase sequence included a series of cutaways to Alma, who falls asleep waiting for her husband and then, intuitively fearing for his safety, prays in front of an icon. This strategy would have augmented suspense while emphasizing how far Arturo has strayed from the idealized home. Fanny's capture, followed by a closing shot of Arturo being welcomed back into the family fold narratively contain Fanny's seductive qualities and physical virtuosity alike, implicitly condemning American cinema's potentially deleterious effects on the stability of the Mexican family.[184] At the same time, the film would have invited audiences to take pleasure in these very characteristics.

Fanny's critical reception highlights this ambivalence through the distinction drawn between the villainous title character and the virtuosic Mexican actress who played her. Writing in *Cine-Mundial*, Soto interpreted *Fanny* as a direct response to "denigrating" Hollywood films, intervening in a rather one-sided war of cinematic representations. Soto contends that many Mexican

FIG 1.14 A chase scene in *Fanny o el robo de los veinte millones* alludes to Mexico's military aviation program. Archivo General de la Nación (México), Fondo Hermanos Mayo, concentrados sobre 363.

productions (including *Fanny*) could be considered "as derogatory as the Yankee" in their depictions of adultery, violence, and military abuses, but seeks to recuperate the film, writing, "Doesn't it seem preferable to you that we forget that Fanny, of the 'Theft of the Twenty Millions,' is an American, in order to remember that her interpreter, Mary Cozzi, is a limber and agreeable girl, with as much capacity to make a thrilling serial as any American 'miss'?"[185] The critic's employment by an American film magazine may explain his attempt to smooth over any conflict created by Mexican productions' efforts to refute—but also compete with—Hollywood. Downplaying *Fanny*'s overt criticism of American cultural influence, Soto claims it as a victory for Mexican cinema precisely because Cozzi's physical virtuosity rivals that of American actresses.

Fanny stages thrilling spectacles of speed, transportation technology, and female criminality, both critiquing and capitalizing on the conventions of Hollywood cinema, even as it addresses the national problem of military misconduct. The film's tenuous links to topical events allowed its concern with Hollywood cinema and American consumer culture's potential impact on conventional gender roles to come to the fore. Yet *Fanny* shares with *La banda del automóvil* and *El automóvil gris* a vision of national modernity structured by pervasive public spectacles of violence.

Conclusion

In early twentieth-century Mexico, media spectacles of violence and criminality gave expression to social conflicts generated by modernization and military conflict, from anxieties surrounding crime in a growing metropolis to a comprehensive challenge to the state's monopoly on legitimate violence during the Revolution and the renegotiation of women's participation in the public sphere in its aftermath. Stretching cinema and photography's uniquely modern capacities to capture elusive, ephemeral, and unpredictable happenings to their limits, these images capitalized on the sense of relentless and quintessentially modern eventfulness linked to a violent present.

In the illustrated press of the late Porfiriato, spontaneous and staged images of murders, accidents, and executions were pivotal to the claims of an emerging mass-circulation, information-oriented press to effectively capture and disseminate topical events. At the same time, these images attested to a desired modernization of policing and punishment that responded to elite anxieties and positivist principles. During the Revolution, the vicissitudes of military conflict set technological, practical, and ideological limits on the photographing and filming of bodily violence and its aftermath. At the same time, filmic documents of the conflict drew on narrative strategies like the apotheosis, and were supplemented with melodramatic rhetoric that framed violent acts in moral and juridical terms. (Melo)dramatization of a violent present worked to discursively contain its potential political meanings.

As the most active phase of the Revolution drew to a close, the increasing presence of Hollywood films on Mexico City screens reconfigured local understandings of cinematic realism and the meanings attached to mass-produced images of violence. Discourses that evoked a human body in mortal peril as a guarantee of the realism of the cinematic image shifted from a focus on the life-threatening exploits of the Revolutionary cameraman to the daredevil stunts of serial actors. Capitalizing on spectacular stunts and location shooting, films that reconstructed or evoked current events displayed local filmmakers' mastery of photographic technique and fictional narrative codes. At the same time, they hearkened back to the public displays of criminality during the Porfiriato and the nonfiction images of Revolutionary conflict, which transformed acts of public violence into marketable spectacles. By the late teens and early twenties, violence was often framed as a sign of local modernity, rather than as a threat to the state's political legitimacy. Within a broader panorama of visual culture, early narrative films exemplified the spectacularization of everyday life through new visual technologies that packaged the profound conflicts of Mexico's modernization for popular consumption.

Chapter 2

ON LOCATION

*Adventure Melodramas in
Postrevolutionary Mexico,
1920–1927*

In a 1920 article entitled "El héroe de la película" (The Hero of the Film), the critic Carlos Noriega Hope spun a playful fiction around an exaggerated piece of news that had been published in local papers: the death of actor Fernando Elizondo, who had in fact been injured but not killed in a railway accident during filming.[1] Requesting tolerance from his readers for an "intrusion of literature on cinema" (justified by the fact that "there is currently no cinematic topic that merits commentary"), Noriega Hope substituted his weekly column of film-related news in the newspaper *El Universal* with a short story that highlights the intersection between two concurrent developments in the 1920s: the production of action-packed adventure melodramas by Mexico City filmmakers and the expanding coverage of cinema in the local press.[2] Framing film production as a subject that held sensational audience appeal, Noriega Hope comments on the shared role of cinema and journalism in dramatizing the everyday as Mexico entered a period of relative peace in the early twenties.

As the story opens, a newspaper reporter named Rodríguez is being scolded by his boss for having lost two important scoops the previous day: "the murder on the Calzada de Tlalpan [a major north-south thoroughfare in Mexico City] and the workers' strike in Tizapán." Rodríguez rushes to follow up on a report that an army official was crushed by a passing trolley. Hurrying to the site of the reported accident, he finds a group of men on horseback in intense combat. Hoping to make up for his lackluster performance, Rodríguez "greedily imagined the 'lead' of the newspaper, in seven columns, with a red headline," "thinking [it was] a new Revolution," before realizing that the battle is in fact a simulation staged for film cameras. When he speaks to the director, Rodríguez learns that the official survived the accident, making the incident one that merits only "an insignificant notice in the police blotter." Disappointed, the reporter decides to embellish the story by falsely reporting the death of a "national artist." The short story ends as the military official regains consciousness, surrounded by a group of hospital nurses who hail him as the "hero of the film."[3]

Implying that a fresh outbreak of revolutionary conflict was the ideal subject for sensational journalism in the early twenties (with criminal acts and labor strikes serving as acceptable substitutes), "The Hero of the Film" signals the popular appeal of simulating violence onscreen and in the press. In the absence of compelling items about the local entertainment scene, "The Hero of the Film" presents filmmaking itself as a newsworthy activity, whose attraction is linked to displays of bodily violence and the perils of modern transportation technologies. The short story also acts as a self-reflexive commentary on anecdotes about filmmaking that circulated widely in the early twenties, in which acts of violence staged for the camera were supposedly confused with real-life (and sometimes, revolutionary) violence. As film criticism expanded in the early 1920s, journalists like Noriega Hope and Rafael Bermúdez Zatarain dramatized the mechanics of film production and linked it to national progress, even as depictions of violence in domestic productions recalled recent military conflict and persistent concerns regarding criminality. In these anecdotes, the risk and injury endured by actors attested to their commitment to the cause of Mexican cinema and to physical prowess equaling that of the stars of popular American westerns, a key point of reference for Mexican adventure melodramas of the 1920s.

Signaling how exaggerated anecdotes of real-life bodily danger had become an integral part of star discourses, in Mexico as well as in the United States, "The Hero of the Film" also alludes to Noriega Hope's specialized knowledge of local film production. The critic reminded readers that he was able to set the record straight regarding the published "news of a cinematic catastrophe" because he "was present at said 'catastrophe.'"[4] Personally acquainted with aspiring actor-directors like Fernando Elizondo and Miguel Contreras Torres, Noriega Hope reported frequently on their activities during a brief boom in production between 1920 and 1922, particularly their excursions outside Mexico City to shoot on location. The critic was active in film production himself, choreographing a fight scene for Contreras Torres's *El Zarco*, whose title refers to the eponymous villain of a novel by Ignacio Altamirano.[5] Between 1921 and 1923, Noriega Hope directed a comic adventure film entitled *La gran noticia* (*The Big News*). Also working closely with Contreras Torres, Bermúdez Zatarain wrote the script for *El Zarco* and served as codirector for Contreras Torres's following film, *El caporal* (*The Foreman*).[6]

Although Mexico City critics often expressed disappointment with the finished films, their on-set accounts and interviews with would-be stars like Contreras Torres and Elizondo fostered ambitions for self-sustaining film production, reinforcing journalists' own role in bolstering these efforts. A series of film-related contests organized by newspapers and magazines during the same years also allowed the press to present itself as a champion of local film production.[7] Even in the absence of commercially successful releases, the closely interconnected activities of production and criticism created a sense of a robust film culture that encompassed the consumption of imported cinema, but attached particular significance to domestic film production.

In this chapter, I trace the close connections between the production of adventure melodramas and the framing of filmmaking as a sensational spectacle in the popular press, examining the often contradictory meanings attached to cinematic depictions of violence in the aftermath of the Revolution and in the light of anti-Mexican bias in the Hollywood films that dominated Mexican exhibition markets. Critics often linked their hopes for a national industry to two types of attractions: landscape views that participated in a broader drive to forge a picturesque imaginary of the nation in the postrevolutionary period; and daring onscreen exploits rivaling those seen in U.S. productions. Echoing tales of the real-life perils faced by the stars of Hollywood serial films and westerns, local critics emphasized the risks to life and limb involved in filmmaking as a measure of commitment to national cinema, as well as proof of a virtuosic masculinity. At the same time, cinematic depictions of violence proved highly problematic, and filmmakers sought to skirt the violent legacy of the Revolution and the "denigrating films" (*películas denigrantes*) produced by North American studios.

Adventure melodramas produced in Mexico in the 1920s intersected with the emerging currents of postrevolutionary nationalism, defined by efforts to modernize and unify the nation by promoting education, public health, transportation infrastructure, and forms of cultural production that constructed a national identity spanning regional, ethnic, and class divides.[8] The visual and narrative strategies of these films, mediated by the popular press, framed violence and physical peril as uniquely cinematic attractions that were closely intertwined with nationalistic conceptions of masculinity and heroism. Peace itself proved precarious in the postrevolutionary period (the term postrevolutionary refers to the cessation of most open hostilities after 1920, though the chronological limits of the Revolution are a matter of debate). In addition to a series of high-profile political assassinations throughout the decade, open conflict erupted with the De la Huerta Rebellion (1923) and the Cristero War (1926–1929), fought by Catholics who objected to the state's aggressive policies of secularization. (Furthermore, the Partido Nacional Revolucionario [National Revolutionary Party], founded in 1929, and its successors the Partido Mexicano de la Revolución [Mexican Revolutionary Party] and Partido Revolucionario Institucional [Institutional Revolutionary Party], which dominated Mexican politics for seven decades, claimed a state of ongoing social revolution, with their party machinery drawing power from unions and peasant leaders). Reimagining Hollywood westerns and crime serials through regional iconographies and works of national literature, the imaginaries of violence and technological disaster cultivated by Mexican adventure melodramas of the 1920s signaled tensions within postrevolutionary modernizing projects, including debates surrounding the role of U.S. cinema within a thriving entertainment scene.

While the action and physical dynamism of Hollywood westerns often appealed to local audiences, these productions were often the most egregious examples of "denigrating films" that depicted Mexicans as lazy, sadistic "greasers" or sultry señoritas. Although such preconceptions long predated the Mexican Revolution, they circulated with renewed intensity in American yellow journalism and sensationalistic films about the conflict.[9] Becoming a staple of Hollywood feature films of the early twenties, these representations generated growing public frustration that culminated in a national boycott of several U.S. production companies declared by President Álvaro Obregón in 1922.[10] In some cases, Mexican films were explicitly viewed as a form of cinematic "revenge" (revancha), which responded to stereotypical Hollywood representations of Mexico with equally unflattering portrayals of the United States. Yet some critics argued that domestically made adventure melodramas veered perilously close to these offensive imports by presenting violence as a pervasive aspect of daily life in Mexico. As Colin Gunckel argues with reference to the 1930s, "revolutionary films (and other historical epics) too closely recalled the excessive visibility of problematic, denigrating images generated by Hollywood in previous decades."[11] Given this issue, as well as the politically sensitive nature of the conflict, most Mexican adventure films of the 1920s avoided direct reference to the Revolution, while still attempting to capitalize on the sensational appeal of cinematic violence.

A notable exception to the rule, the 1921 film *Alas abiertas* (*Wings Outspread*, Ernesto Vollrath and Luis Lezama) centered on government forces' aerial attacks on Zapatista factions, generating press coverage that is particularly suggestive for evaluating the complex meanings attached to onscreen violence in the early twenties. Accounts of *Alas abiertas*'s production highlighted a blurring between real and simulated combat during shooting, attributing the slippage to a "fiery" national character, and presenting the perceived authenticity of the resulting scenes as a source of sensational appeal. Bermúdez Zatarain reports,

> It was a combat between revolutionaries and federal troops and, in effect, [the filmmakers] obtained from the chief of the battalion a sufficient number to achieve a good cinematic fight. The curious thing was that, a half an hour after the simulation [*simulacro*] began, the soldiers attacked each other with real rage, with a truly bellicose ardor, saying things not fit to be transcribed. Perhaps this is due to the fiery spirit that, fortunately, we Mexicans possess. With this, absolute reality for the scene was achieved, although the services of the Red Cross had to be solicited to tend to five or six wounded.[12]

This description suggests the sensational appeal of literally reviving revolutionary conflict onscreen. José Gómez, an actor who participated in the simulated combat, commented, "What can you do! It's our blood that makes us do these things."[13] These press discourses framed physical injury as the guarantor of cinematic authenticity, while attributing the irruption of real-life aggression to an essentialized national "spirit." Journalists' accounts of the filming of *Alas abiertas* signal the attraction, but also the potential pitfalls, of referencing the Revolution onscreen; depictions of physical injury offered sensational authenticity, but also reinforced associations of Mexicanness with unbridled violence.

Two directors can be credited with the majority of Mexican adventure melodramas produced between 1920 and 1922, none of which have survived to the present day. Ernesto Vollrath, director of *La banda del automóvil* (*The Automobile Gang*), filmed a number of rural dramas, first in partnership with the impresario Germán Camus, and later independently: *Alas abiertas*, *En la hacienda* (*On the Estate*, 1922), and *La parcela* (*The Lot*, 1923).[14] The self-styled actor-director Miguel Contreras Torres, who remained active in filmmaking well into the sound era, produced and starred in *El Zarco* (José Manuel Ramos, 1920); *El caporal* (Juan Canal de Holms and Rafael Bermúdez Zatarain, 1921); *De raza azteca* (*Of Aztec Race*, Miguel Contreras Torres and Guillermo Calles, 1922), and *El hombre sin patria* (*The Man Without a Country*, Miguel Contreras Torres, 1922), among other films.[15] A number of these productions were literary adaptations: in addition to Contreras Torres's adaptation of *El Zarco*, *La parcela* was based on an 1898 novel by José López Portillo y Rojas and *Alas abiertas* on a 1920 book by Alfonso Teja Zabre. Yet while advertisements and press coverage of the productions mentioned their literary sources, these were rarely presented as lending cultural legitimacy to the films, perhaps because their connections with the source texts appear to have been somewhat tenuous.[16]

Instead, film critics attributed imported adventure melodramas (particularly westerns) and their stars with a strangely central role in forging viable models for domestic film production, desirable onscreen visions of Mexican manhood, and picturesque images of the nation (themselves in dialogue with Hollywood westerns that deployed scenic landscapes within narratives of territorial expansion and American exceptionalism).[17] The reception of adventure melodramas of the early 1920s suggests that this optimism was misplaced; neither these productions, nor the high-society melodramas produced concurrently by Camus and others, managed to secure sufficient box-office success to ensure continuity in production. In the face of this disappointing performance, the production of adventure films quickly waned, as domestic filmmaking declined overall in 1923 and 1924.[18]

Yet imported adventure melodramas persisted as a point of reference in a small number of films made throughout the decade outside Mexico City, most notably two features directed by Gabriel García Moreno in the city of Orizaba in the state of Veracruz, *El tren fantasma* (*The Ghost Train*, 1926) and *El puño de hierro* (*The Iron Fist*, 1927). Produced with financing from local businessmen, these two titles are rare examples of surviving silent-era features produced in Mexico. By contrast with regional production of the 1920s in Brazil, films made outside Mexico City attracted relatively little attention from critics based in the capital and thus remained at the margins of contemporary debates about viable strategies for establishing a Mexican film industry in the shadow of Hollywood.

Gabriel García Moreno's films capitalized on location shooting and stunt sequences in a manner comparable to the adventure films of the early twenties, and resonated in a similarly complex way with currents of postrevolutionary nationalism. Whereas the Mexico City productions shot on location in the early twenties showed close affinities to the Hollywood western in their emphasis on regional landscapes and dangerous stunts, García Moreno's films drew on the tropes of crime serials and addressed distinctly modern themes in keeping with Veracruz's status as a hub of trade, travel, and industry, including the expansion of transportation infrastructure and the spread of narcotics through urban communities. *El tren fantasma* and *El puño de hierro* evoked the dark underside of modernizing projects that were being renewed under postrevolutionary governments, including the construction of rail lines and roads and public-health and temperance campaigns, initiatives that were reinforced by the exhibition and production of educational films.[19]

The ongoing expansion of transportation infrastructure proves central to the plot of *El tren fantasma*, which pits bandits operating within a railway company against an inspector sent to investigate irregularities in the local office. The railway had played a pivotal role in the expansion of trade and individual mobility in the late nineteenth and early twentieth centuries, and served as an important means of military mobilization during the Revolution. Articulating scenes of action with a heterosexual love triangle, the film was successfully exhibited in Mexico City after screenings in Veracruz. By contrast, *El puño de hierro* drew on the more destabilizing aspects of imported serials—multiple identities, narrative complexity, and ambiguity—and received a less enthusiastic reception. The film incorporated scenes from *El buitre* (*The Vulture*), shot by García Moreno in Mexico City in 1926, within a narrative of drug traffickers and their victims.[20] In the film's conclusion, the villain El Tieso (the Rigid One), owner of the drug den, is revealed to be leading a double life as Dr. Ortiz, leader of a campaign against narcotics. Whether because of its imperfect integration of repurposed and new footage or its potentially subversive approach to modernizing initiatives, *El puño de hierro* was poorly received and never exhibited in the capital, bringing García Moreno's career in Mexican cinema to a close.[21]

Throughout the 1920s, press coverage of Mexican adventure melodramas emphasized the appeal of scenic views captured on location, which were linked with emerging forms of nationalistic cultural production. As the film historian Aurelio de los Reyes notes, despite Camus's much-publicized construction of a studio in Mexico City in 1920, film enthusiasts of the period overwhelmingly preferred shooting outdoors.[22] Crews' excursions outside the capital generated considerable interest in the press at a moment when a growing number of official and commercial initiatives sought to package the scenery, traditional customs, and indigenous past of rural Mexico for both domestic and foreign consumption.[23] Mexican adventure melodramas took an active role in this forging of a national picturesque in close connection with the illustrated press.[24] As in the transnational American-Italian case analyzed by Giorgio Bertellini, the national picturesque forged in post-revolutionary Mexico entailed an aesthetic appreciation of scenic landscapes and stressed ethnic difference (here, of indigenous populations), linking it with supposed primitivism, while framing archaeological sites as evidence of the past glories of a fallen civilization. The 1920s also witnessed the expansion of anthropological and archaeological research in Mexico, most prominently a series of expeditions to the ruins of Teotihuacán organized by the anthropologist and public intellectual Manuel Gamio, in which Noriega Hope also participated.[25]

Alongside contests for aspiring film actresses, the magazine *El Universal Ilustrado* sponsored a search for "La India Bonita," or the most beautiful woman judged to embody indigenous physical characteristics.[26] The contest gave expression to growing efforts to "ethnicize national identity" in the wake of the Revolution, addressing a sense of regional and ethnic fragmentation by encouraging the incorporation of native populations into a Spanish-speaking, *mestizo* (mixed-race white and indigenous) national community.[27] These developments in popular culture built on influential expressions of *indigenismo*, most notably Gamio's 1916 volume *Forjando patria* (*Forging a Nation*) and José Vasconcelos's 1925 essay *La raza cósmica* (*The Cosmic Race*). Despite divergent views regarding the value of indigenous culture, both texts exalted the process of *mestizaje* (racial and cultural mixture).[28] Ironically, press discourses surrounding the Mexican adventure melodramas of the 1920s often reinscribed the "notions of racial inferiority (the discursive 'blackening' suggested by the term 'denigrating')" evident in Hollywood studios' depictions of Mexico; rugged Mexican masculinity was often defined by contrast with indigenous "degeneracy."[29]

The ambivalent stance of postrevolutionary entertainment culture toward indigenous communities is signaled by Noriega Hope's article "The India Bonita in the Theater and the Cinema," which observes how films and Mexico City revue theater were capitalizing on the excitement generated by *El Universal Ilustrado*'s India Bonita contest. He notes that these stage and screen productions "do not insist, fortunately, on extracting all the filth, all the 'humus,' all the rottenness of a suffering and forgotten race, but rather, in the manner of self-declared professors of 'folklore' [in English], recover the lovely legends, the most original songs and episodes of our country," incorporating regional customs and types such as the "charros of Tamaulipas, the songs of Jalisco, the 'típicas' of Chapala."[30] Sidestepping the social marginalization— and perceived racial inferiority—of indigenous populations, Noriega Hope's remarks are suggestive of postrevolutionary cultural production's tendency to synthesize customs and practices from various regions into a palatable whole, while discarding cultural practices deemed alien to modernity.[31]

Press coverage of Vollrath's *En la hacienda* further indicates how melodramas of the early 1920s constructed a vision of Mexico's indigenous populations that at once romanticized and dehumanized them. A photo spread in *El Universal Ilustrado* shows the pale, dark-haired actress Elena Sánchez Valenzuela costumed as a native woman, an early example of the long-standing practice of "whitening" indigenous characters in Mexican cinema through the casting of light-skinned actors.[32] The accompanying text describes how Sánchez Valenzuela "interprets the sweet and long-suffering spirit of our indigenous women. Her role in the work . . . synthesizes our indigenous women, the daughters of this bronze race who within their inner impassivity hold an excess of altruistic sentiments."[33] Characterizing indigenous women as noble, victimized, and fundamentally passive (as well as homogeneous, to the extent that diverse ethnic groups are imagined to be "synthesized" in a single character), the description taps into nostalgia discourses that constructed indigenous populations as fundamental to Mexican national identity, yet slated to disappear as such through linguistic and cultural assimilation.

As often contradictory forms of indigenista rhetoric reshaped notions of national identity, private and public initiatives to increase tourism in the 1920s sought to capitalize on Mexico's regional landscapes and cultural traditions, dovetailing with federal infrastructure projects that created more effective transportation networks.[34] In the mid-1920s, travelogues like Miguel Contreras Torres's *El verdadero México* (*The True Mexico*, 1925) and Gustavo Sáenz de Sicilia's *Maravillas de México* (*Marvels of Mexico*, 1926) showcased the country's natural scenery and historic and modern buildings, in hopes of bolstering foreign tourism and investment.[35] The popularization of the rotogravure printing process led to the expansion of photographic supplements in magazines like *Revista de Revistas*, which, as de los Reyes notes, often featured "popular types and customs, archaeological sites, [and] colonial buildings" associated with Mexico's varied regions.[36] He links this vogue for scenic photography to illustrated magazines' and newspapers' fascination with the mobility offered by modern transportation technologies, signaled by their coverage of automobile races and pioneering flights by Mexican aviators.[37] Similarly, Esther Gabara observes that in the twenties and thirties, "Mexican writers and photographers were fascinated with the idea of being tourists in their own land," emphasizing that the journalistic and photographic discourses of travel in the illustrated press were closely linked with, but not reducible to, officially sanctioned forms of cultural nationalism like the burgeoning muralist movement.[38]

One such travel narrative was a series of humorous chronicles published in the magazine *El Universal Ilustrado* in 1921, which recounted the trip taken by Noriega Hope (who served as the publication's editor-in-chief) to the lakeside town of Chapala in the state of Jalisco to shoot *La gran noticia* in collaboration with a number of other writers from the magazine. The film narrated the adventures of a young reporter (Lauro de Prida) who investigates a series of crimes committed by a mysterious bandit, "El Pintado." This press coverage exemplifies the convergence of filmmaking with film criticism, functioning not only as visible evidence of an incipient national film industry, but also as a form of virtual tourism. In addition to highlighting location shooting as evidence of ongoing film production, critics presented cinematic landscapes as assets for Mexican film production, claiming them as national rather than local or regional attractions. In the adventure melodramas of the postrevolutionary period, this picturesque repertoire was juxtaposed with onscreen cinematic violence, signaling how the filming of adventure melodramas gave expression to the contradictions of a Mexican national identity under construction in the postrevolutionary period.

Filmmaking as (National) Spectacle: Adventure Melodramas and Film Criticism in the Early Twenties

Perhaps encouraged by the box-office successes of Enrique Rosas's *El automóvil gris* and Ernesto Vollrath's *La banda del automóvil* the previous year, in 1920 Mexico City film critics sought to forge a star system that would bolster domestic production, pinning their hopes on Mexicans who had been involved with filmmaking in the United States, however marginally.[39] Initially, one of the most promising candidates was Fernando Elizondo, a railroad employee turned actor who had appeared in *The Ninth Commandment*, directed by the Swiss filmmaker Emil Harder in the United States.[40] When Elizondo's plans for filmmaking in Mexico were frustrated by his accident, the attention of local journalists turned to Miguel Contreras Torres. While Contreras Torres initially lacked direct connections to the U.S. film industry, press coverage of his films frequently referenced the stars of Hollywood westerns, particularly William S. Hart, even as it hailed the rural themes and thrilling action scenes of his films as viable strategies for national film production.[41] Guillermo Calles, Contreras Torres's codirector for *De raza azteca*, had worked with William Duncan, star of Hollywood adventure serials and westerns, a fact that was highlighted in the film's publicity.[42]

Local film critics first expressed interest in Elizondo when he traveled to Mexico City to exhibit *The Ninth Commandment* and stayed on to shoot a film entitled *El tren expreso* (*The Express Train*). He later appeared in the comedy *Mitad y mitad* (*Half and Half*, Enrique J. Vallejo, 1921), which boasted "an exciting aviation scene."[43] In an interview with Elizondo, Noriega Hope frames his physical exploits through reference to a broader culture of sensational news, marshaled to help compensate for the lack of exciting developments in the local entertainment scene. Setting the scene for his meeting with the actor, Noriega Hope admits he was, like other journalists, scouring "Yankee [newspaper] supplements to . . . find each day a thrilling event to exploit in our papers."[44] Elizondo's serendipitous arrival at his office provides him with an improbable story that itself seemed "extracted from the polychrome pages of the 'New York World.'" The interview emphasizes Elizondo's feats of daring—he boasts that he can "change trains, jumping from one car to another, as they pass each other rapidly on parallel tracks"—and his unlikely entry into the film business after a producer spotted him performing these feats in the railyard. The actor claims these feats as a point of national pride, stating, "I learned all these things in Mexico and there's no 'trick' to it; many of our unschooled brakemen do them impeccably every day." With a mixture of irony and hyperbole, the article frames Elizondo's physical virtuosity—and by extension, that of his countrymen—through an imaginary of sensational journalism with an international scope, presenting it as a resource to be exploited by domestic film production.

Elizondo also described plans to use modern transportation technologies to stage thrilling stunts and display Mexico's landscapes, a strategy he claimed would appeal to audiences while disseminating a flattering image of the nation abroad. Declaring his intention to return to New York to continue acting, Elizondo continued, "First I will take isolated scenes in our most beautiful landscapes, publicizing in this way the natural attractions of our Fatherland abroad. I have already obtained all sorts of assistance in this respect, and the current director of the Ferrocarriles Nacionales [National Railway Company] has given me wide latitude to use the necessary railway equipment so that I can show off my daring in sensational scenes."[45] This description suggests that landscape views and action scenes operate as linked but semiautonomous attractions, with modern transportation technology facilitating the display of both. Elizondo's partnership with the railway company also prefigures Gabriel García Moreno's association with the Ferrocarril Mexicano in Veracruz later in the decade.

Although Elizondo's encounter with Mexican cinema was fleeting, film critics continued to frame domestic film production as a newsworthy spectacle throughout the early twenties, especially in their profiles of Contreras Torres, whose tireless efforts to publicize his productions dovetailed with the expansion of coverage of film-related topics in the Mexico City press. In the absence of a steady stream of domestic productions, journalists devoted considerable coverage to Contreras Torres's excursions out of the city to shoot scenes on location, using them as a pretext to emphasize the actor-director's intrepid character. A journalist in *El Universal* chronicled a trip by director José Manuel Ramos to Xochimancas in the state of Morelos, where the novel was set. In the article, Contreras Torres is compared to the stars of Hollywood westerns, described as "a young 'sportman' [sic] who will perform exploits à la Bill Hart, formidable horseman, [a] 'desesperado' in all sorts of sensational acts and who is determined to risk his skin."[46]

Later that month, another journalist chronicled a day of shooting in a villa in Tacuba, just outside Mexico City, that had been designated a "'session' in honor of the press."[47] Although this term usually referred to an advance screening of a completed film, here the filming itself became a spectacle staged for journalists, who were already closely acquainted with the filmmakers. Additional drama was added to the account as the critics are surprised by an outburst of "shots, hoofbeats, imprecations" and one of the actresses working in the film takes "refuge in [one of] the rooms, suspecting some Zapatista attack," while cinematographer Julio Lamadrid continued filming the scene.[48] Although Contreras Torres quickly explains that the disruption was intended to create the proper atmosphere for his performance, the fleeting confusion between simulated and actual violence adds an extra thrill to the description of the shoot and dramatizes the act of film production for readers.

Even as journalists emphasized a sensational sense of realism linked to the blurring of real and simulated violence, they took the opportunity to highlight their specialized knowledge of film production, bolstering their critical

FIG 2.1 "The First Fight as I Saw It." Writing under a pseudonym, Carlos Noriega Hope reports on the staging of fight scenes in *El Zarco*. *El Universal Ilustrado*, 9 September 1920. Nettie Lee Benson Latin American Collection, University of Texas Libraries, University of Texas, Austin.

authority while emphasizing Contreras Torres's willingness to risk life and limb for national cinema. Noriega Hope, who had visited several studios during a trip to Los Angeles, discusses his efforts to educate Contreras Torres on the staging of fight scenes during the filming of *El Zarco*.[49] While Noriega Hope informs him that filmed combats required careful fakery to seem believable, Contreras Torres bombastically insists, "I'm willing to be killed. I want this fight to be real and effective, for blood to flow and injuries to swell up. . . . No tricks or superimpositions. Clean blows!"[50] Star discourses surrounding Contreras Torres stressed physical peril and injury, over and above a mastery of special effects or cinematic technique, as proof of his fanatical commitment to an incipient film industry.

In interviews and articles, Contreras Torres's physical exploits were framed in both nationalistic and international terms, with critics contending that the model of the Hollywood western was (somewhat paradoxically) key for forging an onscreen vision of Mexican masculinity that could win success for domestically produced films. Commenting on Contreras Torres's significance for a national industry in advance of the release of *El Zarco*, the critic Roberto Núñez y Domínguez writes,

> No one before him had managed to transplant to the screen our national type par excellence. For this reason his first film is bound to provoke real admiration not only in this country but far beyond its borders. From today onward, we will have little interest in the dramas of the "Far West" [in English] in which William Hart and William Farnum, those two "cowboy" [in English] artists who with their abilities and energy awaken such sympathy in good-natured North American audiences, which see in them a superior incarnation of their ethnic qualities: action, force, daring.[51]

Rather than advocating that specifically Mexican genres and forms be cultivated, the critic suggests that Contreras Torres's efforts could displace U.S. productions that glorified Americans' "ethnic qualities" precisely by appropriating these films' strategies, forging a "national type" through emulation of popular Hollywood stars.

In a similar vein, another critic predicted that "perhaps, when [*El Zarco*] premieres, some fervent female admirers of [Antonio] Moreno, [William] Hart, [Eddie] Polo and [Tom] Mix—the devotees of force—will think that we, without being masters of cinematography, possess *men* who are ignorant of the existence of rice powder."[52] The reference to rice powder evokes the figure of the *fifí*, or modern dandy, who was criticized as appearance- and consumption-obsessed, and closely linked with the local presence of U.S. cinema.[53] If Contreras Torres's films lacked the technical polish of Hollywood adventure melodramas, they nevertheless promised to showcase a rugged Mexican masculinity defined by contrast with this problematic male type.

Discussing his follow-up to *El Zarco*, Contreras Torres himself claimed, " 'El caporal' fits within the type of 'open air' films that have such success in Mexico. I believe that if the Americans work marvels with a William Hart or a Douglas Fairbanks, we need actors who, like them, synthesize the soul of Mexico."[54] Yet the actor's conception of Mexican masculinity also perpetuates racial hierarchies embedded in the rhetoric of postrevolutionary nationalism.[55] He hastens to assure the journalist, "Don't go thinking that miserable Indians and even more miserable shacks appear in the film. No ... Mexico has imponderable beauties and the true men of the hacienda are not representatives of a degenerate and useless race."[56] Although Contreras Torres co-directed *De raza azteca* the following year with a self-identified Indian actor who was featured in a heroic role, his comments on *El caporal* signal the racist underpinnings of onscreen models of Mexican masculinity that, ironically, were patterned on the protagonists of "denigrating" Hollywood films.

Initially defining his vigorous onscreen persona in opposition to indigenous communities, Contreras Torres also described his productions by contrast with the urbane, cosmopolitan approach of other Mexican films. In the face of the disappointing box-office performance of the features modeled on Italian diva films produced by Enrique Rosas and Mimí Derba's Azteca Films Company in 1917 and the dramas financed by Germán Camus in the early twenties, Contreras Torres commented, "I think it useless to attempt, for the moment, historical reconstructions or high-society films, because we lack efficient cinematic training for this. Our efforts should be directed toward the countryside."[57] Beyond this claim that adventure melodramas with rural settings were most appropriate to the stage of cinema's development in Mexico, Contreras Torres emphasizes the need to cultivate emphatically national topics in order to appeal to spectators at home and abroad. He asserted in a 1921 interview,

> Our films, in order to be Mexican, in order to have a market all over the world, must speak to us of our land. I only make things of the people, without showing "fox-trots" [in English] or grand aristocratic ballrooms. For me, a scene in the country—in our country—is worth more than any city scene, with the stupidly European or Yankee life we lead here [in Mexico City]. Don't you think that the salvation of cinema in Mexico is precisely ... Mexico? This is my belief—I who would give my life for a national film.[58]

Contreras Torres's attempts to forge an export-ready vision of Mexico in dialogue with the Hollywood western are most evident in *El Zarco* and *El caporal*'s depictions of the charro. In the early 1920s, the charro was being transformed from a figure associated with specific regions of Mexico to a national icon, which would be exploited for decades in the *comedia ranchera* of Mexican sound cinema. The Asociación Nacional de Charros (National Charro Association), founded in July 1921, standardized guidelines for horsemanship competitions and promoted a uniform image for the charro by limiting the use of bright colors in their costumes, comprising wide-brimmed sombreros, bolero jackets, and fitted trousers.[59] Significantly, the screen adaptation of *El Zarco* referenced the historical origins of the charro costume:

the gangs of nineteenth-century highwaymen referred to as *plateados*, for the stolen silver they used to decorate their clothing. Set during the Wars of the Reform (1857–1861) between liberals and conservatives, Altamirano's novel critiques the complicity of politicians and bandits in the formation of the *rurales* (mounted police force) by the victorious Benito Juárez.

However, this element of the source text seems not to have been highlighted in the film, which focused on the travails of Manuela (Gilda Chávarri), who is courted by the hero Nicolás (Contreras Torres), but rejects him in favor of the bandit El Zarco (Enrique Cantalauba). She comes to regret her decision after she follows El Zarco to the bandit camp, and her lover is ultimately captured and killed. Meanwhile, Manuela's godsister Pilar (Graziela de Zárate) wins Nicolás's heart, and they marry. *El caporal*, whose plot was original, also narrates the travails of a hero named Nicolás and played by Contreras Torres, "faithfully depicting cattle thieves, showing silent and terrible battles at the edge of precipices; speaking of the spontaneous and sincere love of our men of struggle and action."[60] Nicolás's home is destroyed and his mother murdered by a criminal; the culprit turns out to be a corrupt ranch manager, who had blamed Nicolás for robberies he himself committed.[61] Staging a melodramatic recognition of masculine virtue, the films' plots exalted the figure of the humble rancher, while motivating dynamic fight scenes and feats of horsemanship.[62]

Although extensive press coverage presumably built anticipation for *El Zarco*, its initial run in November 1920 was interrupted when police suspended screenings due to competing copyright claims to Altamirano's novel. The exhibition of the film was delayed until January 1921.[63] Greeted by a lukewarm critical reception, *El Zarco* seems to have enjoyed at least modest box-office success, as is suggested by the fact that International Pictures, known locally for their catalog of American serial films, opted to distribute *El caporal* and *De raza azteca*.[64] (Contreras Torres later complained that exhibitors and distributors had kept the lion's share of the profits from his films.)[65]

While reviews of *El Zarco* were mixed, they singled out the film's display of landscape views as a special attraction.[66] Noriega Hope attributed the film's impressive cinematography to location shooting, noting that *El Zarco* was "composed almost exclusively of exteriors, [and thus the cameraman Julio] Lamadrid did not have to 'force' his lens, which accounts for the absolute clarity and perfect relief of the figures."[67] Other critics judged *El Zarco*'s use of landscape views excessive. Cube Bonifant, a pioneering female film critic known for her sardonic wit, notes that the film begins with "a long, very long, panoramic exhibition of landscapes of Michoacán." In a better humor later in her viewing of the film, Bonifant praises the "beautiful landscapes" with a bit more enthusiasm, while her companion observes that "those backdrops could never have been obtained in the United States."[68] Similarly, a review of *El caporal* noted that "the choice of the sites where the various scenes unfold deserves special mention. One can see reflected there the lovely Tzararacua waterfall, the picturesque lakes of Pátzcuaro y Cuitzeo, and the lovely hacienda of Queréndaro, which was chosen as the setting for some of the principal scenes." The appearance of "professional charros" in the film was also cited as a selling point by the reviewer.[69]

Contreras Torres continued to exploit the perceived audience appeal of picturesque landscapes as he aligned himself more closely with discourses that valorized indigenous peoples and elaborated a more critical take on Hollywood's "denigrating films." *De raza azteca* centered on the friendship between Víctor (Contreras Torres) and Diego (codirector Guillermo Calles), who respectively played "The Charro and the Indian, who are the synthesis of the national soul."[70] Diego saves Víctor and his fiancée Catalina (Irma Domínguez) from drowning when their boat overturns in Xochimilco (an indigenous community located in a network of canals south of Mexico City), and the two join forces to rescue Catalina after she is kidnapped.[71] Tellingly, Contreras Torres cites the recently excavated ruins of Teotihuacán near Mexico City as a key inspiration for *De raza azteca*, noting that the film's contemporary setting nonetheless allowed for the contemplation of historic monuments.[72]

Despite *De raza azteca*'s clear connections with indigenista discourses and the growing public profile of archaeological and anthropological research, some critics found the film's emphasis on violent action counterproductive. Writing for *Cine-Mundial*, the critic Epifanio Soto Jr. lambasted the film.

> Miguel Contreras Torres has just released "De raza azteca," his third production, which he assures [us] is of nationalist tendencies, although we find these only in the protagonist's charro hat. Because the spectator stumbles on a gang of bandits, in the clothing of Texan cowboys, that operates in the vicinity of Chapultepec; witnesses kidnappings and crimes in the most central avenues of the city and has the general impression that, in all the places the plot takes him to, there are no decent people other than the hero and his sidekick. And this leads him to be ignorant of the reality of this poor country that seeks to defend itself, confirming, rather than

destroying, the ideas planted by some Yankee film people, [who are either] ignorant or malicious.[73]

Suggesting that the iconography of Hollywood westerns was incongruous in a Mexico City setting, Soto also expresses concern that *De raza azteca* reproduces Hollywood stereotypes of Mexicans as savage and violent. Perhaps most gravely, in Soto's opinion, Contreras Torres failed to perform "a single feat of horsemanship or athleticism worthy of being photographed." Even as the film evoked a problematic imaginary of urban criminality, for Soto it failed to capture the physical dynamism presented as central to its appeal.

With the release of Contreras Torres's next production, *El hombre sin patria*, Soto's misgivings about his films' implications for the national image intensified, resulting in a brief public debate with Noriega Hope about the value of cinematic "revenge" on the United States. *El hombre sin patria* narrated the travails of a young wastrel who is expelled from the family home and seeks his fortune across the border in the United States. Subjected to discriminatory treatment by a foreman, he reacts by killing his tormentor, and returns home chastened. (Once again, the use of location shooting in the film was widely publicized, with Contreras Torres reportedly filming in Ciudad Juárez, El Paso, Arizona, and Los Angeles.)[74] The film seems to have been the most pointed of a handful of productions that responded to Hollywood stereotypes of Mexicans with negative images of Americans. Following the release of *El hombre sin patria*, Noriega Hope hailed Contreras Torres as the "apostle of our cinematic revenge" in an article entitled "Aggressive Nationalism."[75] Criticizing the public's preference for the elaborate sets and lavish costumes of Hollywood productions, he urges them to view the efforts of the "humble national star" as an embodiment of "the revenge that we carry with us, with the patience of the ant confronted with the clamor of the elephant." Despite the implied disparities between the size and profitability of film production in the two nations, Noriega Hope advocates a tit-for-tat response to Hollywood stereotypes. He writes, "Just as [in Hollywood films] there appear odious types, topped off with 'big sombreros' [in English], here in his latest work there appears the repugnant Yankee foreman, a bit conventional, excessively cruel." Without cherishing illusions about the quality of Contreras Torres's films, Noriega Hope argues that they constitute a worthy blow against a racist system of representation, precisely because of their exaggeratedly negative images of North Americans.

Soto, on the other hand, implied that that cinematic "revenge" was essentially futile, arguing that the anti-American content of *El hombre sin patria* "cannot evoke in us anything but a smile of pity, if it had the purpose attributed to it, which is to make our neighbors rage as they have made us rage." Reversing his position on the portrayal of armed violence in *De raza azteca*, which he had condemned as unflattering, Soto contends, "When there is a direct insult to the nation, of course one should complain ... but protesting the appearance of a group of bandits fit for the gallows, when the newspapers inform us on a daily basis about the exploits of those like them, is unreasonable."[76] Although Soto's public comments may have been informed by his position writing for a U.S. magazine, Noriega Hope suggested in a later column that his colleague's ignorance of the most egregious Hollywood productions, which studios would avoid exporting to Mexico to minimize public relations problems, was to blame. Noriega Hope writes, "Mexican journalists should applaud 'revenge' films, even if they are technically deficient. ... Our duty, as Mexicans, imposes this obligation on us, above all if, in some cheap movie theater in Texas or New Mexico, we have contemplated William Desmond or George Walsh hit a poor extra dressed as a Mexican, with his face painted with grime, with the absurd soul of a prospector."[77] Noriega Hope evokes a discourse of patriotic duty that was frequently referenced in discussions of "denigrating films." As Laura Isabel Serna has shown, governmental bans on Hollywood productions "were effective in uniting Mexican viewers on either side of the border in the defense of the nation." However, nationalistic sentiments could be marshaled for opposing ends; for example, exhibitors hostile to the boycott protested that it was interfering with their contributions to the nation's economy.[78] As the exchange between Soto and Noriega Hope indicates, these debates encompassed not only the regulation and censorship of cinema, but also domestic film production and its conflictual dialogue with Hollywood.

The "open air" adventure melodramas of the 1920s were closely linked to the modernizing projects and nationalistic rhetoric of the postrevolutionary period, even as their dynamic action sequences and emphasis on violence and banditry evoked some of the most egregious Mexican stereotypes in Hollywood cinema, themselves linked with the recent history of Revolution. Within the expanding discourse of film criticism, sympathetic journalists like Noriega Hope and Bermúdez Zatarain attributed patriotic meanings to the activity of film production, framing it as a marker of national modernity in spite of the disappointing reception of the films themselves. Adventure melodramas of the 1920s drew on the rhetoric of postrevolutionary nationalism as they capitalized on the appeal of scenic landscape views and daring stunts, constructing a cinematic "nationalism" whose relationship to U.S. productions was hotly debated in the press. Although hopes for a self-sustaining domestic film industry had waned by the mid-twenties, the regional productions of Gabriel García Moreno signal how adventure melodramas continued to give expression to the contradictions of postrevolutionary modernization through the end of the silent era.

Reformulating the Crime Serial: The Regional Productions of Gabriel García Moreno

In addition to the wave of productions based in Mexico City and filmed on location in nearby states, semi-amateur film enthusiasts across Mexico engaged in the production of feature films throughout the 1920s. By contrast with the regional productions of 1920s Brazil, which were widely discussed in fan magazines with a national circulation, these films had relatively minor repercussions on a national level. Among them, only García Moreno's *El tren fantasma* and *El puño de hierro* have survived to the present day.[79] Like the films of Contreras Torres, García Moreno's features relied heavily on the appeal of location shooting (including dynamic landscape views shot from a moving train) and thrilling physical stunts, characteristic of Hollywood westerns and serials. *El puño de hierro* explicitly references a global imaginary of sensational crime fictions; it features a young aficionado of Nick Carter stories (Guillermo Pacheco) who becomes an amateur detective, unravelling the mystery of the drug den with the help of his sidekick, the chauffeur Perico (Manuel Carrillo).

Beyond his films' emphasis on physical exploits, García Moreno incorporated into his fiction features nonfictional sequences with a prurient appeal, including footage of surgeries and patients suffering from physical deformities that he had shot in Mexico City hospitals.[80] De los Reyes speculates that the filmmaker may have also repurposed material from a promotional film commissioned by the Ferrocarril Mexicano in *El tren fantasma*, which was filmed with the company's cooperation.[81] If so, both of García Moreno's films made in Orizaba reworked elements of educational and promotional film linked with the nation's modernizing projects. Evoking the expansion of transportation infrastructure and campaigns to promote public health and social hygiene, initiatives that were renewed under postrevolutionary governments, García Moreno's films frame the unintended consequences of modernization as a source of sensational narrative thrills.

In the versions restored by the Filmoteca de la Universidad Nacional Autónoma de México, *El tren fantasma* and *El puño de hierro* suggest an impressive mastery of continuity editing conventions and special effects, particularly the miniature used to render a railway crash in the former film. (García Moreno later worked in the Backgrounds and Miniatures Department at the Hal Roach studios in Los Angeles, where he moved in 1929.)[82] Yet as in the case of *El automóvil gris*, the contemporary viewer's experience of these films is shaped by alterations to the texts in the intervening years. David M. J. Wood observes that the restorations of the features completed by Esperanza Vázquez Bernal may unwittingly emphasize the affinities between García Moreno's films and Hollywood cinema of the same period by incorporating suspenseful parallel editing and other hallmarks of classical continuity editing. He indicates that the case of *El tren fantasma*, whose footage was preserved entirely out of order, is especially problematic.[83] De los Reyes also suggests that Vázquez Bernal's final restoration of *El puño de hierro* glosses over the discontinuities that probably resulted from the reuse of the footage from García Moreno's earlier film *El buitre*.[84] In addition, a number of the original intertitles from *El puño de hierro*, and all of those in *El tren fantasma*, have been lost and were later replaced with text drawn from surviving scripts.[85] The films' precarious preservation means that ambiguities inevitably remain regarding their original form; yet the dialogue with North American adventure melodramas remains clear.

A resident of greater Mexico City, García Moreno had moved to the city of Orizaba with hopes of establishing a production company. In seeking financing, he took advantage of business contacts he had previously made while working as a banker. Suggesting the robust development of industry in Orizaba, a center of textile manufacturing, García Moreno's financing came principally from "representatives of the local bourgeoisie—businessmen, lawyers, bankers, high-ranking employees of the Moctezuma Beer Factory or of oil companies," with the most significant investments from the cigar factory owner William Mayer.[86] The productions of García Moreno's company, the Centro Cultural Cinematográfico, may have also been funded in part by the general public, who were offered the opportunity to "collaborate in the aggrandizement of the Fatherland by buying shares in this enterprise."[87] Although his films were financed locally, García Moreno sought national and even international markets. He incorporated bilingual Spanish-English intertitles in his films, and *El tren fantasma* was even shown briefly in Corona, California, in August 1927.[88]

During his time in Orizaba, García Moreno maintained contact with Mexico City's entertainment scene, while also cultivating local talent and connections to the local press. García Moreno employed a number of Mexico City actors: Manuel de los Ríos, who had played one of the bandits in Enrique Rosas's *El automóvil gris*, appeared as *El tren fantasma*'s antihero Paco Mendoza and as the villain El Tieso in *El puño de hierro*. Carlos Villatoro, who played the protagonist of *El tren fantasma*, Adolfo Mariel, had appeared as a bandit in *El buitre* in 1926 and reprised this role in *El puño de hierro*.[89] His love interest in the latter film was played by Lupe Bonilla, winner of the "Estrella Veracruzana" (Starlet of Veracruz) star-search contest sponsored by the newspaper *El Dictamen*.[90] Reminiscent of competitions organized by Mexico City newspapers in the early twenties, this casting practice signals the local press's investment in film production, although this was limited in comparison with the activities of Mexico City critics. A number of local railway employees appeared as themselves in *El tren fantasma*; *El Universal Ilustrado* even described it as "a film made by railroad workers."[91] (The production of the film *Mocidade louca* [*Mad Youth*, Felipe Ricci] in Campinas, Brazil in 1926 resulted from a similar partnership between film enthusiasts and railroad employees.)

According to de los Reyes, *El tren fantasma* became "the first film in which the train, symbol par excellence of the mobility of the Revolution, was the protagonist, and not incidentally, because its manufacture was due to the desire of the railway workers of Orizaba to show, not the Revolution, but the modernization of the railway with electric trains."[92] As numerous scholars have emphasized, the railroad played an outsized role in the economic development of Mexico in the late nineteenth century, as well as in the revolutionary conflict. Hailed as a powerful catalyst for economic growth, the construction of rail lines with foreign capital during the railroad boom of the 1880s was emblematic of the economic policies of Porfirio Díaz's regime. As Lynne Kirby writes, "The development of a railroad system in Mexico between 1876 and 1910 was utterly dependent on foreign investment, primarily American, and oriented the national economy toward export production and the international economy dominated by Western nations (many lines ran into Mexico directly from the United States via railway concessions)."[93] While Díaz's finance minister José Limantour had initiated the nationalization of most of Mexico's U.S.-owned railroads in 1907, the process unfolded slowly, and

FIG 2.2 "A Film Made
by Railway Workers."
El Universal Ilustrado, 24
February 1927. General
Research Division,
the New York Public
Library, Astor, Lenox,
and Tilden Foundations.

negotiations between Álvaro Obregón's government and foreign powers to
resolve the issue of Mexico's external debt assured the eventual reprivatization
of the transportation network.[94] The economic integration of agricultural
hinterlands made possible by the railroad facilitated the private purchase of
communal land, a source of popular unrest leading up to the Revolution; yet
at the same time, in the late nineteenth century "railroad development fostered major public investment in areas that produced least wealth," and those
living along planned rail lines negotiated considerable concessions from railway companies.[95]

The inauguration of the electric railway on the lines of the Ferrocarril
Mexicano in 1923 marked a new phase for the transportation networks that
had long linked the capital with Veracruz, Mexico's major Atlantic port. The
rail connection between the two cities, under construction from the 1840s
through the 1870s, was routed through Orizaba and was joined by several

other lines, including the Tehuantepec route that bridged the Atlantic and Pacific Oceans.[96] Although the federal government's priorities shifted away from rail lines toward the construction of a national highway system beginning in 1925, rail travel remained a powerful signifier of modernity and speed.[97]

El tren fantasma showcases the electric railway as a visible sign of Veracruz's prosperity and modernization, while also highlighting the potential of this infrastructure to facilitate unauthorized traffic.[98] The film's action begins as Adolfo Mariel is dispatched to Orizaba to investigate irregularities in the railway company's local office. Shortly thereafter, we learn that many of its employees lead double lives as bandits under the leadership of Paco Mendoza, alias "El Rubí" (the Ruby). The criminal activities of the gang are dramatized in the following scene, which depicts a robbery of the real-life Moctezuma beer factory (a reference to local industry and the film's financiers, also a common strategy in Brazilian regional productions of the 1920s). With his identity concealed by a black leather mask and bodysuit, reminiscent of the disguises used in French crime serials, El Rubí steals the factory's takings and escapes by rappelling down the side of the building. As he flees, one of his accomplices, sporting a wide-brimmed sombrero with a pointed peak, lassoes a factory guard as he fires, as the scene juxtaposes distinctly national and cosmopolitan iconographies. Paco Mendoza's double identity is communicated to the audience in this scene through an intertitle and a medium shot that shows him unmasking himself. This revelation creates dramatic irony as Paco and Adolfo battle for the affections of the stationmaster's daughter Elena (Clarita Ibáñez), whose short haircut and stylish attire mark her as a pelona (flapper or modern girl).

In the film, criminal activities are closely integrated into the workings of the railway even as they hamper its efficiency; one of the bandits arrives late to his job as an engineer after the factory robbery. There appears to be some historical basis for these irregularities in daily practices on the rail lines of Veracruz in the late nineteenth and early twentieth centuries. By contrast with the rigid controls exercised over railroad workers in the United States and England, absenteeism and the appropriation of company equipment for personal use were relatively common.[99] More improbably, later in the film the bandits take control of a locomotive to kidnap Elena on Paco's orders, allowing him to play the hero in a staged rescue. After Adolfo learns of Paco's identity as El Rubí, Paco convinces Elena to accompany him on a stolen locomotive, which later crashes when he loses control of the vehicle. Finally, in

FIG 2.3 Adolfo (Carlos Villatoro) is framed against a mobile view of the Veracruz landscape. Note the local newspaper *El Dictamen*, which sponsored a star-search contest for García Moreno's *El puño de hierro*. Video still.

El tren fantasma's climax, bandits attempt to derail the train by dynamiting the tracks (a common form of military sabotage during the Revolution).

In addition to highlighting illicit uses of transportation networks, *El tren fantasma*'s dynamic stunt sequences capitalize on the appeal of a gaze harnessed to transportation technologies, incorporating footage taken from a moving train that recall the "phantom ride" films of cinema's earliest years. Beginning with the opening scene, which introduces Adolfo during his journey to Orizaba, scenery is rendered dynamic through the train's movement. Adolfo appears in medium close-up reading a copy of the local newspaper *El Dictamen*, flanked by windows that offer a mobile view of the surrounding landscape. This strategy gives a sense of the "panoramic perception" offered by rail travel, a viewing experience marked by speed and a consciousness of technological mediation, signaled by the presence of telegraph poles and wires.[100]

After the robbery scene that follows Adolfo's arrival, mentioned above, the action doubles back to the railyard. Adolfo discusses his mission with the stationmaster, seizing the opportunity to flirt with Elena. The action then shifts to a series of narratively unmotivated "phantom ride" shots. The first, taken several cars back from the locomotive, captures the length of the train rounding a curve, at once accommodating itself to the topography and slicing through it. In the next shot, a fixed camera captures the oncoming train, followed by another traveling shot taken from the train that shows the vehicle plunging into a tunnel. Offering a vicarious experience of speed, this sequence is linked only tangentially to the narrative action, suggesting how spectacles of transportation technology held the potential to act as semiautonomous attractions.

Publicity for *El tren fantasma* also emphasized scenic landscape views as a key part of its audience appeal. One notice published in Mexico City, where the film was exhibited simultaneously in ten theaters, observes that "*El tren fantasma* has a sensational plot, and one can see in all of its scenes the tropical setting, with advantage taken of the beautiful landscapes that surround the cheerful Pluviosilla [a nickname for Orizaba], inspiration of writers and now filmmakers."[101] Given the promotional tone of this notice, it may have been published at the request of the filmmakers. Yet it nevertheless indicates that both fast-and-furious action and scenic views were considered powerful selling points for the film.[102] In addition to publicity discourses stressing landscape as attraction, local topography and vegetation are highlighted by compositional choices throughout. The actors are often framed against faintly visible ridgelines, a subtle reminder of Veracruz's mountainous terrain. In the scene in which Paco loses control of the engine, spiky maguey plants (a key element of Mexico's visual iconography, prominent in the work of muralist painters), race past the camera, reminding the spectator of the location's specificity even at a moment of considerable suspense.

Regionally specific customs also make an appearance into *El tren fantasma*'s action-driven plot. Following the robbery of the beer factory, an impromptu dance competition breaks out between the bandits; one dances a sensual rumba of Cuban origin, while another demonstrates fast-paced *jarabe* steps. The bandits' costumes, particularly their headgear, evoke a variety of film genres and iconographies, ranging from cowboy hats to broad sombreros and soft caps like those sported by the French *apache*. By contrast with this moment of spectacle, bullfighting plays a more substantial role in the film's plot. Paco receives an invitation to take the place of a professional matador and allows himself to be injured in order to impress Elena. This scene incorporated actuality footage of the toreador Juan Silveti, integrating elements of visual documentation into the narrative.[103] Like *El tren fantasma*'s treatment of landscape, these interludes were integrated with the plot, but offered an appeal rooted in their local specificity.

Functioning as a marker of local modernity and a means of displaying picturesque scenery, the train in *El tren fantasma* is closely linked with the making and unmaking of the romantic couple. Noting how technological and narrative machinery converge to foster heterosexual desire in silent cinema, Lynne Kirby observes, "The train is a social force that puts bodies in relation to each other by chance and joins them together, even if by accident. The train, as such, offers itself as a social ground of integration, a mobile support of attraction, an intermediary term in the engendering and channeling of desire."[104] *El tren fantasma* hews closely to this narrative pattern; Adolfo and Elena meet for the first time upon his arrival to the station, and the locomotive is central to the romantic rivals' attempts to win Elena's affections. Significantly, the train's role as visible sign of local modernization is directly integrated into the romantic plot. A tête-a-tête between Adolfo and Elena, during which she (temporarily) rejects his romantic advances in favor of Paco, takes place in front of a public monument commemorating the completion of the electric railway in 1923.

The railway's role in the romantic rivalry driving *El tren fantasma*'s plot motivates the display of risky stunts and special effects. The scene of Elena's kidnapping, in particular, exemplifies the melodramatic temporality of a rescue "in the nick of time" that allows Adolfo to display his physical prowess.[105] As Adolfo is bidding Elena and her father goodbye in the rail yard, bandits spring out of the train, which fills much of the frame while the struggle is shown in extreme long shot. The bandits beat her father and he falls onto the tracks; meanwhile, Adolfo jumps on board the moving locomotive, where he grapples with one of Paco's accomplices while clinging to a railing. The struggle is shown in a series of mobile long shots taken from onboard the train. As Adolfo clings to the handrail, a series of medium shots show his adversary stomping on his fingers until he loses his grip and falls to the ground. Improbably, Adolfo makes it back to the railyard to save Elena's father, still collapsed on the tracks, from an oncoming engine with seconds to spare.

While investigating Paco's double identity, Adolfo falls into the clutches of the bandits. Paco coerces his love interest into running away with him, but loses control of the locomotive. This loss of control is signaled by shots in which rapid camera movements loosely follow the line of the tracks, suggesting a point of view that has literally run off the rails. Paco jumps from the rear and

FIGS 2.4 AND 2.5 Romance, the rails, and local modernity: Adolfo (Carlos Villatoro) and Elena (Clarita Ibáñez) converse in front of a plaque commemorating the completion of the electric railway. Video stills.

FIG 2.6 A lobby card shows Adolfo's last-minute rescue of the stationmaster. Archivo General de la Nación (México), Fondo Hermanos Mayo, concentrados sobre 363.

tries to convince Elena to follow, but she balks. Meanwhile, Adolfo escapes with the help of Paco's jealous girlfriend, Carmela (Angelita Ibáñez), and pursues the train on horseback. He manages to jump aboard and save Elena before a catastrophic explosion (rendered using a scale model of a railway bridge and a miniature locomotive). Although Adolfo's rescue of Elena cements his triumph over his rival, a final scene redeems Paco through a self-sacrificing act that averts a technological disaster on a mass scale. Having lost Elena, Paco falls into a depression, which alienates his criminal compatriots. To punish him, they conspire to sabotage the train on which Elena and Adolfo are traveling to their honeymoon. Just before the explosion, Paco grabs the dynamite planted by his former associates, saving the train but perishing in the process.

By contrast with the adventure melodramas produced in Mexico City in the early twenties, which were presented as contributions to an emerging national industry, *El tren fantasma* was discussed in the press as a primarily regional achievement. Although advertisements described *El tren fantasma* as a "national film" (*película nacional*), they stressed its production in the state of Veracruz and its inclusion of "natural landscapes of incalculable artistic

FIG 2.7 Bandits dance the rumba and *jarabe* during a brief folkloric interlude in *El tren fantasma*. Video still.

merit."[106] The film enjoyed an enthusiastic reception when it was shown at the Teatro Variedades in the port of Veracruz; a reviewer reported that, despite an early arrival at the theater, his "efforts to enter easily were frustrated by the quantity of people who flooded through the lobby door."[107] Amid the excited chatter of the crowd, the reviewer managed to find a seat and waited along with the rest of the spectators while "they showed an art film, which everyone watched with little interest, wanting above all to see *El tren fantasma*. Intermission comes. Finally the lights go down again and EL TREN FANTASMA appears. Applause and exclamations break out on the spot." Suggesting the excitement generated by the opportunity to see a locally made film, the reviewer does not comment in detail on *El tren fantasma* itself, perhaps skirting the issue of its quality. Instead, the critic assures the reader that "everyone left satisfied, having appreciated the film; we sincerely declare that it is a good production, where the efforts of a group of Orizaba businessmen have been made manifest." The journalist added, "The whole state of Veracruz should see [*El tren fantasma*], as should every good Mexican who can appreciate [good] efforts." Suggesting *El tren fantasma* constituted a worthy endeavor rather than a highly polished product, the reviewer nevertheless framed it as appealing to both a regional and a national public.

By contrast with the positive reception of *El tren fantasma*, García Moreno's next production proved much less palatable for local audiences and was never exhibited in Mexico City. Whereas *El tren fantasma* was structured around a single line of narrative action centered on a heterosexual love triangle, *El puño de hierro* involved multiple romances, insinuations of bestiality and homosexuality, and double identities concealed from the viewer until the final moments of the film. Further confusing matters, in *El puño de hierro*'s final sequence, nearly the entire narrative is revealed to have been a drug-induced hallucination suffered by the protagonist, Carlos (Octavio Valencia), the first time he indulges in narcotics. This action opens the film, setting a precedent for its use of graphic and often unsettling imagery: after yielding to a friend's persuasion, Carlos injects himself with morphine. In the following scene, after an ellipsis in the story time, Carlos is shown in the throes of addiction stroking a donkey that he mistakes for his girlfriend Laura (Hortensia Valencia). Without any clear narrative justification, other unconventional sexual practices are shown as consequences of the consumption of drugs; in a later scene set in the drug den, a group of young men caresses and kisses a mature man dressed only in a loincloth. In this sense, *El puño de hierro* parallels sensational features depicting drug abuse and taboo sexuality produced in Brazil in the late 1920s, including *Vício e beleza* (*Vice and Beauty*, Antônio Tibiriçá, 1926) and *Morfina* (*Morphine*, Francisco Madrigano and Nino Ponti, 1928), which became rare commercial successes of domestic film production.

Perhaps most troublingly for contemporary audiences, *El puño de hierro* undercuts the discourses of social hygiene actively promoted by postrevolutionary governments with the revelation of antidrug campaigner Dr. Ortiz's double life as the drug kingpin El Tieso. Compounding this irony, Ortiz/El Tieso is revealed to suffer from a physical defect, a sign of the "degeneracy" attributed in the film to drug abuse. He suffers from paralysis in one of his hands, a detail that echoes the affliction of the "Clutching Hand," villain of the Pathé Exchange serial *The Exploits of Elaine* (Louis Gasnier and George B. Seitz, 1914). This revelation at once explains his nickname (meaning "The Rigid One") and helps explain the film's title, which recalls another serial distributed by Pathé Exchange, *The Iron Claw* (Edward José, 1916). Furthermore, when Laura visits Dr. Ortiz's home to seek help for Carlos, he lures her to the drug den intending to seduce or assault her. In *El puño de hierro*, physical deformity and moral turpitude are embodied in the very authority charged with extirpating them.

Publicized as a "moral and exciting film" dedicated to showing "the tragic figures of morphine, drunkenness, and gambling, denouncing their effects in Mexican youths of all social classes," *El puño de hierro* manifests a deep ambivalence toward the postrevolutionary rhetoric of social hygiene. This ambivalence is clearest in a sequence that evokes the contemporary practices of public-health campaigns, which incorporated outdoor lectures and the screening of educational films intended to inform the populace about the risks of alcoholism, drug abuse, and venereal disease.[108] Early in the film, Dr. Ortiz gives an antidrug speech in a public plaza, which motivates the insertion of a series of nonfiction images; in effect, the conventions of the educational (or exploitation) film briefly displace those of narrative.[109] Emphasizing narcotics' ambivalent character as both modern malady and advanced medical tool, a sequence demonstrates their use in surgical procedures. Following this scene, images of children with physical deformities, described in an intertitle as the result of their parents' drug use, are presented as evidence of effects of narcotics' pernicious effects on the social body. Beyond arousing pity or revulsion from the spectator, the insertion of these nonfiction sequences within the narrative generates ambivalence within the authoritative scientific discourse in whose service they are mobilized. Even as the sequence unequivocally condemns drugs' negative effects on public health, it suggests the impossibility of untangling the risks and benefits of modern medical treatment, an ambivalence embodied by the double identity of Dr. Ortiz/El Tieso.

Beyond this key narrative reversal, *El puño de hierro* draws on the tropes of the crime serial with its complex subplots, secret identities, and unexpected revelations. The scene of Dr. Ortiz's speech provides a point of connection between the main romantic couple, Carlos and Laura, and the film's other characters. Emphasizing the chance—and sexually charged—encounters possible in urban spaces, during the speech Antonio (Carlos Villatoro), who is secretly the bandit leader "El Murciélago" (the Bat), makes overtures to Esther (Lupe Bonilla), an employee of El Tieso who is implied to be a prostitute. (The lines of action involving El Murciélago's criminal gang rely on repurposed scenes from *El buitre*.)[110] Neither is aware of the other's occupation before they cross paths in the drug den, located not in a populated area, but rather (as is later revealed) in an isolated grotto.

FIG 2.8 Manuel de los Ríos as Dr. Ortiz, showing an example of "degeneration" during an open-air antidrug lecture that recalled public-health campaigns of the period. Video still.

FIG 2.9 De los Ríos as El Tieso, trying to convince the bandit El Murciélago (Carlos Villatoro) to join his operation in a scene in the drug den. Video still.

FIG 2.10 Juanito (Guillermo Pacheco), the young aspiring detective, reads Nick Carter stories. Video still.

Whereas in *El tren fantasma* the train fosters a fluid integration of action and setting, the spatial relationships established through editing in the restored version of *El puño de hierro* are marked by incongruity. This strategy highlights a sense of discontinuity in the local geographies of modernity, conveying how city and countryside entered into unexpected relations in a rapidly industrializing state.

The discontinuities in *El puño de hierro*'s visual construction and its complex, ambiguous narrative likely contributed to its comparatively negative reception by local audiences. After giving mixed praise to the film's cinematography and actors, a reviewer in *El Dictamen* lambasted its narrative construction, judging the plot

> completely deficient. Lacking unity and connection, of very slow and confusing development, at times difficult to understand. . . . It does not offer thesis or action, and limits itself to the presentation of scenes, some very fine, which do not build to a final moral or a defined and solid objective. It is the weakness and total lack of interest of the plot that compromises the success of this production, which boasts quite accomplished artists, beautiful scenes, very intense sequences, and an ensemble that is truly hearten-

ing for the national [cinematic] art, all of which loses its luster due to the lack of action, dynamism, and pleasing unity in the overall work.[111]

While the tediousness of the film's narrative as described by the reviewer certainly sets it apart from imported adventure melodramas that trade on fast-and-furious thrills, the perceived lack of narrative unity and clarity recall criticisms often levied against serial films. Significantly, the reviewer links the lack of a coherent narrative to the absence of an effective moral. *El puño de hierro*'s unsettling scenes of violence, sexual desire, and drug abuse are never recuperated by a clear lesson. For the reviewer, this lack of the moral legibility characteristic of melodrama detracted from the film's appeal.

In the wake of the film's disappointing local run, the Centro Cultural Cinematográfico shut down, and García Moreno moved with his wife to Tijuana, working in Los Angeles between 1929 and 1937.[112] Coincidentally, these years marked the drawn-out period of the development of sound cinema, from the early commercial success of *Santa* (Antonio Moreno, 1931), to the smash hit *Allá en el Rancho Grande* (*Over at the Big Ranch*, Fernando de Fuentes, 1937), which helped consolidate a technically proficient and internationally popular sound film industry in Mexico. Yet while silent-era productions never managed to forge the powerful nationalist myths of Mexican cinema's industrial "Golden Age," they highlighted the conflictual construction of national modernity in the face of North American influence and the limits and contradictions of postrevolutionary modernizing projects.

Conclusion

During the 1920s, adventure melodramas shot on location and regional productions converged in complex ways with the modernizing nationalism of postrevolutionary Mexico. The films of Miguel Contreras Torres and other "open air" productions of the early 1920s reworked the conventions of Hollywood westerns in their focus on scenic landscapes and regional customs, capitalizing on the appeal of cinematic depictions of violence while sidestepping images of revolutionary conflict and "denigrating" Hollywood imports. In this context, emerging discourses of film criticism and ambitions for a national industry were mutually reinforcing, even as critics and filmmakers debated the proper orientation of domestically produced films toward North American cultural products. At a distance from the activities of filmmaking and film criticism centered in the capital, *El tren fantasma* and *El puño de hierro* registered the geographic and social particularities of a modernizing Veracruz, highlighting modernization's complicity with criminal violence and technological disaster, and undercutting progess-oriented discourses of social hygiene. Although none of these films ultimately offered a model for self-sustaining film production, they demonstrate the capacity of sensational adventure melodramas to bolster the cultural projects of postrevolutionary nationalism, while simultaneously highlighting their contradictions.

PART II

*STAGING
SPECTACLES OF
MODERNITY
IN BRAZIL*

Chapter 3

RECONSTRUCTING CRIME IN RIO DE JANEIRO AND SÃO PAULO, 1906–1913

On the morning of 16 October 1906, the first reports appeared in Rio de Janeiro newspapers of a shocking case of robbery and murder, called the "Crime of Carioca Street" after the downtown thoroughfare where it occurred. The body of nineteen-year-old Italian immigrant Paulino Fuoco, a victim of strangulation, was discovered in a ransacked jewelry store belonging to his uncle, and his brother Carluccio had gone missing. After Carluccio's corpse was found floating in Guanabara Bay, an abandoned boat led the authorities to Eugenio Rocca, Justino Carlo (alias Carletto), and Jerónimo Pigato, who eventually confessed to luring the victim out onto the water and taking the keys to the jeweler's before strangling him and disposing of the body. For several days, the front pages of popular local newspapers like the *Gazeta de Notícias*, the *Jornal do Brasil*, and the *Correio da Manhã* featured articles relating to the case, abundantly illustrated with photographs and lithographs showing crime scenes crowded with curious onlookers, images of the victims on the autopsy tables, and portraits of detectives and suspects. The Crime of Carioca Street was quickly adapted to the stage in a series of dramas and musical revues. Two years later, as exhibitors in Rio de Janeiro ventured into film production, the case was adapted to the screen as *Os estranguladores* (*The Stranglers*), a 700-meter film shot by the Portuguese immigrant Antônio Leal that is considered Brazil's first narrative feature.

Violent death was not in itself so unusual in turn-of-the-century Rio de Janeiro, a city of over 800,000 residents that had a per capita murder rate roughly six times that of London.[1] Yet the Crime of Carioca Street and other gruesome cases generated intense media spectacles that highlighted the profound social and spatial divides of Brazil's two fastest-growing cities. As the nation's economy boomed through the export of agricultural commodities, especially coffee and rubber, the city was transformed by large-scale European immigration, internal migration, and urban reforms, inspired in part by Baron Haussmann's remodeling of Paris, which demolished working-class dwellings in the city center to make way for broad avenues and grand buildings. The city of São Paulo, smaller in size but growing more rapidly, was also targeted for urban renewal, although sweeping reforms would not be realized until the 1920s.

In an urbanizing Brazil, narratives of criminal acts committed by newly visible social actors, especially immigrants and young women, proliferated in entertainment culture and the expanding illustrated press. Popular sensationalism capitalized on the unique capacities of cinema, photography, and new printing technologies to capture—or to convincingly reconstruct—unpredictable and often violent events viewed as typifying modern experience. As would be the case with early Mexican fiction films a decade later, police reportage and early narrative cinema simultaneously documented and dramatized current events. Building on the cultural repertoire of stage melodrama and serial literature, these cultural forms encouraged audiences to interpret topical happenings through moralistic frameworks that emphasized individual guilt or innocence, rather than the pervasive social ills that accompanied modernization.

Drawing on a broader public culture of sensationalized violence, filmed reconstructions of real-life cases shaped the emergence of early narrative cinema in Brazil as film producer-exhibitors capitalized on topical subjects. A production of Leal's Photo-Cinematografia Brasileira company, *Os estranguladores* was reportedly exhibited more than 830 times during a three-month run in the capital, attracting over 20,000 spectators in the first month alone and sparking a brief craze for filmed reenactments of real-life crimes that lasted through early 1909.[2] In the wake of *Os estranguladores's* success, Leal and his competitors rushed to adapt a September 1908 case, referred to as the "Crime of the Trunk" because the body of the victim, the Syrian businessman Elias Farhat, was concealed in a steamer trunk. Leal continued to exploit sensational subjects in *Noivado de sangue* (*Bloody Engagement*, 1909), based on the case of a young teacher who murdered a former lover with the complicity of her new husband, and *Um drama na Tijuca* (*A Drama in Tijuca*, 1909), a

O CRIME DA RUA DA CARIOCA

A casa n. 53 da rua da Carioca, onde foi perpetrado o horrível crime e o cadáver de Paulino Fuoco, umas das víctimas dos ladrões.

FIG 3.1 Crime as a public spectacle: crowds gather on the scene of the "Crime of Carioca Street," and graphic images of the victim's corpse are displayed to newspaper readers. *Gazeta de Notícias*, 21 October 1906. Acervo da Fundação Biblioteca Nacional, Brasil.

fictional film whose subject often appeared in the police blotter: the suicide of a woman in the wake of an unhappy love affair. As urban reforms and the expansion of public transportation encouraged women to circulate in urban spaces and participate in novel forms of commercialized leisure, questions of private morality sparked heated public debates.

Alongside the hugely popular *filmes falados e cantantes* (talking and singing films), which were accompanied by actors' performances from behind the screen, reconstructions of real-life cases became the greatest commercial successes of early film production in Brazil. Following the opening of the first permanent venues for film exhibition in Rio de Janeiro in August 1907, the rise of these locally specific genres signaled the emergence of the "movie theater as unit of production [as] an alternative to the predominant system of the movie theater as importer and exhibitor," according to the film historian José Inácio de Melo Souza.[3] He notes that in Rio and São Paulo between 1907 and 1911, "production for local consumption was a marginal activity, but one with a significant impact on the survival of some movie theaters."[4] Following the film scholar Jean-Claude Bernadet, Melo Souza nuances previous characterizations of this period as a "bela época" of Brazilian film—that is, a golden age of national cinema prior to the domination of foreign imports—in the work of the critic Paulo Emílio Salles Gomes and others. Rather, Melo Souza insists, local productions acted as a means of distinguishing particular venues' offerings within an urban exhibition market dependent on foreign (particularly French) films.[5]

By 1911, the Companhia Cinematográfica Brasileira, owned by the Spanish impresario Francisco Serrador, had consolidated a near-monopoly over distribution and exhibition in Rio and São Paulo, putting an end to the vertically integrated, if small-scale, production model of the producer-exhibitors. Significantly, two of the most ambitious attempts to recapture local audiences in the early teens were two reconstructions of real-life cases produced by the brothers Alberto and Paulino Botelho. O caso dos caixotes (The Case of the Strongboxes, 1912), which depicted an audacious payroll robbery on board a steamship, and Um crime sensacional (A Sensational Crime, 1913), a reconstruction of the murder of the businessman Adolfo Freire (supplemented with a train accident scene seemingly unrelated to the case), were in fact the only Brazilian-made fiction films to be exhibited in São Paulo during these two years.[6] Extending the reciprocal exchanges between cinema and the police blotter, these films emphasized the threat of criminality and technological breakdown that accompanied expanding networks of modern traffic.[7]

Like the majority of works of early Brazilian cinema, these filmed reenactments are believed lost to the historical record. Yet analyzing their traces in the illustrated press and their interconnections with popular theater illuminates how entertainment and visual culture rendered spectacular the tensions of everyday life in Brazil's most rapidly modernizing cities, giving rise to forms of film narrative intimately linked to topical events. Referring to Leal's reconstruction of the Crime of the Trunk, Bernadet argues that the restaging of the murder at the actual scene of the crime combines a "desire for the raw document, for 'reality,' with a desire for fiction . . . a double desire already manifest in the press."[8] Indeed, the police blotter offered readers a profusion of verbal and visual documents, even as it indulged in wild speculation. Supposedly faithful transcriptions of autopsy and police reports, interrogations, and reporters' conversations with witnesses were reproduced along with passages that narrated violent events in a novelistic style.

As was also the case in early twentieth-century Mexico City, this local imaginary of sensational crime is clearly in dialogue with the "spectacular realities" of fin-de-siècle Paris analyzed by Vanessa Schwartz.[9] To a greater extent than in Mexico, French dailies like Le Figaro and its competitor Le Petit Jour-

nal were influential in the development of Brazilian newspapers, and Paris was a key point of reference for elite-driven modernization projects during what Jeffrey Needell calls a "tropical Belle Époque."[10] Influencing urban reforms, architectural styles, fashion, and leisure, European models also shaped elite attitudes toward crime, which was paradoxically hailed as a marker of urban modernity. The French expression *grandes crimes* was used frequently in the popular press, indicating a distinction between the forms of violence that elites associated with the working classes—bar fights, disputes over personal honor, and "crimes of passion"—and often characterized by the press as sudden and senseless explosions of violence, and intriguingly mysterious, gruesome, or perverse criminal acts of the type committed in U.S. and European cities, which received international publicity.[11]

Ironic in tone, discourses that framed crime as a herald of progress signal elite acceptance of modernization's social costs, suggesting how, as Jean Franco argues in the context of twentieth-century Latin America more broadly, "the pressures of modernization and the lure of modernity" have perpetuated structural inequality and the extrajudicial use of state violence against citizens.[12] While reminiscent in many ways of the cosmopolitan imaginaries of crime that circulated in Porfirian and revolutionary Mexico City, the sensational journalism and cinema that flourished in turn-of-the-century Rio de Janeiro and São Paulo were shaped by a distinct brand of modernizing euphoria that followed Brazil's relatively peaceful transition from empire to republic in 1889. Following a period of initial political and economic volatility, marked by speculation and inflation followed by financial crisis, renewed alliances between the federal government and regional agrarian elites fostered greater political stability, setting the stage for ambitious modernizing initiatives. Exemplifying a mode of modernization premised on social exclusion along racial and class lines, the sweeping transformations of Rio de Janeiro were accompanied by the growth of entertainment culture, including film exhibition and production.

Giving expression to elite ambitions and anxieties accompanying rapid urbanization, cinematic and theatrical spectacles of real-life crime participated in a broader tendency to criminalize the working classes, evident in journalistic and scientific discourses as well as in practices of arbitrary policing, such as arrests for vagrancy or other minor offenses. Yet while their content emphasized class disparities, sensational narratives were viewed as possessing a broad appeal across social sectors. Graphic news photography and topical films promised to expand cultural markets to illiterate consumers, although their limited purchasing power was also an obstacle. Only 31 percent of Brazil's population could read and write in 1900, although the percentage was higher in large cities.[13] Unfolding in the press, onstage, and onscreen, public spectacles of violence reinforced social divisions by fostering anxieties regarding particular classes and areas of the city. At the same time, they worked to build a mass audience across these divides in the face of the impossibility of effectively segregating elite and working-class spaces in rapidly expanding cities. In turn-of-the-century Rio and São Paulo, the massification of the illustrated press and the development of local film production helped forge a public sphere conditioned by violence and economic inequality.

The occurrence—and perhaps more important, the news coverage—of sensational cases was frequently linked by journalists to ambitions for national progress, measured against the models of more industrialized nations. After the discovery of the Crime of the Trunk, the São Paulo newspaper *Correio Paulistano* noted ironically, "There are those who affirm that sensational grand crimes are indices marking the degree of civilization of the milieu where such refinements of cruelty occur with frequency. If this phrase we have recalled is not a paradox, it can be said without exaggeration that S. Paulo, day by day, is becoming civilized, competing with the great centers."[14] In a similar vein, after the Crime of Carioca Street, a writer for the *Gazeta de Notícias* declared, "One of the characteristics of the greatest and most refined civilizations are [*sic*] grand crimes. In this respect, and under this aspect, we have the right to consider ourselves among the most advanced of civilized peoples. We are not lacking in what journalistic technology calls sensational crimes."[15] The reference to "journalistic technology" evokes a self-conscious local adoption of investigative reporting techniques characteristic of sensational journalism in the United States and France.[16] At the same time, the term also recalls the growing industrialization of the press, including the introduction of rotary presses, which allowed for increased print runs, and the adoption of halftone photographic reproductions. Staking a claim to topicality, photography and cinema staged quotidian experience as thrillingly modern by spectacularizing violent and socially disruptive events.

In Brazil's expanding cities, the overwhelming and enervating qualities of a highly industrialized metropolis were as much an object of longing as an element of daily experience. As in the case of Mexico City, the greatest threats to health and safety were often posed by the lack of adequate infrastructure and public services in the face of rapid urban growth. Although some cartoons from the period depict the distinctly modern hazards of urban traffic, more

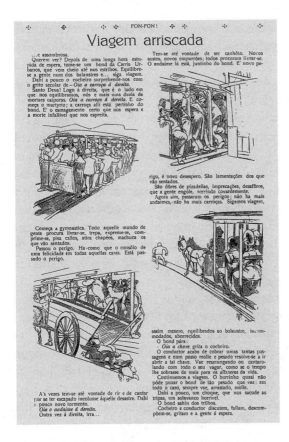

FIG 3.2 "A Risky Trip": overcrowding and accidents on an outdated mode of public transportation. *Fon-Fon*, 13 July 1907. Acervo da Fundação Biblioteca Nacional, Brasil.

representative is a humorous illustrated narrative entitled "Viagem arriscada" (Risky Trip), which describes slow and hazardous travel on a mule-powered tram, a mode of transportation that coexisted with an expanding network of electric trolleys. Rather than an overwhelming experience of speed and mobility, the text and accompanying illustrations depict a transit system slowed to a crawl by overcapacity and ineffective management of traffic flows, leading to long waits, overcrowding, collisions, and derailments.

Such inconveniences, along with more pressing social problems, were partly a consequence of rapid population growth in the two cities at the turn of the twentieth century. Between 1890 and 1900, Rio de Janeiro almost doubled in size, growing from over 522,600 to more than 811,400 residents, while São Paulo's population exploded from just under 65,000 in 1890 to nearly 240,000 by 1900, mainly due to the arrival of large numbers of European immigrants.[17] Plagued by chronic overcrowding and contagious diseases, the two cities lacked adequate housing, transportation, lighting, sanitation, and policing, especially in the expanding suburbs and favelas (informal communities or shantytowns), where new arrivals and working-class residents displaced from other areas often took up residence. Infrastructural improvements were concentrated in city centers and wealthy neighborhoods like the new residential districts constructed in Rio's Zona Sul (Southern Zone) during the first decade of the twentieth century. Following the 1889 Proclamation of the Republic, the export of agricultural products and the construction of transportation infrastructure—often bankrolled by foreign capital—fueled Brazil's economic expansion, without leading to significant gains in wages for workers or the nation's small middle class. Nor did liberal-democratic ideals translate into the enfranchisement of broad sectors of the population; suffrage was limited to literate males, and the number of actual voters in presidential elections never exceeded 3.4 percent of the population during the republic.[18]

As the nation's capital (prior to the 1960 inauguration of Brasília), Rio de Janeiro served as the most visible site of Brazil's modernization and economic prosperity. The campaigns of urban reform initiated in 1903 by the city prefect Francisco Pereira Passos were designed to showcase the nation's progress to both domestic and foreign observers.[19] Densely clustered buildings, some dating from the colonial era, that served as tenements (cortiços) were demolished to make way for broad thoroughfares, most notably the Avenida Central (later Avenida Rio Branco), which ran through the heart of Rio's shopping and entertainment district, and the Avenida Beira Mar (Shoreline Avenue), which linked the city center to new neighborhoods in the Zona Sul. These urban reforms increasingly displaced the informally employed and the working classes to distant suburbs and the northern area of the city, while elite citydwellers gravitated toward developing residential areas in the southern zone.

The sweeping transformations of downtown Rio de Janeiro were justified by hygienic concerns—high population density and unsanitary living conditions exacerbated outbreaks of yellow fever and other infectious diseases—and for cosmetic reasons. Local journalists formed the League against Ugliness (Liga contra o Feio), waging newspaper campaigns against "unattractive" aspects of the cityscape such as cramped, narrow streets and the presence of beggars in the central districts.[20] In her analysis of urban reform and social dissent in republican Rio, the historian Teresa A. Meade suggests that affluent residents were more troubled by the visibility of crime and prostitution, especially in central areas that might be frequented by foreigners, than by its actual existence. She writes, "There are indications that the city's elite then, as now, was less concerned with an increase in vice so long as it remained contained to the poorer neighborhoods. The real problem in Rio was that the city had grown so rapidly and haphazardly that congested areas brought the diverse social classes and races into close proximity."[21] Yet entirely excluding the poor from the modern city was an economic impossibility: Marcos Luiz Bretas notes, "They could not be eliminated pure and simple, since they provided the cheap labor indispensable to the elites. In the first years of urban reform, the role of the police grew considerably, with the end of controlling this mass of poor workers."[22] Attempts to professionalize Rio de Janeiro's police began in 1903 and became more pressing in the wake of collective uprisings, most notably the 1904 Revolt of the Vaccine, a weeklong riot sparked by a campaign of forced smallpox vaccination.[23]

Even as elites and the police force worked to suppress visible signs of poverty and crime, emerging forms of popular sensationalism actively linked criminality to the modernity promised by urban renewal and demographic shifts. Even as urban reforms sought to reinforce spatial divisions between classes, the police blotter highlighted the permeability of public spaces. A key element of the disturbing appeal that the Crime of Carioca Street held for newspaper readers was the fact that it took place on a heavily traveled street in the city center. The *Jornal do Brasil* suggested that the perpetrators of the Crime of Carioca Street might lurk among the crowds circulating on the capital's newly constructed avenues, aligning the physical transformations of the city and the emergence of novel forms of leisure with the threat of violent crime.

> With the modification of the habits of our tranquil and utterly bourgeois city, due to its radical transformation, with the new arteries that already lend it the aspect of a European city, day by day, European immigration grows, and as is natural, on par with the arrival of new elements good for our prosperity, it brings some bad ones as well.
>
> New types make their appearance daily, giving preference to places of entertainment [*casas de espectáculos*], confectioneries, and fashionable cafés, in order to promenade on the avenues in automobiles and luxurious carriages, without anyone knowing their provenance or how they maintain the lifestyle of wealthy persons.[24]

The journalist establishes a parallel between the physiognomy of public spaces and of those that populate them, associating the city's newly Europeanized appearance with an influx of immigrants. Elites influenced by social Darwinism and scientific racism had encouraged these migratory flows as a means of effacing slavery's demographic legacy in Brazil, claiming that African-descended workers were naturally indolent and would be unproductive when liberated from forced labor. By subsidizing immigrants' transportation costs, federal and state governments aimed to provide a supply of cheap labor while "whitening" the nation's population.[25] Yet by suggesting that the masses of otherwise desirable white immigrants might conceal dangerous elements, the article alludes to fears regarding foreigners' criminal tendencies, a key concern for police reformers of the period.[26] The description also speaks to the difficulty of visually distinguishing between social classes, given that "the abolition of slavery in 1888 and the continuous flow of European immigrants forced a complete restructuring of social behaviors, introducing new and not immediately classifiable individuals in public space."[27]

Anxieties regarding criminal behavior and the difficulties of determining class identities within urban crowds were partially countered by the visual classification of potential offenders through the growing use of police photography.[28] In 1907, the photographic department of Rio de Janeiro's police force created images of 3,141 suspects.[29] Even those who were arrested for minor offenses were photographed, fingerprinted, and classified as "known criminals."[30] Yet affluent *carioca* (Rio de Janeiro) residents were also captured by the camera lens on a mass scale, as street photography, illustrated magazines, and actuality films documenting upper-class diversions forged an unprecedented "visibility of the elite."[31] The visual culture of turn-of-the-century Rio and São Paulo insistently displayed both working-class criminality and elite leisure culture, rendering literal the continuum that, according to Allan J. Sekula, links the criminal mug shot with the bourgeois portrait photograph, as both are informed by conceptions of individuality grounded in private-property rights.[32] Images of these polarized social classes mark the emergence of a mass culture that was paradoxically premised on social divides.

As demographic shifts transformed Rio and São Paulo, commentators raised the alarm about the presence of anarcho-syndicalists among the ranks of recent immigrants, who were often blamed for popular uprisings.[33] Yet much of the dissent in the period can be traced to deep-rooted inequalities in Brazilian society. Internal tensions in the nation's racially stratified military fueled the November 1910 Revolta da Chibata (Revolt of the Whip), in which a group of sailors rose up to protest abuses by officers—most immediately, a punishment of more than two hundred lashes administered to the sailor Marcelino Rodrigues Menezes—seizing control of the nation's fleet and training their guns on the capital. Arising from a local backlash against public-health campaigns, the 1904 Revolt of the Vaccine grew into a mass protest against elite-driven modernization. Meade finds special significance in the fact that rioters targeted the most visible elements of urban reform, rather than the public-health institutions directly responsible for the vaccination program: they "overturned and set ablaze streetcars, brok[e] gas and electric streetlights, erected barricades to cut off access to the main arteries in the vital business districts near the docks and trading houses, invaded construction sites to tear apart newly constructed walls and floors, and vandalized train stations on lines out to the rapidly expanding *subúrbios* on the outskirts of downtown."[34] Meade argues that these actions are indicative of public consciousness that elites' modernization programs were furthering the spatial exclusion of broad sectors of the population.

While nonviolent and lacking political motives, huge crowds also flocked to the scenes of infamous crimes and, later, to the films based on them. As images from the police blotter attest, masses of curious onlookers would cluster at crime scenes, the morgue, and the Casa de Detenção (House of Detention). Due to their sheer numbers, moviegoers occasionally obstructed traffic on central streets. Schwartz suggests that the emergence of mass entertainments in Paris at the turn of the twentieth century is indicative of the pacification of the Parisian masses by the last third of the nineteenth century.[35] By contrast, in turn-of-the-century Rio de Janeiro, elite hegemony was precarious, and the threat of mass mobilization a very real one. As a compensatory measure, police reportage and crime-themed films evoked the moral polarities of melodrama, emphasizing individual guilt over broader social ills.

Charting the role of sensational depictions of violence in the emergence of mass culture in turn-of-the-century Rio de Janeiro and São Paulo, I first turn to print media, examining how the police reportage and the *crônica* (a short journalistic text in an essayistic style) intersected with photography and cinema in the documentation of quotidian experience.[36] Drawing on novel visual technologies and reporting techniques, these journalistic genres also incorporated elements of a preexisting melodramatic repertoire, particularly aspects of the folhetim (serial novel), attributed with the capacity to attract a reading public that encompassed both the elites and the working classes. Focusing on how the strategies of investigative reporting, street photography, and topical films offered consumers a means of vicariously navigating the city, I show how these interconnected cultural forms cut across social classes, even as they highlighted the social and spatial divisions that shaped urban life in turn-of-the-century Rio and São Paulo.

In the following section, I examine how popular entertainments cultivated a mass public by dramatizing violent events and rendering them morally legible. Tracing the journalistic and theatrical precursors of Leal's *Os estranguladores*, I argue that its focus on real-life events and locations helped forge an audience for locally made films. Examining the strategies used by exhibitor-producers to market their films as both timely and authentic, I observe how elements of visual documentation (reenactment and landscape views) and dramatization (tinted sequences and apotheoses, or allegorical tableaux vivants) enhanced the appeal of topical narratives and constituted audience attractions in their own right. In the Botelho brothers' filmed reconstructions of the early teens, the restaging of events sensationalized by the illustrated press fostered further experiments with film narrative and style. By reading early film production in Rio and São Paulo through the lens of popular sensationalism, I illuminate how public spectacles of violence capitalized on the perceived affinity between visual technologies and topical events to stage daily experience as thrillingly modern, working to forge a mass audience in Brazil's rapidly growing metropolises.

Spectacularizing the Everyday: The Crônica,
The Police Blotter, and the Actuality Film

Sensational journalism operates at the intersection of the melodramatic and the topical; it invests quotidian experience with shocking, thrilling, and disturbing characteristics through rhetorical excesses and moral polarities. In turn-of-the-century Rio de Janeiro and São Paulo, the emergence of sensational police reportage rendered daily life an unfolding drama on the model of the folhetim. Beginning in the late nineteenth century, the growing massification of the press and the introduction of illustrations helped periodicals cultivate an appetite for news among illiterate consumers, even as both working-class and elite residents were captured by new visual technologies. In turn-of-the-century visual media, an incipient mass culture that highlighted, yet often failed to critique, violence and social inequality addressed a socially stratified audience.

Traversing urban spaces and shifting between cultural registers, the work of João do Rio—a pseudonym of the writer Paulo Barreto, perhaps the period's most celebrated writer of crônicas—offers a point of departure for examining how emerging mass cultural forms addressed social and spatial transformations in a modernizing Brazil. Borrowing the French term *flâneur* to describe his methods of moving through and observing the metropolis, João do Rio celebrated in his writings both the visible triumphs of modernization and urban reform—the Avenida Central, the electrified pavilions of the 1908 National Exposition—and their dark underside.[37] He penned a recurring section entitled No Jardim do Crime (In the Garden of Crime) in the *Gazeta de Notícias* beginning in 1905, and brought together a series of crônicas focused on the working classes and on the inmates of Rio's House of Detention in his 1908 collection *A alma encantadora das ruas* (*The Enchanting Soul of the Streets*).[38] Documenting the reshaping of daily life in turn-of-the-century Rio de Janeiro, João do Rio's writings signal the privileged role of narratives of criminality and violence in cultivating a mass public and in making sense of urban experience.

In a 1907 crônica, João do Rio draws attention to the subterranean connections between the police blotter's visual reportage and the portraits of the elite that circulated in the illustrated press. He writes,

> Take note of the newspapers and magazines. They are replete with halftones [*fotogravuras*] and with names, names and faces, many names and many faces! This generation makes, on its own initiative, its anthropometric identification for the future. But the curious thing is to see how the publication of these names is requested, is implored in newsrooms.... The interesting thing is to observe how they long for a portrait in the papers, from the dark promenades of the gardens of crime to the charity 'garden-parties' [in English], from criminals to angelic souls who think only of doing good. Appear! Appear![39]

In this account, rather than resisting new forms of surveillance enacted by visual technologies, members of both the upper and "criminal" classes eagerly participate in their "anthropometric identification"; that is, the observation and classification of their physical characteristics. If individuality is affirmed by the public circulation of one's image, these novel forms of individual visibility encompass both elites and denizens of the "lower depths," with these polarized social groups implied to be both subjects and consumers of print culture.

As is suggested by João do Rio's reference to the halftone process, the impulse to "appear" was fueled by the introduction of new printing technologies and business strategies in the local press. In the last quarter of the nineteenth century, Brazilian periodicals had begun to shift away from politically oriented publications printed on a relatively small scale toward modern-format papers with large circulations. Major Rio de Janeiro newspapers introduced high-volume printing presses, lithographic printing using zinc plates, and cartoons in the final years of the nineteenth century.[40] The popular daily *O Estado de São Paulo* was founded in 1875, with the inexpensive *Gazeta de Notícias* appearing in Rio the same year. By January 1878, the latter paper reached a circulation of 18,000 copies, which the newspaper claimed was a number unprecedented in the history of Brazilian journalism.[41] First published in 1891, the *Jornal do Brasil* introduced a number of innovations, including a novel method of quickly distributing papers throughout the capital using horse-drawn carts, reaching a circulation of 50,000 in 1900.[42] Founded in 1901, the *Correio da Manhã* became one of Rio de Janeiro's most politically combative and sensationalistic newspapers, competing aggressively for market share. The magazine *Revista da Semana* had debuted the previous year, becoming the first in the nation to reproduce large numbers of photographs. Exemplifying a broader shift toward abundant illustrations, the publication promised to "multiply its printed images in such a way, choosing them so well that they dispense with commentary," suggesting that the written texts inaccessible to illiterate consumers could be superseded by an eloquent sequence of photographs.[43] Toward the end of the decade, illustrated magazines like *Fon-Fon* and *Careta* won wide popularity among more affluent readers with their mixture of political commentary, caricatures, crônicas, and photographs that documented current events, urban reforms, and elite diversions.

The growing fascination with the image in the popular press ultimately worked to transform the verbal style of journalistic genres, including the crônica itself. Flora Süssekind argues that the ornate language of premodernist writers like João do Rio and Olavo Bilac gradually gave way to the development of a telegraphic style "suggestive of a snapshot."[44] Süssekind links this tendency to the growing professionalization of writers, who were increasingly able to earn a living wage by publishing in newspapers and magazines, and to their encounters with new technologies like the cinema, the gramophone, and the typewriter. Although turn-of-the-century writers had yet to experiment with modernist literary techniques that emulated photographic or cinematic procedures like fragmentation and montage, they noted affinities between the topical genre of the crônica and the novel medium of film. In the oft-cited introduction to his 1909 collection *Cinematógrafo*, João do Rio writes,

> The crônica evolved toward the cinema. . . . It passed through drawing and caricature. Lately, it has been photography, retouched but lifeless. With the delirious haste of us all, it has now become cinematic—a cinematograph of words, the story [*romance*] of the operator in the labyrinth of events, of others' lives, and of fantasy, but a story in which the operator is a secondary character dragged along in the rush of events.[45]

Suggesting that the genre has evolved toward ever-greater detail and immediacy, João do Rio contends that both the crônica and cinema blur the distinction between observer and observed as both are caught up in the accelerating rhythm of daily life. For the writer, the pleasures of both cinema and journalism are rooted in their ephemerality. Describing the fleeting sensations offered by a variety program, he writes, "A film, another, yet another. . . . We don't like the first? On to the second. The second's no good? Onward then!"[46] Discounting cinema's potential to preserve historical time, he concludes his comparison of film and the crônica by noting, "It follows that, just as the film is not re-viewed, this page resembling life is not reread. It displeased, or it enchanted. There was no time to reread it to note its defects—simply because there is no time for anything."[47] Cinema and the crônica preclude reflection, exemplifying—but also actively constructing—a modern temporality defined by fleeting impressions.

Taking the variety program as a metaphor for his journalistic activity and the quotidian experience it documents, João do Rio makes reference to a unique aspect of the moviegoing experience for affluent spectators in turn-of-the-century Rio de Janeiro, stating, "Perhaps you will see people you know, who do not speak to you, which is a blessing."[48] Commenting on the frequent interaction demanded by circulation in public spaces that were far from anonymous—he suggests one might be hailed in the street by numerous bothersome acquaintances—the writer also alludes to the experience of seeing familiar faces onscreen, which would not have been unusual for upper-class moviegoers in the period. As film exhibition in Rio de Janeiro expanded in late 1907 and early 1908, producer-exhibitors like Leal and Júlio Ferrez (who belonged to a family of French emigrés who served as Pathé Frères's agents in Brazil) filmed and screened actualities that displayed urban reforms and the leisure activities of the Rio de Janeiro elite: carriage rides, boat races, and a confetti-throwing "battle" during Carnival. These examples of "local films" offered elite spectators the thrill of recognizing themselves in moving images as "both the subject and the object of the show."[49] More than an "alternative public sphere," the movie theater became a privileged site of upper-class visibility.[50]

Signaling the early embrace of the cinema by Rio de Janeiro elites, a popular society column in the *Gazeta de Notícias* entitled Binóculo (Opera Glass) discussed the production and exhibition of local films with avid interest. Penned by Figueiredo Pimentel, the daily column not only reported on society gatherings, but also actively promoted new social practices among elites. Pimentel helped popularize moviegoing among affluent cariocas by setting the "fashionable" times to attend film screenings (called *soirées da moda*), thus helping his readers potentially avoid spectators of other classes who also flocked to new downtown movie theaters.[51] In his column, Pimentel announced that Júlio Ferrez would film the well-to-do families who participated in a weekly carriage promenade, specifying the time when the carriages should circulate in order to be recorded.[52]

The production of these actualities can be viewed as an extension of the "visibility of the elite" that Pimentel cultivated in his column.[53] Binóculo featured a section entitled Vimos ontem (Yesterday We Saw), which listed the ladies and gentlemen of local society who had passed in front of the *Gazeta de Notícias*'s newsroom, including descriptions of their fashionable attire, modeled on European fashions that were famously impractical in Rio's tropical climate.[54] In a visual counterpart to this practice, photographs of local notables, posing or caught unawares, proliferated in the pages of illustrated magazines. The magazine *Fon-Fon* accompanied these images with the caption "O Rio em flagrante: os nossos instantâneos" (Rio in flagrante: our snapshots). The caption emphasizes the camera's unique capacity to document ephemeral moments and chance encounters by capturing events in medias res. Yet *em flagrante* also literally refers to the idea of being caught red-handed, again evoking the hidden kinship between the mug shot and the bourgeois portrait.

While illustrated magazines and actualities focused almost exclusively on elite diversions and affluent areas of the city, the crônica, like police reportage, traversed class and spatial divisions within the city. In his many texts addressing urban crime and poverty, João do Rio positioned himself as the reader's guide through the urban underworld, linking his investigations to a sensational imaginary with an international scope. A crônica ironically titled "Sono calmo" (Peaceful Slumber) begins with an invitation by a police officer to accompany him on a tour of cut-rate lodging houses. João do Rio writes, "In French plays of ten years ago, there already appeared the journalist who brings fashionable people to macabre places; in Paris the reporters of [*Le Petit*] *Journal* move about accompanied by an authentic *apache*. I merely repeated a gesture that is almost a law. I accepted."[55] Witnessing the filthy, overcrowded conditions, João do Rio makes clear how the police's criminalization of the working classes—in this case, forcing them into lodging houses by arresting those who sleep outdoors—exacerbates their misery. Yet by framing his expedition into the lower depths of Rio de Janeiro through references to French journalism and theater, the journalist also associates these inhumane conditions with Paris's uniquely modern ills. Early in the crônica, he cites a companion's conviction that "misery is proportional to civilization."[56]

Adopting a self-consciously blasé tone, João do Rio posits the impossibility of separating urbanization and modernization from its social costs. In a text on child murderers from *Cinematógrafo*, he writes, "Given the current level of civilization, a civilization that carries with it the seeds of every kind of decadence, crime tends to increase, as the budgets of great powers increase, and with an ever greater percentage of impunity."[57] In terms reminiscent of the critique of modernity developed by the Marxist critics of the Frankfurt School, João do Rio suggests that the "progress" represented by industrialized nations' capitalist expansion, which helped drive Brazil's increasing integration into the global economy, is in fact an implacable evolution toward barbarism.[58] In his crônicas, João do Rio acts as both a critic of and an apologist for the structural violence of modernization in Brazil. His work participates in broader currents in the incipient mass culture of Rio de Janeiro and São Paulo, which framed violence as inseparable from progress and as a defining feature of public life.

Appearing alongside the crônicas of João do Rio and other premodernist writers in popular newspapers, the emergent genre of the police blotter was indebted to these journalists' role as guides through the cityscape and their ornate rhetorical style. Reporting on the minute details of cases (and often supplementing the information provided by the authorities with independent inquiries), the police blotter also narratively reconstructed events in a literary style. The critic Valéria Guimarães observes that in sensational reportage, "confusion between the employment of a rhetoric committed to information and a literary tone, long used in the crônica," creates "a dialogue with fiction that slips into pure invention."[59] Sensational reportage purveyed a heightened, dramatized "truth" that owed much to popular literature, narrating and fictionalizing events rather than simply enumerating facts. The initial report on the Crime of Carioca Street published in the *Gazeta de Notícias* sets the scene for the crime in a highly imaginative fashion.

> The last stragglers emerging from places of entertainment [*casas de espetáculos*] on the nearby square were passing by. In the new street lamps, the yellowed light of the Auer bulbs softly lit the street. . . .
>
> It was a horrifying crime at the classic hour of horrifying crimes, accentuated by the audacious circumstance of having taken place in the heart of the city. . . .
>
> The flash of diamonds in a *vitrine*, the profusion of jewels lined up on the shelves, with fat figures attesting to their value, from that brilliant, illuminated rectangle arose a hallucinatory fascination that tempted a group of bandits, whose number is not yet known, to crime.[60]

The *Gazeta de Notícias*'s account is framed by references to novel practices of urban diversion and consumption, which are in turn associated with new technologies of light (the illumination of the centrally located street and the glow of the jeweler's shop window, itself a close analog to the film screen).[61] This description links the display of commodities and the increasing circulation of city residents in spaces of commercialized leisure to the growing incidence of crime, suggesting that unexpected dangers accompanied emerging forms of urban mobility and visibility. Yet these novel elements of urban life are also situated within an established cultural repertoire: the journalist describes the murder as a "horrifying crime at the classic hour of horrifying crimes," situating real-life events within a horizon of expectations shaped by popular narratives that blended fact, speculation, and outright invention.

In her taxonomy of journalistic genres in nineteenth- and early twentieth-century Brazil, Marlyse Meyer traces a complex web of relationships between police reportage, the crônica, and the folhetim, arguing they have a common point of origin in the *variedades* (varieties, or miscellaneous news items) that began to appear in Brazilian newspapers in the first decades of the nineteenth century.[62] The characteristics of the variedades—brevity, topicality, and the ability to draw the reader's attention—would continue to unite the *faits divers* (a section comprising short, often sensational news stories), the crônica, and the folhetim in its many incarnations. Although many key figures of nineteenth-century Brazilian literature, including Machado de Assis and José de Alencar, had published novels in the space at the foot of the page reserved for the folhetim, the format was also closely associated with novels by French authors like Émile Gaboriau and Pierre Alexis Ponson du Terrail, published locally in translation. Unfolding their suspenseful plots through daily install-ments in the newspaper, the serial format proved ideal for framing daily life as a series of shocking and often violent happenings. In fact, the literary his-torian Brito Broca describes the folhetim as a precursor of the police blotter.

> The *romance-folhetim* was perhaps the first element of sensationalism to be introduced into the press. It preceded police reportage, offering readers a dish identical to the one that it would later provide them. So much so that when the newspaper took on a new profile, approaching the modern model, the attraction of novels at the foot of the page began to decline. Today, the reader no longer seeks the continuation of a novel, but rather follows the police blotter, curious to know how the investigation is pro-ceeding, if the criminal has been caught.[63]

The substitution of the police blotter for the folhetim is literalized in the satirical newsroom novel *Recordações do escrivão Isaías Caminha* (Recol-lections of the Scrivener Isaías Caminha). Published in 1907 by the Afro-Brazilian writer Lima Barreto, the autobiographical novel exemplifies his bit-ing critiques of republican Rio de Janeiro, which draw on his experiences of racial discrimination and exclusion from the elite networks of power, wealth, and favor that governed the political and intellectual life of the Republic.[64] Isaías, who serves as the novel's narrator, describes how a "grand crime"—the discovery of a wealthy couple's decapitated bodies in an isolated suburb—reshaped the content of a daily newspaper (a thinly veiled version of the *Correio da Manhã*): "On the day of the crime . . . the editor-in-chief did not spare his vastly amusing folhetim. He ordered that it not be published, as he wanted a page and a half about the crime; let it be invented, the most minute details given, the wildest conjectures. . . . Whatever it took, he wanted a page-and-a-half and twenty-five thousand copies for single-issue sales."[65] As de-scribed by Barreto, the sensational news item includes many elements directly cannibalized from the serial novel: one journalist settles on "a Rocambole-esque title of a popular novel" as the headline, while another who has been charged with the duty of writing the lead-in draws on his "reading of *folhet-ins policiais*" (serial novels with criminal themes).[66]

Mining an existing cultural repertoire of sensational tropes facilitated the expansion of the illustrated press at a moment when literacy remained lim-ited. Guimarães argues that the presence of clichés in the serialized novel and police reportage signals the incorporation of elements of oral culture in the popular press. She writes, "When the editor or *cronista* takes up the traditional narrative formula, he opens a channel of dialogue with the reader, even if this reader is little acquainted with the realm of writing. . . . [T]he *faits divers* and other sensationalist formulas reveal the duality of the operation of cultural exchange between producer and receiver."[67] At times consumed indirectly by illiterate consumers through collective reading aloud, serial novels were imagined to enjoy a cross-class appeal.[68] João do Rio noted criminals' fondness for violent, melodramatic narratives in his crônica "The Book-merchants and the Readings of the Streets," while the magazine *Fon-Fon* declared that well-to-do women "only read the society section, Binóculo, and all of them, without exception, simply die for the folhetins. The more violent and full of tragic peripeties the folhetim is, the more it absorbs them."[69]

Suggesting how the appeal of melodramatic narratives spanned social divides, in Barreto's novel sensational news both shapes and is shaped by the mass audience. The narrator comments, "Due to this strange, mysterious faculty of the masses, this case, banal a month earlier or later, on that day took on the proportions of an event, an uncommon happening."[70] Significantly, the crowd that gathers to gaze at the successive bulletins posted outside the newsroom is imagined as a heterogeneous one, composed of "all sorts of people: old, young, bourgeois, workers, ladies—people of all ages and conditions."[71] In contrast to the increasing spatial segregation of the city, the voyeuristic participation in spectacles of sensational violence—as imagined by Barreto—temporarily dissolves class boundaries in a mass moved by curiosity and horror. In practice, these groups may have been more homogeneous; in a photograph published in the *Correio da Manhã*, the crowd gathered around a posted bulletin offering updates on the case that inspired the film *Um crime sensacional* appears to be comprised exclusively of men.[72] Elsewhere in the novel, mass gatherings take on more actively threatening qualities in a fictionalized description of the Revolt of the Vaccine, a collective mobilization against processes of modernization imposed from above.

Although the use of conventions familiar from the folhetim in the police blotter may have helped newspapers attract some newly literate consumers, graphic visual content held the potential to further expand their audience. In 1907, a journalist identified only as "Zig-Zag" discussed the tendency of serial literature and the police blotter to crowd out the literary texts that had dominated the newspaper in past years. Zig-Zag notes that "homeopathic doses of strong sensations and dramatic sallies" provided by the serial novel were essential to a daily's hold on its public: "A newspaper can lack a telegraphic service, it can be weak in its information, it can lack grammar . . . but take away its folhetim, and you will see if this is not the same as taking away its life."[73] Despite the popularity of the serial novel, Zig-Zag notes that the front page was increasingly dedicated to examples of the illustrated crime report, which he refers to as the *calunga*, using a contemporary term for a cartoon or caricature. The journalist suggests that visual reportage offers a graphic message that is grasped instantaneously rather than read, noting consumers' preference for

> the synthesis of the calunga that informs and updates [readers] on events with the speed and penetration of a lightning bolt. One does not need time to read the calunga. It is enough to see it, enough to glance at it and make out, on the page blackened by the traces of the artist's pencil, a face, a prone body, with a name and some suggestive headlines underneath, for the reader to come to know of the latest murder committed against a man, and, also, ordinarily, against the art of drawing and engraving on cheap paper.

Declaring that "the masses are omnipotent and if they love and adore the calunga, what is not only practical for them, but also humane, is to give them their fill of it," Zig-Zag suggests that the police blotter, with its graphic, crudely rendered images, was legible to the large number of consumers who were wholly or partially illiterate.

Similarly, a caricature from the magazine *Fon-Fon* evokes the consumption of sensational news by illiterate audiences by means of the image and reading aloud. Alongside an image of the "nervous and impressionable reader whose facial expression accompanies all the details of 'Frightful Fires' or 'Barbarous Murders' described in pathetic terms in the *Jornal do Brasil*," the cartoon features a "reader who is . . . illiterate, who only *listens* to [others] reading . . . and grimaces when he cannot understand . . . the explanatory figures of the sensational news."[74] The cartoon highlights the role of sensational police reportage in general, and its visual elements in particular, in expanding the audience for the illustrated press.

Stoking a demand for information and graphic visual detail, the police blotter utilized a wide variety of photographic images and drawings with varied visual conventions, ranging from forensic images with a juridical purpose (mug shots and photographs of crime scenes and autopsies) to preexisting studio portraits of victims and images of other locations connected to the crime. For instance, the front page of a Sunday edition of the *Correio da Manhã* reporting on the Crime of Carioca Street featured portraits of the victims

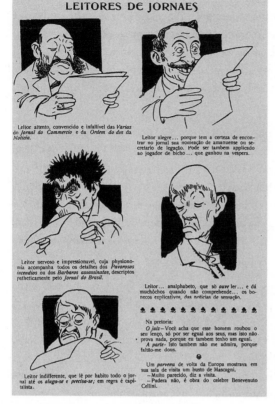

FIG 3.3 A gallery of "newspaper readers," including a "nervous and impressionable reader" (center left) and an "illiterate reader" (center right) of sensational news. *Fon-Fon*, 8 June 1907. Acervo da Fundação Biblioteca Nacional, Brasil.

and their uncle, images of the three suspects and an accomplice, and images of the boat used in the crime and the bridge where it was moored, arranged symmetrically around a large central image of onlookers posing outside the building where the crime took place. Photos on subsequent pages showed Carluccio's corpse, a crowd outside the morgue, and the victim's funeral procession.[75] As this example suggests, photographers occasionally captured unfolding—if not particularly gripping—actions. Yet in most cases, they were confined to documenting locations in the aftermath of events, locations that were charged with meaning through their connection with violent happenings. Signaling the challenges in capturing unpredictable events with the camera, illustrations in the police blotter manifest a range of weak and strong "reality effects," from drawn reconstructions of events that resisted capture by the camera—most often the moment of death itself—to lithographs (often, but not always, based on photographs) and halftone photographic reproduc-

FIG 3.4 News photographs and drawn reconstructions dramatize events surrounding the "Crime of the Trunk." *Gazeta de Notícias*, 13 September 1908. Acervo da Fundação Biblioteca Nacional, Brasil.

tions, usually reserved for newspapers' more elaborate weekend editions. For example, the first report on the Crime of Carioca Street in the *Gazeta de Notícias* was illustrated with engravings based on the photographs of the crime scene that were published as halftones in the paper's Saturday edition (see figure 3.1). Supplementing newspaper reporters' investigative narratives, these images traced itineraries through urban space that (as in the case of the crônica) crossed spatial and social divides.

Two years later, the *Gazeta de Notícias* published an illustration of the Crime of the Trunk that exemplifies the police blotter's mixed representational strategies and its moralistic framing of violent events. The page contains two photographs of the infamous trunk—closed, and opened to reveal the dismembered body of the victim—a portrait of "The Murderer Michel Traad," and an image of a crowd waiting on the docks for his arrival for police interrogation in Rio de Janeiro. However, the layout is dominated by two drawn reconstructions of pivotal moments of the case: the moment when "the wretched man suddenly throws himself at Elias Farhat, rapidly encircling his neck and strangling him with the cord," and his apprehension when he attempts to throw the trunk overboard.[76] Offering graphic but entirely speculative depictions of violent events, sensational police reportage quickly attributed them with moral meanings.

Documenting and dramatizing quotidian experience through a combination of visual documents and fictionalized images and narratives, the illustrated press insistently staged disparities between social classes while framing urban space and quotidian experience as thrilling, threatening, and distinctly modern. Newspapers and magazines developed a complex mode of address that made use of abundant illustration and the conventions of popular literature to dramatize quotidian experience, catering to educated as well as illiterate or barely literate consumers. In this context, photography and cinema proved pivotal in fostering the collective consumption of spectacles of violence that addressed a divided citizenry as a mass audience.

From Front Page to Stage to Screen: *Os estranguladores*

The close connections between journalism and early cinema in turn-of-the-century Brazil are evident not only in a shared affinity for sensational subjects, but also in the professional trajectories of local camera operators, which help account for the significance of topical subjects for early film production. Both Antônio Leal and rival camera operators Alberto and Paulino Botelho also worked as news photographers.[77] Reflecting on his career later in life, Leal linked his filmmaking activities to his work as a photojournalist, noting, "Perhaps because I worked for a time with the press, I developed a taste for opportunities; I was attracted by filmed reportage, the animated documentation of interesting things."[78] In 1916, Leal discussed the potential of films based on current events to attract local audiences in the face of financial and technical constraints on film production:

> The best stimulants to spectators' abundant attendance at the cinema are films of their own social life, live reportage. . . . We have already verified this here: films produced in 1908 and 1909 about more or less interesting

occurrences, some of them taking advantage of the popular excitement left in the wake of great crimes, achieved in Rio and the states a success never equaled by great works of art, made with expense and care, executed in the great European studios.[79]

Local productions could not hope to match the technical sophistication of imported films; yet they could take advantage of the "popular excitements" fostered by the press and popular theater, as well as the unique capacities of cinema to thrillingly reanimate topical happenings. Significantly, the most popular productions of early Brazilian cinema arose at the intersection of the press, popular theater, and cinema, as Maite Conde has shown in the case of the 1910 film *Paz e amor* (*Peace and Love*). Shot by Alberto Botelho for the impresario William Auler, the film was shown over a thousand times in Rio de Janeiro.[80] This satire of president Nilo Peçanha's administration, accompanied by vocal and musical performances from behind the screen, was modeled on the *teatro de revista* (revue theater) and drew on humorous writings in the illustrated magazine *Careta*.

Signaling their investment in dramatizing current events, cinematic and journalistic crime narratives were permeated with the terminology of the stage. In newspaper reports, the site of violent events was often referred to as the *cenário do crime* (setting or backdrop of the crime) or as the *teatro do crime* (theater of the crime). A columnist in the *Jornal do Brasil* linked the theatrical rhetoric of the police blotter to stage adaptations that capitalized on current events. Referring to the insertion of sensational scenes dealing with the crime into an existing musical revue, the journalist writes, "The artists of the Palace Theater had their own idea about the horrifying case of Carioca Street. If from the true theater of events things passed into the theater of exploitation and the ridiculous, they, too, resolved to take advantage of the situation."[81] Like advertisements for theatrical productions, publicity for crime-themed films included lists of the tableaux or single-shot scenes (*quadros*) of which they were composed. Filmic reconstructions of real-life cases capitalized on the unique possibilities of the moving image to restage topical events, participating in a broader tendency to dramatize daily life.

As suggested by the sardonic comments in the *Jornal do Brasil*, the Crime of Carioca Street was heavily exploited on local stages almost from the very first reports well into the following year. It even became the subject of an unusual form of printed theater: the playwright Artur Azevedo comically portrayed the collective obsession with the case in short vignettes, part of a long-running series of topical dialogues published in the newspaper *O Século*, entitled Teatro a vapor (Steam-powered Theater). In the first of the sketches related to the Crime of Carioca Street, entitled "Um desesperado" (A Desperate Man), a genteel male caller named Dr. Chiquinho pays a visit to a well-off lady and her four daughters. On entering, he complains,

> At home, over lunch, in the office, in court, on the Rua do Ouvidor [a downtown commercial street], on the Avenida [Central], at my tailor's, at my barber's . . . everywhere, in short, no one talks of anything but the crime of Carioca Street! . . . And then I remembered your ladyships. There, I said to myself, I will certainly hear nothing of Carletto and Rocca. . . . [T]hese ladies only enjoy speaking of fashion, balls, the theater, excursions, etc. There I will be free of this cursed subject![82]

In Dr. Chiquinho's account, discussions of the case permeate social interactions across urban spaces. His attempt to avoid the rumors by calling on these young women assumes a gendered separation between the public and domestic spheres, which was in fact being increasingly eroded in turn-of-the-century Rio de Janeiro as new means of transportation, especially the electric trolley, facilitated women's movements outside the home.[83] Oblivious to their guest's frustration, the young ladies do nothing but discuss graphic details of the case until he is once again driven out into the street. Suggesting the newspaper's role as a proxy for mobility in public space, one of them even sends a passing boy to determine whether a second edition has been printed with new information about the case.

Whereas "Um desesperado" suggests the newspaper's capacity to bring the violent events that characterized public life into the private sphere, a second dialogue entitled "Depois do espectáculo" (After the Theater) highlights how popular entertainments capitalized on—and distorted—topical events. In this dialogue between two working-class men—their class is suggested by their nonstandard grammar and pronunciation—Azevedo mocks a less-than-faithful adaptation of the Crime of Carioca Street by a local theatrical company. Returning from a performance, one of the men complains: "They changed everything . . . and it ended up a mess not even the devil could understand!"[84] The disgruntled spectator ultimately concludes that the alterations are due to the producers' unwillingness to "stir up the people."[85] Azevedo's vignette hints at practical and political reasons for fictionalizing real-life events at a moment when working-class mobilizations posed a threat to public order as defined and enforced by elites. At the same time, the dialogues highlight the imagined appeal of sensationalistic narratives across social classes: proper young ladies thirst for gruesome details, while a working-class man attends and critiques a theatrical performance, albeit one catering to popular tastes.

Details of Azevedo's "Depois do espetáculo" suggest that it referred to an actual play entitled "Os estranguladores," which like competing theatrical performances and later films, claimed to faithfully reconstruct current events while framing them in highly melodramatic terms. A commentator noted that the play, staged by the Dias Braga Company less than three weeks after the case broke, capitalized on the lingering "impression of the horrendous crime," whose sensational impact was compounded by its melodramatic structure: "Go see it because its shocking tableaux produce strong emotions, of revolt and then relief when we see virtue rewarded and infamy punished."[86] Two other theatrical adaptations of the Crime of Carioca Street were announced in November 1906, while a third production based on the case was presented at the Teatro São José in January 1907.[87]

Concurrently with these stage productions, a local theater exhibited an actuality film showing the three suspects in the crime, *Rocca—Carletto—Pigato na Casa de Detenção (Rocca, Carletto, Pigato in the House of Detention)*, filmed by an unidentified camera operator in November 1906. A report in the *Gazeta de Notícias* evokes journalists' frenzy to capture the unfolding events of the case following a promise by Rocca to

> make important declarations and clear up obscure and mysterious points of this tenebrous crime. . . . This was the sensational news, promised and awaited, with the possibility of a dash of scandal. . . . Thus, from early in the morning, all who managed to gain entry into the house of detention were there. Journalists, the authorities, photographers, even a camera operator [*cinegrafista*] with his apparatus, there they were, thrilling with the same curiosity, the same eager expectation.[88]

In this vivid description, the camera operator takes a position among the other purveyors of visual and verbal information jockeying for access to Rocca's declarations, suggesting the close affinities between the filmed actuality, news photography, and written reportage. According to advertisements, the film was exhibited for a week in the Teatro Maison Moderne, a variety theater owned by the Italian impresario Paschoal Segreto.[89] This run suggests its considerable appeal for audiences at a moment prior to the emergence of dedicated, permanent movie theaters, when individual films were rarely advertised by title.

By contrast with the actuality's highly topical nature, Leal's reconstruction, *Os estranguladores*, mined the recent past for subjects that would captivate local audiences. After going into business with the Italian immigrant Giuseppe Labanca, Leal aimed to entice spectators to his venue, the Cinema Palace, with "national films," including dramas, comedies, and actualities. Produced nearly two years after the commission of the crime, *Os estranguladores* was advertised as "a magnificent reconstitution of the exciting drama for which Rio de Janeiro served as theater."[90] Participating in the theatricalization of real-life crime, the film's source text is believed by some scholars to be a play penned by the local writers Figueiredo Pimentel (of the Binóculo column) and Rafael Pinheiro.[91]

Beyond his possible creative contribution to *Os estranguladores*, Pimentel publicized it in his column, describing it as "a film that will attract the attention of all the people [*todo o povo*] of the capital. . . . It is nothing more and nothing less than the reproduction of the exciting tragedy of the Deathly Gang. All the peripeties of the horrible crime of Rocca, Carletto & Co. are there reproduced."[92] Although the Binóculo column was addressed primarily to elites, the film's potential audience is described as encompassing the entire population of the capital, and is implied to be the working classes (*povo*). The journalist suggests that *Os estranguladores*'s drawing power is grounded both in moral outrage and morbid appeal, as is implied by the phrase "exciting tragedy." Positioned within a panorama of popular entertainments that dramatized violent events, the film is attributed with a unique ability to "reproduce" these happenings by means of the camera.

The available information on *Os estranguladores*'s cost, profits, and exhibition suggests a fairly modest investment that reaped immense monetary and popular success over an extensive box-office run. According to an estimate given by Leal in 1915, *Os estranguladores* raked in fourteen times the original budget in his movie theater alone; three other copies were also rented out to exhibitors in other states, who gave him a 50 percent share of the profits.[93] The first advertisements for the film appeared in early July 1908; the day after its premiere, the suspension of the exhibition by the police "until further notice" was announced.[94] The film was exhibited at Leal and Labanca's Cinema Palace for two weeks in early August (after which it was "temporarily withdrawn for the improvement of various tableaux") and another two weeks in September, with a brief reprise later in the year.[95] On 12 September, an advertisement described *Os estranguladores* as "the film that has achieved the greatest success both in Rio and in the [s]tates.[96] Suggesting the extent of

Os estranguladores's travels, the film was still being shown in 1910 in Fortaleza, capital of the state of Ceará in northeastern Brazil.[97]

Like sensational news reportage, *Os estranguladores* combined the reconstruction of real-life events and the documentation of actual locations. The list of tableaux published in advertisements for the film notes the reenactment of key events ("the first strangling," "arrest of the second criminal").[98] At the same time, it highlights the precise locations where the events of the case unfolded, including the Avenida Central, where one of the victims, Carluccio, had arranged a rendezvous with the robbers; the Prainha pier, where he embarked on his fatal voyage; and the suburb of Jacarepaguá, to the west of the city, where Carletto, the last of the suspects to be captured, was detained by police.[99] Like the investigation and its press coverage, the film linked sites in the heart of the capital's commercial districts, where the importation and consumption of goods was concentrated, with its margins, including distant suburbs connected to the city center by train lines. Containing violent happenings through the threat of juridical punishment, the film's final tableau, entitled "In prison," likely provided a sense of narrative closure. Capitalizing on a case that had been previously transformed into a public spectacle in the local press and onstage, *Os estranguladores* restaged violent events for the camera and stressed location shooting, echoing practices of policing and investigative reporting that promised to map a deeply divided and sometimes threatening urban space. By evoking "popular excitement" stoked by journalism and theater, *Os estranguladores* helped forge a mass audience for locally produced films.

The Crime of the Trunk: Competing Adaptations
and Narrative Experiments

In September 1908, during the wildly successful run of *Os estranguladores*, news of another sensational crime swept São Paulo, where the Syrian businessman Elias Farhat was murdered by his secretary, Michel Traad, as well as Rio de Janeiro, where Traad was taken for questioning after he was caught trying to jettison the trunk containing Farhat's corpse from the deck of the steamship *Cordillière*. The case inspired a series of films, plays, and novels that sought to capitalize on the murder, supposedly motivated by Traad's attraction to Farhat's wife, Carolina. It also gave rise to an aggressive competition to capture and stage visual material related to the case: the news photographer and filmmaker Paulino Botelho boasted that he had managed in a surprise ambush to photograph the coach and driver that had transported the infamous trunk, where Leal had failed to gain the driver's cooperation through an offer of money.[100] Within a week of the first reports of the crime on 5 September, Leal's Cinema Palace began to advertise a filmed reconstruction of the events entitled *A mala sinistra* (*The Sinister Trunk*).[101] Yet by the time Leal's version was first exhibited at the Cinema Palace in mid-October of 1908, its novelty value had been lessened by a rival adaptation by Júlio Ferrez (also entitled *A mala sinistra*) that premiered eleven days earlier.[102] In São Paulo, an actuality documenting legal proceedings related to the case was also screened, and the Spanish impresario Francisco Serrador produced a reconstruction of the crime, his first venture into narrative filmmaking.[103] The decreasing lag between the events depicted and their adaptation to the screen strengthened perceived affinities between filmed reconstructions and journalistic coverage, and the reception of the multiple film adaptations of the Crime of the Trunk register their competing claims to realism and spectacle.

While the most elaborate filmed reconstructions of the case were produced in Rio de Janeiro, writers, theatrical companies, and camera operators in São Paulo quickly capitalized on the gruesome events that had taken place in their city.[104] Although popular São Paulo dailies like the *Correio Paulistano* and the *Estado de São Paulo* did not illustrate their crime reports at this time, photographic images relating to the crime circulated in magazines like *A Ronda*. The *Estado de São Paulo* described a proliferation of literary texts based on the crime, noting, "The publications on the shocking crime of Boa Vista Street grow and multiply.... An anonymous prose writer has written the history of the victim and now three more novels are being announced, all concording in the reconstitution of the horrifying scene of the strangulation and in decorating themselves with the most fantastic settings."[105] The journalist singled out one work as literally sensational, since it recounted the commission of the murder "in such brilliant and striking tints that we came to feel a *frison* [*sic*] of terror run down the spine." The case was also adapted to the stage, but the production passed municipal censorship in São Paulo only on 2 December.[106]

By contrast, just five days after the announcement of a judgment in favor of the victim's wife, who was suspected of helping him to plan the crime, the Edison Cinema announced, "The actuality film THE CRIME OF THE TRUNK. Habeas-corpus of the innocent widow, filmed from nature [*tirada do natural*]."[107] While the actuality appears to have been an ephemeral novelty (it was exhibited for only three days), the magazine *A Ronda* claimed that its appeal to "public curiosity" led it to "break the record for cinematography in S. Paulo."[108] Less successful was the filmed reconstruction of the case produced by Francisco Serrador, whose negative reception, as Melo Souza points out, signals the limits of sensationalistic content as an audience draw at a moment when conventions of spatial and temporal continuity were being consolidated in imported cinema.[109] Shot by Alberto Botelho, *O crime da mala* was a first venture into fiction for Serrador, who had recently invested in the construction of a film studio after producing a small number of actualities.[110] Melo Souza speculates that Serrador's film was prohibited by the police not because of concerns about its content—both film adaptations of the case made in Rio de Janeiro were shown in São Paulo as well—but rather because of the negative reaction to a private screening for journalists and authorities.[111] On the basis of a review published in the magazine *Cri-Cri*, Melo Souza argues that the film failed both to establish the relations of narrative and spatial continuity that were becoming standard in imported films and to effectively simulate the locations and persons involved in the crime. The review noted unconvincing sets, gaps in the narrative, and a lack of resemblance between the actors used in the film and their real-life counterparts.[112] (Apparently, Serrador cast members of his own staff in the film, rather than casting a wider net.)[113] Melo Souza suggests that the "lack of verisimilitude of the actors (the police official, the widow, the scribe), which could have passed merely as a (tolerable) sign of an incipient film production, is surpassed by the narrative 'holes' and 'jumps,' whose 'filling-in' by the spectators forced them into an exercise of comparison between reality and fiction, with a serious loss on Serrador's part."[114] Failing to create a self-contained diegesis that would reduce the need for references to current events to ensure audience comprehension, Serrador's film failed to offer either a convincing document or a viable fiction.

By contrast with Serrador's attempt, the cinematic reconstructions of the crime shot by Leal and Ferrez in Rio placed a premium on location shooting, while also incorporating elements associated with fiction films, most notably tinted sequences and apotheoses. The *Gazeta de Notícias* claimed that Ferrez's version of *A mala sinistra* "demanded great sacrifice on the part of the company, which had to send camera operators to São Paulo and Santos to photograph all the minutiae of the reconstitution of the nefarious crime."[115] However, Melo Souza concludes that "the number of tableaux, the fact it was programmed with five other films, and the small number of days of exhibition indicate a modest production with little appeal."[116] Yet the Ferrez version of *A mala sinistra* still posed a potential threat to the novelty, and thus the box-office attraction, of Leal's version. A series of advertisements aggressively asserted the latter's superior virtues, including the sense of authenticity produced by shooting on location and the appeal offered by the use of color.

> Notice: This film has nothing in common with that exhibited in other movie theaters. A unique composition of the Photo-cinematografia Brasileira and the Cinema Palace: first exhibition of this grand tragedy of furor and ruthlessness, composed of twenty-some tableaux, some colored and others natural, taken in the city of S. Paulo and Santos, on board, and in Rio. Performed entirely by national artists, whose impeccable work is just and exuberant proof of how much we have advanced in cinematic art.[117]

Emphasizing its authentic settings, the advertisement also highlights acting technique, suggesting a tension between the documentation of actual crime scenes and the fictionalization of events through reenactment. The distinction made between "colored" and "natural" scenes also suggests an ambiguity in the film's orientation toward current events: the term *natural* was used to indicate nonfiction images, as in the case of the actuality film *O crime da mala*. Yet as Joshua Yumibe argues, color can create both "a verisimilar effect and a dazzling, spectacular quality," a tension that was particularly evident in the " 'spectacular realities' of fin-de-siècle representation."[118]

Although advertisements for Leal's *A mala sinistra* suggested a conjunction of visual documentation with spectacularization, coverage of the film in local newspapers emphasized its close affinities to the popular press. The *Correio da Manhã* observed that

> profound excitement still persists in carioca and paulista [São Paulo residents'] minds regarding the sorrowful scene occasioned by the infamous Traad, since it has been reported in detail by all the papers, this crime that captured the attention of the public for a long period due to the circumstances surrounding it. Today, if you would like to see in person [ao vivo, literally "live"] everything that happened from the murder to the latest declarations of the notorious bandit, go to the Cinema Palace.[119]

According to this description, the film is able to literally revive the events of the crime, whose impact on residents of the two cities is attributed to sensational newspaper coverage. The *Jornal do Brasil* directly compared the work of the camera operator to that of the journalist, noting that, "in the production of this film, the cinematic press [imprensa do Cinema] labored to accomplish the best reconstruction of this tragedy."[120] Binóculo columnist Figueiredo Pimentel described *A mala sinistra* as an "exact reproduction of the crime.... [I]t could be said that it is a true film, *d'apres-nature*."[121] After the day of its premiere, Pimentel noted its sweeping success, commenting that "The Rua do Ouvidor was almost impassable yesterday in the area of the Largo de São Francisco. This was because of people who wanted to enter the Cinema Palace. There, for the first time, the film *A mala sinistra* was being exhibited, a surprising film that reanimates [*revive*], minute by minute, the celebrated crime."[122] Like the *Correio da Manhã* reporter, Pimentel attributes filmed reconstructions of real-life crimes with the ability to reanimate topical events, suggesting how cinema functioned to restage and thus commodify an eventful present.

Although newspapers were quick to align Leal's film with their own efforts at information gathering, *A mala sinistra* also interpreted topical happenings through reference to moral polarities. According to advertisements, the film concluded with "a lovely apotheosis, also colored: VIRTUE CRUSHES CALUMNY."[123] (The title probably referred to the eventual vindication of Farhat's wife, Carolina.) The convention of the climactic apotheosis would have been familiar to local audiences from the endings of *féeries* (fantasy films that drew on stage melodrama and operetta, produced principally by the French Méliès and Pathé companies) and religious passion plays. The fact that this sequence was advertised as a colored apotheosis also suggests an attempt by Leal to emulate a special attraction of the Pathé films distributed by his competitors, the Ferrez family.

The inclusion of the apotheosis in Leal's version of *A mala sinistra* is also linked to exhibition practices that repackaged imported films for local audiences, circumscribing their possible meanings in the process. In March 1908, a Gaumont actuality depicting the funerals of King Carlos I of Portugal and his heir (who had been assassinated by antimonarchists) was exhibited at the Cinema Palace, with an apotheosis made in-house that glorified "THE PORTUGUESE FATHERLAND—THE BRAZILIAN FATHERLAND."[124] Affirming connections between Portugal and its former colony, the apotheosis presumably would have evoked patriotic sentiments in response to a violent disruption of state power. While Nöel Burch describes apotheoses as "open endings" that exemplify the lack of a clear dénouement characteristic of pre-classical cinema, I speculate that in *A mala sinistra*, the apotheosis would have provided a form of ideological closure that mitigated the disruptive impact of public violence.[125] Like the endings of other filmed reconstructions—*Os estranguladores*'s ending scene "In prison," the concluding tableau "Remorse" in

Ferrez's version of *A mala sinistra*—the apotheosis scene in Leal's film likely encouraged audiences to interpret current events in terms of unequivocal moral meanings.

The varied strategies adopted in the three reconstructions of the Crime of the Trunk indicate that maintaining novelty in the face of competitors entailed a delicate negotiation between fictional strategies and perceived visual authenticity, which gave expression to locally specific understandings of cinema's relationship to topical events. As Leal continued to offer "national" films as a means of differentiating his venue's offerings, efforts to appeal to local audiences encouraged a shift toward fiction as Leal continued to exploit sensational subjects through early 1909.

Violence and Female Honor:
Noivado de sangue and *Um drama na Tijuca*

Playing a prominent role in ongoing attempts to attract local spectators, Leal produced his final two crime-themed films shortly after opening a new studio on the Rua dos Invalidos in central Rio, where, according to advertisements, he was producing new films on a weekly basis.[126] The filmed reconstruction *Noivado de sangue* and the fictional *Um drama na Tijuca* addressed questions of female morality in the light of broader debates about marriage and sexuality in a modernizing Brazil. While less ambitious than Leal's earlier filmed reconstructions in terms of their length, these films signal the continuing importance of sensational subjects and scenic landscape views, which began to be advertised as an attraction for audiences in their own right.

Based on a murder referred to as the "Crime of the Crystal Arcade"— it took place in a hotel adjacent to a modern glass-and-steel shopping gallery—*Noivado de sangue* was exhibited only eight days after the news of the case broke in February 1909, allowing the company to advertise it as the "recent tragedy of love and blood that unfolded in São Paulo last week."[127] Surprisingly, given this rapid turnaround, Leal again claimed that he filmed on location.[128] Yet even as *Noivado de sangue* capitalized on onsite reporting and a sense of topicality, it was the first of Leal's filmed reconstructions whose advertisements mentioned the names of onscreen performers (who were active in popular theater) and the fact that it had been "coordinated and rehearsed by the actor Antonio Serra."[129] This division of labor between camera operator and a role resembling a director was novel within Leal's production model, suggesting a shift toward fiction that was extended in *Um drama na Tijuca*.

Where *Os estranguladores* and the adaptations of the Crime of the Trunk had focused on the Italian and Syrian communities, highlighting public concerns regarding migratory flows, *Noivado de sangue* and *Um drama na Tijuca* depicted women's transgressions of dominant sexual mores, with fatal consequences. The latter focused on an unfaithful woman who is spurned by both her suitors and commits suicide by poisoning. For its part, *Noivado de sangue* capitalized on a striking gender reversal of the typical "crime of passion," most often an act of violence committed against a woman by her husband or lover. While reformers condemned men's violence against women as a troubling sign of the "retrocession of civilization" in a modernizing Brazil, the fact that the perpetrator was a woman lent the Crime of the Crystal Arcade a thrilling novelty.[130]

The case also crystallized ongoing debates about the crime of deflowering (*defloramento*), legally punishable in the case of seduction or false promises of marriage, which brought into focus questions of female honor and agency at a moment when patriarchal power structures were being contested—but also reaffirmed—within discourses of national modernization.[131] The killer, Albertina Barbosa, a young schoolteacher, confessed to having shot her former lover, Arthur Malheiros de Oliveira, a law student who had lived as a tenant in the home she shared with her mother. An affair between Albertina and Arthur produced a child, but he refused to marry her; their son was placed in an orphanage, where he later died. Shortly after Barbosa's marriage to another teacher, Elízio Bonilha, she confessed her previous relationship, and they jointly planned to kill de Oliveira. Despite the four years that had passed since the "seduction," Barbosa was initially acquitted of the murder in June 1909 on the grounds it constituted a legitimate defense of her honor, although she would undergo two more trials before being exonerated in April 1910.[132]

By contrast with the publicity for *Os estranguladores* and *A mala sinistra*, which emphasized the specific events and sites displayed in the films, advertisements for *Noivado de sangue* "dispense with a lengthy description since the subject of this film is too well known to the public."[133] The film's journalistic intertext likely ensured its initial success; the *Gazeta de Notícias* reported, "A great number of persons could be observed yesterday in the Rua do Ouvidor, in their efforts to see the reconstruction of the recent bloody tragedy that took place in São Paulo . . . now on view at the Cinema Palace

A VINGANÇA DA PROFESSORA

FIG 3.5 "The Teacher's Revenge: Reconstruction of the Crime of the Crystal Arcade, in São Paulo, According to the Latest Police Reports." *Gazeta de Notícias*, 7 March 1909. Acervo da Fundação Biblioteca Nacional, Brasil.

in a splendid film of 500 meters which has nothing to fear from a comparison with those of the best foreign producers."[134] The newspaper attributed the venue's ongoing success to its program of film production, noting that "new national films are now being made with all the trimmings in the new studios of the Cinema Palace." Like Leal's *A mala sinistra*, *Noivado de sangue* was shown for just under two weeks in the Cinema Palace, screening for only a day in São Paulo, where the subject matter may have been considered too inflammatory.[135]

Lacking another sensational case to adapt, Leal turned to a fictional narrative of female sexual transgression set in a traditional upper-class neighborhood, whose picturesque scenery motivated the inclusion of landscape views. *Um drama na Tijuca* was advertised as a "real and characteristic scene of the intimate life of Rio's finest society, with tableaux of astonishing artistic effect, some taken on the natural sites of that fantastic mountain, full of beauty and a witness to innumerable amorous adventures."[136] Seeking its source in the police blotter, Conde has speculated that *Um drama na Tijuca* was based on the sensational 1906 case of a young student who murdered his rival for the affections of an attractive widow, wounding her as well.[137] However, these events do not closely correspond to the plot of *Um drama na Tijuca* as described in the *Jornal do Brasil*: after becoming "engaged or more than engaged" to a lover who departs on a trip, the protagonist Dolores takes up with another man. When her first suitor returns and learns of the betrayal, the two romantic rivals "come to an understanding like men. The other learns of the relations that the faithless woman had before him." Rejected by both her suitors, Dolores poisons herself.[138] Like *Noivado de sangue*, the film was advertised as "rehearsed by Antonio Serra," and advertisements refer to the actor João Barbosa as the author of its plot.[139] In the apparent absence of a real-life referent, advertisements stress melodramatic plot events staged in picturesque settings.

Tableaux descriptions for *Um drama na Tijuca* pair key plot events with the display of scenic views, suggesting that displays of local landscapes offered an appeal beyond the fascination attached to the scene of the crime. A tableau entitled "Lovers' walk, how happy they are!" incorporated "Views taken in the caverns and other sites in Tijuca."[140] Even the confrontation between the two romantic rivals takes place in a scenic location: the advertisement specifies it is a "View taken on the path to the Cascatinha waterfall."[141] Extending the interest of earlier reconstructions of real-life crimes in mapping and displaying urban space, *Um drama na Tijuca* indicates a shift in production practices from reenactments of topical events to the rehearsal and direction of theatrical actors in a scripted narrative. This strategy, however, may not have held the same attraction; *Um drama na Tijuca* was initially screened for a single week, although it was reprised the following month.[142]

Um drama na Tijuca brought the cycle of sensational narrative films produced in late 1908 to 1909 to a close. A falling-out between Leal and his business partner led to the dissolution of the Photo-cinematografia Brasileira, marking the end of one of the most successful examples of the producer-exhibitor model that defined the "bela época" of filmmaking in Rio de Janeiro and São Paulo.[143] The popularity of "talking and singing films" based on revues and operettas would continue to attract huge audiences throughout 1909 and 1910. Yet the consolidation of integrated circuits for the importation, distribution, and exhibition of foreign films through Serrador's Companhia Cinematográfica Brasileira would sharply limit exhibition opportunities for locally made films. In the teens, a pair of productions by the camera operators Alberto and Paulino Botelho aimed to revive the popularity of filmed reconstructions of real-life crimes, continuing to capitalize on public spectacles of violence while developing more complex narrative forms.

Coda: True-Crime Film after the "Bela Época"

Remaining active in the production of newsreels, Alberto and Paulino Botelho continued to produce and market films for local audiences in the 1910s.[144] In 1912 and 1913, the Botelho brothers built on the exchanges between cinema, the illustrated press, and popular theater in two dramatic reconstitutions. Their first effort, *O caso dos caixotes*, depicted a robbery of funds belonging to the national treasury on board the steamboat *Saturno*, accomplished by swapping convincing replicas for the coffers of money. The following year, the brothers produced *Um crime sensacional*, a filmed reenactment of the murder of the businessman Adolfo Freire by his gardener Secundino Augusto Henriques, with Freire's lover also wounded in the struggle. Deviating from the facts of the case as reported in local newspapers, the Botelho brothers drew on sensational imaginaries of technological disaster. Their reconstruction of the crime inserted a railway accident at the film's climax, which evoked a series of recent crashes on the Estrada de Ferro Central (Central Railway) that had sparked outcry in local newspapers.

Signaling the increasing complexity of narrative film language—the films were advertised as double the length of Leal's *Os estranguladores* and contained hundreds of tableaux (shots)—*O caso dos caixotes* and *Um crime sensacional* were completed under the instructions of actors, with Paulino operating the camera for both films.[145] Framed as a distinctly national accomplishment, *O caso dos caixotes*'s publicity also indicates a foreign antecedent: an advertisement compared it to the "reconstruction of the *celebrated Bonnot case*," a reference to one in a series of French films that capitalized on a panic provoked by the anarchist Bonnot gang, motorized bandits who terrorized Paris by committing robberies and kidnappings).[146] Adding another element of sensationalism, transportation technologies motivated the inclusion of daring stunts, including a scene in which one of the thieves escaped by sliding down the side of the steamship on a rope.[147]

As with earlier films depicting real-life crimes, the "Case of the Strongboxes" built on news coverage and appeared alongside a theatrical production based on the same events. Committed in June 1912, the theft of the payroll payments had captured public attention due to its audacity and ingenuity. The case was not solved until August of that year, when the robbery turned deadly: one of the thieves, João dos Santos Barata Ribeiro, was spotted burying his share of the money and murdered the witness, giving rise to a police investigation that uncovered the theft.[148] However, evidence quickly surfaced that the authorities had misappropriated a portion of the recovered money. Police corruption became the principal target of the satirical revue "1.400 Contos," whose title referenced the amount of money stolen in the original heist. Despite protests by Barata Ribeiro, the revue was performed over a hundred times in a mixed-use venue, the Cinema Teatro Rio Branco.[149]

In addition to restaging events as reported by the press, *O caso dos caixotes* incorporated reportage directly into its structure, signaling how ongoing exchanges between cinema and journalism facilitated experiments with narrative form. One advertisement stated, "The portion that unfolds in São Paulo is narrated by bulletins from the newspaper, which the present film illustrates, showing to the public the locations where the events occurred in their everyday existence [*vida normal*]."[150] Providing an armature for the events shown onscreen, journalistic discourse helped bridge the temporal discontinuity between the events of the crime and the same locations captured at a later date, an effect apparently accomplished in other scenes through reenactment. Alluding to the potential for confusion between the crime and its reconstruction, a reviewer observes, "The most interesting thing is that the actors . . . were walking about in Santos, in S. Paulo, and here in false beards, with strongboxes and suitcases, here and there, without the police suspecting anything, or even taking an interest in whether it was a film or something more serious." Noting the film's "minute reconstruction of the theft," the journalist also highlights "the landscapes captured there, which are most beautiful."[151] An advertisement for the film also singles out "majestic panoramas" of the mountains near Santos.[152] These press discourses suggest that two distinct but potentially overlapping notions of location—as sites given significance by current events and as picturesque landscape views—were at work in *O caso dos caixotes*. Landscapes might function as "authentic" settings for reenactments or as audience attractions in their own right, prefiguring the strategies of sensational Brazilian fiction films of the late teens and twenties, whose appeal was closely tied to location shooting.

Recalling the moralistic framing of earlier filmed reconstructions, *O caso dos caixotes* ended with a jailhouse fantasy sequence that dramatized the criminal's remorse. An advertisement describes the film as "ending with a segment of fantasy in which João Carocho [the fictionalized version of Barata Ribeiro], in prison, recalls the principal moments of his crime and sees, in a cruel dream, the astute Picolo [his accomplice, whose real name was Piccoli Vicenza], enjoying the results of his audacity in the company of beautiful women—TERRIBLE DREAM!! TERRIBLE AWAKENING!!"[153] Although this flashback/fantasy sequence would have showed the spoils of crime as well as its punishment, it recalls the morally charged endings of earlier films based on real-life crimes, whose narrative closure seems to have relied on melodramatic logic.

Suggesting profound shifts in the local exhibition market, *O caso dos caixotes* was considered a success after being exhibited in two theaters owned by the Companhia Cinematográfica Brasileira for only three and five days, respectively, before being screened briefly at two other venues later in the month.[154] The film was also shown in São Paulo in three different theaters for a total of five nights, and was later reprised, in 1914 and 1918.[155] Despite its comparative brevity, the run of *O caso dos caixotes* was seemingly profitable enough to prompt the Botelho brothers to produce another example of what they referred to as an "actuality film," *Um crime sensacional.*[156] The film was based on a case referred to as the "Crime of Paula Matos" (after the location where it occurred), which generated such a furor in the popular press that it was portrayed as distracting the populace from pressing public matters. A satirical cartoon portrays a figure labeled "the people" engrossed in a newspaper report on the crime, while a lit fuse attached to the head of president Hermes da Fonseca burns, suggesting that sensational news deflected attention from an imminent political crisis.[157] The crime was widely covered in the newspaper *A Noite*, founded in 1911 and often considered the city's most sensationalistic.

Signaling how both film and theater continued to forge a cross-class culture of popular sensationalism, the play *O crime do jardineiro* (The Gardener's Crime) premiered the day after the release of the Botelho brother's *Um crime sensacional*, perhaps in an attempt to capitalize on its publicity campaign. The play was performed in one of Rio's prestigious legitimate theaters, a decision that seemed incongruous for one critic, who noted that "in the Lírico, in spite of 'O crime do jardineiro' having been announced at popular prices, and as presented by a popular company, ladies appeared in '*toilette*' and gentlemen in '*smoking*.'"[158] Yet the apparent mismatch between the play's subject and its audience suggests the persistent cross-class appeal of popular sensationalism. Highlighting *O crime do jardineiro*'s topical origins and viscerally thrilling qualities, *A Noite* described it as a "drama of profound actuality" that was "intense, vibrant and exciting."[159]

Capitalizing on this sense of topicality, *Um crime sensacional* again included reenactments of violent events in the actual locations where they unfolded. Stills from the film's production later appeared in print, bringing reciprocal exchanges between cinema and the press to new heights. In an article on the film (likely a promotional text provided by the filmmakers), *A Noite* praised its "true *clou*: the reconstitution of the crime in the actual location— in the house, on the roof, in the mango tree, in the bedroom, in the bathroom, it was here the crime occurred, the environment is the same, the situation identical."[160] This step-by-step recreation of the violent events parallels the minute detail on the crime provided in *A Noite*, which published an image of the house's floor plan marked with the exact trajectories of the murderer and victim, even including an image of a bloody footprint left by Freire's lover Maria Antonia.[161] On the Sunday following the crime, the *Gazeta de Notícias* published an extensive sequence of drawings that recreated the struggle between Freire and his killer, imaginatively reconstructing events to create a protocinematic visual narrative of the crime.[162] Later that month, the newspaper further blurred the line between reportage and cinematic reconstruction by illustrating an article on the case with an image drawn from *Um crime sensacional*. While credited to the Botelhos' Brazil-Film production company, the still nevertheless incorporates the filmed reconstruction into the newspaper's informational discourse.[163]

Yet as in the case of previous filmed reconstructions of real-life cases, the production practices adopted in the face of a rapid turnaround time—the film premiered a month and a half after the first reports of the case—were often at odds with a faithful rendering of the real-life events.[164] A review of the film observes, "The landscapes are varied and very well chosen. There are two good interiors, quite acceptable. Painted cloth never gives a good impression, and Brasil Film [*sic*] should avoid it. It is so easy to put together folding screens, covered in painted paper. The interiors betray the precipitousness with which the film was made."[165] Mixing location shooting with painted sets, the Botelhos' mode of production apparently created uneven effects of verisimilitude, which corresponded to liberties taken with the actual events of the crime.

Um crime sensacional deviated in a number of ways from a factual reconstruction of the case, not only incorporating the railway accident, but also introducing a fictional character without a clear counterpart in the real-life

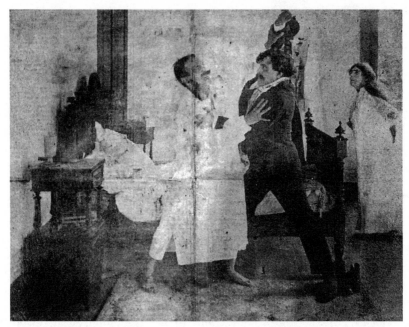

FIG 3.6 The Botelho brothers' filmed reconstruction of the "Crime of Paula Matos" adds visual drama to the informational discourse of the newspaper. *Gazeta de Notícias*, 26 July 1913. Acervo da Fundação Biblioteca Nacional, Brasil.

cast of characters: "Rosa, the demon woman," a role played by the actress Judith Saldanha, who also appeared in "O crime do jardineiro" as the gardener's lover Julia.[166] Adding the frisson of an illicit relationship to the motive for Henriques's crime, the tableaux list for the film suggests that Julia is the figure responsible for goading him into murder.[167] The added attraction of "the accident on the famous track of the Conde de Frontin"—a reference to the engineer and politician Count Paulo de Frontin, who administered the railway network surrounding Rio de Janeiro—appears to have been linked to the demise of the villainess, allowing for narrative closure while also capitalizing on the sensational appeal of technological breakdown.[168] This plot point is suggested by a series of tableau titles in the film's third and final part: "The flight of the demon woman, Waiting for the train, The beast [Henriques] becomes agitated, The demon who departs, The punishment begins! . . . The accident, The hand of God, I am avenged." The film's final tableau, entitled "Divine justice," recalls the moralistic framing of earlier reconstructions of real-life cases.[169] In addition to meting out "justice" to the gardener's lover, the accident scene would have resonated with public concern regarding the grave problems with the local rail system. In the three months preceding the release of the film, there were three serious collisions on the railway lines surrounding Rio, including a fatal crash.[170] The *Correio da Manhã* called the system "A Estrada da Morte" (Rails of Death), ironically describing it as "a funeral business run by the Count of Frontin with rare skill."[171]

Further suggesting the role of modern transportation technologies in the film's production, *A Noite* reported an incident in which the cast and crew of Brazil-Film boarded a train operated by the railway company in order to "shoot a film of the landscape with the train in motion" and to record a scene featuring their "artists inside the train car."[172] However, an employee of the company protested, and the filmmakers were ejected from the car. This anecdote suggests how the Botelho brothers may have incorporated landscape views rendered dynamic by the vehicle's motion—both as backdrops for the narrative action and as attractions in themselves—into narrative productions whose appeal was premised on their spectacularization of a violent, eventful present.

Whether as a consequence of its sensationalistic subject or of its combined display of cinematic and transportation technology, *Um crime sensacional* enjoyed a longer run than *O caso dos caixotes*. Initially shown in the Pavilhão Internacional and the Teatro São Pedro, both owned by the impresario Paschoal Segreto, *Um crime sensacional* was exhibited for four days in the first venue, where it was held over "by request," and ten in the second.[173] In São Paulo, it was shown over four nights in two theaters.[174] Although the Botelho brothers' attempt to capitalize on sensational events was relatively short-lived and only modestly successful in comparison with the initial cycle of crime-themed films, it indicates the persistence of restaging public violence as a means of appealing to local audiences through the early 1910s.

Conclusion

If in 1913 spectators in Rio and São Paulo still showed interest in violent actualities produced locally, these films occupied a marginal position within the increasingly centralized distribution-exhibition circuits that were consolidated at the beginning of the teens. While filmed reenactments of local, topical events could be extremely profitable as part of the vertically integrated business model of the producer-exhibitor, who had the flexibility to take advantage of spectacular box-office successes, such adaptations had difficulty gaining traction within theater chains focused almost exclusively on the distribution of foreign films. However, local desire to produce thrilling narratives of adventure and crime with local settings would in fact be stimulated by the North American and European serials that quickly gained popularity with Rio de Janeiro audiences in the late teens.

Indicative of the precarious character of early film production in Rio de Janeiro and São Paulo, the short-lived genre of the filmed reconstruction is deeply revealing of the role of public spectacles of violence in the emergence of a mass culture premised on social divisions. Like the narratives of police reportage and crônicas that traversed the social and spatial divides of Brazil's modernizing cities, these reenactments imbued familiar locations with a morbid fascination and forged a temporality perceived as distinctly modern by framing daily experience as a succession of contingent, unpredictable, and shocking events. Taking the scene of the crime as a point of departure for narrative, reconstructions of real-life cases facilitated a transition from actuality to more complex narratives that combined visual documentation, reenactment, and wholly fictional material. Like illustrated magazines and actualities, these films accorded an unprecedented visibility to both elites and marginalized social actors—immigrants, women, and the working classes. Cinema and the illustrated press addressed polarized social sectors as consumers of an emergent mass culture through the use of melodramatic conventions and the intervention of new visual technologies. Sensational visual culture openly acknowledged the social stratification and violence—individual and structural—that accompanied modernization in early twentieth-century Brazil, framing public violence as perhaps the most unequivocal sign of local modernity.

Chapter 4

THE SERIAL CRAZE IN
RIO DE JANEIRO, 1915–1924
Reception, Production, Paraliterature

Between January and April 1920, the Rio de Janeiro entertainment magazine *Palcos e Telas* (Stages and Screens) published weekly installments of a story entitled "Um caso estranho" (A Strange Case), focused on the murder of an American film distributor living in Rio. Advertised as "full of improbabilities, perhaps, but sensationally mysterious," the story was described as a *"folhetim cinematográfico,"* or cinematic serial novel.[1] However, unlike the tie-in novelizations of American serial films published widely in local newspapers a few years earlier, the story was not associated with any existing film. Instead, "Um caso estranho" transplanted the tropes of imported serials and detective stories to Brazil's then capital. This strategy is especially apparent in the first installment, in which a police interrogation reconstructing the victim's movements motivates references to several sites linked to the local entertainment world. These included Praça Tiradentes, a square around which several popular theaters and cinemas were clustered, and the elegant Odeon movie palace.[2] Such references to actual locations likely added to the thrill for local readers, who could imagine the kind of detective story more frequently set in London or New York unfolding in their midst. Yet it is a fictional site that plays the most central role in the story: the imaginary Brazilian-Film studio, where the distributor's murder (by a director in the pay of German spies, as it turns out) was serendipitously captured on film.

Published in one of Rio de Janeiro's first specialized film magazines, "Um caso estranho" exemplifies the interconnections between popular serial crime and adventure narratives and local ambitions for film production. The story renders Brazil's capital a setting for tales of criminality and intrigue with cosmopolitan associations, a strategy it shared with a series of crime and adventure films produced in the city in 1917, all considered lost: *A quadrilha do esqueleto* (*The Skeleton Gang,* Eduardo Arouca and Carlos Comelli), *Le film du diable* (*The Devil's Film* [released locally with the French title], Louis Monfits and [first name unknown] Dillac), and *Os mistérios do Rio de Janeiro* (*The Mysteries of Rio de Janeiro,* Coelho Neto and Alfredo Musso). The latter two films were originally conceived as serials, though neither continued beyond an initial episode.

Like "Um caso estranho," *Os mistérios do Rio de Janeiro* and *Le film du diable* incorporated references to the First World War. In this respect, the story recalls French and American serials and their tie-in novelizations, which often used the war as the backdrop for death-defying adventures. Although Brazil maintained neutrality in the conflict until late 1917, sensational fictions produced before its entry evoked the events of the war. *Le film du diable* depicted German atrocities in war-torn Belgium despite being shot in a number of recognizable locations in Rio de Janeiro, while the plot of *Os mistérios do Rio de Janeiro* centered on German ships stranded in Guanabara Bay. By chance, the film premiered, along with *A quadrilha do esqueleto*, the day before the country announced its entry into the war.[3]

Taking its cue from a local craze for serials in the mid-teens, "Um caso estranho" seeks to provide similarly addictive narrative thrills, explicitly modeling itself on the novelizations published in local newspapers. As Rafael de Luna Freire has shown, this practice was pioneered in Rio de Janeiro by the sensationalistic newspaper *A Noite*. The paper began publishing a novelization of *Os mistérios de Nova York* (*The Mysteries of New York*) in March 1916, based on the Pathé Exchange serial released locally with the same title (which was compiled from select episodes of *The Exploits of Elaine, The Romance of Elaine,* and *The New Exploits of Elaine*). The practice was swiftly adapted by a wide array of publications.[4] According to Luna Freire, *A Noite*'s founding editor, Irineu Marinho, later participated to varying degrees in the production of *A quadrilha do esqueleto* and *Os mistérios do Rio de Janeiro* in collaboration with Antônio Leal, camera operator for several filmed reconstructions of real-life crimes in the previous decade.[5]

The magazine's description of "Um caso estranho" as a "folhetim cinematográfico," despite the absence of an accompanying film text, signals how globally popular forms of serial narrative were assimilated locally within the "codes of reception" established by the literary tradition of the folhetim, which had played a pivotal role in the emergence of a self-consciously national literature in Brazil in the latter half of the nineteenth century. If films like *Os mistérios do Rio de Janeiro* and *A quadrilha do esqueleto* sought to capitalize on the local popularity of imported serials, adaptations of Joaquim Manuel de Macedo's 1844 *A moreninha* (*The Little Brunette*, 1915) and José de Alencar's 1862 *Lucióla* (1916), both filmed by Leal, drew on a national tradition of melodramatic literature with both cultural cachet and popular appeal. Significantly, these canonical works are both set in Rio de Janeiro, by contrast with indigenista "foundational fictions" by Alencar like *O guarani* (*The Guaraní*, 1857) and *Iracema* (1865), which were adapted to the screen a number of times during the silent era.[6] Like the crime and adventure films produced in Rio de Janeiro shortly after, these films share an interest in highlighting the local setting through landscape views and on-location shooting in the homes of wealthy residents.

Perhaps recalling these recent efforts at film production, "Um caso estranho" mobilizes fantasies about the possibility of a local industry that had been increasingly stifled by the consolidation of exhibition interests aligned with foreign film producers after 1911. Self-sustaining local production seemed ever more improbable in the face of the onslaught of American films that accompanied the First World War. As exports of French and Italian films declined as a result of the conflict, American producers took advantage of the disruption to expand aggressively overseas, especially in the lucrative markets of South America.[7] A number of Hollywood studios established their first Brazilian branch offices in Rio de Janeiro in the mid-teens: Universal was the first to do so, in May 1915, followed by Fox and then Paramount.[8] As I have observed in the case of Mexico City during the same period, in Rio de Janeiro the popularity of serials was perhaps the most visible sign of North American cinema's expanded presence. A story focused on an American film distributor's murder in a local film studio might be considered a macabre bit of wishful thinking, signaling a desire to reclaim a market dominated by Hollywood cinema for national productions that had been disappointingly slow to materialize.

At the same time, the episodic structure of the story itself highlights the generative potential of serial forms for local film culture. One of the first serials to be screened in Rio de Janeiro, *Lucille Love, the Girl of Mystery* (Francis Ford, 1914), exhibited in June 1915 with the title *A rapariga misteriosa*, was promoted with a contest that invited fans to predict the ending of the film, part of a publicity campaign surrounding the debut of Universal's recently opened local distribution branch.[9] A similar contest accompanied the publication of "Um caso estranho," which invited its readers to compete for a golden medallion and the title of "first national detective" by guessing the murderer's identity.[10] Both contests solicited participatory engagement from local consumers; the second borrowed an imported advertising strategy to promote a locally themed crime story.

I have chosen to linger on "Um caso estranho" because it crystallizes a set of desires linked to the staging of local modernity through the exhibition and production of crime films in Brazil's capital during the late teens and early twenties. I argue that the broad popularity of serial narratives, and their privileged role in these sporadic efforts to produce fiction films in Rio de Janeiro in the period can be attributed to two factors: their association between criminality and modernity, which built on discourses in the local press; and the paraliterary character of these fictions, which lent them a special degree of cultural productivity. I understand the category of paraliterature in two senses: on one hand, it refers to the formulaic and "subliterary" nature of crime narratives; on the other, it refers to the "parasitic" interdependence between film serials and their tie-in novelizations, on which they sometimes relied to achieve narrative intelligibility.[11] As the intertwined forms of serial films and tie-in novelizations were appropriated in the local context, they gave rise to folhetins cinematográficos without corresponding films and to locally produced crime and adventure films without tie-ins novelizations, both of which capitalized on the local popularity of imported crime fictions.

The dissemination of imported serials and their tie-in in Rio de Janeiro exemplifies processes of cultural massification, which were characterized by intertextual relationships across media that signaled "the increased mobility and circulation of all 'social things.'"[12] In the Brazilian context, the dynamics of massification were inseparable from the presence of American cultural products. Yet the functioning of serials as "heterogeneous text[s]" characterized by "openness and intertextuality," in Shelley Stamp's words, also meant that they provided multiple entry points for spectators and readers in Rio de Janeiro, who took them as points of departure for varied forms of cultural production across print and film.[13] The case of serial culture in Rio de Janeiro in the late teens provides additional impetus for rethinking the long-standing association between serial forms and the industrialization of the creative process.

The tendency to understand serial culture as a series of formulaic narratives with homogenizing effects overshadows the complex ways that serial literature and other paraliterary forms solicit participatory engagement from audiences. Jennifer Hayward has traced this former position in Marxist criticism from Antonio Gramsci to Max Horkheimer and Theodor Adorno, arguing that far from being passive dupes of the culture industry, "serial audiences use their texts" in "processes of collaborative interpretation, prediction, metacommentary, and creation."[14] In some cases written collectively, serial narratives invite reader engagement through a segmented, long-term mode of dissemination that gives the public the opportunity to comment on and, potentially, to affect the development of a serial narrative still in progress. Unlike most serial fans in major film-producing countries, spectators in Rio de Janeiro managed to produce paraliterary narratives and serial-influenced films that had a considerable, if short-lived, local impact.

In this chapter, I examine the cross-medial form of the cinematic serial novel as a site where the national literary tradition of the folhetim intersected with the exhibition of imported crime and adventure serials, fostering the local production of paraliterature and fiction films in the interstices of the increasingly regularized (and implicitly Americanized) mode of cultural production and consumption embodied by the serial. Rudmer Canjels argues that the distribution of serials became a key site at which imported cinema was reimagined through local cultural forms, a dynamic that often acted as a stimulus to local production.[15] In crime films produced in Rio de Janeiro, key "semantic elements" of imported serials—insidious criminal organizations, international intrigue, modern technologies used for nefarious ends—appeared alongside scenic views of well-known local sites.[16] Showcasing urban spaces and featuring fantastic stunts, these productions capitalized on varied forms of cinematic realism, even as their plots defied verisimilitude.

The production and reception of crime films in Rio was shaped by emerging discourses of film criticism and in particular, by the concept of the *truc*. Appearing frequently in reference to film serials and their tie-ins, this French loanword was understood in Brazil to encompass cinematic displays of physical prowess, special effects, and thrilling plot developments. The spectacular quality of the truc was often in tension with locally produced crime films' claims to document the local, evident in publicity discourses. Yet at the same time, the cinematic spectacle of the truc functioned as a sign of technological mastery, as becomes clear in press coverage of the adventure melodramas produced in Rio de Janeiro by Luiz de Barros in the wake of the crime films of the late teens.

The case of *Le film du diable* exemplifies how location shooting and the truc were framed as audience attractions in the context of attempts at serial film production. Produced by the short-lived Nacional-Film Company, *Le film du diable* combined panoramas of local landscapes with a narrative of the European conflict. An advertisement described the film as a "sensational and exciting narrative [*romance*] that unfolds, in imagination, in the martyred lands of Belgium."[17] The unlikely "place substitution" of Rio de Janeiro for Belgium was made even less plausible by press discourses that advertised scenic views as a key element of *Le film du diable*'s audience appeal.[18] Further blurring the distinction between fictional setting and scenic view, an exhibition of the film began with "prises de vue" that showed Guanabara Bay, the neighborhoods of Gávea and Tijuca, as well as Santos harbor and the Cubatão mountains in the state of São Paulo.[19] (A U.S. film journalist present at the screening noted that these "had nothing to do with the [photo]play.")[20]

Combining panoramas of Brazilian landscapes with European points of reference, *Le film du diable* took a highly unusual approach to the global conflict of the First World War. According to an article in the American trade publication *Moving Picture World*, which discussed *Le film du diable* alongside other local filmmaking initiatives, its plot focused on a young woman who suffers abuse at the hands of a German commander after her family is killed by his troops. (The leading role was played by an American actress, a fact that publicity discourses cited as a coup for local film production in a manner similar to the case of the unproduced Mexican serial *Chucho el Roto*.)[21] After her escape, "while asleep her spirit is made to leave the body and go out to seek revenge for the infamies perpetrated against her and her parents."[22] In a series of unusual allegorical sequences, the forces of good and evil, represented by Satan and a nude woman, debated her course of action.[23]

Although these sequences clearly deviate from the cinematic conventions dominant in the period—*Moving Picture World* noted that *Le film du diable* "did not follow closely the rules of the game"—it nevertheless sought to capitalize on the fast-and-furious action associated with imported serials, with their emphasis on technological disaster.[24] (One article emphasized its setting in a context where "all the marvels of science are being applied to human destruction.")[25] A notice about the film (likely a promotional text published at the producers' request) praised its " 'trucs' of perfect execution, and scenes that excite for their grandeur, for example the fall of an automobile that plunges from the bluffs of Gávea, into a profound grotto . . . until the motor explodes there below."[26] (The accident takes place after the heroine kills her captor and escapes in the vehicle, from which she is forced to leap under a hail of bullets when it runs out of fuel).[27] If the picturesque views of Brazilian scenery that preceded the narrative were presented as autonomous attractions, this sequence would have integrated the dramatic local topography into the stunt itself. According to one report (which was likely exaggerated), an actual automobile was destroyed during filming, with eight camera operators present to capture the vehicle's fall.[28]

Capitalizing on the appeal of the truc associated with imported serials, *Le film du diable* was also intended to duplicate their episodic structure. Although a review of the film in *A Noite* emphasized that *Le film du diable* was merely "the first [part] of a long projected series," which would give the filmmakers an opportunity to correct the defects evident in this first installment, *Moving Picture World* had no such optimism. The reviewer noted that at the end of the film's exhibition, a final intertitle "puts an end to the misery of the audience by saying 'The rest of this play will appear soon.' Nothing more has followed."[29] For this observer, far from encouraging ongoing consumption, the unfulfilled promise of a narrative "to be continued" justified intense skepticism about the prospects of Brazilian film production. Indeed, the film's impact seems to have been fairly modest, although advertisements claimed that *Le film du diable* drew full houses for a week, double the three- or four-day run of most programs.[30] Capitalizing on its connection to the events of the First World War, the film was also screened at a benefit for Portuguese war orphans and later shown alongside actualities documenting the aftermath of the sinking of a Brazilian steamship, the *Paraná*, by a German submarine, an incident that contributed to the severing of diplomatic relations between the two countries.[31]

While imported adventure serials offered visual and narrative conventions for displaying physical and technological virtuosity in Rio de Janeiro crime films, these local productions were unable to achieve the continuity and regularity of production that underpinned the serial craze in the United States. Contrasting Italian serials with their North American counterparts, Monica Dall'Asta notes that the Italian industry's "lack of financial organisation, standardisation and rationalisation" precluded "reaching levels of industrial, thus serial, manufacturing."[32] The fact that both *Le film du diable* and *Os mistérios do Rio de Janeiro* were planned as serials but released as features suggests the far greater obstacles faced by Brazilian film producers in their attempts to achieve self-sustaining production. Releasing the films in this format was a logical way to recuperate some of the producers' investment, and *Os mistérios do*

Rio de Janeiro and *A quadrilha do esqueleto* both achieved considerable box-office success. Yet this strategy also signals the particularities of imported serials' local exhibition, which were usually shown in two-episode blocks approximating a feature-length program, though not always according to a regular exhibition schedule. Furthermore, advertisements for serial films emphasized closure rather than cliffhangers, emphasizing the narrative pleasures available to viewers in a single sitting in a context where the continuity of exhibition was not always guaranteed. These practices may have also influenced the manner in which locally produced crime films were ultimately released. Although they did not ultimately manage to replicate serial structure, these texts asserted Rio de Janeiro's place in a cosmopolitan imaginary of crime and staked its claim to the status of a producer of thrilling cinematic entertainment.

Positioning these films within a broader context of serial and paraliterary culture in early twentieth-century Rio, I begin by discussing the imaginary of crime and technological modernity cultivated by American and French serials and referenced in local newspapers, moving on to discuss the production of both sentimental and sensational melodramas shaped by the precedent of the folhetim, and the afterlife of the local serial craze in the films of Luiz de Barros. As in the previous decade, criminal activity was presented as an ambivalent marker of urban modernity in the local press; however, the charge of collective anxiety and fascination attached to real-life cases seems to have lessened. The historian Marcos Luiz Bretas suggests that in Rio de Janeiro "in the 1910s . . . there was a change in the type of preoccupation with the maintenance of order, since the flow of immigrants was subsiding and the city was developing better-defined behaviors and routines in the redesigned public space."[33] By 1917, crime was more likely to be discussed in the context of new technologies of communication and transportation that forged international networks, facilitating the circulation of goods and persons, but also bringing about a "globalization of risk," in Anthony Giddens's phrase, or accelerating the pace at which catastrophic events unfolded, as Stephen Kern has argued in the case of the outbreak of the First World War.[34] Despite serials' overt capitalization on the "terrors of technology," little public outcry against the genre was made in Rio de Janeiro, apart from the occasional condemnation in the press as a school for criminals.[35] I speculate that their suspenseful, addictive structure was mitigated somewhat by the particularities of serial exhibition in Rio de Janeiro. (It is important to note that the serial craze of the late teens was initially centered in the capital. While serial films and tie-in novelizations were disseminated in other Brazilian cities in the teens and early twenties, the ambitions of serial-influenced films produced in Rio de Janeiro were principally local in scope.)

In Brazil's capital in the latter half of the teens, the popularity of serial films and fictional tie-ins allowed local writers and producers to imagine inserting their own narratives within a mode of imported serial culture, which was itself characterized by repetition and the constant recycling of iconographies and narrative tropes. The literary and cinematic crime narratives produced in Rio de Janeiro certainly do not approximate the industrial regularity of production, exhibition, and cross-promotion between film and print media that characterized most American serials; yet this is precisely why they can offer fresh insights regarding the relationship between mass media and modernization. Examining serial production from the perspective of its interstices and from the margins of global culture industries can help further nuance interpretations that reduce it to a capitalist rationalization—or, in the case of Brazil, a colonization—of cultural forms.

Sensational Journalism, Serials, and the *Cine-Folhetim*, 1916–1918

At the turn of the twentieth century, Brazil's capital nurtured a culture of popular sensationalism that framed public spectacles of violence as signs of local modernity in print, onstage, and onscreen. Extending this tendency, in the latter half of the teens, local audiences developed a fascination with crime films' exploration of the dark side of modern transportation and communication technologies. As these imported crime series and serials gained popularity with local audiences, their possible effects on audiences became a matter for debate. In 1915, an article in the illustrated magazine *Selecta* discussed the ambivalent effects of cinematic crime narratives, noting that "[t]he cinematograph, with its frequent reproductions of crimes and Rocambolesque enterprises, has been considered by many modern Catos as the most efficient school of crime."[36] Yet in addition to "enriching the repertory of [criminals'] audacities" by providing them with models, it could also be mobilized as a crime-fighting tool.[37] The article goes on to relate the (probably apocryphal) tale of a group of police officers in a small town outside New York who filmed a reconstruction of a crime, screened it in a local theater, and caught the curious robbers as they tried to flee the cinema.[38]

Expanding this reflection on the cinema to the question of criminality more broadly defined, the magazine mused two weeks later, "[I]f civilization has forged new instruments of criminality, such as firearms, the press, photography, dynamite, the wireless telegraph, the automobile, hypnotism, new poisons, microbial infections, etc., in science itself we have found valuable, efficient resources, which are capable, to a greater extent than penal repression, of attenuating the effects, diminishing the successes, combating the results of contemporary criminality."[39] The magazine's discussion presents modern transportation and media technologies as "instruments of criminality" as much as signs of progress. This ambivalence was implicit in the serial film genre, which consistently "flaunt[ed] catastrophe, disorder and disaster rather than continuity and regulation," emphasizing the rapid flow of unpredictable events that characterized modern life.[40] As Tom Gunning observes in his analysis of D. W. Griffith's *The Lonely Villa* (1909), the use of communication technologies as a means of structuring the narrative works to highlight "the darker aspects of . . . instant communication and the annihilation of space and time," hinting at the possibility of catastrophic reversals. In the film's plot, centered on a father's frantic "race to the rescue" after he receives a telephone call from his wife and daughters, who are being menaced by criminals who cut the phone line, Gunning argues, "the smooth functioning of technology glides over the abyss of anxiety at its sudden failure."[41] Playing a pivotal role in early adventure melodramas like Griffith's, this ambivalent imaginary of technology was exploited to the hilt in Hollywood crime and adventure serials.

The fascination with the multivalence of technology, which could be enlisted either to commit or to combat nefarious crimes, and which played a central role in the mass violence and destruction of the First World War, shaped the local reception of *Os mistérios de Nova York*, which had been imported from France by the Ferrez family for exhibition in their Cinema Pathé. In local newspapers, the serial's "absolutely ingenious and unprecedented applications of science" were billed a key selling point.[42] While locally made crime films do not appear to have imitated the fantastical array of inventions featured in the Pathé Exchange serial, press accounts indicate an interest in the destructive effects of modern weaponry and transportation technologies. *Os mistérios do Rio de Janeiro* evoked the First World War in a scene featuring poison gas attacks, while *A quadrilha do esqueleto* featured a gruesome automobile accident that would have recalled the sharp rise of traffic accidents and deaths in Rio de Janeiro in the early teens, as the number of automobiles soared, a problem exacerbated by the city's topography and poor road conditions.[43] Perhaps most spectacularly, the latter film incorporated a chase sequence and fatal fall from the gondola used to transport sightseers to the top of the Pão de Açúcar (Sugarloaf Mountain).

The strategies of *A quadrilha do esqueleto* and other crime-themed films of the late teens signal a desire to sensationalize everyday life in Rio de Janeiro through the tropes of imported serial films. The police blotter of *A Noite* often referenced characters from imported crime narratives in both print and cinematic form, playing into perceived popular tastes. (One 1914 article alleged that even the "children of Rio have a true and ardent passion for the *folhetim policial*," including tales featuring Sherlock Holmes and Fantômas.)[44] Indeed, the case of *Fantômas*, a series of novels by Marcel Allain and Pierre Souvestre adapted to the screen in a 1915 Gaumont serial directed by Louis Feuillade, exemplifies convergences between the press, crime fiction, and crime films. In November 1915, *A Noite* referred to a recently released criminal as a "new Fantômas," a reference that may have been inspired by (or designed to publicize) the local re-exhibition of the Gaumont serial.[45] In July 1916, *A Noite* described the theft of a cigarette case and a pearl necklace as a "case à la 'Devil's Hand,'" which was the name given locally to the villain of *The Exploits of Elaine*, the "Clutching Hand."[46] Evoking the serial's hero (Justin Clarel in the French novelization), the newspaper described the robbery as "a difficult problem even for the cunning of a Justino Clarel with all his extraordinary coincidences." Even as the article comments ironically on the serial's lack of verisimilitude, it also suggests that the real-life crime partakes in the thrilling intrigue offered by the film. This confusion between life and cinema might even manifest itself literally. In 1918, *A Noite* published an article entitled "Like in *Os mistérios de Nova York*," about a group of students who heard strange noises from the building next door and called the police, supposedly thinking that it might be the criminal gang from the film.[47]

The police blotter cultivated a sense that the uniquely modern thrills and anxieties associated with crime serials were part of quotidian experience in Rio de Janeiro, an impulse that also informed the production of films that capitalized on serial conventions. The practice of exhibiting serials in blocks of two episodes, rather than one episode a week, may have made the genre seem more feasible for local producers.[48] First used by Universal in the exhibition of *A rapariga misteriosa* in June 1915, this strategy persisted through the end of the serial craze in late 1918. By contrast, many French series films, and even serials such as Feuillade's *Les vampires*, had been shown with markedly irregular release schedules, at times in multiple movie theaters. The model

FIG 4.1 Technology as thrilling threat: the façade of the Cinema Pathé decorated to advertise the "Death Ray" ("Radiações mortais") episode of *Os mistérios de Nova York* in 1916. Arquivo Nacional, Brasil.

of irregular exhibition in feature-length programs would have made serial production seem more attainable for local film producers than the standardized schedule of serial exhibition in the United States, where single episodes were usually shown on a weekly basis.

The novelty of exhibition in episodes quickly caught the public's attention, and was creatively adapted as a marketing technique. French series and serial films from previous years were retrospectively linked to the new vogue for serials. Episodes of *Fantômas*, which had first been shown in Rio in 1913, were re-exhibited multiple times between November 1915 and February 1916.[49] When the series of Zigomar crime films produced by the French studio Éclair—each film was an autonomous narrative, rather than an installment of a serial—was re-exhibited in September 1916, it was advertised as "the first crime film [*film policial*] exhibited in distinct chapters."[50] In addition to the re-exhibitions of series films repackaged as serials, serial films were shown somewhat haphazardly. For example, Feuillade's *Les vampires* (*Os vampiros*) was announced first in January, then in February 1916, but not actually shown until March, when it was exhibited concurrently with *Os mistérios de Nova York*. After a series of irregularly spaced screenings, the run of the serial finally concluded in January 1917.[51] The intermittent practice of showing two episodes of a serial at a time may have mitigated the potentially unpleasant experience of a cliffhanger without a clear timetable for resolution.

Accordingly, when the publication of *Os mistérios de Nova York* began in *A Noite* in March 1916, an explanatory preface stressed that each installment and episode was an autonomous unit, reassuring audiences they would not be subjected to perpetually unresolved suspense.[52] Similarly, an advertisement in the entertainment section stated that "each episode, which can be read separately, constitutes a film, to be exhibited in the Cinema-Pathé."[53] The episodes of *Os mistérios de Nova York* were shown between 16 March and 23 July, always in pairs, and always at two-week intervals. An advertisement for the film emphasized that "accompanying *without a single interruption* the publication of *A Noite*, the Cinema Pathé presents on fixed dates the famous romance chronicling the exploits of the Devil's Hand, a new, enigmatic, attractive, plot."[54] In this case, regular exhibition and thus consistent audience expectations were maintained.

The publication of tie-in novelizations established affinities to the form of the folhetim, without making other concessions to local specificity. Installments of the story were published on a daily basis in a format characteristic of the folhetim, which occupied the bottom quarter of the newspaper's back page, rather than an entire sheet, as was the case with the weekly tie-ins published in American newspapers. However, by contrast with the French novelization, from which the Brazilian tie-in was apparently translated, the story does not appear to have been modified to include local references. As Canjels has pointed out, Pierre Decourcelle's French-language novelization of the same Pathé Exchange serial, *Les mystères de New-York*, draws on Arthur B. Reeve's original fictional texts but incorporates references to France (including a flashback conversation between Justin Clarel and the celebrated French criminologist Alphonse Bertillon) and incorporates subtly expressed anti-German sentiments.[55] By contrast, an initial comparison between the Brazilian and the Mexican versions of the tie-ins reveals texts that are almost identical beyond the languages of their publication.[56]

Although the local publication of tie-in novelizations appears to have been less carefully tailored to Brazilian audiences than to those in France, where

FIG 4.2 Cross-promotion in an advertisement for *Os mistérios de Nova York*: "See it in the Cinema Ideal, Read the Folhetim in A Noite." *A Noite*, 15 March 1916. Acervo da Fundação Biblioteca Nacional, Brasil.

FIG 4.3 The first installment of the tie-in novelization of *Os mistérios de Nova York* closely mimics the format of serial novels published in the "rodapé" (bottom quarter of the page). *A Noite*, 9 March 1916. Acervo da Fundação Biblioteca Nacional, Brasil.

Pathé Exchange's parent company was based, a craze for the genre swiftly took hold in Rio de Janeiro. While Pathé's productions were extensively promoted in the tie-in novelizations published by *A Noite*, Universal serials also enjoyed great popularity with local audiences. An informal rivalry between fans of the two companies' films gives an indication of the sweeping popularity of the genre in Rio in the late teens. According to the journalist Pedro Lima, the Rua da Carioca was flooded with cinemagoers on Mondays, the days that new episodes of serials were first shown, due to the exhibition of Universal and Pathé programs in two rival movie theaters: "The audience of the Iris mixed with that of the Ideal, since they were almost directly in front of each other. The showings began at 1 p.m. and interrupted the traffic, no one could get by," until a bell rang announcing the start of the screening and the crowd rushed inside.[57]

While local exhibition practices reconfigured the release schedule of imported serials and its forms of narrative suspense, Rio de Janeiro audiences seem to have shared an enthusiasm for dynamic "serial queens" like White, Ruth Roland, Grace Cunard, and Helen Holmes, whose star personas resonated across the globe.[58] Attempts to capitalize on the success of *Os mistérios de Nova York* suggest the enthusiastic local reception of Pearl White in particular. After the serial's conclusion, the Cinema Pathé exhibited *Aventuras de Elaine* (*The Perils of Pauline*) in November 1916, with advertisements emphasizing White's reappearance onscreen.[59] The Cinema Ideal responded by showing another episodic narrative featuring a daring female protagonist, exhibiting fifteen installments extracted from the series *The Hazards of Helen* under the title *A mulher audaciosa* (*The Audacious Woman*).[60]

Even after the serial craze had passed, Pearl White continued to captivate the imagination of modernist writers, who discussed her dynamic persona as the epitome both of quintessentially American traits and of the modern medium of the cinema itself. According to the writer Pedro Nava, the attractions of French serials paled beside their American counterparts starring White, who he called "the synonym of the happiness, health, sportiveness, and courage of the American girl. And what eyes. Not even *Os vampiros* and the French suggestiveness of the clinging suit of old Musidora could prevail against her and against *Os mistérios de Nova York*."[61] In 1922, a collectively authored manifesto in the first issue of celebrated modernist magazine *Klaxon* affirms that "cinematography is the most representative artistic creation of our age." The manifesto's authors suggest cinema's unique qualities through a series of contrasts between the serial queen and Sarah Bernhardt, held to embody an outmoded model of femininity: "Pearl White is preferable to Sarah Bernhardt. Sarah is tragedy, sentimental and technical romanticism. Pearl is ratiocination, instruction, sport, rapidity, joy, life. Sarah Bernhardt=nineteenth century. Pearl White=twentieth century."[62] For these modernist writers, Pearl White's physical feats epitomized the uniquely modern physical dynamism embodied by the cinema.

Beyond the links between the figure of the serial queen and discussions of film as a quintessentially modern medium, the craze for imported serials and tie-in novelizations fostered critical discussions of the truc, discussed as a marker of physical and technological virtuosity in film. First appearing widely in Rio de Janeiro newspapers at the turn of the century, the term usually referred to an act of subterfuge or deception (often in the political realm, though at times for criminal ends) and more occasionally to various types of stage illusions. In the context of serial films, it was used to describe the abundant disguises and traps (literal and figurative) laid for characters and, by extension, the physical exploits and cinematic illusions that accompanied them. In a text announcing its launch of the novelization of *Os mistérios de Nova York*, *A Noite* suggested that the novelization held an attraction that surpassed the gimmicks abounding in the genre: "When the 'trucs' and 'ficelles' intended to engage readers' curiosity could no longer offer any new configuration whatsoever, there appeared in the United States a novelty that achieved stupendous success in just a few days," that is, the serial and its tie-in.[63] As this description suggests, the truc was associated with the production of novel thrills and sensations in the context of a commodified mass culture. By contrast, as Luna Freire has pointed out, in April 1916, an episode of Feuillade's *Les vampires* was marketed as gritty and realistic in comparison with the improbable plots of U.S.-produced serials; it was advertised as "the story [*romance*] of an evildoer, just as he is; without trucs or impossible events."[64] Emerging from promotional discourses on imported serial films and tie-ins, the Brazilian conception of the truc has clear points of contact with the global reception of serials. Yuri Tsivian has noted the fascination evident in pre-1924 Soviet cinema and film criticism with American serial films marked by "the prevalence of outdoor locations, event-filled narratives and physical stunts (*tryuk*)."[65] *Os mistérios do Rio de Janeiro*, *A quadrilha do esqueleto*, and especially *Le film du diable* capitalized on a conception of the truc that encompassed both physical exploits and cinematic special effects.

Capitalizing on the popularity of serials featuring White and other serial queens to promote its paper, *A Noite* printed a second tie-in in April 1917, continuing the practice through early 1918. These included *O enigma da mascara ou a garra de ferro* (*The Iron Claw*, a.k.a. *The Laughing Mask*, Edward José, 1916), starring White; *O Estigma ou a malha rubra* (*The Red Circle*, Sherwood MacDonald, 1915), with Ruth Roland; *Ravengar* (*The Shielding Shadow*, Louis Gasnier and Donald MacKenzie, 1916); *O mistério da dupla cruz* (*The Mystery of the Double Cross*, William Parke, 1917), featuring Mollie King; and an Italian film in episodes, *O Fiacre n. 13* (*Cab N. 13*, Alberto Capozzi and Gero Zambuto, 1917). Luna Freire observes a dizzying variety of print material linked to crime and adventure films: the 1917 serialization of *O telefone da morte* (*The Voice on the Wire*, Stuart Paton, 1917) in the *Correio da Manhã*; the publication of summaries of *Os estranguladores de New-York ou o mistério da mancha vermelha* (*The Crimson Stain Mystery*, T. Hayes Hunter, 1916) in the newspaper *A Rua*, as well as handbills; and the publication of tie-ins in book form, beginning with *Os mistérios de Nova York*.[66] The popularity of tie-novelizations reached its peak in 1917, coinciding with the high point of crime-film production in Rio.

In Rio de Janeiro, the publication of tie-ins synchronized precisely to the exhibition of serial films was relatively short-lived, continuing for approximately two years, from early 1916 to early 1918. However, beginning with its founding in March 1918, *Palcos e Telas* almost invariably published some form of verbal supplement to local serial exhibitions, whether in the form of lengthy summaries or text-heavy advertisements placed by exhibitors. The magazine also featured more imaginative fictional texts that appropriated the stars and conventions of Hollywood adventure melodramas. Shortly after its founding, *Palcos e Telas* began to publish installments of a curious story entitled "Film em séries" (Serial Film). Resembling the sensational "jungle films" popular in the United States in the early teens, the story features a heroine named Ruth who is menaced by wild beasts.[67] Three years later, in March 1921, *Palcos e Telas* published the first installment of "Sidney, the Bandit, a cinematographic novel dedicated to the great actor William S. Hart." The text was accompanied by a cast list dreamed up by the author, who paired the characters' names with the popular American actors she imagined playing each role.[68]

A recurring feature of the magazine was a section entitled Plots in the Genre of . . . (Argumentos gênero . . .); each installment included a short story evoking the types of narratives closely associated with certain Hollywood stars. "Plots in the Genre of Pearl White," for example, involved a wealthy young heiress whose life was in peril. She becomes involved in a car chase whose stakes are abruptly raised by the discovery of a bomb attached to her car; she deliberately wrecks her vehicle, plunging into the water; then, in a final plot twist, one of her captors tricks the other, then reveals himself to be her fiancé.[69] These reimaginings of the sensationalistic tropes of Hollywood serials suggest the fascination that imported cinema held for local audiences, even as they mark a certain ironic distance from the stars and imported films that inspired these texts.

The vogue for serials in Brazil's capital began to wane in early 1918, signaled by *A Noite*'s decision to stop publishing tie-in novelizations; by this point, they had almost completely fallen out of favor in the United States.[70] In June of that year, a critic in *Palcos e Telas* displayed fatigue with the format, describing *Seven Pearls*, a 1917 Pathé Exchange serial directed by Donald MacKenzie and starring Mollie King, as just another instance of "the eternal and ultra-Rocambolesque adventures of the *cine-folhetim*" which failed to present any exciting novelties for audiences.[71] In the same issue, an Italian serial starring Emilio Ghione was criticized for its "impossible scenes with truly miraculous coincidences, intended to prolong the series with an eye on the biggest profit possible, which for this very reason no longer move us."[72] Local critics had begun to draw connections between the serial film's *coups-de-théâtre*, its addictive and repetitive narrative structures, and its rationalized mode of production and cross-promotion. While Rio de Janeiro film producers could hardly hope to flood the local market with episodes of locally made serials, their products vied for local success by combining spectacular stunts and fast-and-furious narrative action with landscape views and, in some cases, by drawing connections to literary works belonging to a nationally specific repertoire of melodramatic narratives.

As North American film distributors gained a firm foothold in the Brazilian capital's exhibition market, Antônio Leal, who had recently returned to Brazil from Europe, proposed a series of strategies to stimulate local film production.[73] In two interviews given in late 1915 and early 1916, Leal suggested that the local audiences' interest would most effectively be captured by films that acted as a "living newspaper" (*jornal vivo*), depicting topical events like natural or transportation disasters, and by adaptations of national literature.[74] Whereas Leal had capitalized handsomely on the first strategy in 1908 and 1909, in 1915 and 1916 he adopted the latter, producing literary adaptations contextually linked to the tradition of the folhetim. In 1915, Leal produced *A moreninha*, based on the popular 1844 novel narrating a romance between members of the Rio de Janeiro elite. *A moreninha* was one of the first Brazilian novels to be set in contemporary Rio de Janeiro, rather than in the historical settings favored by José de Alencar and other Romantic writers. Financed by the film exhibitor Gustavo José de Mattos, the film was exhibited in the Cine Palais and, according to a retrospective account by Leal, had a profitable run in São Paulo, Bahía, and a number of other states.[75] By aligning the film with the cultural prestige enjoyed by the novel, *A Noite* also linked it with ambitions for national film production, citing a "desire to see established among us the lucrative and useful industry of the cinematograph, which is transformed, when it is well oriented, into an instrument of civic and literary education."[76] Although the article is unsigned, it echoes the editor-in-chief Irineu Marinho's interest in establishing local film production, which would come to fruition in *Os mistérios do Rio de Janeiro* and *A quadrilha do esqueleto*. Although little is known about Leal's adaptation of *A moreninha*, he later noted the production's reliance on the good will of wealthy locals: a number of sequences were filmed in a mansion belonging to the president of the Banco do Brasil, Custodio de Almeida Magalhães, who joined forces with Mattos and Leal to create a production company. In preparation for more ambitious undertakings, Leal resolved to film *Lucíola* to test his technical abilities.[77]

Like *A moreninha*, *Lucíola* was a romantic narrative that had been elevated to the status of a literary classic; it was a highly sentimental, if also risqué, tale of a love affair between a courtesan and a young man recently arrived in Rio de Janeiro. Promotional discourses on the film emphasized the film's erotic appeal—it included a scene where Lucíola, temporarily spurned by the hero, disrobes at a party—and its use of location shooting. Highlighting the film's status as a literary adaptation, an article in *A Noite* also emphasized that both the film and source text are "full of highly dramatic situations and take place in local settings."[78] An advertisement stressed the film's production on location, providing the names of wealthy locals who had opened their homes for filming.[79] Combining sexually suggestive content with sentimentality, and unfolding in the social world of Rio de Janeiro's elites, *Lucíola* appears to have enjoyed considerable success during its weeklong run in the capital, attracting nearly 20,000 spectators.[80]

The publicity surrounding *Lucíola* exemplifies the intersection of the folhetim and the imported serial film, and their role in shaping horizons of production and reception in Rio de Janeiro in the late teens. Advertisements for the film serialized a summary of its plot over three days in *A Noite*, evoking literary tradition, while linking the film to the current vogue for "romances cinematográficos."[81] The considerable space allotted to the plot summaries of *Lucíola*, whose folhetim format occupied a much greater portion of the page than did standard advertisements, may be a function of the working relationship between Leal and the newspaper's editor-in-chief though it should be noted that the newspaper also printed a review condemning *Lucíola*'s sexually charged subject matter.[82] According to Luna Freire, Marinho had already become a financial partner in the Leal-Film production company, although their business relationship was dissolved before the production of *A quadrilha do esqueleto*. Although the nature of Leal's involvement in the latter film is not entirely clear, there is evidence that it was developed and copied in his laboratory, if not shot in his studio as well.[83] Marinho continued to take advantage of his position at *A Noite* to promote *A quadrilha do esqueleto*. As Luna Freire notes, the paper essentially provided free publicity for the film, publishing an extensive interview with one of the founders of its production company, Veritas, as well as short profiles of some of the actors and other items.[84] The interpenetration of journalism and sensational cinema, evident in news stories, also demonstrates the close links between the local press and filmmaking activities.

Informed, like locally produced crime films, by the intermedial form of the folhetim cinematográfico, Leal's films sought audience appeal and legitimacy by invoking literary tradition and grounding in the local context. Some period observers, however, suggest that productions like Leal's had limited success in attracting spectators whose tastes were shaped by sensational serials. In 1917, a commentator blamed the limited success of local productions on the fact that they were "in their totality, taken from old novels," and predicted a much warmer reception for *Os mistérios do Rio de Janeiro*, which was based on an original script by the celebrated author Coelho Neto.[85] Although the film's literary source may have been up-to-date, its title refers back to a much longer tradition of serial literature. It recalls not only the serial *Os mistérios de Nova York*, but also multiple nineteenth-century serial novels entitled *Os mistérios do Rio de Janeiro* and, more broadly, the extensive "mysteries-of-the-city" genre inaugurated by Eugène Sue's 1843 *Les mystères de Paris*.[86] A book entitled *Os mistérios do Rio de Janeiro*, sold in installments by its publishers, was advertised in the capital in February 1918, after the film's run; it featured stories based on infamous real-life cases, including the Crime of Carioca Street and the Crime of Paula Matos, reconstructed for the screen in 1908 and 1913.[87]

Refiguring the Serial: *Os mistérios do Rio de Janeiro* and *A quadrilha do esqueleto*

Despite these clear affinities to serial literature with a transatlantic scope, *Os mistérios do Rio de Janeiro*'s fantastical plot was nominally grounded in contemporary events. The film's lone episode was entitled "The Treasure of the German Ships," a reference to the German vessels stranded in Brazilian harbors by military blockades. Summaries of the film take the First World War as the backdrop for a criminal conspiracy: the film's villain, a false Tunisian prince named Djalmo, is described as "an audacious thief, linked to an international gang organized to operate in the great capitals during the war."[88] Insinuating himself into local high society, the prince meets "a widowed consul" and his daughter, Hilda, and learns that the *Viking*, a ship under the consul's guard, holds a fortune in gold.[89] Like the journalistic discourses that publicized turn-of-the-century "grand crimes," this description suggests that the presence of ultramodern criminality testified to Rio de Janeiro's status as a world capital. Press coverage of the film also emphasized the film's close connection to current events, though in rather vague terms. In April 1917, when the project had still been conceived of as a multiepisode film, a newspaper article described it as "a serial drama [*drama em séries*], but, as each episode is a drama on a different subject of thrilling actuality, the public is now notified that the second episode will reflect the latest sensational events in Brazilian life."[90]

Although this second episode was never completed, summaries of *Os mistérios do Rio de Janeiro* indicate that the film nonetheless drew on the convoluted narrative logic of imported crime and adventure serials, featuring multiple kidnappings, interlocking love triangles, and betrayals piled on betrayals. According to a summary published in a review of the film, a series of romantic rivalries develops: Hilda falls in love with the villain, arousing the jealousy of Djalmo's lover, Fiammetta; in turn, Bracco, one of Djalmo's criminal associates, falls in love with Fiammetta.[91] During a party at the consul's house, Djalmo drugs his host in order to kidnap Hilda. Suspicious of his motives, Fiammetta enlists the gang of thieves to kill Djalmo. (This scene may correspond to a surviving still in which Fiammetta appears surrounded by criminal associates.) Finding the boxes of stolen gold empty, Bracco suspects Fiammetta; during a confrontation in which poison gas is released, Bracco tries to carry her to safety and is stabbed for his trouble. Hilda is then kidnapped again by Bracco, who mistakes her for Fiammetta, and the episode (and ultimately, the film) ends with no apparent resolution to these conflicts.

FIG 4.4 Fiammetta makes a pact with a group of bandits in a disreputable watering hole. Publicity still, *Os mistérios do Rio de Janeiro*. Museu da Imagem e do Som do Estado do Rio de Janeiro, Coleção Jurandyr Noronha.

Although this description recalls the "intensity and polyvalence of the hostility" that Ben Singer notes are characteristic of American serials, *Os mistérios do Rio de Janeiro* also established a dialogue with the French and Italian productions that had dominated local markets only a few years before.[92] The historian Alex Viany cites a sensuous scene involving Djalmo and Fiammetta as evidence of the impact of the Italian diva film, citing a description from a program of the period: "The two laugh, with her seated on the knees of the prince. He, picking up a glass of champagne, takes a sip and, with a kiss, transfers it to the mouth of his lover, the two of them in this way drinking to fortune!"[93] A curious detail from the beginning of the film also recalls the fifth episode of Feuillade's *Les vampires*, "The Eyes that Fascinate," exhibited in Rio de Janeiro in June 1916.[94] In a scene with Orientalist overtones, the prince is able to "only with his look, detach a branch of flowers that the maiden [Hilda] had admired from the tree," explaining this feat by noting that "he had learned, with the fakirs in India, to dominate nature."[95] In addition to these exoticized elements, the discursive traces left by the film signal a navigation between the reference points of North American and European cinema—what Paul Schroeder-Rodríguez calls a process of "triangulation."[96]

Although they were not accompanied by tie-in novelizations, *Os mistérios do Rio de Janeiro* and *A quadrilha do esqueleto* were both characterized by the narrative twists and turns that linked imported serial films with the tradition of the folhetim. An article discussing both films indicates the plot of *A quadrilha do esqueleto* was similarly convoluted, cautioning that it will not even attempt to provide "a complete summary, which would be impossible," suggesting a "narrative unmappability" characteristic of North American serial films.[97] The description goes on to introduce the principal characters, whose desires and conflicts are strongly reminiscent of the Pearl White serial *The Iron Claw*, exhibited in Rio with a tie-in in 1917: "Rodrigo is an unscrupulous type who, feigning friendship for the capitalist Peixoto, had long been obsessed with the idea of stealing his wife and fortune, taking advantage of his intimacy with those of the house to carry out his doubly shameful plan. As an obstacle to this, Rodrigo constantly encountered the resistance of Emilia, a virtuous woman incapable of betrayal."[98] Frustrated in these attempts and in need of money, Rodrigo plans to murder Peixoto with the help of the Skeleton Gang at a secret meeting. Rodrigo's nefarious plans are discovered by the Dwarf, who lives in Peixoto's home as a sort of court jester, and who follows Rodrigo to the location of the secret meeting. However, instead of trying to foil the plot, the Dwarf "preferred to accompany the entire crime, enjoying the vengeance it represented for him."[99] After Peixoto is murdered by the gang's leader, Skeleton, a "struggle, a real duel between the police and the bandits is established, ending after a series of peripeties . . . with the arrest of the gang."[100] According to another account, these included the "imprisonment of a police officer" in the bandits' hideout, a car chase in Tijuca, and a scene filmed in the Casa de Detenção (House of Detention).[101] The reference to a "series of peripeties"—implying an episodic narrative structure punctuated by climactic and unexpected events—suggests the film's affinities with serial literature and cinema, while references to on-location shooting indicate connections with local filmmaking activities of the previous decade.

As Luna Freire observes, the display of views of local spaces, framed as sites of sensationalized violence, signals continuities between the serial-influenced films of the late teens and the filmed reenactments of real-life cases made nearly a decade earlier. While he is careful to distinguish between the preclassical form of the filmed reconstructions and the feature-length crime films made in 1917, Luna Freire speculates that both groups of films were "sustained by sensationalistic cultural matrices," by "the desire to really *see* or *feel* a reality that is unknown (or undergoing a process of rapid change), transformed into a spectacle."[102] Reviews and advertisements for *Os mistérios do Rio de Janeiro* and *A quadrilha do esqueleto* demonstrate how their use of location shooting worked to showcase the class-stratified spaces of early twentieth-century Rio de Janeiro.

Press coverage of *Os mistérios do Rio de Janeiro* highlights filming in affluent homes and the display of local scenery. One review, in *O Imparcial*, suggestively described the film as "a romance of adventures . . . of the most convoluted sort, which, because it takes place in well-known locations, will arouse great interest, always maintaining the spectator's attention, one moment in tragic romantic situations, the next in the splendor of our dwellings which are as lavish and tasteful as the most opulent in Europe, or in the marvelous exuberance of our incomparable landscapes."[103] As was also the case with the adventure melodramas of the 1920s, *Os mistérios do Rio de Janeiro*, according to this description, juxtaposed sentimentality with vertiginous action and framed location shooting as a semiautonomous attraction, rather than as a mere setting for narrative events. Significantly, while some sites highlighted in advertisements were known for their dramatic scenery (such as the Pão de Açúcar and the Tijuca and Gávea neighborhoods), most were residential neighborhoods firmly associated either with the elites or working classes, or, as one advertisement put it, "high society and the 'bas fonds.'"[104] The *O Imparcial* reviewer's summary of *Os mistérios do Rio de Janeiro* notes that Prince Djalmo resides in the traditional neighborhood of Cosme Velho, while advertisements list the film's locations as "Tijuca, Pão de Açúcar, Gávea, Furnas [the caverns located in Tijuca], Santa Teresa, Guanabara Bay, Leme, Copacabana, Ipanema, Fluminense Football Club, Jockey Club."[105] The film also featured "the Botequim da Revira," a tavern in the working-class neighborhood of Saúde described as "authentic."[106] The remainder of the sites listed are either located in the city's wealthy southern zone (Leme, Copacabana, Ipanema), which had been expanded in the urban reforms of the previous decade, or in older neighborhoods like Santa Teresa, Cosme Velho, and Laranjeiras, known for their historic mansions. The athletic venues mentioned were also spaces for elite diversions; Jeffrey Needell cites the Jockey Club in particular as a point of rendezvous for the upper classes.[107]

While also capitalizing on an imaginary of Rio de Janeiro as a divided city, publicity for *A quadrilha do esqueleto* promised a grittier approach to the capital's lower depths. One advertisement emphasized that the film's "plot, images, types, landscapes, in short, everything [was] genuinely carioca."[108] In an interview in *A Noite*, one of the directors of Veritas described the release as "a crime film, of a kind that pleases everyone, like the police blotter in their newspaper. The company preferred to debut in this way, because we wanted to reproduce onscreen some very characteristic aspects of Rio de Janeiro."[109] In a phrase that strongly evokes French serials like *Fantômas* and *Les vampires*, exhibited in the capital in 1915 and 1916, the director goes on to comment, "It would doubtless be easy to make films with terrifying bandits, who commit holdups with black sacks over their heads. But that is for other milieus; we wanted to produce excitement only with our types, our habits, our police, our milieu, in short."[110] To a greater extent than *Os mistérios do Rio de Janeiro*, publicity for *A quadrilha do esqueleto* highlighted the film's grounding in the local context. An advertisement listing the actors and their roles cited a number of nonprofessionals among their ranks, including "patrons of the Hunchback's Tavern (authentic), reporters (one authentic), civil guards (authentic), police, passersby, etc."[111] In an interview given about the film, the director admitted that the barroom where the "authentic" patrons gathered was reconstructed in their studio, but that the clients were real, and given copious amounts to drink to render the scene more convincing.[112] An advertisement for *A quadrilha do esqueleto* boasted that it showcased the following locations.

> A great part of the Quinta da Boa Vista [a large park in the northern section of the city, originally part of the grounds of the imperial palace], the Misericordia neighborhood, showing the ruins that exist in front of the Central Market, a beautiful section of the garden in the Plaza of the Republic, the great extension of Conde do Bomfim Street, various sections of Tijuca, Pão de Açúcar and its proud Aerial Way, the secular ruins of Brás de Pina, about which there is an interesting controversy and where a lovely garden will be constructed, the House of Detention, with its corridors and cells, innumerable city streets, various private residences, etc., etc.[113]

Although there is some overlap in the sights shown by the two simultaneously released films (Tijuca, Sugarloaf Mountain), *A quadrilha do esqueleto* focuses principally on working-class neighborhoods in the northern zone of the city and, intriguingly, on a pair of ruins, one of which served as the bandits' hideout in the film, and both of which were slated for demolition, according to the film's director.[114] The use of these ruins was likely an inexpensive way to add a sense of atmosphere bolstered by press discourses: according to *A Noite*, a "gang of telegraph wire thieves" had recently been apprehended there.[115] Yet the ruins also would have inscribed into the film vestiges of the destructive, as well as constructive, processes that transformed Rio de Janeiro in the first decade of the twentieth century, which has been described as "the era of demolitions."[116]

Alongside this interest in ruins, *A quadrilha do esqueleto* showcased the modern transportation technologies that were continuing to transform daily experience in Brazil's then capital. According to Pedro Lima, spectators were particularly impressed with a scene in which an automobile appeared to crush a character's leg, an effect accomplished with the help of the journalist Inácio de Carvalho, who had suffered an amputation and used a prosthetic leg.[117] A vertiginous chase sequence was staged on the gondola used to transport sightseers to the top of Sugarloaf Mountain, which had been opened to the public in 1912. Even as the high-wire pursuit recalls the dangerous stunts of imported serials, it highlighted a distinctly modern feature of Rio de Janeiro's cityscape. Like moving images themselves, the gondola produced an exciting mobile view by means of modern machinery. In 1917, the ride was still being advertised (albeit at "reduced prices") as a "splendid, enchanting, refreshing excursion" that offered "the most thrilling panorama!!"[118] The gondola was thus presented not only as an engineering feat, but also as a means of making the local landscape spectacularly and even sensationally visible, a project that the serial-influenced local films shared.

Despite their shared dialogue with imported serial films, *Os mistérios do Rio de Janeiro* and *A quadrilha do esqueleto* positioned themselves in distinct ways within global imaginaries of war, criminality, and technology, and within local discourses and iconographies that sketched spatial and class divisions within Brazil's modernizing capital. The films also differed in regard to the precariousness of their production: plans to produce *Os mistérios do Rio de Janeiro* as a serial never materialized, whereas the producers of *A quadrilha do esqueleto* completed two additional releases, a comedy and a drama written by a prominent local author.

Premiering on the same day, both films were received enthusiastically by audiences. *A quadrilha do esqueleto* was shown simultaneously in two of the most elegant cinemas in Rio, the Avenida and the Ideal, while *Os mistérios do Rio de Janeiro* was exhibited in the slightly less prestigious Cine Palais, owned by Mattos. On 28 October, the final day of exhibition for *Os mistérios do Rio de Janeiro*, an advertisement for the film boasted that "defying the inclement weather, [the film] has attracted to the Cine Palais 13,964 persons, anxious

FIG 4.5 "A Pursuit on the Pão de Açúcar's Aerial Way" in *A quadrilha do esqueleto*. *A Noite*, 24 October 1917. Acervo da Fundação Biblioteca Nacional, Brasil.

to acclaim the ingenious creation of the prince of Brazilian novelists."[119] Reports and publicity for *A quadrilha do esqueleto* did not cite exact audience numbers, but provided verbal and visual evidence of massive crowds. Ticket sales were temporarily suspended in both the cinemas exhibiting the film, and in "the Ideal, the attendance was so great, that the public had to wait in the street, blocking traffic, and making necessary the police's intervention to regulate the circulation."[120] The pressure of the crowd was even reported to have broken a mirror in the Ideal's waiting room.[121] *A quadrilha do esqueleto* was exhibited in a series of neighborhood cities and the nearby city of Petrópolis through 4 November, eventually screening at ten cinemas in São Paulo and one in the port city of Santos.[122] *Os mistérios do Rio de Janeiro* received a more modest exhibition in São Paulo, appearing in two cinemas over four days in April.[123]

A quadrilha do esqueleto and *Os mistérios do Rio de Janeiro* won a place alongside the customary foreign offerings of these movie theaters; yet their relatively brief runs suggest the sweeping transformation of the infrastructure of distribution and exhibition after 1911. Despite intermittent discussions attempts to establish self-sustaining film production, local productions remained marginal in local markets, even if they were greeted with intense (if fleeting) popular excitement. Like regional productions of the 1920s, they were the product of semi-amateur initiatives that had difficulty achieving continuity. In the end, neither company was able to effectively build on the audience excitement generated by serial narratives, which itself was short-lived.[124]

While local efforts at filmmaking failed to achieve the industrial regularity of serial film production and distribution evident in the United States, the particularities of local exhibition and the local circulation of paraliterary texts provided openings for local writers and filmmakers to insert their own locally inflected narratives. The adaptation of serial structure and conventions in Rio de Janeiro constitutes one of the most productive sites of Brazilian film culture's engagement with the presence of American and European cinema in the teens. Negotiating the new rhythms of urban life and the nation's involvement in the First World War *Os mistérios do Rio de Janeiro*, *A quadrilha do esqueleto*, and *Le film du diable* established a dialogue with popular serial forms that simultaneously reveled in and critiqued the violence of modernity, from criminal acts and mechanical disaster to a global military conflict that had been fostered and intensified by new technologies. Although these efforts were limited and short-lived, their legacy was keenly felt in Rio and São Paulo in the early twenties, and increasingly outside these major cities in the remainder of the decade.

Coda: The Afterlife of the Serial Craze

Prolific filmmaker Luiz de Barros, who had shot a number of society dramas and literary adaptations in the teens, directed a series of sensational melodramas that became some of the more successful efforts at film production in Brazil in the early twenties. Barros had been approached by would-be director Antônio Tibiriça, who was later involved in the production of sensationalistic features in the late twenties, with the project that became the adventure film *A jóia maldita* (*The Accursed Gem*).[125] Filmed in Santos in 1920 by the camera operator Paulino Botelho, who had shot reconstructions of real-life crimes in the early teens, *A jóia maldita* depicted the exploits of a "jewel thief

who reaches the extreme of robbing his own wife and becomes a fugitive."[126] In her comments on the film, the historian Maria Rita Galvão observes that it was composed of a "series of incidents and peripeties that motivate the display of landscapes of São Paulo, Alto de Santana, and Rio de Janeiro," suggesting that *A jóia maldita* extended the combination of frenetic action with picturesque views that appears to have characterized the serial-influenced films of the late teens.[127] A surviving still suggests it drew on the fantastic disguises and exoticized iconographies of the American adventure serial: an actor in old-age makeup holding a dagger is shown entering a room through the window, while a second actor holds him at bay with a vaguely Oriental-looking urn from which steam is pouring.[128]

The following year, Barros directed *O cavaleiro negro* (*The Black Rider*), which featured a physically dynamic female heroine reminiscent of an American serial queen. The local actress Antonia Denegri performed stunt scenes that wedded physical virtuosity with precarious technological mastery. A retrospective account published in the fan magazine *Selecta* in 1927 recounts a humorous anecdote about the film's production, noting that Barros "wanted to make [a film] where he could apply some cinematic 'trucs.' He wanted to show that not only the Americans, but he, too, could make use of all these effects."[129] The article provides considerable detail about the artificial rain and wind used to stage a scene where the hero and heroine ride through a torrential rainstorm, noting an oversight that spoiled the illusion: a dust trail visible in the wake of the galloping horse. Although here the term *truc* apparently refers to the special effects used to create the false rainstorm, it is closely linked to a physical exploit performed by Denegri—the "vertiginous gallop" on horseback.

In another article published in the magazine, which claims that "Antonia Denegri admires the cinema, because it has an infinity of sensations," the actress recounts how one of her stunts went dreadfully awry, evoking the tales of real-life threats to life and limb suffered by American stars of adventure melodramas. During a staged tumble off her horse, Denegri overshot the spot that had been prepared in advance to break her fall, suffering serious injuries.[130] These narratives linked Denegri's performances to the earlier press coverage of American serial queens, which Jennifer Bean argues inaugurated a model of stardom grounded in a "semiotics of catastrophe," advancing the realistic imperative of the cinematic medium by displacing spectatorial attention from the mechanical and economic machinery of filmmaking onto the physical peril endured by the "extraordinary body" of the film star.[131] Yet the notion of the truc invoked in coverage of film production in the 1920s implied a more self-conscious relationship between the physical virtuosity of actors and cinematic special effects. Given the economic and practical obstacles faced by filmmakers in Brazil, special effects became pivotal to claims of technological proficiency.

Barros's most elaborate foray into adventure melodrama came in 1924 with *Hei de vencer* (*I Will Triumph*), which was celebrated in the press as a victory for Brazilian film production because of its risky stunts. The film's hero, Alberto, a would-be journalist, must unravel the mystery of a woman's murder when the police accuse his friend of the crime. Alberto begins to investigate the victim's husband, triggering a series of sensational chase sequences. In one of these scenes, the aspiring reporter follows the husband by jumping onto the moving car in which he is traveling, later leaping from the roof onto an overpass near the train station. Alberto later tracks the husband to an airfield where he is attempting to make his escape, resulting in an airborne pursuit during which the villain is accidentally killed.[132] *Selecta* described *Hei de vencer* as "a film of sensational adventures, such as an actor's passage from one airplane to another at a height of 800 meters, and the 'barrel roll of death,' filmed inside the vehicle itself, which serves to prove that among us, as well, there is no lack of courage and perseverance to obtain what is desired."[133] Another reviewer in the magazine commented, "The scenes with the airplanes are one of the best parts of the film, we never imagined this would be done here!," signaling how the physical and technical exploits of film production became a point of pride for local audiences.[134] Signaling the appeal of daring stunts across genres, a thrilling aviation sequence also played a prominent role in the sentimental melodrama *Quando elas querem* (*When Women Love*, 1925), shot in São Paulo by an Italian immigrant who called himself E. C. Kerrigan.[135] In the film's climax, the heroine enlists her friend, a female pilot, in order to reach a wealthy suitor (who has the power to save her father's business) before he leaves the country on a steamer. The gondola on the Pão de Açúcar would make an appearance in another romantic drama made in Rio de Janeiro the same year, *A esposa do solteiro* (*The Bachelor's Wife*, Paulo Benedetti).[136] As the film's heroine is about to commit suicide by jumping from the summit, the hero leaps onto the outside of the moving car from a high pole in order to reach the top in time to save her.

Although their impact on film production outside Rio de Janeiro and São Paulo was not fully felt until the mid-1920s, serials and adventure melodramas were shown in regional capitals and smaller cities shortly after their rise to popularity in the capital in 1916. *Les vampires* was shown in Porto Alegre, capital of the southern state of Rio Grande do Sul in 1916, followed by *Os mistérios de Nova York* in 1917. The exhibition of serials in the city was often accompanied by the publication of tie-in novelizations.[137] Following the exhibition in Recife of *Os mistérios de Nova York* in the final months of 1916, the serials *O enigma da máscara* (*The Iron Claw*) and *A malha rubra* (*The Red Circle*) were shown in weekly sessions of two episodes each, concurrently with the daily publication of their novelizations in the newspapers *A Provincia* and *A Ordem*, respectively.[138] The series *The Hazards of Helen*, exhibited in Rio with the title *A mulher audaciosa* (*The Audacious Woman*), was shown in Recife beginning in May 1918, accompanied by summaries printed in a pamphlet distributed free to spectators at the Teatro Moderno.[139] While exhibitions of serials in regional capitals were not always timely, they do appear to have enjoyed considerable popularity in these cities by the late teens.

While the appeal of serials waned quickly in Rio de Janeiro after 1918, the dynamics of film distribution in Brazil, dependent on often inadequate transportation networks, kept action-oriented films like serials and westerns on movie screens in areas of the northeast, north, and the interior of southeast and central states well into the 1920s. In the following chapter, I examine the cultural afterlife of "outmoded" forms of adventure melodrama in regions outside Rio de Janeiro and São Paulo, which were viewed as the privileged sites of Brazilian modernity. In semi-amateur efforts at establishing film production across the country, the spectacles of violence and technology linked with these genres were staged in local landscapes, asserting, like the would-be serials made in the capital in the late teens, a physical virtuosity and technological mastery felt to be quintessentially modern.

Chapter 5

REGIONAL MODERNITIES

Sensational Cinema
Outside Rio de Janeiro and
São Paulo, 1923–1930

In October 1924, nine months into a campaign promoting Brazilian cinema led by the journalists Pedro Lima and Adhemar Gonzaga, the Rio de Janeiro-based magazine *Selecta* made a curious distinction regarding the correspondence received from aspiring film actors. The magazine notes that such letters "principally come from the interior of the states. It seems the film, there in the hinterlands [*sertão*], turns the heads of lots of people, much more than here in Rio."[1] Implying that fans outside Brazil's rapidly growing cities were uniquely susceptible to dubious fantasies of stardom, this comment highlights how an imagined geography that divided the nation's cosmopolitan capital from its provincial sertão shaped both filmmaking and discourses on cinema in the 1920s. In the pages of Brazilian fan magazines that chronicled filmmaking activity across the country, clear tensions emerge between carioca critics' efforts to foster forms of film culture they viewed as modern in the service of national progress, and the efforts of enthusiasts outside Rio and São Paulo to stage local and regional modernities through film production.

Historical evidence indeed suggests that producing and appearing in films held a particularly powerful appeal for Brazilians living outside the rapidly growing cities of Rio de Janeiro and São Paulo. During the 1920s, groups of semi-amateur film enthusiasts produced fiction features in regional capitals and small towns, from Porto Alegre in the far south to Recife in the northeast, including the city of Campinas in São Paulo and several towns in the state of Minas Gerais. Even as urbanization and industrialization concentrated much of

Brazil's economic growth in the southeast, the production of regional films, as I will call them, outstripped the combined output of Rio and São Paulo in the period. Produced under great economic and technical constraints, these films constituted utopian attempts by working- and lower-middle-class actors, directors, and camera operators to actively participate in the technological modernity embodied by the cinema. Presenting their efforts as sources of civic pride, regional filmmakers often enlisted financial support from wealthy locals. In some cases, their efforts attracted the attention of prominent politicians, including the governors of the states of Pernambuco and Minas Gerais.[2]

As Paulo Carneiro da Cunha Filho argues in the case of filmmaking in Recife in the 1920s, the mere "fact of there being cinema, of there being a technological visual culture" was marshaled as proof of local modernization; independent of commercial or critical success, film production enacted "the inclusion of those on periphery of capitalism as subjects of the gaze."[3] In this sense, regional films show clear affinities to the early genre of the "local film," which has received a growing amount of scholarly attention over the past decade.[4] Produced in close proximity to the intended site of consumption, local films offered audiences the pleasure of recognizing familiar spaces, their neighbors, or even themselves onscreen. Emphasizing the continuing significance of local filmmaking practices after the early cinema period, Martin L. Johnson argues that the local film relies on "place recognition, which combines audience recognition of local people and spaces with [multiple] interpretative frameworks" for assigning meanings to place.[5] Yet while regional productions held special appeal for local spectators, film enthusiasts often expressed ambitions to exhibit their films on the state, regional, and national level. As no clear center of film production had emerged in Brazil in the 1920s, cities and towns could aspire (however improbably) to become "the Los Angeles of Brazil" or "Hollywood in Miniature."[6] Reporting on developments across the country, illustrated magazines framed regional filmmakers' efforts as steps toward the forging of a national cinema. Identifying shared strategies for constructing cinematic visions of local modernity among geographically dispersed groups of filmmakers, I define regional films as texts that highlight their perceived position outside the geographic, economic, or cultural "centers" of a nation, laying claim both to local difference and to belonging to modernity. Presenting the sites of their production as both picturesque and economically productive, most Brazilian regional films of the 1920s wove images of landscapes, industry, and agricultural production into action-packed narratives. These productions drew heavily on the conventions of imported adventure melodramas, particularly westerns and serials. Considered outdated in major urban areas, these films' emphasis on physical dynamism and technical mastery (embodied by stunt sequences and special effects) led them to be received elsewhere as quintessentially cinematic and uniquely modern.

Contemporary but rarely intersecting with the modernist and regionalist literary movements debated by intellectual elites in the 1920s, the efforts of regional filmmakers took on special significance in locations where modernization was experienced as delayed or interrupted, often as a consequence of unstable economic growth driven by the export of agricultural commodities.[7] The links between uneven development and the local desires for modernity manifest in regional films are signaled by the term used to describe them by Brazilian film historians: *ciclos regionais* (regional cycles). Describing successive waves of filmmaking in each city, as production companies quickly went bankrupt and new ones emerged, the term evokes the boom-and-bust cycles of export commodity production that fueled Brazil's economic expansion in the nineteenth and early twentieth centuries, before the collapse of the coffee boom due to worldwide economic depression. These developments helped trigger the fall of the Republic and Getúlio Vargas's rise to power in the Revolution of 1930.

As the term *regional cycles* suggests, historians of Brazilian silent cinema have highlighted the discontinuous character of filmmaking in the 1920s, attributed to the structural disadvantages faced by domestic productions in the face of Hollywood's market dominance (by 1922, 80 percent of the films shown in Rio de Janeiro were of North American origin).[8] The film historian Maria Rita Galvão writes, "Perhaps better than any other, the phenomenon of the regional cycles typifies a situation of underdevelopment in film production. This production does not present itself as a straight line; it does not effectively constitute a movement. Outside of Rio and São Paulo . . . Brazilian silent cinema is made up of experiences that exhausted themselves, isolated from each other and in most cases mutually ignorant of each other."[9] Yet further research, including recent scholarship that reevaluates the regional films of the 1920s, suggests that the phenomenon of regional production in the 1920s cannot be reduced to a marker of cultural dependency conditioned by neocolonial economic exchanges.[10] Galvão's statements exemplify a critical trap observed by Ana M. López, who notes that linear narratives of development are unable to account for the trajectories of silent cinema in Latin America. López argues that "because of temporal ambiguity and asynchronicity, teleological narratives of evolution become mired in dead ends and failed efforts and do not do justice to the circuitous routes of Latin American modernity."[11] In this chapter, I trace the "circuitous routes" of cinematic modernity in Brazil in the 1920s, marked by the drawn-out circulation of imported adventure melodramas through national territory, and the adaption of these films' conventions in secondary cities across the nation.

Dismissed by carioca journalists as hopelessly outdated by 1920, action-packed genres were closely associated with marginal exhibition spaces—working-class neighborhood movie theaters, geographically isolated cities and towns—where they circulated well into the decade, functioning as highly generative models for regional films. (By contrast with the United States, in Brazil serials were not initially linked with working-class audiences.)[12] Closely associated with the practice of outdoor location shooting, which was attractive to regional filmmakers because it showcased local scenery and reduced the need for studios and artificial lighting, these genres also offered abundant opportunities for stunts and special effects in their depictions of violence and physical peril. In the face of technological limitations—camera equipment that was decades old or intended for amateur use, inadequate film stock, improvised facilities for developing and editing—stunts and special effects asserted local camera operators' mastery of a highly spectacular mode of cinematic realism that relied on "the affective sensation of realistic thrills . . . grounded in the practice of on-location shooting."[13] Yet rather than simply utilizing exterior spaces as "setting" (rendering place a backdrop for, and function of, narrative events), as was customary in Hollywood cinema, Brazilian regional films often foreground "landscape" as a semiautonomous attraction, which may be granted the capacity to temporarily suspend the narrative through the exercise of a spectator's contemplative gaze, as Martin Lefebvre argues.[14] Both press accounts and surviving footage from regional films suggest the appeal of scenic views, most immediately for local spectators, but potentially for national audiences as well.

In some cases, regional films' formal strategies—particularly slow panning shots displaying outdoor spaces—encouraged the contemplation of landscape in a manner akin to the spectatorial address of filmed travelogues.[15] At the same time, extratextual discourses also primed audience members to "direct the 'landscape gaze' onto the narrative spaces of fiction films despite the absence of strategies or intentions to make them autonomous."[16] Fan magazines discussed Brazil's picturesque scenery as a natural resource on which film production could capitalize, while newspapers framed local sites as sources of civic pride. Regional films also made use of cinematic codes associated in other national contexts with industrial and educational films. In addition to incorporating local agriculture and industry as plot elements, some regional films devoted considerable screen time to displaying production processes. In this sense, regional fiction features incorporated conventions linked to the *filme natural* (nonfiction film), a category that encompassed travelogues and sponsored promotional films. Often dismissively described as the *filme de cavação* (cavação literally means digging; figuratively, it connotes hustling), the filme natural was harshly criticized by many Brazilian film critics, both because they viewed nonfiction as incapable of attracting a mass audience, and because unstaged images of daily life in Brazil (especially footage that displayed the country's large population of African and indigenous descent) could undercut elites' desires to present Brazil as an industrialized and Europeanized nation.[17]

Regional films' articulation of landscape and action—panoramic shots of local scenery minimally integrated with the narrative, dynamic chase and fight scenes—often parallels the oppositions between rural and urban space that structure many of their plots. At a moment when 70 percent of Brazilians still lived in the countryside, urban imaginaries and experiences took on powerful associations with modernity.[18] In productions that adapt "semantic elements" of the Hollywood western, such as *João da Mata* (*John of the Bush*, Amilcar Alves, 1923), produced in the city of Campinas, and *Revezes* (*Reversals*, Chagas Ribeiro, 1927), made in Recife, violent clashes between courageous heroes and villainous landowners evoke the residual forms of power exercised by land-owning elites in an industrializing Brazil.[19] Regional films influenced by crime and adventure serials, including *Retribuição* (*Retribution*, Gentil Roiz, Recife, 1925) and *Tesouro perdido* (*Lost Treasure*, Humberto Mauro, Cataguases, 1927), focus on suspenseful scenes and daring stunts, while productions like *Mocidade louca* (*Mad Youth*, Campinas, Felipe Ricci, 1927) and *Entre as montanhas de Minas* (*Between the Mountains of Minas* [Gerais], Belo Horizonte, Manoel Talon, 1928) integrate thrilling displays of transportation technology into romantic plotlines.

Sensational scenes often showcased social practices associated with modern models of femininity (the figure of the *melindrosa*, a "modern girl" analogous to the flapper, was often placed at the wheel of an automobile), in addition to acts of male aggression that signaled a need to reform modern masculinity. In alternating urban with rural settings, these films stage reconciliations between city and country through the formation of a heterosexual couple.[20] Sentimental and sensational elements both highlight, and tentatively resolve, the economic disparities heightened by capitalist industrialization. These romantic dramas are punctuated with a surprising number of scenes of murder, brutal beatings, and accidents, which seem to have been viewed by regional filmmakers as essential ingredients for fiction films. At the same time, depictions of violence staged confrontations between a desired modernization and modes of production and social organization seen as archaic.[21]

During the 1920s, industrialization and export commodity production, especially the cultivation of coffee in Brazil's southeast, fostered growing divisions between rural and urban spaces and between geographic regions. As Marly Rodrigues observes, "The expansion of capitalism in Brazil . . . the construction of railroads, the opening of new areas of coffee cultivation, the concentration of labor power, the growth of electrical potential, of the industrial sector and of cities, sealed the distinction between the south and the other regions of the country."[22] Economic prospects were particularly disheartening in the north and the northeast, where the principal agricultural products (rubber in the Amazon, sugar on the northeastern coast) were no longer competitive on the global market and did not enjoy the protectionist measures often granted to the coffee plantations of the southeast, whose owners were key power players in the First Republic.[23] According to Durval Muniz de Albuquerque Jr., the 1920s witnessed the emergence of a new imagined geography of the northeast as a space of grinding poverty and drought starkly opposed to the prosperous south and particularly São Paulo, which emerged as "a highly differentiated space as a result of such patterned developments as industrialization, urbanization and immigration from Europe, as well as the effects of the abolition of slavery," which reshaped Brazil's labor market.[24] He attributes this "invention of the Northeast" to the emergence of new modes of nationalist discourse, particularly modernist writers' efforts to forge a unified national tradition by drawing on forms of popular culture identified with varied regions.[25]

Although the discursive opposition between the stricken northeast and the industrializing south functioned as a key trope of regionalist discourses in the 1920s, anxieties surrounding economic decline were present in multiple regions. Cunha Filho argues that film production in Recife, a center of economic and political power in the colonial period that declined as Brazil's sugar economy waned in the eighteenth and early nineteenth centuries, responded to a profound "melancholia" linked to the city's struggles to effectively modernize and retain transatlantic trade.[26] Even in the wealthy and political powerful states of Rio de Janeiro, São Paulo, and Minas Gerais, which dominated Brazilian politics during the Republic, the cultivation of coffee had depleted the soil in some areas by the late nineteenth century, plunging previously prosperous locales into economic stagnation. In his 1919 story collection *Cidades mortas* (*Dead Towns*), the writer Monteiro Lobato describes coffee-growing areas of the state of São Paulo experiencing premature decline, where growth had stagnated before modernization could fully arrive. "Progress in Brazil," Lobato writes, "is nomadic and subject to sudden attacks of paralysis."[27] Paulo Emílio Salles Gomes contends that a desire for technological modernity in the face of economic stagnancy motivated the filmmaking activities of Humberto Mauro, a key figure of both silent and sound cinema in Brazil who directed three features in the small city of Cataguases in Minas Gerais.[28] Although some scholars suggest that these descriptions of decline in coffee-growing zones are exaggerated, the volatility of economic growth does appear to have shaped perceptions of uneven modernization across Brazil's regions.[29]

Within this context of unstable and unevenly distributed economic expansion, the size and prosperity of the cities and towns where regional films were produced varied considerably. In the late twenties, a number of films were made in Porto Alegre in Rio Grande do Sul in Brazil's extreme south, where cattle raising was complemented by food production and other profitable economic activities. Many regional productions were shot in the states of São Paulo and Minas Gerais, considered part of Brazil's prosperous southeast. Campinas, the second-largest city in the state of São Paulo, had expanded apace with the coffee boom, though without equaling the state capital's vertiginous growth. Films shot wholly or partially in Belo Horizonte, the recently constructed capital of Minas Gerais, including *Entre as montanhas de Minas* and Humberto Mauro's *Sangue mineiro* (*Blood of Minas Gerais*, 1929), intersected with a project of regional modernization through urban development. The organization of the city on an orderly grid provided a symbolic break with the colonial past and its baroque architecture, embodied by the former capital, Ouro Preto.[30] In addition to these filmmaking activities in Belo Horizonte and Cataguases, production took place in small towns across Minas Gerais, including Ouro Fino, Pouso Alegre, and Guaranésia.

Just as the economic prosperity of sites of regional production varied, so did the technical sophistication of the films themselves, which ranged from the beautifully photographed melodramas of Humberto Mauro to the series of films made in Recife, whose visual language fails to conform to the continuity editing codes that were internationally dominant in the period. Whether marshaled to display an emerging urban modernity or to counteract a sense of stalled economic development, regional films worked to stage local progress in the face of uneven modernization. A suggestive review of the lost film *Alma gentil* (*Kind Soul*, Antonio Dardes Netto), produced in Campinas in 1924, signals how regional films might serve both as visible evidence of local modernization, and as pedagogical tools that could aid viewers in negotiating incipient social and economic transformations. A local journalist describes the film, which narrated the love affair between a shepherd who rescues an heiress and her uncle from drowning and later follows her into the city to continue the courtship, as "an easy narrative [*novela*], within the reach of any public, and very much of the moment [*de atualidade*] in this time of transition through which we are passing, from village life to the accelerated existence that progress imposes on great centers."[31] Considering that the description of Campinas as one of Brazil's "great centers" was something of an overstatement, the review suggests how the film might have portrayed, but also helped invent, experiences of a modernization that had yet to be fully realized.

While they faced considerable obstacles to national distribution, many regional films were received enthusiastically (though not uncritically) in the cities of their production as thrilling demonstrations of physical and technological virtuosity on the level of their plots and cinematic technique. These productions refashioned an index of local "backwardness"—a temporal lag in film distribution and exhibition, signaled by the presence of imported serials and westerns—into a visible sign of regional modernity in the form of adventure melodramas that were viewed as both emphatically local and quintessentially cinematic. A handful of films made in Rio and São Paulo in the 1920s also incorporated daring stunts: most spectacularly, a foiled suicide attempt on the Pão de Açúcar gondola in *A esposa do solteiro* (*The Bachelor's Wife*, Paulo Benedetti, 1925), and a last-minute plane ride in *Quando elas querem* (*When Women Love*, E. C. Kerrigan, 1925). Yet the prominence of elements of adventure melodrama in films made in Recife, Porto Alegre, Campinas, Cataguases, and elsewhere suggests that action-oriented genres resonated most powerfully on the economic and geographic margins of Brazil.

Although their production companies were financially precarious and usually short-lived, regional filmmakers implicitly contested the cultural centrality of Rio de Janeiro and São Paulo by aspiring to transform their cities and towns into hubs of film production, even as they often aligned their efforts with carioca publications that called for the consolidation of a national film

FIG 5.1 A publicity still for the melodrama *Alma gentil* (1924) shows a daring rescue. *Selecta,* 7 March 1925. Acervo Cinemateca Brasileira/SaV/MinC.

industry. The fan magazines *Selecta, Para Todos . . .* , and *Cinearte* presented themselves as both promoters and arbiters of domestic film production. Their silent-era campaign in favor of Brazilian cinema proved highly influential in other periodicals, particularly their well-known slogan "Every Brazilian film should be seen." Gonzaga and Lima carried on a lively correspondence with regional filmmakers, and the magazines' pages became a clearinghouse for news, gossip, and publicity stills relating to filmmaking activities across Brazil. In monthly columns on Brazilian cinema, which were first published in *Selecta* and *Para Todos . . .* in early 1924 and later appeared in the magazine *Cinearte* (founded in 1926), the two journalists sought to mold regional films in accordance with aesthetic criteria shaped by their familiarity with North American fan magazines and their viewing experiences in Rio de Janeiro's well-served exhibition market.[32] The magazines also defended standards of film exhibition modeled on U.S. practices, advocating the construction of lavish movie palaces in Rio de Janeiro (a goal that came to fruition in Cinelândia, a complex of theaters built by impresario Francisco Serrador) and the timely release of Hollywood "superproductions" across the nation.

Hailed by these Rio de Janeiro fan magazines as both a sign of national modernization and a tool of national propaganda, film production in Brazil was conceived as part of a broader program to foster a modern film culture. In a typical statement from 1928, Lima calls for

> a serious cinema, with criteria, with a story and acting, on a par with our environment, our possibilities, our natural beauties . . . not only to create a most profitable industry, but to bring civilization to the most recondite region of our territory, conquering all distances with a single sentiment of nationality, fortifying national unity in a single conviction, and making us known, admired, and respected abroad.[33]

This rather dizzying list of fiction film's possibilities indicates the interconnected ambitions and desires attached to cinema in the period. In addition to reaping profits at the box office, fiction features should stage a desirable image of Brazil as both picturesque and visibly modern (for the journalists, this meant industrialized and racially white) for spectators abroad. At the same time, cinema should facilitate national solidarity and progress by overcoming geographic distance and regional backwardness. In this passage and elsewhere in the pages of *Cinearte*, cinema was discussed as a means of modernizing social practices (through exposure to the fashions and habits portrayed in Hollywood films) and as a vehicle for producing and disseminating knowledge about Brazil's diverse regions. Yet as the campaign against the *filme natural* signals, carioca journalists often proved resistant to cinematic visions of Brazil articulated from its geographic margins, even when regional filmmakers sought to align themselves with the modernizing projects articulated by the fan magazines. Favoring polished production values, elaborate mise-en-scène, and careful attention to films' scripts and visual language, Lima and Gonzaga alternately praised regional filmmakers' ambition and criticized their final products as uncinematic: technically deficient, stylistically primitive, and reminiscent of outdated forms of adventure melodrama. At once intensely nationalistic and closely aligned with Hollywood aesthetics and production practices, the journalists' campaign often clashed with filmmaking initiatives that set their sights on primarily local and regional horizons.

Beginning with an account of the circulation of serials and westerns throughout Brazil in the 1920s, I analyze three groups of regional films that strategically adapted these imported genres to showcase local landscapes, to display thrilling special effects, and to give expression to the dynamics of modernization in Brazil. Working across geographic regions and in roughly chronological order, I analyze films made in Campinas and Recife that drew on the conventions of the western as they addressed problems of land distribution and legal impunity in rural settings, followed by features made in Recife and in Cataguases that mined the improbable plot devices and dynamic stunts of adventure serials in a bid for popular success, even as they emphasized scenic landscape views and made oblique references to a national past. Finally, focusing on the cases of Campinas and Belo Horizonte, I examine productions from the late twenties that emphasized dynamic female characters and modern men out of control, noting how melodramatic plots that united heterosexual couples moved between major metropolises and bucolic settings, suggesting that each of these spaces had a role to play in Brazil's emerging modernity.

Before turning my attention to regional film production, I trace the prolonged and productive circulation of Hollywood adventure melodramas outside first-run exhibition markets in the 1920s, arguing that they played a pivotal role in both the experience and the discursive construction of film culture outside Rio de Janeiro and São Paulo. Building on Kaveh Askari's approach to film exhibition in early twentieth-century Iran, "rather than thinking about the interruptions to circulation and damage to prints negatively, as incomplete steps towards more developed national film cultures," I contend that the prolonged circulation of serials and westerns outside Rio de Janeiro and São Paulo, cited by illustrated magazines as evidence of the backwardness of exhibition outside these metropolises, proved to be a productive point of departure for staging regional modernities.[34]

"Obscure Neighborhoods, Backward Towns": Mapping Regional Film Exhibition in the 1920s

In 1926, the illustrated magazine *A Pilhéria*, printed in Recife, published a story entitled "A estrela morta" (The Dead Star) that betrays a fascination with American adventure melodramas and their circulation through time and space. The story narrates a love affair between two film actors with distinctly American-sounding names: Dick, "the fearless *cowboy* [in English] who rode wild broncos, lassoed trains, drove off his enemies with blows, and made dreamy young ladies sigh," and Alice, "who worked in the 'dangerous' genre, as the principal figure of serial films [*films em série*], those that feature disasters and assaults at every turn."[35] After Alice is killed in a horseback-riding accident during shooting, Dick becomes obsessed with going to the movies to watch her screen appearances. Increasingly aware that "cinema had evolved, progressing incessantly, and new stars had emerged, making [everyone] forget the old," Dick wanders through "humble towns in the interior," attempting to catch an exhibition of Alice's now-outmoded films. He eventually happens upon a screening in the unnamed location where the story is set, but to his horror, as he watches, the film featuring his beloved catches fire and disintegrates before his very eyes.

Highlighting the shifting fortunes of film stars, genres, and formats, "The Dead Star" is also a self-conscious commentary on the dynamics of exhibition in Brazil's secondary and tertiary film markets, where the sensational melodramas in which the hero and heroine starred continued to be shown long after they were considered hopelessly outdated in Rio de Janeiro and São Paulo. The story's ending also suggests how film distribution in the interior highlighted the fragility of celluloid, which came to bear the physical traces of its drawn-out circulation through vast expanses of national territory. In 1924, the magazine *Selecta* complained about re-exhibitions of damaged film prints that had circulated through the country on the *linha* (line) before eventually being reprised in Rio de Janeiro. The magazine described film prints' trajectory through the urban margins and the geographic extremes of the country in suggestive terms that are worth quoting at length.

> Everyone knows that the film is damaged by its passage through the projection machine, to the extent that seeing it is no longer the same after some time in the cinemas on the outskirts [*arrabaldes*]. Even worse is seeing it in the interior, where not-always-capable hands do progressively more and more damage. When a film returns from its excursion on the "line," having passed through the interior of the central states, or when it comes from the North or South, and is tossed onto the platter—its miserable state is quite advanced. It is "rainy," that is, scratched along its length, giving a detestable impression in the light areas; pieces are missing, making the figures, from moment to moment, jump and change position (this as a consequence of the cuts made, due to the damage to the perforations of the film).[36]

In some cases, carioca magazines noted that exhibitors in markets perceived as less lucrative, such as the northeast, were often sent films that had already been heavily used during their runs in the Southeast.[37] Yet in other cases, journalists blamed the damage to prints on their passage through space and time as they circulated through the interior. An article in *Para Todos . . .* observes that "copies . . . pass from state to state, pass from town to town, from theater to theater, from projector to projector, losing a few centimeters here, a few meters there . . . these linhas depend on railway connections in central states, [with films] being exhibited at night and then on the following morning they are dispatched to a nearby town, on this interminable peregrination."[38] Reliant on existing transportation networks, this mode of exhibition was described as having an insistently linear character (as the term used to describe it suggests), in sharp contrast to the simultaneity of film releases in hundreds of first-run theaters in the United States. In comparison, according to *Para Todos* . . . , only two or three prints of each release were sent to Brazil, likely because the limited revenues that could be collected in rural areas did not make it cost-effective to purchase additional copies.[39] The magazines suggested that, given the limited number of prints in circulation and the vastness of Brazil's territory, this linear form of exhibition would inevitably lead to an experience of temporal delay. Although the dynamics of film distribution in Brazil were undoubtedly more complex than these descriptions suggest, with the business practices of local distributors and exhibitors leading to significant variations, discussions of the linha in carioca magazines indicate how the circulation of films was constructed as a marker of geographic isolation and backwardness.

Logically enough, Rio de Janeiro film magazines focused on exhibition in the capital, including its rivalry with São Paulo, which threatened to edge out Brazil's then capital as the most robust market and the city where imported films premiered. More intermittently, the magazines called for the reform of exhibition in the hinterlands, often in response to readers' reports on local entertainment scenes. As early as 1920, *Para Todos* . . . criticized exhibitors who "first, to the public of this city [Rio de Janeiro], and then through movie theaters spread through the vastness of the entire national territory, offer as modern works of 'yankee' cinema, real antiques exhumed from the museums of prehistory."[40] The following year, the magazine published a letter from a reader in the southern city of Curitiba, who noted that its reviews helped viewers identify and avoid outdated films.[41] Similarly, *Cinearte* stated in 1928 that readers used its illustrated summaries to identify scenes missing from the copies they saw locally, which had suffered "real mutilations that transform [them] into absolutely absurd things, without meaning, without sequence, without concatenation."[42] *Cinearte* blamed the heavy damage to films on exhibitors, particularly in the North, whom they claimed refused to pay competitive prices for newer programs, and argued that it was spectators' duty to demand

FIG 5.2 *Cinearte*'s feature "Cinemas e cinematografistas" displays exhibition spaces across Brazil—such as this movie theater in Belém in the Amazonian region—as signs of the nation's cultural modernity. *Cinearte*, 10 November 1926. Hemeroteca Digital Brasileira.

new releases from exhibitors, forcing them to negotiate more favorable distribution agreements.[43] The magazine framed a thriving, up-to-date exhibition culture as a sign of national modernity. Maintaining that "the progress of a country can be measured by its number of movie theaters," *Cinearte* showcased exhibition venues all over the country, whose photographs were published in a weekly section entitled "Cinemas e Cinematografistas" (Movie Theaters and Exhibitors).[44]

If these images of local movie theaters that appeared in the magazine were intended to demonstrate the progress of film exhibition in Brazil, letters from geographically dispersed readers preserve evidence of its irregularities and delays. In these sections, which either responded to readers' questions or (supposedly) reprinted their letters verbatim, clear distinctions emerge between the tastes of Rio de Janeiro journalists, who preferred romantic dramas with big budgets, and their widely scattered audience, who often (but not universally) viewed and enjoyed action-packed adventure melodramas. In these spaces of reader interaction, journalists constructed and enforced hierarchies of taste that linked serials and westerns to working-class and geographically isolated audiences. Suggesting both the geographic extension of its readership and the popularity of Hollywood westerns across the country, in 1919 *Para Todos*... reported on actor Tom Mix's marital status, "in response to hundreds of questions we have received from the capital and twenty Brazilian states, including faraway Acre," located on the border with Bolivia and Peru.[45] Despite many of its readers' enthusiasm for American adventure melodramas, by late 1920 *Para Todos*... had made clear its editors' distaste for serials. In a typical statement, the magazine declared, "We know nothing about serial films. We never watch this genre, which decidedly does not seduce us."[46] Considered outmoded in Rio de Janeiro's first-run venues, serials nevertheless dominated the programs of the city's suburban cinemas.[47]

While critics presented the exhibition of serials as a marker of the "backwardness" of local exhibition markets, readers manifested both frustration and enthusiasm with the presence of the format in local movie theaters. In a June 1923 editorial, *Para Todos*... harshly criticized the products of the French studio where Louis Feuillade directed serials like *Judex* (1916) and *Barrabas* (1919). The magazine declared, "The perfectly imbecilic Gaumont serials have deserted the Avenida [Rio Branco, Rio's central thoroughfare] in search of obscure neighborhoods, backward towns."[48] A year and a half later, a loyal *Para Todos*... correspondent in Recife, who used the pseudonym of "Cyclone Smith" (the hero of a serial starring Eddie Polo), made a number of observations about local film offerings, including the presentation of "various Gaumont serials" and the exhibition of Hollywood superproductions with a lag of as much as two years behind Rio de Janeiro.[49] Similarly, *Pearl of the Army*, exhibited in Brazil with the title *O correio de Washington*, was shown in Rio de Janeiro beginning in March 1918.[50] Almost exactly three years later, *Para Todos*... published a sonnet in praise of Pearl White by a reader in Belém, located near the mouth of the Amazon River in northern Brazil, which had been composed "on the occasion of the exhibition in this [state] capital of the serial film *O correio de Washington*."[51] This notice suggests both the degree to which exhibition in remote cities lagged behind that of southern capitals and the devotion to the star that persisted among fans.[52] Evidence of how the structure of serial films was reworked during their travels can also be found in the magazine's pages; in 1923, *Para Todos*... responded to an inquiry from a reader in the state of Paraíba in the northeast, exclaiming, "How delayed [*atrasados*] films are being exhibited, there! *Amotinação* [*Mutiny*] was a reduction of the serial film *O fantasma pardo* [*The Grey Ghost*]," a serial starring Eddie Polo that premiered in the United States in 1917.[53] Imported adventure melodramas arrived in northern Brazil not only with a considerable lag, but at times, significantly transformed.

Press discourses on the prolonged circulation of imported adventure melodramas in carioca magazines suggests how understandings of the western genre and the serial format often overlapped in the minds of critics, who associated North American cinema with fast-and-furious violence and action. In turn, this phenomenon helps account for the tendency of many regional films to mix syntactic elements associated with the serial (particularly its episodic structure, characterized by cliffhangers and abrupt narrative reversals) and the semantic elements of the western. In 1924, *Para Todos . . .* used the term *serial* (*film de séries*) to describe "*cow-boy* [in English] films with shootouts and chase scenes." Further deviating from understandings of the serial format developed in major film-producing countries, the magazine continues, "*The Count of Monte Cristo, Robinson Crusoe, Judex*, and *The Mysteries of New York* are not serials [*seriados*], they are novels [*romances*]."[54] Paradoxically, *Judex* and *The Mysteries of New York* in fact had a more properly serial structure than most westerns, as they were released in multiple installments.[55] Recalling their affinities to literary classics (some published in serial form), the magazine compares them to the novel, suggesting that they held greater cultural prestige than the series of action-packed westerns starring actors like Tom Mix and Buck Jones. Renewing perceived connections between the folhetim and serial cinema, the practice of publishing tie-in novelizations of serial films also persisted outside Rio and São Paulo throughout the 1920s. In January 1922, the first issue of the weekly Campinas publication *Cine-Jornal* published a cine-folhetim of Pathé's production of the *Three Musketeers*, although its synchronization with the screening of the film's episodes seems to have been short-lived.[56] As late as 1928, the comedic horror film *The Cat and the Canary* (Paul Leni, United States, 1927), advertised as a "sensational novel of love, adventures and mysteries," was accompanied by a tie-in published in installments in the *Diário de Notícias* in Porto Alegre.[57]

The magazine *Selecta* also assumed a close link between the multipart serial film and the series western, making some creative (though misleading) deductions about the development of film genres and formats in the United States. Although one- and two-reel westerns had in fact become popular in the United States by 1909, before the emergence of the serial format, *Selecta* concluded that it was the rise of the western that was responsible for the "decadence" of "adventures that left one's mind in suspense at the end of each episode" (serials). The journalist declares in reference to the latter, "This vulgar phase of cinema which still persists, for the consolation of a naïve public, improved its deplorable proportions somewhat, since it has reduced itself to its current length, which alone is a great victory, and has come to be shown in cinemas of abysmal category, always latecomers when it comes to accepting innovations."[58] The associations between "vulgar" action-oriented cinema, marginal exhibition spaces, and cultural "backwardness" could not be more clear. Indeed, by the mid-twenties, most Hollywood westerns were produced exclusively for second-run movie theaters in the United States; they had a long cultural afterlife in Brazil, where silent westerns were shown in the interior as late as 1941.[59]

The perceived connection between action-oriented genres and local "backwardness" was most often stressed by the journalists themselves. Yet readers also expressed dissatisfaction and desires for more recent releases. In 1923, a reader in Maceió, capital of the northeastern state of Alagoas, complained, "We have to put up with the pathetic whacks taken by Universal, the incorrigible mania of old Carl Laemmle for blows, bullets, and horseback rides. Serials, struggles, punches, and the eternal final kiss!"[60] Two years later, a reader in the town of Gravatá, located in the neighboring state of Pernambuco, expressed frustration with the local exhibition of serials (even as he praised the regional film *Jurando vingar* [*Swearing Revenge*, Ary Severo, 1925]).

> We have only one movie theater here, quite average, by the way. So we put up with the most irritating kind of filler. This theater has a mania for serials, and what serials! . . . [R]eal stinkers [*borracheiras*]. If it had a competitor, perhaps they would show good films, but it doesn't. . . . We have to bear with patience what it shows us. After all, we thank God, because it's the only amusement we have here on Sundays.[61]

For this reader, a lack of competition in the local entertainment scene led him to grudgingly accept the films offered. In the case of more robust exhibition markets, fans might evoke the negative connotations of serials and westerns as a means of making class-based distinctions between movie theaters. Aligning herself with the fan magazines' campaigns to improve exhibition culture, a female reader from Belo Horizonte wrote to complain that a local exhibitor had begun to show Paramount, First National, and UFA (Universum Film-Aktien) superproductions in a new movie theater located near two working-class neighborhoods. As a consequence, she writes, "the best families of Belo Horizonte society are forced to attend the new movie theater, sitting in the same rows as the riff-raff [*escória*] . . . people without composure who only understand the ridiculous chase scenes of Tom Mix and similar!"[62] While this letter sparked a series of indignant rebuttals by readers in Belo Horizonte, who defended the residents of the neighborhoods in question, its publication indicates that some members of the magazines' audience also viewed the presence and popularity of imported adventure melodramas as a marker of lower-class status and cultural backwardness.

Having traced the social meanings attached to the presence of imported adventure melodramas in the pages of illustrated magazines and on film screens outside Rio and São Paulo, I want to examine an inverse phenomenon: the marketing of a regional film, *O vale dos martírios* (*The Valley of Martyrdom*, Almeida Fleming, 1926), in a manner that attempted to reconcile the persistent appeal of the serial film with the imperative to modernize Brazilian film culture articulated by fan magazines. Produced in the small town of Pouso Alegre in Minas Gerais, this tale of star-crossed lovers menaced by the machinations of a villainous doctor recalled both serial films and melodramatic serial novels, especially in the scene of the heroine's race to the hero's rescue in an automobile, just before she collapses due to the effects of a poison. (Apparently dead, she is in fact unconscious, and narrowly escapes being buried alive.) While Salles Gomes compares these plot devices to "Italian and French folhetins," a promotional circular for the film recalls the marketing campaigns of serials like Gaumont's *Les vampires*, which sought to pique moviegoers' curiosity by withholding key details, in its use of a giant question mark that envelops a figure of a man on horseback with a cape concealing his face. The drawing's caption reads, "Heavy black clouds block the brilliance of the stars on a horrific night in whose shadow a mysterious figure will perpetrate a heinous crime! WHO CAN THIS MYSTERIOUS FIGURE BE? SEE *O Vale dos Martírios*."[63]

Despite hostility toward serials and westerns in carioca fan magazines, *O vale dos martírios*' affinities with these adventure melodramas did not prevent its producers from invoking the discourse of national progress through film production espoused in illustrated magazines. *Cinearte*'s slogans are quoted abundantly in the promotional circular, which claims that "the vertiginous action of some of its scenes, the dramatic paroxysms of which it is full, the tenderness of its romantic parts, the unexpected denouement of its sequences, all this makes 'O Vale dos Martírios' the true consecration of the

Brazilian film industry and a legitimate source of pride for every Brazilian whose heart thrills [*estremece*] for his fatherland." Here, nationalistic sentiments are themselves described as literally sensational—*estremece* means to "shudder" or "shiver." However, carioca critics proved skeptical of the film's narrative strategies. A reviewer in the newspaper *Correio da Manhã* judged *O vale dos martírios* "quite good for a work from a little town in the interior, where the lack of technical resources must be enormous," while lamenting that "the final scenes are a bit long and tend toward the serial genre, with forced and almost unbelievable situations."[64] While *Cinearte* praised the film's producers for their promotional initiative, the magazine lambasted the film for its "ridiculous story," noting that "its motifs are anticinematic, like the burial of the ingénue."[65] If *O vale dos martírios*'s publicity materials suggest how the conventions of adventure melodrama might be used to assert modernity in the face of profound technological limitations, the review indicates how these tropes became a point of contention between regional filmmakers and Rio de Janeiro journalists.

The working-class, "backward," and geographically marginal connotations attached to the serial and the western were transformed into markers of local progress by regional productions that capitalized on these imported films' emphasis on physical and technical virtuosity. Films produced in Campinas, Recife, and Porto Alegre appropriated conventions of the Hollywood western to integrate depictions of rural customs and local landscapes with dynamic action sequences. In some cases, these conventions were marshaled in a critique of the vestiges of an authoritarian social order. By contrast, other films made few concessions to the local context, generating debates surrounding the possibilities that imported adventure melodramas offered for regional production.

Picturesque Landscapes and Rural Villains: Reimagining the Western in Campinas and Recife, 1923–1927

In the first regional film to enjoy significant commercial success, *João da Mata,* produced in Campinas in 1923, idealized images of rural spaces are juxtaposed with exciting stunts and fight scenes. As suggested by the film's title (which translates to "John of the Bush"), *João da Mata* focuses on rural life, despite being produced in the city of Campinas, which had expanded into a sizeable city in the early twentieth century as it increasingly incorporated small-scale manufacturing into its economy. Despite these developments, the polarization between the interior and the metropolis seems to have resonated with the local writer Amilcar Alves, who wrote the play on which *João da Mata* was based in 1921, later adapting it to the screen with the help of the Phenix-Film production company, a group of local film enthusiasts. When Alves's play won a national contest sponsored by the Academia Brasileira de Letras (Brazilian Academy of Letters), the judges praised it for showing "an impressive piece of the true Brazil, with its good native people who are overrun and despoiled at every turn by the brutality of the intruders who come from the city to dispossess the legitimate landowners of the hinterland [*sertão*]."[66] While the play explicitly opposed wealthy city-dwellers to poor farmers, it also evoked the persistence in rural communities of *coronelismo*, the tendency of local political bosses (*coronéis*) drawn from the ranks of land-owning elites to exercise outsized political and economic influence, often reinforced by the extrajudicial use of violence.

The land dispute that drives the plot of *João da Mata* dramatized this so-cial conflict through a series of fight scenes that drew on the conventions of the American western. Lacking an official deed to the house where he and his mother live, the eponymous farmer (Angelo Forti) loses his property to the villainous coronel Viga (José Rodrigues), who bribes witnesses to provide false testimony. After the trial, the two become embroiled in a physical con-frontation; Viga then falsely accuses João of robbery. Fleeing to the state of Bahia in order to avoid imprisonment, João fortuitously discovers evidence there that the coronel is guilty of a previous robbery and murder. Returning to Campinas, João confronts Viga, leading to a final struggle. This sequence, one of a few surviving fragments of the film, is consistent with the visual language of most regional productions, which tend to use wide shot scales and static tableau framing.[67] A series of long shots, punctuated with a few medium shots and a single close-up of João, shows the two men grappling with each other in standing and prone positions. In the scene's conclusion, the police burst in to find João collapsed on top of Viga's corpse; the young farmer has beaten him to death unwittingly. In an intertitle, an official comments to João's mother, "Your son killed an extremely dangerous thief; he'll be acquitted," suggesting a reversal of the miscarriages of justice shown throughout the film.

Beyond its allusions to corruption in the handling of property disputes, *João da Mata* showcased local agriculture, emphasizing both the scenic ap-peal and the economic productivity of the region. Evoking picturesque views and sensational action side by side, an article about the film in *Para Todos* . . .

(most likely a promotional text inserted by request) listed its chief attractions as "the plantation houses and their well-observed interiors, the coffee groves and their details, the characters' costumes which do not plagiarize that of the American cowboy, the automobile accident and the real fight scenes, impeccably photographed." The same article praises *João da Mata*'s display of the "natural beauty that should characterize our films so that they have the double effect of appeal and propaganda," linking its strategies to press discourses that framed cinema as the ideal means for projecting a vision of Brazil as both picturesque and modern.[68]

In *João da Mata*, sensational scenes seem to have functioned both as a source of thrills and as a demonstration of the mastery of cinematic technique; in the press, they were often discussed as semiautonomous attractions with little connection to the plot. For example, the scene of the automobile accident, in which a car collides with the coronel's son, seems to have served little narrative purpose beyond emphasizing Viga's villainy. Although he is not responsible for the accident, Viga kicks over a container of medicine while the boy is being treated for his injuries.[69] The sequence, which survives, builds suspense by intercutting a long shot of the boy walking along a curve in the road with images of the approaching car. In a medium long shot, he is shown bending down to tie his shoe; a cut back to long shot displays a rather unconvincing collision between the car and the boy (the vehicle obviously stops short of the actor). Although this scene seems gratuitous, it would have demonstrated the local capacity to stage stunts using modern transportation technologies, however precariously. Significantly, the promotional notice insists that *João da Mata* offers the dynamic appeal of American adventure genres without their narrative excesses, describing the film as characterized by "intense sentiment and natural emotions, a story in the same genre at times so brutally exploited by the Americans."[70] A local review of the film also affirmed both the influence of Hollywood conventions and the superiority of the local product, commenting, "The two fight scenes are impeccable, better than those presented by the Americans, who are unquestionably experts in this particularity."[71]

The film's combination of thrills and action sequences with local spaces and concerns seems to have appealed to audiences in the region. Carlos Roberto de Souza has traced the fairly extensive exhibition circuit of *João da Mata*, which was shown in Rio and São Paulo and circulated along railroad lines in the state of its production. (The producers offered stationmasters a commission to distribute the film.) However, only a little over a tenth of the capital invested in the film was ever returned to the producers, and Phenix-Film was liquidated without the possibility of making a second film.[72] At this juncture, film production in Campinas was renewed by one of Brazilian silent cinema's most curious figures, an itinerant director and occasional con man named Eugenio Centaro. Born in Italy, he billed himself as E. C. Kerrigan and claimed to have worked for Paramount, using these credentials to create film schools and direct feature films in Campinas, the city of São Paulo, Guarnésia in Minas Gerais, and Porto Alegre in Rio Grande do Sul.[73] After founding the Escola Cinematográfica Campineira, Kerrigan recruited personnel from the defunct Phenix-Film to shoot a fiction feature, *Sofrer para gozar* (*Suffer to Enjoy*) beginning in late 1923.[74]

In contrast with *João da Mata*, *Sofrer para gozar* seems not to have drawn its plot from the local context, instead narrating a melodramatic tale of female suffering through the conventions of the Hollywood western. A program leaflet for the film, which is presumed lost, sketches its plot in language replete with melodramatic extremes: "Edith Barros, a rare example of virtue and abnegation, lives in constant martyrdom at the hands of her husband Tim, a rough man and habitual drunk. With the resignation of a saint, she bears all of her husband's brutality, without paying heed to Jacques Fernandes, an evil and unscrupulous man, who courts her constantly."[75] In the face of her resistance, Jacques (José Rodrigues) arranges to have a group of men ambush and kill Tim (Lincoln Garrido). Edith (Cacilda Alencar) is forced to accept an offer of employment from Jacques, working in a bar "where dancers, landowners, peons, and adventurers intoxicate themselves in disgusting promiscuity, stupefied by the flash of roulette chips, glasses of stimulants, and the beauty of women," according to the program. Further suggesting the borrowing of semantic elements from the Hollywood western, another summary of the film further specifies that it is "a bar on the American system, with women, alcohol, and gambling."[76] With the introduction of the hero, the cattle rancher Jayme (Ricardo Zarattini), into this unsavory atmosphere, the summary of the film provided in the program ends, inviting the reader to view the film in order to "follow point by point all the peripeties of the film, extremely felicitous scenes of natural landscapes, and the most exciting touches, which will capture the complete attention of the public." Suggesting an episodic narrative structure marked by a succession of melodramatic "peripeties," the description foregrounds the camera's capture of landscape, as well as particularly thrilling scenes that promised to arouse strong sensations in the spectator.

The film's climactic moments combined dynamic physical action with cinematic special effects. When police agents arrive to investigate the death of Edith's husband, Jacques shoots one of them and tries to rape Edith before being overpowered by Jayme. According to the program, this "tremendous struggle" is characterized by "a perfect labor of technique and by an excitement so intense that the spectator will feel a 'frison' [*sic*] of enthusiasm and indescribable anxiety run up his spine."[77] Drawing on interviews with participants in the filming, Souza describes the choreography and special effects that went into the sequence.

> A violent blow from the hero was to have made the villain break the railing and fall on his back onto a table full of bottles, which, in turn, would shatter as well. The hero jumps from the upper level and the fight ends on the ground floor. The action was carefully prepared: the railing and the table were previously sawed down so that, at the right moment, they would break without difficulty and the villain's fall was decomposed by the camera, first falling from the upper floor, caught by a thick tarp below, and then shattering the table, rolling from a small platform constructed especially for the take.[78]

The program leaflet advertises this scene as offering two intertwined thrills to the audience: the excitement generated by the violent physical combat, and the spectacle of cinematic effects that maximized its visceral impact, priming spectators to note and appreciate the filmmakers' "perfect labor of technique."

While *Sofrer para gozar*'s local reviewers did not single out this scene for special praise, they did stress the film's affinities to Hollywood westerns, praising or criticizing the film in accord with their perceptions of these genre conventions' value as a model for local productions. One critic observed the film's "preoccupation with Americanizing everything, from the costumes to the gestures, and from the gestures to the action; this, however, will never be a grave defect, since we know that 'household gods work no miracles.'"[79] The reviewer associates North American cinema with action-packed narrative and with a distinctive style of corporeal performance, suggesting it provides useful models for local productions. Other spectators, however, rejected this strategy and the incongruities with the local context it produced. Three years after *Sofrer para gozar*'s initial release, when it was still being shown in small towns in the interior, Diogo de Mariz, a reader from the small town of Ouro Fino in Minas Gerais, wrote to *Selecta* to criticize the film. He complained of

FIG 5.3 Production still, *Sofrer para gozar*. The platform shown may have been used to simulate a fall during the climactic fight scene. Acervo Cinemateca Brasileira/SaV/MinC.

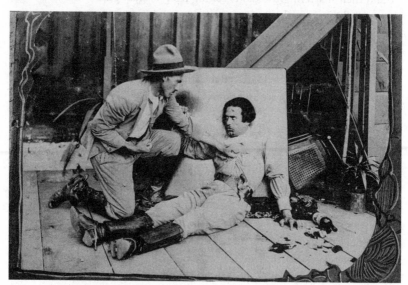

FIG 5.4 A publicity still shows the aftermath of the fight scene in *Sofrer para gozar*. Acervo Cinemateca Brasileira/SaV/MinC.

[c]haracters with names like Edith, Tim, Jack, Bill and others with re-
volvers in holsters fallen almost to the knee, blows, fights, the manner of
throwing a drink in the face of an insolent joker, pulling a revolver and . . .
hands up, half a dozen shots and the escape on horseback. . . . [I]t could
be that this pleases the general public, but those who are familiar with
the great difference between our customs and those of the folks up north
simply think it a great absurdity.[80]

Indicating the extended circulation of regional films in their areas of production, this comment also locates the Americanization of the film in its costuming, gesture, and narrative action. Suggesting that these aspects would appeal
only to an undiscriminating "general public," Mariz draws attention to the
"misplaced" quality of the film's visual and narrative codes.[81] In the same issue
of the magazine, a native of Campinas declared that, considering his home-
town's scenic beauty and "luxury," "I don't think it's necessary to make 'Far-
west' [in English] films."[82] Whether guided by the illustrated magazines' negative attitudes toward these genres or by a sense of incongruity between local
settings and the tropes of imported adventure melodramas, for these spectators *Sofrer para gozar* failed to offer a viable model for an incipient Brazilian
cinema.

Although *Sofrer para gozar*'s circulation was limited and reactions to it
were mixed, an interview with the principal actress, Cacilda Alencar, suggested that the act of participating in filmmaking itself held a transformative
potential for those involved in regional productions. Alencar, whose sister
had appeared in *João da Mata*, invokes narratives of a rapid rise to stardom,
which were staples of both North American and Brazilian fan magazines. She
writes, "It's true that I was always a great admirer of the silent art, fervently so,
and I considered it an inaccessible pinnacle, without ever imagining one day
being a film star! So you can well imagine the impression it made on me to
find myself, from one moment to the next, posing in front of a camera lens!"[83]
Alencar may have been downplaying previous acting experience, considered a
morally suspect activity for women at the time.[84] Yet she also seems to marvel
at the mere presence of the cinematic apparatus, itself attributed with star-
making power. Alencar describes her motivations and those of her collabora-
tors in terms that are highly suggestive of the seductive qualities of fantasies of
film production outside Brazil's largest cities: "We acted, yes, in these films
to satisfy a desire and for experience; we want to collaborate, with our efforts,
in showing the world that if Brazil wishes, it too can produce this art."[85] In

addition to the echoes of nationalistic discourses on cinema promoted by the illustrated magazines, Alencar's interview suggests a potent desire to appropriate cinematic technology to stage and participate in local modernity.

Shortly after the premiere of *Sofrer para gozar*, E. C. Kerrigan left Campinas for the city of São Paulo, where he would direct the romantic melodrama *Quando elas querem*. Following the production of *Alma gentil* and the filming of *A carne* (*The Flesh*, Felipe Ricci, 1925), an adaptation of a risqué naturalist novel by Júlio Ribeiro, a final fiction film, *Mocidade louca* (*Mad Youth*, 1927), was produced in Campinas in 1927. In *Mocidade louca*, an industrialized Campinas served as the backdrop for a romance that united a dissolute member of the urban elite with the daughter of a local businessman. Suggesting a shift in local filmmakers' aesthetics in accord with the goals of carioca fan magazines—the production company even adopted the name Selecta Film, seemingly in honor of the publication—*Mocidade louca* maintains the investment in dynamic action articulated with local spaces evident from the earliest narrative features produced in Campinas.[86]

Concurrently with the production of *João da Mata* in Campinas, shooting began in Recife on *Retribuição*, a production of the Aurora-Film Company and the first narrative film of one of Brazil's most prolific regional cycles. Thirteen fiction features and as many nonfiction films were made in Recife and nearby towns between 1922 and 1931, expressions, according to Cunha Filho, of a strong desire to modernize in the face of the city's reduced importance to the national economy. Significantly, filmmaking was spearheaded by working-class film enthusiasts rather than by elites, who sought to maintain their historical privilege by clinging to traditional cultural forms, an impulse that informed the regionalist literary movement of the 1920s.[87]

An early site of European colonization, Recife became a center of sugar production, the primary basis of Brazil's colonial economy.[88] Due both to declining sugar prices and the exhaustion of the soil, sugar production declined as coffee cultivation in the southeast expanded, and northeastern Brazil slipped into an economic depression. The abolition of slavery in 1888 further weakened the region's plantation economy, while Recife's significance as a port was eclipsed by the rise of steam-powered ocean vessels, since its harbor was too shallow to accommodate them. Beginning in the late nineteenth century, a series of devastating droughts consolidated an image of the northeast as an arid sertão (backlands), characterized by traditional forms of social organization and religious belief, and plagued by poverty, scarcity, and marauding bandits (*cangaceiros*).[89] Seeking renewed prosperity and insertion in the global economy, local officials initiated a series of reforms, modernizing the port's facilities and constructing broad avenues in the downtown districts between 1906 and 1914. By the time *A filha do advogado* (*The Lawyer's Daughter*, Jota Soares) was produced in 1926, local productions showcased Recife's accelerating modernization; images of metropolitan transport and bustling streets appear throughout the film.[90]

Earlier films produced in Recife, however, avoided urban spaces in favor of open landscapes that provided a backdrop for dynamic action sequences while also showcasing the trademark product of the local economy. Produced on the heels of *Retribuição*, described by its director, Gentil Roiz, as "a story that resulted from the assimilation of American films," *Jurando vingar* was "an attempt to register the Northeast, its cane fields."[91] Less than twenty minutes of the film have survived, but extant sequences make it clear that the film drew on the semantic elements of Hollywood westerns—bitter vendettas, showdowns in saloons, and races to the rescue on horseback—to thrill audiences and showcase local landscapes and economies.

Disregarding the rigid class stratification characteristic of the Northeast's plantation economy, the protagonist Júlio (Gentil Roiz), the owner of a sugar plantation, courts Bertha (Rilda Fernandes), who works as a waitress in a local bar, and who is coveted by a criminal nicknamed Avião (José Lira). Following a confrontation between Júlio and Avião in the bar, the latter seeks revenge. When Júlio travels to a refinery to sell the year's harvest, Avião murders his sister Maria (Iara de Alencar) and has Bertha abducted on her way home from work. In a scene that strongly evokes crime serial conventions, filmed in long shot, the bandits ambush her from behind, drag her into a car, and speed away. Learning of the kidnapping from Bertha's mother, Júlio races to the rescue on horseback; the camera pans to follow his trajectory through the rolling hills of the surrounding countryside. Bursting through the door, Júlio is ambushed by Avião, who brandishes a knife. Consistent with a tendency toward tableau framing throughout the film, the fight is depicted entirely in long shot, with the exception of two medium close-ups showing their struggle over the weapon. Júlio kills Avião during the struggle before rushing to free Bertha. While the couple's troubles are not quite over—they are nearly poisoned at their own wedding by one of the bandit's accomplices—this climactic scene offered visceral thrills that local spectators understood as closely linked to Hollywood conventions.

In a letter to *Para Todos . . .* , a reader in the nearby town of Gravatá observed *Jurando vingar*'s "Americanized fights," judging the film "three times better than *Retribuição*." Yet the letter-writer expressed disappointment at the bar scenes, observing, "It seems like the clients had no taste for posing for the lens, as they were stock still."[92] Similar to Cacilda Alencar's account of her transformation into a film actress, this review highlights the presence of the camera, which marks an encounter with technologies of mechanical reproduction. In this case, the encounter is infelicitous: the camera's presence creates a visible discomfort in the actors, which interferes with the desired illusionism. Yet the prospect of becoming a film actor retains its fascination for this reader, who, while acknowledging that *Jurando vingar*'s production values cannot compare to those of imported films, notes that the "audience received the film with a loud round of applause. I thought it fitting and grew enthusiastic, since I have always dreamed of Brazilian cinema. It is a pity not to be part of it." The reader's comment suggests how local film production fostered not only ambitions for the progress of a national cinema, but also participatory fantasies articulated on a local level. The film's reception in Recife was also exuberant; during its exhibition at the Cinema Royal, there was reportedly "no space to contain the audience, which got to the point of interrupting the traffic on the Rua Nova," the central street where the movie theater was located.[93]

Building on the excitement surrounding filmmaking in Recife, production companies proliferated in and around the city through the end of the 1920s. A number of these were formed by former members of the troubled Aurora-Film Company, giving rise to Planeta-Film, founded by actors from *Retribuição*, and to Liberdade Film, which was organized after the closure of Aurora in 1927. Others emerged independently, including the Olinda-Film Company, which focused its energies on nonfiction films like *As grandezas de Pernambuco* (*The Grandeur of Pernambuco*, Chagas Ribeiro, 1925). The company's lone fiction film was the 1927 *Revezes*, which, like *João da Mata*, idealizes agricultural life while criticizing the authoritarian abuses of the landowning class. Directed by Chagas Ribeiro, the film is set in the Agreste region between the coast and the arid sertão.[94] *Revezes*'s opening intertitle, while acknowledging the production's flaws, asserts its value by insisting that "the Pernambucan landscape is wonderfully taken advantage of" in its scenes. Driving home this claim, the film opens with a slow pan of a field where farmhands are shown in extreme long shot planting cane.

The rural setting of *Revezes*, described in an intertitle as "The Serra dos Quilombos, on whose slopes the sun of civilization has not yet shone," is quickly linked to the indiscriminate use of physical force by despotic landowners.

After a series of images in long shot and extreme long shot introduces the estate where the film's action unfolds, an intertitle describes the acts of brutality perpetrated by its authoritarian owner, Jacinto (Antonio Pinto). This brutality is quickly demonstrated with the beating of an intruder, which acts as a moment of sadistic spectacle. Jacinto shakes and kicks the man, then orders a group of workers to drag him to a fallen tree, where he is whipped. His expressions of pain are highlighted by medium close-ups on his face, unusual in a film framed mostly in long shot and extreme long shot. Despite this graphic depiction of physical violence, it is not Jacinto's abuses, but the sexual desires of his morally corrupt son, Jayme (Ernani Outran), that set the film's tragic plot in motion. Returning from his studies in Recife, Jayme sets his sights on a peasant girl, Célia (Marinha Marrocos), who is in love with a young farmhand named Carlos (Anísio Moreira). When his attempts to seduce her fail, Jayme shoots and kills Carlos from behind with a rifle. Carlos's brother confronts Jayme; in the struggle, he fatally stabs Jayme. Célia pines for Carlos and eventually dies, while Jacinto's workers revolt and his ranch goes bankrupt; he ends the film an impoverished beggar. Although fate punishes the members of the landowning class for their transgressions, their legal impunity is assumed, and the authorities are entirely absent from the film.

Prominent during the early years of film production in Campinas and Recife, the conventions of the western also played a key role in regional production in Porto Alegre, where they were reconfigured through the regional iconography of the *gaúcho* (cattle wrangler). In 1926, the automobile salesman Eduardo Abelim produced *Em defeza da irmã* (*In a Sister's Defense*), which reduced the drama of offended female virtue and male villainy to its barest elements. After a stranger attempts to rape his sister, the hero hunts him down with the help of a group of local men. Reminiscing about the film, an observer described the actors' motley costumes, which indicate a hybridization of imported and local iconographies: "some dressed perfectly in the *gaúcho* mode, others in a mixture of *guasca* [a synonym for *gaúcho*] and 'cow boy' (a figure of great influence at the time, which was the age of Tom Mix, Eddie Polo, Buck Jones, and others)."[95] The following year, Walter Medeiros, son of a local landowner, filmed *Um drama nos pampas* (*A Drama in the Pampas*), advertised as a "super-production of regional customs."[96] Recalling the land disputes and sexual threats of other regional films, *Um drama nos pampas* recounted the tribulations of a widow (Sara Olmo) and her daughter, Célia (Betty Fernandes), who have mortgaged their farm to an unscrupulous local landowner, Antônio Guerra (Catharino Azambuja). Guerra asks for the girl's hand in marriage in exchange for forgiveness of the debt, and does not hesitate to murder Célia's brother when he opposes his designs. Ultimately, in accordance with the episodic structure and moral logic of melodrama, "after a thousand peripeties, love and justice triumph."[97]

In Campinas, Recife, and Porto Alegre, the adaptation of the tropes of the western dramatized the class inequalities generated and maintained by the dynamics of Brazil's agrarian economy in thrilling and melodramatic terms. Providing pretexts for physical and technological feats—scenes of brutality, daring stunts, and spectacular special effects—*João da Mata*, *Jurando vingar*, and *Revezes* highlight the economic productivity of their regions of origin, even as they suggest the persistence of authoritarian forms of local power in a modernizing Brazil.

Bandits, Bullets, and Buried Treasure: Adapting the Adventure Serial in Recife and Cataguases, 1923–1927

In a series of nostalgic articles published in 1963, director Jota Soares reminisced about the early days of film production in Recife, recalling how enthusiastic viewings of "the adventures of Grace Cunard, Eddie Polo, Noble Johnson, Pearl White, Ruth Roland, Jack Perrin, and other experts in the art of confronting the greatest of perils" provided a key impetus for filmmaking activities.[98] Surviving only in fragments that total thirty minutes, *Retribuição* used narrative devices familiar from imported serials: an adventurous female orphan and a struggle over a coveted object, in this case a treasure map.[99] Soares reminisced that *Retribuição* "had everything: trains, boats, chase scenes, torture, and love too. The public thrilled [*vibrou*] and began to believe in Cinema in Pernambuco. And how the courageous bandits of the film walked proudly through the streets of Recife! They wore their caps and everything, just as they acted on the screen."[100] While retrospective, Soares's comments suggest how appropriating the iconographies of the serial, both onscreen and off, added a participatory dimension to local film culture.

Retribuição opens with a prologue that introduces the characters through intertitles and medium close-up shots of the actors looking directly into the camera. While this device was common in works of transitional-era cinema, such as Louis Feuillade's *Fantômas* (1913), the practice would have been out of place in most American and European films of the 1920s.[101] Furthermore, *Retribuição*'s opening differs from the typical prologue in that the first figure to be introduced is not an actor-character, but rather cameraman Edson Chagas.[102]

This choice suggests the pivotal role of the camera operator, whose technical mastery renders film production possible. However, unlike the actors who appear in the following shots, Chagas does not look directly into the lens, instead manifesting shyness when confronted by the camera. As in reviews of regional films like *Jurando vingar*, the gaze directly at, or noticeably averted from, the camera highlights its offscreen presence and the significance attributed to it.[103] While reviews of regional productions often called for actors to eliminate their self-consciousness in front of the camera, this uncertainty about how to return the camera's gaze in a fashion that conformed to prevailing cinematic codes foregrounds the moment of encounter with cinematic technology.

After the prologue scene, a brief series of high-angle panning shots establishes the location of the action, displaying the domes of several baroque churches in Recife. Reviews of the film suggest that these images, along with other moments that solicited a "landscape gaze," were appreciated as semiautonomous views. One reviewer contended that deficiencies in the script were compensated for by "natural scenes of the most beautiful aspects of Pernambuco's nature."[104] Another noted *Retribuição*'s "lovely panoramas, exciting struggles." Whether appreciating these elements as independent or interconnected attractions, the critic judged that "nothing was lacking for a perfect film."[105]

Retribuição's narrative is set in motion with two events typical of the serial: the death of the heroine's father (Ferreira da Graça) and the introduction of a love interest.[106] Just before expiring, he entrusts Edith (Almery Steves) with a map showing the hidden location of "a fortune in gold coins that circulated in Brazil during the Empire" (according to an intertitle), forging a tenuous connection to national history within the plot. Despite this revelation, the search for the treasure begins only a year later. The catalyst is the appearance of the hero, Artur (Barreto Júnior), in Edith's garden, where he has wandered after being deceived and beaten by the villain of the film, Curisco (Tancredo Seabra). Curisco shares a name with a well-known real-life cangaceiro, but more closely resembles a Parisian apache in his vest, tie, and flat cap.[107] After this action is presented in flashback (shown in a single long shot whose distant framing lessens the visual impact of the violence), the focus of the action shifts to Curisco and his gang. A series of intertitles and close-ups introduce the bandits as they sit playing cards; the outlaws appear in caps, shirtsleeves, and vests, while one of them wears a broader-brimmed hat. Curisco berates one of the gang (Mário Freitas Cardoso), Espião (the Spy) for not having found a target for the gang's next robbery. Leaving the hideout, Espião inevitably ends up at the bench where Edith and Artur are discussing the treasure, setting the stage for a series of dynamic chases and struggles.

In the following sequence, the "Ruins of Palmyra" (in fact a chalk mine in the neighboring town of Olinda), becomes the backdrop for a series of chases and struggles, constituting the film's most dynamic articulation of local landscapes with thrilling action.[108] Edith and Artur hire a car, which according to an intertitle waits for them "in front of the Elixir Americano factory," an allusion to local industry.[109] They set off to search for the treasure, unaware the bandits are lying in wait. The two separate and Artur begins to dig, but is soon interrupted by Edith's cries for help as she is pursued by the bandits. Artur turns, pulls out a pistol, and fires at one of the gang, who dramatically tumbles down the slope as he expires. Yet the gun jams or runs out of bullets, as indicated by a rare close-up. Artur scrambles up the embankment after the outlaws, not realizing that several are lying in wait for him. As Edith runs toward the ledge, Artur is shown in long shot fighting off his pursuers with his fists. Curisco enters the frame to subdue him at gunpoint, and Edith is quickly captured as well.

In the following scene, the captives are transported to the bandits' hideout, located on an island, imprisoned, and in Artur's case, tortured. The couple is rescued from their predicament by the intervention of Espião, who secretly consults with Edith in her cell. The heroine sends the repentant bandit to seek help at her home; learning her brother Roberto (Oséias Torres de Lima) is set to arrive on the next train, Espião hurries to the station to explain her plight. Roberto rushes off to free the captives on the island, while Espião contacts the police. Played by a real-life boxer, Roberto fends off the bandits with impressive physical skill; at one point, he throws two of them over his shoulders.[110] Meanwhile, a procession of policemen arrives at the dock; one bandit is fatally shot, the rest apprehended, and Curisco "seeing the end of the gang, ends his existence," according to an intertitle. Echoing the conventions of the North American serial, these peripeties conclude with a romantic union between the hero and heroine.[111] As Edith walks with Artur by the edge of a lake, Artur notes that he must soon leave the city, prompting a confession of love from Edith. Roberto, surprising the two lovers in the midst of their conversation, notes that he must leave on the next steamship for Rio de Janeiro and hopes to see his sister married before he does. Eliding the wedding sequence, the film moves directly to the newlyweds' departure in an automobile, a distinctly "American-style" ending criticized by the local intellectual Samuel Campello in a suggestive review.

Published in the *Diário de Pernambuco*, Campello's review complimented the film's clear photography and its images of "the Beberibe woods, the Palmyra ruins, in Olinda, Pina Beach, and Dois Irmãos" (a neighborhood in Recife), suggesting that the scenic views were presented with satisfying technical competency.[112] Yet this praise for the film was preceded by a long tirade on the unfortunate state of cinema after the First World War, when the United States flooded the market with "cunning propaganda against Mexico and those films, the so-called *policiais* [detective films], with an infinity of series. Nothing more unrealistic, nothing more dangerous to society's customs, than these adventure films. Who can deny their pernicious influence on weak brains?" To support his case, Campello cites cases of crimes inspired by the cinema in Mexico, New York, and Rio de Janeiro, evoking a cosmopolitan imaginary of crime that spans Latin America and the United States. Complaining that imported serials had driven him away from the movies, Campello makes an exception for the premiere of *Retribuição*, which he describes as taking place in an overheated cinema packed with eager spectators. Bitterly disappointed, he writes, "The plot, my God! It has nothing of ours in it; it's an imitation of American films, the so-called 'policiais.' Blows, punches, gangs of bandits, impossible sequences, and even a marriage in the American style, with a declaration of love made to the hero by the heroine, immediately followed by an automobile ride."[113] Rejecting the film's action-oriented aesthetic as both derivative and dangerous, Campello criticizes Hollywood's influence and, implicitly, the renegotiation of gender roles that it might entail. Although Edith lacks the physical dynamism characteristic of the Hollywood "serial queen"— as Lucilla Ribeiro Bernadet points out, neither she nor Artur performs any particularly impressive physical feats within the course of the film—her exercise of control over her romantic destiny was likely appealing to local audiences for the very reasons that Campello rejected it: it alluded to the "new immediacy, energy and sexual economy" embodied by imported serials.[114]

Perhaps in response to such criticisms, Aurora-Film's next production *Jurando vingar*, focused more closely on local themes. Yet the iconography and narrative thrills of American adventure films remained a key point of reference among local film producers. Discontented with the leadership of Aurora-Film, Barreto Júnior and Tancredo Seabra, who respectively played the hero and the villain of *Retribuição*, left to found their own company,

Planeta-Film, in 1925. Although very little is known about their first production, *Filho sem mãe* (*Motherless Child*), surviving publicity stills suggest it juxtaposed the figure of the cangaceiro with the codes of the Hollywood adventure film. Planeta-Film's next project, never completed, was a serial film entitled *Herança perdida* (*Lost Inheritance*), according to a local reader of *Selecta* who criticized the folly of embarking on such a lengthy, ambitious project.[115]

Contracted to direct a film in the nearby town of Gôiana in 1926, Jota Soares noted that "the Goianenses wanted a film of the American type called 'mustang' [in English], with adventures, fight scenes, shootouts with autos, peripeties." (Here, "mustang" may be a reference to a brand name associated with the American Film Manufacturing Company.)[116] The result was *Sangue de irmão* (*Brother's Blood*), which, according to the director, "was about land disputes and the resulting kidnapping of a nine-year-old child. Lots of action."[117] Evoking the themes of rural authoritarianism present in *João da Mata* and *Revezes*, the film ended with the lynching of a brutal local bandit. As in the case of Campinas, later productions in Recife would focus on the tension between urban and rural spaces and values, articulated through heterosexual romance. In *Aitaré da praia* (*Aitaré of the Beach*, Gentil Roiz, 1927–1928), the *jangadeiro* (raft fisherman) of the title travels to the city after a romantic disappointment, while *A filha do advogado*, directed by Soares, contrasts the depravity of an urban youth with the innocence of his illegitimate sister, raised in the countryside. While neither film sought to directly thrill audiences with sensational stunts, they continued to draw on melodramatic oppositions to address the geographic and social divides that shaped regional modernities.

During the final years of film production in Recife, one of the most technically sophisticated regional cycles was emerging in Cataguases. In 1926, Humberto Mauro and the local photographer Pedro Comello shot the adventure film *Na primavera da vida* (*In the Springtime of Life*), set in an invented town on the border of two unnamed Brazilian states. Neither a copy of the film nor a detailed summary survives, but it appears that the plot centered on the activities of a group of smugglers who kidnap the heroine, necessitating her rescue by the hero.[118] The following year, the two film enthusiasts embarked on the production of another adventure melodrama scripted by Comello, *Os mistérios de São Matheus* (*The Mysteries of St. Matthew*), which also focused on the nefarious activities of a group of local bandits. The film remained unfinished when Mauro chose to focus his energies on the production of

Tesouro perdido (*Lost Treasure*), apparently leading to the end of the professional relationship between Mauro and Comello.[119]

The first production made in Cataguases to have a successful commercial run outside the city, *Tesouro perdido* was set in the small town of Arraial do Príncipe, "a hamlet that is picturesque, healthy, but of stationary development."[120] Opening with a series of static establishing shots displaying its setting at "the foot of the majestic Camparaó mountains, in Minas," the film depicts rural space as plagued by both anachronistic and ultramodern forms of lawlessness. These are embodied, respectively, by the brutal bandit Manoel Faca (played by Humberto Mauro himself) and the cosmopolitan criminal Raul Litz (Alzir Arruda), an international thief on the run under an assumed name, as a later sequence in Rio reveals. The criminals are pitted against two young brothers, Braúlio (Bruno Mauro) and Pedro (Máximo Serrano), who are searching for a buried treasure obsessively sought by their late father. Functioning as the coveted object on which the melodramatic plot turns, the treasure is also linked to the forging of the Brazilian nation.[121] An intertitle explains that the treasure's original owner "had enlisted with the Portuguese forces that rose up against the idea of Independence, in 1822, and before fleeing to Lisbon buried the fortune, being unable to carry it." Unfortunately for the brothers, Manoel Faca and Raul Litz have learned of the treasure's existence and covet it for themselves. After tracking down and killing a traveler who had previously stolen half the map, the two conspire to kidnap their adopted sister Suzanna (Lola Lys, the pseudonym of Mauro's wife Maria Vilela de Almeida), demanding the second half of the map as ransom. Pedro, the younger brother, rushes off to rescue Suzanna, refusing to wait for help. As reinforcements race to the rescue on horseback, with suspense emphasized by close-ups of galloping hooves, the bandits wound Pedro and burn down the shack where Suzanna is being held. The young girl is rescued, but Pedro expires in his brother's arms. Bráulio decides to burn the map, and the film ends with his obligatory romantic union with Suzanna.

In *Tesouro perdido* the mastery of adventure melodrama conventions allowed for the articulation of local landscapes with dynamic narrative action viewed as specifically cinematic. Reporting that the local audience received *Tesouro perdido* with a round of applause, the newspaper *O Cataguazes* noted that the "plot of the film is well-enchained, flowing through the most breathtaking landscapes of our State."[122] In a similar vein, the Rio de Janeiro newspaper *Correio da Manhã* noted, "This picture is really a film. By this, we mean that it is presented in the mold of the Americans'.... Our environments should be respected, and the rest can perfectly well be taken and copied from American films."[123] Similarly, one São Paulo journalist wrote, "In the serial films that make up the dross of 'yankee' cinema we have already seen, many times, similar things." Yet noting other appealing aspects of the production, especially the scenic backdrops, the reviewer suggests that *Tesouro perdido* "leads toward another cinema that obliges us to forget the American silent scene and the plots of its serial films."[124]

The conjunction of Hollywood narrative structures with regional landscapes was hailed by journalists as a productive model for national film production. When the journalists at *Cinearte* declared *Tesouro perdido* the winner in a 1927 competition for the best Brazilian film, they hailed its portrayal of the "true interior of our country," integrated into its suspenseful narrative.[125] As Paulo Emílio Salles Gomes and Sheila Schvarzman show, the friendship between Humberto Mauro and the carioca journalist Adhemar Gonzaga would actively shape Mauro's final two films in Cataguases, which integrate dynamic stunt sequences into romantic dramas that stage oppositions between Brazil's largest metropolises and its countryside.[126]

Errant Youths and Active Heroines: Sentimental and Sensational
Melodrama in Minas Gerais and Campinas, 1927–1930

Toward the close of the decade, a number of regional films narrated tales of errant youths reformed by the love of melindrosas, who, as the daughters of capitalists, provide the aristocratic heroes with an opportunity to marry into a new regime of industrial productivity. Many of these films featured physically dynamic heroines who, like American "serial queens," engage in independent behaviors that place them in harm's way. In *Mocidade louca*, produced in Campinas, the romantic plot is sparked by a dramatic automobile accident suffered by the heroine, who has a fondness for taking pleasure drives alone. In the film *Senhorita Agora Mesmo* (*Miss Right Now*, Pedro Comello, Cataguases, 1927), the heroine Lili (Eva Nil), an orphan who runs her late father's rural estate, is described as possessing an "energetic temperament, always prompt and decisive."[127] She single-handedly pursues a gang of bandits who have attacked the farm; a production still shows the heroine holding two robbers at gunpoint. However, like many of the heroines of American serials, she eventually needs rescuing herself—at the hands of a young man whose affections she has previously refused. Although the film's costumes and

FIG 5.5 Eva Nil briefly gains the upper hand over a pair of thieves in *Senhorita Agora Mesmo*. Acervo Arquivo Geral da Cidade do Rio de Janeiro, Coleção Pedro Lima.

rural setting most closely recall the Hollywood western, Lili's fatherlessness, her resistance to romantic relationships, and her impulsive involvement in adventures (requiring her rescue by a male figure), all strongly evoke North American serials, a connection made explicit in the press of the period.[128]

Independent and physically dynamic heroines also figured prominently in two features made by the director of *Sofrer para gozar* while working in Porto Alegre. The premise of E. C. Kerrigan's film *Revelação* (*Revelation*, 1929) recalls serial conventions in its focus on an independent young woman (Marta Soares) who lacks a father figure. The heroine is a recent orphan who inherits a cloth factory and an agricultural estate; she becomes entangled in a love triangle between the hero (Ivo Morgowa), a worker accused of her father's murder, and the villain (Roberto Zango), "an international vagabond, the bandit Sanchez."[129] In *Amor que redime* (*Redeeming Love*, 1928), also directed by Kerrigan, the innocent young Nora (Rina Lara) becomes embroiled in a gang of criminals led by her unscrupulous lover. According to a summary of the film, considered lost, Nora's first appearance in the film comes as she leaps down from a high wall after a robbery and speeds away in a waiting automobile.[130]

Perhaps surprisingly, it is not these fatherless heroines, nor the ultramodern figure of the melindrosa, who is presented as the greatest threat to the social order in regional films; rather, it is the male *estróina* (wastrel), a young man from an urban, aristocratic background who refuses to assimilate bourgeois values of hard work. In several of the regional films, these dissolute young men are either punished or, more frequently, reformed in the course of the narrative, with their desire for the heroine acting as a catalyst for the narrative action. *A filha do advogado* is perhaps the most extreme example of this narrative paradigm. The antihero, Helvécio, played by the director Jota Soares, is the pampered son of the eponymous lawyer; he is described in an intertitle as a "libertine and wastrel, victim of the madness of the world." Helvécio develops a powerful sexual attraction to the heroine Heloísa (Guiomar Teixeira), who has recently arrived in Recife. In true folhetim-esque fashion, unbeknownst to him, she is his half-sister, raised in secret in the countryside and recently sent to the city at her father's request. The climax of the melodramatic narrative comes when Helvécio bribes her manservant to lock him in a room with Heloísa, where he attempts to rape her. (Ferreira de Castro, who played the manservant—one of a handful of Afro-descended villains who appeared in the regional productions—was singled out for special praise by a reviewer.)[131] Heloísa fatally shoots her half-brother in self-defense and is tried for murder. During the trial, a mysterious lawyer, who is ultimately revealed to be her father in disguise, successfully defends her. While the degenerate figure of the estróina is physically eliminated in the narrative, Heloísa is progressively integrated into an urban, modern social order, a process that culminates in the public recognition of her virtue characteristic of melodrama.[132]

This plot inverts the narrative pattern seen in a number of regional films, including Humberto Mauro's *Braza dormida* (*Sleeping Ember*, 1928) and *Sangue mineiro*, Manoel Talon's *Entre as montanhas de Minas*, and Felipe Ricci's *Mocidade louca*. In these productions, upper-class youths from the city are expelled from the family fold, migrating to rural areas or secondary cities where they develop a work ethic and find love and happiness. Significantly, this trajectory reverses the trend toward urbanization that increasingly concentrated Brazil's population in urban centers. The melodramatic reconciliations of the regional films propose a path toward a modernization that overcame the polarization of urban and rural space through economic development.

Produced in the wake of *Tesouro perdido*, Mauro's *Braza dormida* and *Sangue mineiro* establish more systematic antimonies between city and countryside, linking the former with emotional turmoil and the latter with personal renewal. Extending the practice of on-location shooting used in *Tesouro perdido*, the opening scenes of *Braza dormida* take the bustling streets and elegant Jockey Club of Rio de Janeiro as a backdrop for the wanderings of Luiz (Luis Soares), a dissolute young man who is expelled from the family fold. In a plot that highlights local industry, Luiz responds to a newspaper advertisement seeking a manager for a sugar refinery "in the interior" (according to an intertitle) and falls in love with the owner's daughter Anita (Nita Ney). In this movement between city and country, the latter is portrayed as both pastoral and economically productive, particularly in a lyrical sequence that displays the refinery's machinery.[133] At the same time, rural life continues to be associated with the brutal physical violence manifest in earlier regional productions. The former refinery manager (Pedro Fantol) savagely beats another employee and later sabotages the factory with a bomb, before finally perishing in a cauldron of boiling sugar syrup during a final struggle with Luiz. Like *Retribuição*, *Braza dormida* ends with the marriage of the couple and their departure in an automobile.

In *Sangue mineiro*, the protagonist's romantic happiness is also assured by a movement from urban to rural space: fleeing a crushing romantic disappointment in Belo Horizonte, the film's melindrosa heroine, Carmem (Carmen Santos), seeks refuge on an isolated farm and eventually finds romantic happiness. The adopted daughter of an industrial tycoon, Carmem is cast aside by her lover in favor of her sister (Nita Ney). When Carmem attempts to drown herself, she is rescued by a pair of cousins: Máximo (Máximo Serrano), whose once-aristocratic family has been reduced to living in a cottage on their estate, Acaba-Mundo (World's End), and the wealthy Christovam (Maury Bueno), who is visiting from Rio. Despite an unsettling incident in which Christovam physically forces Carmem to kiss him, he ultimately wins her heart, staging, as in *Braza dormida*, *Mocidade louca*, and *Entre as montanhas de Minas*, a union between the patrician elite and the emerging industrial class. In the film's final scene, Carmem and Christovam, having returned to the city, receive a letter from the farm. The film ends on a melancholy note, as Carmem declares, "I miss Acaba-Mundo," and a close-up on her soulful expression is held for several seconds. This ending suggests a more ambivalent posture toward rural space, gesturing toward its renunciation, and prefiguring Mauro's own decision to abandon filmmaking in Cataguases and move to Rio, where he worked as a director in Adhemar Gonzaga's newly created Cinédia studios.

As Mauro worked on *Braza dormida*, another cinematic tale of errant youth reformed by rural life was being filmed three hundred kilometers away in Minas's capital, Belo Horizonte. The film's production was spearheaded by an Argentine immigrant (described in some sources as being of Spanish origin), Manoel Talon, with the participation of a group of students at the film school he had established.[134] In late January 1928, local newspapers began to report on the shooting of a film initially titled *Entre as montanhas de Belo Horizonte* (*Between the Mountains of Belo Horizonte*), which, fittingly, was to be "produced exclusively in the Capital and its surroundings, being a production of Adventures and sensations new to our public."[135] Another newspaper emphasized the selection of "a subject that can dispense with artificial sets, taking advantage of the panoramic beauty of our fields and our mountain ranges, unequalled in their proud grandiosity."[136] Suggesting how regional productions tapped into civic pride, Talon's film was advertised as featuring "lovely segments of Belo Horizonte, which should be excellent propaganda for the beauties of the Capital of Minas."[137] The film was screened for the state's governor, Antônio Carlos, who had also visited the set of *Sangue mineiro*.[138]

Now considered lost, *Entre as montanhas de Minas*, as the film was ultimately titled, alternated spectacular stunts with sentimental scenes. The film also combined scenes of the state's recently constructed capital and an estate located in the interior, where, as in *Braza dormida*, a "rich, dissipated young man" is reformed through hard work and love for the owner's daughter.[139] The film begins with an encounter between the hero, Hugo (played by Talon himself), and his love interest, Geny (Edla Guimarães), in the amusement park of a local agricultural exposition, which sets the stage for an eventual romantic and economic union between the state's industrial bourgeoisie and agrarian elite. Hugo is described as "the son of a rich businessman from the capital of Minas," while Geny's father is a "rich landowner from the south of Minas" who is in town to exhibit his livestock at the agricultural fair.[140]

The flirtation between Geny and Hugo is "quickly interrupted by a sensational scene": while they are dining in a restaurant on the fairgrounds, Geny attracts unwanted attention from another young man.[141] A physical struggle between Hugo and Geny's unwelcome suitor ensues; the hero, who has been drinking, takes out his gun and fires at his adversary, who falls to the ground. Believing he has killed his opponent, Hugo flees the scene of the shooting, giving rise to what was likely one of the film's most striking scenes, and one of the most challenging to shoot.[142] Pursued by a policeman on a motorcycle, "after many peripeties" Hugo makes a definitive escape by jumping onto a passing train.[143] A surviving production still from this chase shows the automobile with motorcycle in hot pursuit, traveling along a dusty road against a backdrop of low hills. While this scenery does not exactly embody the picturesque "grandiosity" evoked in press notices on the film, it framed local topography as the backdrop for dynamic action.

Through an unlikely coincidence typical of melodrama, Hugo happens to find work at the estate owned by Geny's father (which, according to a summary of the film, is free of the abuses depicted in other regional productions).[144] This idyllic picture is complemented by the arrival of Geny, who excuses Hugo's crime as an act of self-defense; encouraged, "the young man, impassioned, attempted to conquer the heart of his beloved, completely forgetting the mad life he had led up to that point."[145] Interrupting the regeneration of the protagonist, a group of cattle thieves led by the bandit Águia Preta (O. Almeida) threatens the tranquility of the estate. The bandit kidnaps Geny, carrying her off on horseback to his hiding place in an abandoned mill. (This detail recalls a salient element of *Braza dormida*; fired from the sugar refinery, the villain also lives in a mill [*engenho*], literally in the ruins of an earlier mode of production.) A series of fight scenes would have followed; a surviving still shows Hugo and Águia Preta tussling on the ground; Hugo holds Águia Preta down, while the latter thrusts his thumb into the corner of his adversary's mouth. Another image shows Hugo at an even greater disadvantage: the hero has been tied up and suspended upside down from the mill wheel, while Geny has been lashed to a post.[146] While the particulars of the villain's defeat are unclear, it leads to the obligatory outcome—the union of the couple. The legal obstacle to their happiness conveniently evaporates with the appearance of Hugo's friend Júlio, who brings him a letter from his father containing the good news that the man he shot has completely recovered.

In contrast with American serials and westerns exhibited locally, a reviewer observed that in *Entre as montanhas de Minas*, "The scenes unfold at the pace necessary for them to be comprehended, without excesses that fatigue one's attention." The journalist described the film as a "simple romance," associating its melodramatic narrative with a lack of pretension.[147] According to one of its financiers, J. H. Penna, the film attracted ten thousand spectators and yielded twenty contos in profits in Belo Horizonte, but it seems not to have

FIG 5.6 A publicity still shows a moment from a chase scene involving a motorcycle, automobile, and train (not pictured) in *Entre as montanhas de Minas*. Acervo Arquivo Geral da Cidade do Rio de Janeiro, Coleção Pedro Lima.

been shown outside the state of Minas Gerais, despite Penna's efforts to exhibit it in Rio de Janeiro.[148] Yet its melodramatic reconciliation of city and interior through the union of two privileged youths emblematic of Minas's past and present, suggest how film production engaged with ongoing modernization processes in the state.

With its focus on physical action and its emphasis on the romantic reconciliation of the state's agricultural and industrial economies, *Entre as montanhas de Minas* bears a striking resemblance to *Mocidade louca*, the final silent fiction film made in Campinas. *Mocidade louca* was financed by a group of employees from the Mogyana Railway Company, suggesting a desire to publicize Campinas's modern transportation infrastructure.[149] The film is considered lost, but a summary published in *Cinearte* suggests its affinities to other narratives of wayward young men: "If, instead of having satisfied his spendthrift inclinations, they had tried to divert him from the path of dissipation, putting in his hands an instrument of work, perhaps the young Newton Rios [the film's protagonist, played by Antônio Fido] would not have caused his parents the displeasure of revealing himself to be a wastrel and an

FIG 5.7 Hugo, played by the director Manoel Talon, tussles with the villain Águia Preta in a publicity still for *Entre as Montanhas de Minas*. Acervo Arquivo Geral da Cidade do Rio de Janeiro, Coleção Pedro Lima.

ingrate."[150] Banished from his parents' home, the prodigal Newton wanders through the interior of São Paulo, eventually heading to Campinas to devote himself to gainful employment. Once there, Newton embarks on a series of adventures that offered the following sensational spectacles, according to a promotional notice for the film:

In *Mocidade louca* we will see:

- an ascension to and struggle at 60 meters off the ground in the great facilities of the important Portland Brasileira Cement Factory
- a magnificent and extremely risky shot of a wild bull very close to the camera
- an accident in which a train collides with an automobile on a bridge, with the heroine left hanging from it, later falling into the water, where she is saved by the hero.[151]

This list of attractions that are only minimally integrated with the plot recalls Ben Singer's characterization of sensational melodrama, in both its stage
and screen incarnations, as an often disjointed collection of suspenseful situations.[152] Yet the description of the attractions also stresses the significance
of local industry, framing the mastery of cinematic technique as inseparable
from these action-packed scenes.

In addition, *Mocidade louca* prominently featured the figure of the melindrosa, while also incorporating elements of the dynamic femininity constructed by earlier serial films. In publicity photographs, the heroine, Yvone
(Isa Lins), sports bobbed hair, a cloche hat, and a short print dress. Like the
sensation-seeking heroines of American serials, Yvone's independent ways
place her in mortal danger; she is described as having a "weakness for going
on rides through the country, driving her jalopy herself, with confidence in
her own abilities."[153] Trouble arises when the vehicle's motor grinds to a halt
as she is crossing a bridge; investigating the problem, she finds herself menaced by a bull. To make matters implausibly worse, the heroine hears a train
approaching the bridge (the summary explains that it has been dispatched for
an emergency track repair). She throws herself out of the way, managing to
grab onto the bridge, but reaches the point of exhaustion and falls into the
water, where she is rescued by the hero. As in the case of *Fanny or the Theft of
the Twenty Millions* in Mexico, the filming of the locomotive crash with the
cooperation of the Mogyana Railway Company itself became a public spectacle, with over two hundred locals reportedly gathering to observe the scene.[154]

Newton's rescue of Yvone helps facilitate his regeneration, which itself
combines romance and business. Offered a position in her father's silk factory, Newton must foil a commercial rival's attempts to commit industrial
sabotage. While he is at a company picnic, two intruders kill a guard and
break into the factory with the intent of ruining the textiles with a corrosive
fluid. Newton realizes that he has left the keys to the office in the lock and
races back in his automobile.[155] He catches one of the saboteurs (played by the
local boxer Bellini) in the act and chases him to a nearby cement factory, site
of the struggle and deadly fall emphasized in the advertisement. In addition
to presenting Campinas as an industrialized city, this description suggests
how cinematic realism was not only guaranteed by the sight of an imperiled
human body, but also through extratextual discourses that emphasized the
technique behind cinematic special effects. A local reviewer lists the optical
feats involved in the film's production.

In *Mocidade louca* the spectator will have opportunity to appreciate the most cunning "trucs," the most ingenious artifices of cinematography, such as: automobile chases filmed with a telephoto lens—super-vision; marvelous photographic work with miniatures; extremely felicitous shots—a railway disaster, authentic, formidable—struggles at a great height, unique in national films.

In short, these were the details that astonished the film critics of the capital, and Selecta Film calls the public's attention to the attentive observation of these shots, which constitute the triumph of *Mocidade louca*, and the rosy victory of cinema in Campinas.[156]

As in the case of *Sofrer para gozar*, released three years earlier, the audience is invited to carefully observe the "perfect labor of technique" involved in producing spectacular and thrilling sequences that articulate transportation technology with visual technology. Significantly, the review claims that these visual effects favorably impressed film critics in Rio. Indeed, *Cinearte* praised its "scenes of 'suspense' and a variety of those 'trucs' that Cinema accomplishes to perfection," reserving special praise for the use of miniatures for an automobile accident and a fantasy scene set against the backdrop of a castle (executed using a miniature).[157] Suggesting a perceived need to legitimate *Mocidade louca* in the eyes of critics from the capital, the review ultimately presents the spectacular stunts and effects as constituting a triumph of local, rather than national, film production.

In another review of *Mocidade louca* published in Campinas, sentimental and sensational scenes are discussed side by side as sources of excitement for audiences, precisely because both attested to the mastery of cinematic technique. The reviewer writes, "Especially in the scene in the boat, in which she listens to the impassioned declarations of her beloved (Antônio Fido), Isa Lins is truly admirable. . . . Another exciting scene is the train wreck, which due to the perfection with which it was captured, left us breathless for a number of seconds."[158] As in the case of *Sofrer para gozar*, the visceral thrills offered by the display of physical violence or technological breakdown are framed as inseparable from the mastery of special effects. In similar terms, the reviewer notes that Fido excelled "both in his performance in the love scenes and in the formidable struggle with the well-known boxer Belline [*sic*]. The camera operator of Selecta [Film] was quite felicitous in capturing the scene of Bellini's fall, as well as the chase that follows."[159] *Mocidade louca* was perhaps the most striking example of a film that adapted a range

FIG 5.8 A summary of *Mocidade louca* displays the heroine's modern attire and a daring rescue. *Cinearte*, 7 September 1927. Hemeroteca Digital Brasileira.

of iconographies from Hollywood cinema, from daring stunt sequences to emphatically modern models of femininity, to stage a modernity that reconciled rather than polarized the privileged and marginal sites of Brazil's modernization.

Conclusion

1930, a year of sweeping change in both cinema and politics, marked the close of the first wave of regional filmmaking in Brazil. A conflict over the presidential succession provoked a crisis in the regional alliance between São Paulo and Minas Gerais (the "cafe com leite" policy) that had prevailed throughout the Republic, resulting in the Revolution of 1930. Led by defeated presidential candidate Getúlio Vargas of Rio Grande do Sul, this military revolt toppled the government, establishing a populist regime that nationalized petroleum,

FIG 5.9 A scene of a deadly fall in *Mocidade louca* showcased local industry and the actors' physical virtuosity. Publicity still, Acervo Arquivo Geral da Cidade do Rio de Janeiro, Coleção Pedro Lima.

mining, and other industries, and created state institutions to regulate and promote culture, centralizing and nationalizing cultural production. The year 1930 also witnessed an acceleration of the transition to sound films, which had made their debut in April 1929 in São Paulo. Although the transition unfolded at a measured pace—notably, the silent *Sangue mineiro* was still being exhibited in 1930—synchronized sound would transform the economics of film production and exhibition in Brazil. The expense of sound equipment forced many neighborhood and rural movie theaters to close, and all but extinguished regional production. At least one group of regional filmmakers experimented with ad-hoc synchronization using gramophone records, in the 1930 film *No cenário da vida* (*On the Stage of Life*, Jota Soares and Luis Maranhão). Yet with large movie theaters in major cities wired for sound, the prospects of reaching a broad audience with relatively economical silent productions were dimmer than ever. Instead, efforts to establish a self-sustaining industry were increasingly concentrated in Rio de Janeiro. Most notably,

Humberto Mauro abandoned filmmaking in Cataguases for the capital, joining forces with the journalists behind the campaign in support of Brazilian cinema at Adhemar Gonzaga's Cinédia studios. Early sound cinema dovetailed with emerging forms of cultural nationalism in its focus on musical genres, particularly samba, hailed as aural expressions of Brazilian identity. Cinédia shot one of the first productions to capitalize on popular music, the 1933 film *A voz do carnaval* (*The Voice of Carnival*), featuring Carmen Miranda and other celebrated singers, and codirected by Mauro and Gonzaga.

In contrast with these productions, which capitalized on forms of popular music mediated by novel sound technologies, and which inaugurated a self-sustaining (if precarious) film industry in Brazil's then capital, the regional productions of the 1920s had remained marginal, shot in locations that were viewed, to a greater or lesser degree, as occupying the periphery of a modernizing Brazil. Strategically drawing on the conventions of imported adventure melodramas that, depending on the cultural positioning of the viewer, signified either an undesirable sign of cultural delay or a uniquely cinematic and quintessentially modern dynamism, regional films addressed the uneven and unstable trajectories of modernization in Brazil. Recovering regional productions' shared aesthetic strategies and preoccupations in the face of the nationalistic—yet U.S.-oriented—discourses of carioca magazines illuminates the complex operation of staging regional modernities in the face of both Hollywood influence and hegemonic forms of cultural nationalism.

CONCLUSION

In October 1928, twenty years after the murder of Elias Farhat sparked a wave of filmed reconstructions, a second "Crime of the Trunk" was committed in São Paulo, again involving the immigrant community. The *Correio Paulistano* reported, "An Italian recently arrived in São Paulo repeats, along general lines, the sensational crime of Miguel Traad."[1] A young woman, Maria Fêa Pistone, was murdered by her husband, José Pistone, who placed her body in a trunk and brought it aboard the steamship *Massilia*, headed to Bordeaux. Generating sensational press coverage, the case also inspired two competing screen adaptations, both entitled *O crime da mala* (*The Crime of the Trunk*). The two versions were produced by Antonio Tibiriça and Francisco Madrigano, who had achieved impressive box-office profits with the sensationalistic *Vício e beleza* (*Vice and Beauty*, Antonio Tibiriça, 1926) and *Morfina* (*Morphine*, Francisco Madrigano and Nino Ponti, 1928); *Vício e beleza* was even shown with spectacular success in Buenos Aires and Montevideo.[2] Now believed lost, these titillating films offered spectacles of drug abuse and taboo sexual behavior to audiences (usually restricted to adult males).

Although the two 1928 versions of *O crime da mala* are also believed lost, a suggestive account of Madrigano's version of the film written by a reader of the magazine *Cinearte* signals how the regime of sensational reality exploited by "violent actualities" in the early twentieth century persisted through the end of the 1920s, even as carioca film critics advocated the production of quality fiction films in order to establish a national industry and disseminate a desirable image of Brazil. According to the spectator, who signed the letter with the pseudonym "Nick Carter" (after the fictional detective), *O crime da mala* was "ready in the blink of an eye."[3] Like filmed reenactments of real-life cases from the first decade of the twentieth century, it yielded a movie theater "packed with spectators." Despite *O crime da mala*'s apparent popular appeal, "Nick Carter" criticizes the manner in which it capitalized on topical events. He writes, "All this is exploitation. . . . As a Brazilian I went to see it. I did my duty. I thought I'd be seeing a good film. Not the tragedy in all its details. Instead, a nonfiction film [*filme natural*]. I wanted to see the infamous bandit up close. So I ended up seeing the bad example set by those individuals, who instead of making a narrative film [*filme de enredo*] make this."

Echoing the vehement rejection of nonfiction in Rio de Janeiro fan magazines, "Nick Carter" criticizes Madrigano's failure to make a well-executed narrative feature, even as he expresses a desire to see images of the real-life criminal. His description suggests that the film itself mingled fictional narrative with visual document. He notes "horrifying scenes intermixed," such as a "*clos-up* [*sic*] of the criminal hand with the murdering knife in its fist." Yet he also comments on the display of locations and objects that corresponded closely to journalistic accounts of the crime: "Details of Santos captured on the site of the tragedy. . . . The fatal trunk. The carriage [that transported the trunk] framed so that it can be seen it was really this one. 716 [the license number]. Ha!" The strategies of Madrigano's *O crime da mala* and the conflicting expectations of "Nick Carter," who wanted to see both a "good" (that is, narrative) film and the actual face of the accused criminal, demonstrate that documentation and dramatization could not be so easily disentangled in Brazilian cinema, even two decades after the premiere of *Os estranguladores*. The fan's description signals that the sensational mixture of reenactment and fiction, of fast-and-furious action and scenic view, persisted as a locally specific mode of representation through the end of the silent period.

By the early thirties, the fascination with real-life and fictional spectacles of violence in Mexican and Brazilian silent cinema was largely displaced by new strategies for attracting local audiences that were closely linked with ascendant forms of popular nationalism. With the introduction of sound cinema in Mexico and Brazil—fully synchronized feature films made their debut in São Paulo in April 1929, and in Mexico City in July of the same year—commercial ambitions for national film industries were increasingly tied to popular musical genres. The Brazilian samba and the Mexican ranchera were popularized through the expanding media of radio and early sound cinema, coming to function as powerful aural signifiers of national identity. These musical genres were pivotal in forging two of the most popular and enduring genres of these nations' film industries from the 1930s through the 1950s: the *chanchada* (musical comedy) in Brazil, and the *comedia ranchera*, or rural musical, in Mexico. In comparison with the intermittent attempts at film production in Mexico and Brazil during the silent era, these musical genres offered a much more consistent means of attracting domestic audiences—and in the case of Mexico, exporting films throughout the Spanish-speaking world.

In the 1940s and 1950s, filmmaking on an industrial model, emblematized by features with nationalistic themes and high production values, was hailed in Mexico and Brazil as a sign of national progress. In Mexico, the highly patriotic narratives and iconic visual style cultivated by the director Emilio Fernández in his collaborations with the cinematographer Gabriel Figueroa became the most prominent examples of this tendency.[4] In Brazil, this model was exemplified by the short-lived Vera Cruz studio that operated in São Paulo between 1949 and 1954, filming historical epics and other prestige pictures, while continuing to draw on popular genres.[5] With the establishment of self-sustaining—if often precarious—film industries, a silent-era mode of film production that was markedly permeable to topical events and local spaces was replaced by a model that successfully forged marketable cinematic icons of the nation.

Prior to the emergence of national sound film industries, cinema in Mexico and Brazil (as elsewhere in Latin America) manifested a strong investment in topical events and local settings, an impulse to sensationalize quotidian experience through the capture, reenactment, and staging of violent and unpredictable events. In the emerging mass cultures of early twentieth-century Mexico and Brazil, the use of novel visual technologies pleasurably framed the present as thrillingly eventful and thus demonstrably modern. At the same time, sensational visual culture brought to the fore the social costs of modernization, which accentuated disparities between classes, races, city neighborhoods, and geographic regions.

Sensational visual culture in early twentieth-century Mexico and Brazil developed along distinct but parallel trajectories that were shaped by the particularities of each nation's political and social development. The comparison of sensational visual culture in the two nations sheds light on broader tendencies in early twentieth-century Latin America, where accelerated modernization coexisted with differential experiences of citizenship and pervasive public violence. In both Mexico and Brazil, a fascination with spectacles of violence persists from the emergence of narrative cinema in close connection with topical events and illustrated journalism, through the 1920s, when the dominant genre of the fiction film was linked to national and regional modernization by emerging forms of film criticism. Through the end of the silent era, the capture, reenactment, and staging of bodily violence remained central to cinema's claims of realism, to its appeal to audiences through an emphasis on the topical and the local, and to the pleasures of dynamic physical performance and technological mastery.

In Mexico, cinema and illustrated journalism were shaped by the sweeping violence of the Revolution and the nationalist discourses that marked its aftermath, as sensational cinema gave expression to ambiguity regarding the legitimacy of violence and ambivalence surrounding the programs of modernization and social hygiene enacted by postrevolutionary governments. The spectacular staging of public violence during the Porfiriato and the revolutionary conflict was closely linked to the expansion of the illustrated press and the emergence of domestic film production, particularly the widespread production of nonfiction films documenting topical events. Photographic and cinematic records of criminal and military aggression were framed with melodramatic rhetoric that helped circumscribe the range of political meanings that might be attached to them, often shoring up the perceived legitimacy of state violence. The crisis of political authority that arose from the difficulty in distinguishing between military and criminal aggression in occupied Mexico City found expression in the highly successful *El automóvil gris*, which, like *La banda del automóvil, Fanny o el robo de los veinte millones*, and other productions that dramatized real-life criminal cases and political scandals, framed acts of violence less as threats to political legitimacy and social stability than as signs of urban modernity, linked with a cosmopolitan imaginary of crime that circulated on a global scale.

In postrevolutionary Mexico, the staging of physical violence remained pivotal in early attempts to establish a national cinema, and played a prominent role in journalistic accounts that framed filmmaking as a newsworthy event and a sign of national progress. Helping to frame the regional figure of the charro as a national icon, adventure films produced by Miguel Contreras Torres and others in the early 1920s engaged in a conflictual dialogue with North American cinema and its "denigrating" representations of Mexicans. Adventure films of the early 1920s offered audiences two forms of pleasurable realism: virtuoso physical performances (often compared with Hollywood westerns and serials) and landscape views shot on location, which were aligned with the forging of a picturesque iconography of the nation. Although this cycle of adventure films was short-lived, dynamic physical action and location shooting shaped ambivalent visions of technological and social progress in Gabriel García Moreno's *El tren fantasma* and *El puño de hierro*. Thrilling audiences with the display of transportation technologies and hyperkinetic physical exploits, these films highlighted the dark underside of modernization in a regional center of trade and transportation. These adventure melodramas and their press coverage intersected with dominant currents of postrevolutionary nationalism while highlighting their tensions, signaling the persistent appeal of staging bodily violence and peril in Mexican cinema into the late 1920s.

While to some degree the sensational visual culture of early twentieth-century Mexico can be productively read through the lens of nation, analyzing the sensational cinema and journalism of republican Brazil requires close attention to the metropolis and the region as imagined sites of modernization. In turn-of-the-century Rio de Janeiro and São Paulo, sensational visual culture both reinforced and tentatively bridged class and spatial divides within rapidly growing cities. Crônicas, police reportage, literary works, and illustrated magazines cultivated thrilling narratives of criminality that were framed as markers of local modernity, linked with urban reforms and new modes of consumer and entertainment culture. Stage productions and filmed reconstructions of real-life crimes rendered metropolitan experience a sensational spectacle, highlighting the social transformations that accompanied immigration, internal migration, and the growing presence of women in public space. Journalistic and cinematic narratives of crime bolstered emerging mass media's claims to accurately capture a rapid flow of topical events, while also foregrounding the social costs of modernization in rapidly growing cities.

By the mid-teens, the intermedial imaginary of sensational visual culture articulated between the illustrated press, popular theater, and cinema took on a new profile in Rio de Janeiro with the popularity of French and North American serials and their tie-in novelizations. Drawing on a national tradition of serial literature and domesticating imported forms of serial entertainment, paraliterary texts published in specialized film magazines and would-be serial films framed Rio de Janeiro as the backdrop for sensational narratives. These texts were underpinned by novel conceptions of cinematic realism, particularly the notion of the truc, which encompassed virtuoso physical stunts, special effects, and unexpected narrative twists. The interconnected production and consumption of literary and filmic texts that constituted the serial craze in Rio de Janeiro demonstrate how serial forms provide multiple entry points for spectators and creators, allowing for complex articulations between global and local. In this context, locally made adventure melodramas emphasized physical performance and location shooting, offering thrilling forms of verisimilitude closely linked to the cinematic staging of bodily violence.

In the latter half of the 1920s across Brazil, the production of sensational fiction films continued to play a key role in the staging of local modernity, even as film production was increasingly mediated by fan magazines that defined normative models of film production in the service of national progress. Regional filmmakers and carioca critics formulated competing models of "modern" cinema, which was charged with demonstrating the technological and economic development of their place of production, or of Brazil as a whole. While *Selecta, Para Todos . . . ,* and *Cinearte* advocated the production of romantic dramas with elaborate costumes and sets, the popularity of imported serial films and westerns outside of Brazil's industrialized southeastern cities led regional filmmakers to strategically repurpose their conventions in cost-effective adventure melodramas shot on location, whose dynamic stunt sequences, special effects, and references to local industry attested to the advancement of their sites of production. Asserting local modernities at a moment when economic factors favored the southeast over other regions of Brazil, the regional production of adventure melodramas indicates the persistence of sensational genres as a strategy for attracting local audiences, and the ongoing role of print culture in mediating imported forms of mass culture and framing them as germane to local and national modernization.

Although the sensational visual culture of early twentieth-century Mexico and Brazil has been largely overshadowed by the later developments of sound film industries, the legacy of the public spectacles of violence forged by cinema and the illustrated press is keenly felt in the two nations' present-day media cultures, which are marked by public displays of violence perpetrated by the military, paramilitary groups, police, private security forces, and organized crime. In their analysis of the dynamics of violence in contemporary Latin America, Enrique Desmond Arias and Daniel M. Goldstein describe democracies in the region as characterized by "violent pluralism," with "states, social elites, and subalterns employing violence in the quest to establish or contest regimes of citizenship, justice, rights, and a democratic social order."[6] Both Brazil and Mexico have experienced democratic openings in recent decades;

Brazil's military dictatorship, which came to power in 1964, was dissolved in 1983, while the seven-decade dominance of the PRI (Institutional Revolutionary Party) and its precursors in Mexico was interrupted between 2000 and 2012 by the presidencies of Vicente Fox and Felipe Calderón of the PAN (National Action Party). (The country returned to PRI rule in 2013 with the presidency of Enrique Peña Nieto.) In both nations, public violence persists on a mass scale, often exceeding clear oppositions between legitimate and illegitimate uses of force. Organized crime has mounted a formidable challenge to these states' historically precarious monopolies on violence and become ever more intimately entwined with the apparatus of the state itself, with the incidence of violence often heightening divisions in urban space and national territory.

In Brazil's major cities, favelas have persisted as spaces all but abandoned by the state, where basic infrastructure, public services, and education are lacking. In marginalized areas, nonstate actors—including drug traffickers and *milicias* (vigilante groups, often composed of law enforcement officers acting in an extrajudicial capacity)—have challenged the state's sovereign monopoly on violence. In some contexts, the interplay between state and nonstate actors may constitute a form of "sovereignty by consensus" in which "the regulation of life and death is carried out not by one but two violent parties."[7] Graham Denyer Willis argues that in present-day São Paulo, the regulation of death is shared by São Paulo civil police and the organized crime group Primeiro Comando da Capital, who operate under a tacit agreement about who may be killed with impunity (young men presumed to be involved in criminal activity), a precarious agreement interrupted by intense periods of violent confrontation between these two forces.

Focusing on public discussions of criminality in São Paulo, Teresa P. R. Caldeira argues that this "talk of crime" works to "organize the urban landscape and public space, shaping the scenario for social interactions, which acquire new meanings in a city becoming progressively walled.... Moreover, the talk of crime exacerbates violence by legitimating private or illegal reactions—such as hiring guards or supporting death squads or vigilantism—when institutions of order seem to fail."[8] Caldeira demonstrates how public discourses of crime reinforce social and spatial segregation, critiquing (but also legitimizing) varied forms of extralegal aggression, and signaling the inextricability of violence and inequality in contemporary Brazil.

Profound divisions within Brazil's cities have been brought to the fore by high-profile international sporting events like the 2014 World Cup, which have once again rendered Brazil's cityscapes (and particularly Rio de Janeiro, site of the 2016 Summer Olympics) showcases for national progress on the world stage. Favelas have been slated for demolition or subjected to "pacification" through military occupations and the presence of Unidades de Policia Pacificadora (Pacifying Police Units). Recalling the confluence of urban reforms, working-class displacement, and sensational visual culture at the turn of the twentieth century, lurid coverage in print media and television news accompanied these occupations and their repercussions, such as the November 2010 security crisis that accompanied the invasion of the Complexo do Alemão (a conglomeration of several favelas in Rio's Northern Zone). Erika Robb Larkins has recently argued that "entangled forms of violence, spectacle, and commodification" shape daily life in Rio's favelas and media images of these spaces disseminated on a local, national, and international scale.[9] She contends that both drug traffickers and state security forces "perform violent acts in such a way as to ensure they reach broader audiences; they author violent spectacles. Because performative violence is so spectacular, it diverts attention from the social relationships that enable such violence in the first place."[10]

In parallel with the spectacularization of the favela in daily life and news media, these informal communities have been framed as an iconically Brazilian space in globally successful feature films like *Cidade de Deus* (*City of God*, Fernando Meirelles and Kátia Lund, 2002) and the two *Tropa de elite* (*Elite Squad*) films directed by José Padilha and released in 2007 and 2010. These productions exemplify the new global profile of Brazilian cinema enabled by the so-called *retomada* (resurgence) of domestic film production. After the dismantling of the infrastructure of state-sponsored cinema under President Fernando Collor de Mello, the Audiovisual Law of 1993 created new subsidies that encouraged international coproductions and helped forge a new international profile for Brazilian film. These productions are often associated with a globalized "MTV aesthetic," in that they depict graphic violence in a highly stylized manner, making use of rapid editing, saturated colors, and hyperkinetic handheld camera movements. To use Ivana Bentes's terms, a "cosmetics of hunger" arguably displaces the openly politicized "aesthetic of hunger" cultivated by Cinema Novo.[11]

As Laura Podalsky observes, Latin American filmmakers who have risen to new global prominence in the twenty-first century, including figures like Brazilian Walter Salles and Mexicans Alfonso Cuarón, Alejandro González Iñárritu, and Guillermo del Toro have distanced themselves not only from

the model of a state-supported national cinema, but also from the overtly political projects of the leftist New Latin American Cinema movements of the
1960s and beyond. Rather than viewing these commercially successful films as
complicit with the homogenizing forces of cultural globalization, associated
by many critics with historical amnesia, Podalsky argues for the significance
of their emotional appeals to audiences, asserting that "only by acknowledging the sociocultural work being carried out in specific geohistorical contexts
by those films' affective engagements can we debate their social and political
significance in a substantive way."[12] For Podalsky, films such as Iñárritu's visually striking and graphically violent *Amores perros* (2000) do not simply
aestheticize quotidian violence and economic inequality, but rather prompt a
visceral engagement with these social conditions.

In Mexico, depictions of sensationalized violence in audiovisual, print, and
online media are configuring new regimes of emotion and sensation as public life is radically transformed by the devastation of the U.S.-Mexico drug
war. The public staging of violence had remained prevalent throughout the
twentieth century, as the *nota roja* (police blotter) expanded in the 1930s and
beyond with specialized publications like *Detectives, Seguridad Pública, Revista de Policía*, and the infamous *Alarma!* (1963–2014), as well as present-day
newspapers like Mexico City's *Metro*, which features graphic images of recent murders or accidents on most covers of its daily issues. Pablo Piccato has
observed the ambivalent role of sensationalistic police news in shaping the
public sphere in Mexico, noting its capacity to foster "the critical engagement
of readers in public affairs" and to denounce corruption and incompetence
by the authorities with little fear of censorship. Yet he also contends that the
nota roja "justified the use of violence as part of public life," including its extrajudicial use by state actors, reinforcing "the generally accepted premise that
justice seldom came formally from the state."[13] By the 1970s, Piccato notes,
the critical potential of the nota roja was eroded by increasing state influence
over the media.[14] Conversely, weakening one-party rule and media privatization contributed to the "tabloidization" of television news in the 1990s, as a
newly competitive market encouraged the use of sensationalistic strategies.[15]

Beyond these historical continuities, public spectacles of violence in Mexico have been qualitatively transformed by the explosion of armed conflict
involving drug traffickers and government forces over the past decade. In December 2006, President Felipe Calderón launched a military campaign against
powerful drug cartels that engulfed the country in a wave of armed struggles
between cartels (which have increasingly splintered into rival organizations

and loosely affiliated gangs), human-rights abuses and torture by military and police forces, and persistent links between the state and organized crime. Killings and forced disappearances associated with organized crime have exploded over the past decade, with an estimated toll of 100,000 deaths and 25,000 disappearances during Calderón's six-year term in office.[16]

The escalating conflict is intimately linked to the United States, which is a major market for narcotics, a source of smuggled weapons (weapons originating in the United States accounting for 80 percent of those seized by Mexican authorities during a three-year period in Calderón's presidency), and a partner in the Mérida Initiative. Since 2008, this bilateral security program has provided the Mexican authorities with over $2.3 billion (as of this writing) for military equipment and infrastructure, training, and other programs, which many observers believe has contributed to an escalation of the conflict.[17] Furthermore, scholars trace the radical shifts in the character of drug trafficking in Mexico to the North American Free Trade Agreement enacted in 1994. Alan Knight stresses that "NAFTA and neoliberalism have, of course, facilitated the drug trade by boosting cross-border trade and migration," with drug trafficking embodying "a very successful manifestation of neoliberal economics, of free trade and comparative advantage."[18] In Mexico, neoliberal economic reforms also entailed "the progressive dismantling of agrarian ejidos [communal plots], unions, and many of the government's longstanding mechanisms for distributing wealth and supporting subsistence and employment," leading to the creation of a "reserve army of young unemployed or underemployed men, some of whom found work with the traffickers."[19] Fueled by growing profits not only from the sale of drugs, but also human trafficking, kidnapping, and protection rackets, the activities of the cartels exemplify, according to the journalist Ed Vulliamy, the rapacious logic of global capitalism in a neoliberal era.[20]

Recent works of film and television—from arthouse films like Gerardo Naranjo's *Miss Bala* (2011) and Amat Escalante's *Heli* (2013) to hugely popular narco-themed telenovelas like *La reina del sur* (*Queen of the South*, Telemundo/RTI/Antena 3, 2011) and *El señor de los cielos* (*Lord of the Skies*, Telemundo/Caracol TV, 2013–present)—have recast the imaginaries of drug trafficking forged by a low-budget "border cinema" that emerged in the 1970s, giving expression to a new regime of spectacular public violence in Mexico.[21] Hector Amaya argues that "drug cartels use spectacular forms of violence (e.g., bombs, beheadings, mass murders) to advertise the cartels' new social and economic power. The violence has constituted new and grotesque social aesthetics of blood, damaged bodies, uniforms, and guns that function as a stage for novel forms of being in public."[22] Amaya emphasizes that the circulation of *narcocorridos* (narco-ballads), in defiance of bans by various Mexican states and municipalities, facilitates "public performances of power that cannot be incorporated by the nation," as singers and producers take advantage of transnational and digital media circuits to circumvent the state's regulation of culture.[23] Hermann Herlinghaus argues that these musical forms speak to "the moral dispossession of a growing part of the Mexican population, by both the state and the neoliberal economy."[24] Yet literary scholar Oswaldo Zavala critiques binary oppositions between the state and organized crime established by popular narconarratives in which "the criminal organizations profiting from the drug trade are a threat relegated to the discursive *exteriority*—outside the borders—of the power and reason of the state," insisting that drug trafficking is "a social construct always *inside* the state, with organized structures that also fulfill the roles of the state when needed."[25]

The mediation of violence in Mexican public life has increasingly circumvented traditional print media and television news outlets such as the duopoly of Televisa and TV Azteca. As Internet access increases, a development itself tied to the neoliberal privatization of communication infrastructure, public spectacles of violence increasingly take on digital forms, signaling "a deepening crisis in Mexico's public sphere and . . . the simultaneous emergence of counterpublics—narcopublics, perhaps—in response."[26] As assassinations of journalists become increasingly common (in some cases with the suspected involvement of the authorities), news media have begun to avoid covering certain aspects of the conflict and to censor news reports in response to cartel pressure.[27] In March 2011, more than sixty Mexican media organizations collectively agreed not to publicize content considered cartel propaganda, including the content of *narcomensajes* (verbal statements often displayed with, and sometimes even written on, the corpses of victims) and *narcomantas* (narcobanners) hung in public places. Citizen reporters active on social media have played an increasingly important role in reporting on the conflict, in some cases providing real-time information on unfolding confrontations between cartels or with authorities, even as the online presence and influence of cartels has expanded.[28] Websites such as *El blog del narco* disseminate highly graphic photographs and *narcovideos* (including unstaged executions) that are not publicized by conventional media outlets.

Paul K. Eiss stresses that digital images of horrifying cruelty are inextricably linked with public displays like narcomensajes and narcomantas, which are calculated for maximum impact and circulation, arguing that "the narco-media must be read *through* the mass media; it is precisely their presence or reproduction in the mainstream that holds the potential to trigger deep crises in their role as mediators between government and 'public opinion.'"[29] As "distinguishing legitimate from illegitimate media and political constituencies" became increasingly difficult, complicity between the state and organized crime in Mexico was rendered starkly apparent in September 2014 with the forced disappearance and presumed massacre of forty-three students from a teachers' college located in Ayotzinapa in the state of Guerrero.[30] According to a report by international human-rights investigators that contradicts official accounts of the crime by Mexican authorities, buses that the students had commandeered for transportation to a protest were violently detained by municipal police in coordination with other authorities, with evidence of brutal torture committed during the night of the students' disappearance and in the course of the subsequent investigation of the crime.[31]

The pervasive exercise of violence by both state and nonstate actors in contemporary Mexico and Brazil's "violent democracies" and the hypervisibility of this violence in the public sphere resonate with early twentieth-century forms of mass culture that framed violence as an acceptable consequence of industrialization and urbanization. Modernization in both Mexico and Brazil has been deeply marked by profound inequalities conditioned by class, race, and region. In this context, sensational visual culture has framed spectacles of bodily violence as a means of attesting to local modernity, at once foregrounding and reinforcing social and spatial divides in rapidly modernizing nations. Depictions of violence have thus played a pivotal role in forging modern public spheres mediated by visual and print technologies, and continue to chart the dynamics of structural violence and inequality in everyday life.

NOTES

Introduction

1. *Correio da Manhã*, 12 November 1908, 10.

2. *Excélsior*, 15 January 1920, 8.

3. On sensationalism and melodrama as distinctly modern modes of cultural production, see Wiltenburg, "True Crime," 1378–80, and Brooks, *The Melodramatic Imagination*, 14–17.

4. García Canclini, *Hybrid Cultures*, 1–3.

5. Instituto Nacional de Estadística, Geografía e Informática, *Estadísticas Históricas de México*, 90. Ministério da Agricultura, Indústria e Comércio, *Recenseamento do Brasil realizado em 1 de Setembro de 1920*, vol. IV, part IV, ix. Literacy rates tended to be considerably higher in urban areas. On crime statistics, see Piccato, *City of Suspects*, 52–55, 79, 221–36; and Bretas, *Ordem na cidade*, 69, 83–86.

6. Haber, "Financial Markets and Industrial Development," 147.

7. McCann, *Hello, Hello, Brazil*; Garramuño, *Primitive Modernities*.

8. Navitski, "Silent and Early Sound Cinema," forthcoming.

9. I thank Juan Sebastián Ospina León for his input on this point. On Argentine silent cinema, see Losada, "Allegories of Authenticity in Argentine Cinema of the 1910s"; Tucker, "*Páginas libres*," 132–36; Cuarterolo, *Del foto al fotograma*, 135–47.

10. For a sampling of key texts in this debate, see Vitali and Willemen, *Theorising National Cinemas* and Hjort and MacKenzie, *Cinema and Nation*.

11. Debord, *Society of the Spectacle*, 2.

12. Gallo, *Mexican Modernity*; Borge, *Latin American Writers and the Rise of Hollywood Cinema*; Gabara, *Errant Modernism*; Conde, *Consuming Visions*.

13. Monica Dall'Asta, "Italian Serial Films and 'International-Popular Culture,'" 305.

14. Schroeder-Rodríguez, "Latin American Silent Cinema," 36. See also Paranaguá, *Tradición y modernidad*.

15. See Vega Alfaro, *Microhistorias del cine en México*; de los Reyes, *Cine y sociedad en México* 2:255–61; Ramírez, *El cine yucateco*; Tuñón, *Historia de un sueño*.

16. On U.S. film producers' expansion into Mexico, see Serna, *Making Cinelandia*, 19–46.
17. Suárez, *Critical Essays on Colombian Cinema and Culture*, 28. Suárez refers to the films *Bajo el cielo antioqueño* (*Beneath the Sky of Antioquia*, Arturo Acevedo Vallarino, 1925), set between Medellín and the countryside of the province of Antioquia, and *Alma provinciana* (*Provincial Soul*, Félix Joaquín Rodríguez, 1925), which moves between the capital city of Bogotá and rural areas in the department of Santander.
18. For a Chinese parallel, see Bao, *Fiery Cinema*, 49.
19. Gunning, "Before Documentary," 14.
20. See Lefebvre, "Between Setting and Landscape in the Cinema," 22, on the distinction between setting (a representation of place subordinated to its narrative function) and landscape as "space freed from eventhood."
21. Altman, "A Semantic/Syntactic Approach to Film Genre," 10–12.
22. On the impact of newspapers on U.S. film culture, see Abel, *Menus for Movieland*.
23. Cuarterolo traces the relationship between actualities and early narrative films and the visual strategies of illustrated magazines that used series of staged photographs to narrate topical, historical, and fictional events, in *De la foto al fotograma*, 191–222.
24. Gunning, "The Cinema of Attraction[s]"; Bordwell, Staiger, and Thompson, *The Classical Hollywood Cinema*; Bean, "Technologies of Early Stardom and the Extraordinary Body."
25. Serna, *Making Cinelandia*, 6.
26. See Gaudreault and Marion, "The Cinema as a Model of the Genealogy of Media." On intermediality in Latin American visual culture, see López, "Calling for Intermediality."
27. See Bruno, *Streetwalking on a Ruined Map*.
28. Field, *Uplift Cinema*, 25. See also Bao, *Fiery Cinema*, 40.
29. Gerow, *Visions of Japanese Modernity*, 1, 3.
30. Díaz's close ally Manuel González held the presidency from 1880–1884.
31. The Constitutionalist movement takes its name from Carranza's 1913 "Plan de Guadalupe," announcing the formation of an army to oust Huerta and defend the constitutional principles violated by his seizure of power.
32. Daryle Williams, *Culture Wars in Brazil*, 2.
33. For a comparative approach to Mexican and Brazilian patron-client networks, see Roniger, "Caciquismo and Coronelismo." The classic text on *coronelismo* in Brazil is Victor Nunes Leal's *Coronelismo*; see also Woodward, "Coronelismo in Theory and Practice."
34. On the impact of European models of urban planning in Latin America, see Jorge E. Hardoy, "Theory and Practice of Urban Planning in Europe." On the case of Mexico City, see Tenorio Trillo, "1910 Mexico City," 81–90; Tenenbaum, "Streetwise History." On Rio de Janeiro, see Needell, *A Tropical Belle Époque*, 22–51.

35. Nelson Werneck Sodré cites a circulation of 50,000 for Rio's *Jornal do Brasil* at the turn of the century in *Historia da imprensa no Brasil*, 313. Whereas the most widely read Mexican newspapers of the late nineteenth century had an average circulation of 20,000, *El Imparcial* topped 125,000 by 1907. Toussaint Alcaraz, *Escenario de la prensa en el Porfiriato*, 31–32.

36. Piccato, *Public Sphere in Latin America*, 187.

37. On anxieties surrounding crime in Rio de Janeiro, see Bretas, *Ordem na cidade*, 85–86. On the case of Mexico City in the late Porfiriato, see Piccato, *City of Suspects*, 52–53, 136; Castillo Troncoso, "El surgimiento del reportaje policíaco en México," 163.

38. Hansen, "The Mass Production of the Senses," 60.

39. An exception is the modernist group based in Cataguases, Brazil, whose members had social contact with filmmaker Humberto Mauro and published comments on his film *Tesouro perdido* in their magazine *Verde*. R.F., "Música e cinema," *Verde*, September 1927, 31; Salles Gomes, *Humberto Mauro, Cataguases, Cinearte*, 172–73.

40. Hansen, "The Mass Production of the Senses," 70.

41. Hansen, "The Mass Production of the Senses," 70.

42. Andrew, "An Atlas of World Cinema," 24.

43. Gerow, *Visions of Japanese Modernity*, 23.

44. Hansen, "The Mass Production of the Senses," 68.

45. Schwartz, *Spectacular Realities*, 6.

46. On conceptions of cinema as a storage medium for contingent moments, particularly the moment of death, see Doane, *The Emergence of Cinematic Time*, 140–71.

47. On the reenactment of battle in Edison films, see Whissel, *Picturing American Modernity*, 83–89; on *Execution of Mary, Queen of Scots* and other early execution films, see Combs, *Deathwatch*, 27–64, especially 31–35.

48. On moral legibility in fictional melodrama, see Linda Williams, *Playing the Race Card*, 30.

49. Streeby, *Radical Sensations*, 18.

50. Schwartz, *Spectacular Realities*, 11.

51. The literature on this topic is vast. See, in particular, Kern, *The Culture of Time and Space, 1880–1918*; Schivelbusch, *The Railway Journey*; Crary, *Techniques of the Observer*.

52. Singer, *Melodrama and Modernity*, 101–30.

53. Singer, *Melodrama and Modernity*, 102–3.

54. Ana M. López, "Early Cinema and Modernity in Latin America," 49.

55. Wiltenburg, "True Crime," 1378–79. These forms of early modern print culture have affinities with Brazilian *cordel* literature (illustrated pamphlets designed to be declaimed or sung aloud) and Mexican *corridos* (folk ballads based on real-life events).

56. Wiltenburg, "True Crime," 1379, 1378; Brooks, *The Melodramatic Imagination*, 15.

57. Monsiváis, *Los mil y un velorios*, 12.

58. Monsiváis, *Los mil y un velorios*, 13.

59. Mark Seltzer, "Wound Culture," 4. See also Seltzer, *True Crime*.

60. Anderson, *Imagined Communities*, 22–26, 33–36.
61. On literacy and visual elements in Mexican print culture, see Hershfield, *Imagining la Chica Moderna*, 12, 28.
62. Rick A. López, *Crafting Mexico*, 14.
63. Hansen, *Babel and Babylon*, 118, 90–125.
64. Ana M. López, "Early Cinema and Modernity," 61–62.
65. Martín Barbero, *De los medios a las mediaciones*, 243.
66. Herlinghaus, "La imaginación melodramática," 40. Christine Gledhill makes a similar argument for the U.S., U.K., and French contexts in "The Melodramatic Field," 37.
67. Sommer, *Foundational Fictions*. On the folletín in Latin America, see Rivera, *El folletín y la novela popular*; Barros Lémez, *Vidas de papel*. On the Brazilian case, see Meyer, *Folhetim*, 281–404.
68. Martín Barbero, "Memory and Form in the Latin American Soap Opera," 277.
69. Meyer, *Folhetim*, 341–42.
70. On serial form and competition between media, see Hagedorn, "Technological and Economic Exploitation." On the role of iconic characters in serial narratives' self-perpetuating structure, see Mayer, *Serial Fu Manchu*; Abel, "The Thrills of *Grande Peur.*"
71. Dall'Asta, "Italian Serial Films and 'International Popular Culture,'" 302. On the global circulation of serial films and serial stars such as Pearl White, see Canjels, *Distributing Silent Film Serials*; Dahlquist, *Exporting Perilous Pauline*.
72. On reader interaction in serial fiction by Charles Dickens, see Hayward, *Consuming Pleasures*, 21–83; on the participatory aspects of film serials, see Stamp, *Movie-Struck Girls*, 102–75.
73. I use the term "trope of film reception" in the sense outlined by Yuri Tsivian in *Early Cinema in Russia*, 3.
74. F. Ortiga Anckermann, "Notas y comentarios de actualidad," *El Hogar*, 18 December 1914, quoted in Tucker, "*Páginas libres*," 129.
75. Marco-Aurelio Galindo, "Los estrenos cinematográficos: La mujer y el cadáver," *El Universal Ilustrado*, 15 September 1921, 1–2.
76. Fósforo [pseud. Alfonso Reyes and Martín Luis Guzmán], "El cine y el folletín," *España* (Madrid), 25 November 1915, reprinted in González Casanova, *El cine que vió Fósforo*, 135.
77. Fósforo [pseud. Alfonso Reyes and Martín Luis Guzmán], "El cine y el folletín," *España* (Madrid), 25 November 1915, reprinted in González Casanova, *El cine que vió Fósforo*, 135.
78. Raúl Silva Castro, "Entre el cine y el folletín," *Atenea* (Concepción, Chile), August 1931, reprinted in Borge, *Avances de Hollywood*, 92.
79. Castro, "Entre el cine y el folletín," *Atenea* (Concepción, Chile), August 1931, reprinted in Borge, *Avances de Hollywood*, 93.
80. Castro, "Entre el cine y el folletín," *Atenea* (Concepción, Chile), August 1931, reprinted in Borge, *Avances de Hollywood*, 94.

81. Castro, "Entre el cine y el folletín," *Atenea* (Concepción, Chile), August 1931, reprinted in Borge, *Avances de Hollywood*, 91. M. Delly is the shared pseudonym of the siblings Fréderic Henri Petitjean de la Rosière and Jeanne Marie Henriette Petitjean de la Rosière.

82. Ángel Rama discusses forms of power exercised by *letrados* (lettered elites) in Latin America in his influential book *The Lettered City*.

83. Ludmer, *The* Corpus Delicti, 5, emphasis in original.

84. On the role of race and class in defining the boundaries of citizenship in Mexico, see Buffington, *Criminal and Citizen in Modern Mexico*.

85. Piccato, *City of Suspects*, 34–49; Meade, *"Civilizing" Rio*, 33–37.

86. Bretas, *Ordem na cidade*, 70, 132–34; Piccato, *City of Suspects*, 17–49, 170–71.

87. Bretas, *Ordem na cidade*, 43–63, 206–7; Piccato, *City of Suspects*, 41–42; Santoni, "La policía de la Ciudad de México durante el Porfiriato," 104–11.

88. Franco, *Cruel Modernity*, 2.

89. Holden, *Armies without Nations*, 22.

90. Quoted in Nieto and Rojas, *Tiempos del Olympia*, 100.

91. *El Diario Nacional* (Bogotá), reprinted in "Galarza y Carvajal explotan su triste celebridad," *El Cine Gráfico* (Cúcuta), 12 May 1916, n.p. I thank Juan Sebastián Ospina León for sharing the materials from *El Cine Gráfico* cited here and below. A striking parallel case in Spain is *Asesinato y entierro de Don José Canalejas* (*Assassination and Burial of José Canalejas*, Enrique Blanco and Adelardo Fernández Arias, 1912), which combined a reenactment of the assassination of Spain's prime minister with actuality footage of his funeral.

92. The apotheosis is believed to be the only surviving fragment of the film. Nieto and Rojas, *Tiempos del Olympia*, 100–101.

93. "Consecuentes," *El Cine Gráfico*, 28 January 1916, n.p. In his memoir *El águila y la serpiente* (*The Eagle and the Serpent*), Martín Luis Guzmán reports a similar incident involving film images of Venustiano Carranza projected during the 1917 Constitutional Convention. Guzmán, *El águila y la serpiente*, 340; Guzmán, *The Eagle and the Serpent*, 291.

94. The debate about the film and its prohibition in several cities are recorded in "La película inmoral," *El Cine Gráfico*, 5 May 1916, n.p.

95. Martínez Pardo, *Historia del cine colombiano*, 39.

96. The film's credits attribute the direction to P. P. Jambrina, a pseudonym of Martínez Velasco. Suárez and Arbeláez, *"Garras de Oro,"* 59.

97. Martínez Carril, "El pequeño héroe del Arroyo de Oro," 293. A version of the film without intertitles survives at the Cinemateca Uruguaya.

98. Gumucio Dagron, *Historia del cine boliviano*, 83. Portions of Castillo's film survive and have been restored recently by the Cinemateca Boliviana.

99. *La Razón* (La Paz), 30 November 1927, quoted in Gumucio Dagron, *Historia del cine boliviano*, 81.

100. Gumucio Dagron, *Historia del cine boliviano*, 83.

1. Staging Public Violence in Porfirian and Revolutionary Mexico, 1896–1922

1. On the conventions used to create the sense of an unfolding event in early actualities, see Levy, "Re-constituted Newsreels."

2. The footage closely resembles still photographs of the execution that can be viewed in the online catalog of the Fototeca Nacional of the Instituto Nacional de Antropología e Historia. See, for example, the photos numbered 63672, 72252, and 72273.

3. Jablonska and Leal, *La Revolución Mexicana en el cine nacional*, 69.

4. Ramírez Berg, "*El automóvil gris* and the Advent of Mexican Classicism," 8.

5. The sociologist Max Weber considered the monopoly of legitimate violence within a territory to be the foundation of the modern-nation state. See his 1919 lecture "Politics as a Vocation," 33.

6. Vanderwood, *Disorder and Progress*, xi.

7. Debroise, *Mexican Suite*, 175.

8. See Lerner, *El impacto de la modernidad*. The Mexico City newspaper *El Correo Español* makes reference to halftone images showing a reconstruction of the murder of Maria Poucel, published in the local newspaper *El noticiero*. "El noticiero," *El Correo Español*, 20 December 1907, 2.

9. Advertisement, *Excélsior*, 11 September 1919, 8.

10. J. L. del C. [pseud.], "El año cinematográfico," *Don Quijote*, 31 December 1919, n.p. On Necoechea's career as a police reporter, see Federico Gutiérrez, "Páginas truculentas," *El Universal Ilustrado*, 26 October 1922, 37, 61.

11. Hansen, *Babel and Babylon*, 31.

12. Doane, *The Emergence of Cinematic Time*, 158.

13. Doane, *The Emergence of Cinematic Time*, 169.

14. *1810 o los libertadores* (*1810 or the Liberators*), believed to be the first feature-length film made in Mexico, was produced in Mérida, Yucatán, in 1916 by Carlos Martínez de Arredondo and Manuel Cirerol Sansores.

15. Barthes, "The Reality Effect."

16. DVD release of *El automóvil gris*, Filmoteca de la Universidad Nacional Autónoma de México.

17. Miquel, "Las historias completas de la Revolución de Salvador Toscano."

18. The first of these films was based on the films of the cameraman Salvador Toscano and assembled by his daughter; the second was based on the films of Jesús H. Abitia and assembled by Gustavo Carrero.

19. De los Reyes, *Cine y sociedad en México*, 2:91–92. Carranza was assassinated en route to Veracruz by troops loyal to Álvaro Obregón.

20. Script, attributed to Ángel Álvarez, Archivo General de la Nación (Mexico), GD126, Propiedad Artística y Literaria, Caja 393, Expediente 2077, fs. 7.

21. De los Reyes, *Cine y sociedad en México*, 2:78, 88–90. The exhibition of *El proceso de Magdalena Jurado* was advertised in *Excélsior*, 13 April 1922, 8.

22. Gerow, *Visions of Japanese Modernity*, 52–65.

23. Mraz, *Photographing the Mexican Revolution*; Berumen and Canales, *México*; Luna, *La batalla y su sombra*; Orellana, *La mirada circular*, revised and translated

as *Filming Pancho*; Pick, *Constructing the Image of the Mexican Revolution*; Jablonska and Leal, *La Revolución Mexicana en el cine nacional*; Fabio Sánchez and García Muñoz, *La luz y la guerra*; Juan Felipe Leal, *El documental nacional de la Revolución Mexicana*.

24. Lomnitz, *Death and the Idea of Mexico*, 58.

25. A key tenet of Mexican liberal thought was a ban on reelection; for this reason, Díaz encouraged the election of General Manuel González, who served as president from 1880–1884, although Díaz remained in the cabinet. Díaz returned to the presidency in 1884 and would remain in office until 1911.

26. De los Reyes, "Gabriel Veyre y Fernand Bon Bernard," 123, 127–28.

27. For example, *Viaje a Yucatán* (*Trip to the Yucatán*, Salvador Toscano, 1906), *Inauguración del tráfico internacional por el Istmo de Tehuantepec* (*Inauguration of International Traffic on the Isthmus of Tehuantepec*, two versions by the Alva Brothers and Toscano), and *Fiestas del Centenario de la Independencia* (*Festivities of the Centenary of Independence*, multiple versions by the Alva Brothers, Salvador Toscano, and Antonio Ocañas). See de los Reyes, *Filmografía del cine mudo en mexicano, 1896–1920*, 35–36, 39, 58.

28. Lomnitz, *Death and the Idea of Mexico*, 383.

29. Lomnitz, *Death and the Idea of Mexico*, 377–78.

30. Streeby, *Radical Sensations*, 112–72.

31. Buffington, *A Sentimental Education for the Working Man*.

32. Toussaint Alcaraz, *Escenario de la prensa en el Porfiriato*, 31–36.

33. Armando Bartra estimates the proportion of newspaper readers in Mexico at 5 percent of the population in the 1920s, while Florence Toussaint Alcaraz places that of magazine readers at 10 percent in 1910. Bartra, "The Seduction of the Innocents," 302; and Toussaint Alcaraz, *Escenario de la prensa en el Porfiriato*, 69.

34. Torre Rendón, "Las imágenes fotográficas de la sociedad mexicana en la prensa gráfica del porfiriato," 355–65.

35. On journalistic discourses on criminality during the Porfiriato, see Garza, *The Imagined Underworld*; Pérez Montfort, *Hábitos, normas y escándalo*.

36. Castillo Troncoso, "El surgimiento del reportaje policíaco," 167–68.

37. Mraz, *Photographing the Mexican Revolution*, 28.

38. Quoted in Castillo Troncoso, "El surgimiento del reportaje policíaco," 169.

39. Bunker, *Creating Mexican Consumer Culture in the Age of Porfirio Díaz*, 200.

40. Cestas el Roto [pseud.], "La evolución del robo," *El Imparcial*, 7 September 1897, 3.

41. Lerner, *El impacto de la modernidad*, 44.

42. Buffington, *Criminal and Citizen in Modern Mexico*, 38–63.

43. Buffington, *Criminal and Citizen in Modern Mexico*, 8.

44. Piccato, *City of Suspects*, 17–49, especially 26–33. On the "ideal city" in the late Porfiriato, see Tenorio Trillo, "1910 Mexico City," 79–93.

45. Piccato, *City of Suspects*, 41.

46. Piccato, *City of Suspects*, 17–49.

47. Lerner, *El impacto de la modernidad*, 25–26.

48. See Santoni, "La policía de la Ciudad de México durante el Porfiriato."

49. Lerner, *El impacto de la modernidad,* 31–32.

50. Padilla Arroyo, *De Belém a Lecumberri,* 7.

51. Buffington, *Criminal and Citizen in Modern Mexico,* 80.

52. "Nuestro periódico: Su programa," *Gaceta de Policía,* 8 October 1905, 2.

53. The magazine's content was quite heterogeneous; it also published sections on entertainment and sports.

54. Piccato, *City of Suspects,* 77–88.

55. "Asesinato y suicidio," *Gaceta de Policia,* 28 January 1906, 7–8.

56. Castillo Troncoso, "El surgimiento del reportaje policíaco," 179–80.

57. Lerner, *El impacto de la modernidad,* 48–49.

58. See "El último crimen de la Alameda," *El Tiempo,* 8 December 1908, 2.

59. "Reconstrucción del asesinato de Francisco Oviedo," *El Pueblo,* 22 January 1919, 6; "La reconstrucción de la tragedia Serrano Ortiz-Olvera se efectuó ayer por la mañana," *El Universal,* 30 October 1921, 11. A selection of photographic reconstructions from the Casasola archive can be found in Lerner, *El impacto de la modernidad.* However, many of these images are undated, making the history of the practice difficult to trace.

60. See Mraz, *Photographing the Mexican Revolution,* 21; Castillo Troncoso, "El surgimiento del reportaje policíaco," 163–65.

61. Ortiz Gaitán, *Imágenes del deseo,* 40–50; Timoteo Álvarez and Martínez Riaza, *Historia de la prensa hispanoamericana,* 217–18.

62. Casasola has been hailed as the most important photographer of the Revolution, but recent research suggests that he took credit for images taken by his many correspondents. See Gutiérrez Ruvalcaba, "A Fresh Look at the Casasola Archive."

63. Gautreau, "La Revolución Mexicana a los ojos del mundo," 119.

64. Mraz, *Photographing the Mexican Revolution,* 2.

65. Gautreau, "La Revolución Mexicana a los ojos del mundo," 121.

66. Vanderwood and Samponaro, *Border Fury.* Precedents of this practice can be found in the Porfiriato, when photographs of bandits' corpses were presented to authorities as proof of their deaths, and were also sold commercially. Matabuena Peláez, *Algunos usos y conceptos de la fotografía durante el Porfiriato,* 90–92.

67. Vanderwood and Samponaro, *Border Fury,* 68, 94–95, 98.

68. Mraz, *Photographing the Mexican Revolution,* 17, 12. See also Gutiérrez Ruvalcaba, "A Fresh Look at the Casasola Archive," 191.

69. Mraz, *Photographing the Mexican Revolution,* 102–4.

70. Orellana, *Filming Pancho,* especially 79–85.

71. See Pick, *Constructing the Image of the Mexican Revolution,* 40. The contract is reproduced in Delgadillo et al., *La mirada desenterrada,* 163–73. See also de los Reyes, *Con Villa en México.*

72. Like the Revolutionary nonfiction films, *The Life of General Villa* was cannibalized for later use. It was reedited with images from other sources, including the anti-Mexican serial *Liberty, a Daughter of the U.S.A.,* and screened as *La venganza de*

Pancho Villa (*The Revenge of Pancho Villa*) by the itinerant exhibitor Félix Padilla in the 1930s. See Serna, *"La venganza de Pancho Villa."*

73. Advertisement, *El Imparcial*, 14 February 1914, 5.

74. "Correo de espectáculos," *El Imparcial*, 7 November 1912, 7.

75. De los Reyes, *Filmografía del cine mudo mexicano, 1896–1920*, 104.

76. De los Reyes, *Cine y sociedad en México*, 1:92–93; de los Reyes, "The Silent Cinema," 65.

77. Fullerton, *Picturing Mexico*, 152–53.

78. De los Reyes, *Cine y sociedad en México*, 1:96–98.

79. De los Reyes, *Cine y sociedad en México*, 2:119; Juan Felipe Leal, *El documental nacional de la Revolución Mexicana*, 28.

80. Fabio Sánchez, "Vistas de modernidad y guerra," *La luz y la guerra*, 128–29.

81. Miquel, "Las historias completas de la Revolución de Salvador Toscano," 66. Juan Felipe Leal gives the alternate titles *Revolución felicista* (*The Revolution of Félix Díaz*) and *La caída del gobierno de Madero* (*The Fall of Madero's Government*) for this film. Juan Felipe Leal, *El documental nacional de la Revolución Mexicana*, 148.

82. Ortiz Monasterio, *Fragmentos*, 122–23.

83. *El Independiente*, 16 February 1914, quoted in Jablonska and Leal, *La Revolución Mexicana en el cine nacional*, 53.

84. *El Imparcial*, 15 February 1914, 6.

85. Meade, "Modern Warfare Meets 'Mexico's Evil Tradition,'" 123, 133.

86. Meade, "Modern Warfare Meets 'Mexico's Evil Tradition,'" 133.

87. Quoted in de los Reyes, *Filmografía del cine mudo mexicano, 1896–1920*, 104.

88. Jablonska and Leal, *La Revolución Mexicana en el cine nacional*, 69; Juan Felipe Leal, *El documental nacional de la Revolución Mexicana*, 33.

89. Ana M. López, "Early Cinema and Modernity in Latin America," 69; de los Reyes, "The Silent Cinema," 71.

90. De los Reyes, "The Silent Cinema," 71; de los Reyes, *Cine y sociedad en México*, 1:95–98, 209.

91. "¡Basta de Crímenes!," *El Universal*, 29 October 1919, 3.

92. For a discussion of the term *ratero* and the 1917–1918 campaign against rateros in *El Universal*, see Piccato, *City of Suspects*, 163–88.

93. "El Bautizo de Sangre," *El Universal*, 4 November 1919, 3.

94. Piccato, *City of Suspects*, 176.

95. Piccato, *City of Suspects*, 5, 99–100, 177–79.

96. "Enfermedades Citadinas," *Revista de Revistas*, 1 October 1916, 1.

97. See Silvestre Paradox [pseud. Arqueles Vela Salvatierra], "Los crímenes modernos," *El Universal Ilustrado*, 28 December 1922, 31; Silvestre Bonnard [pseud. Carlos Noriega Hope], "El asesinato en el cine," *El Universal Ilustrado*, 25 March 1920, 6; Fígaro [pseud. Porfirio Hernández], "El raterismo considerado como una de las bellas artes," *El Universal*, 3 May 1922, 9; and *El Universal Ilustrado*, "El suicidio considerado como una de las bellas artes," 1 February 1923, 11.

98. For example, a 1921 headline promised to describe "the Rocambolesque escape of the Famous and Celebrated Chato Bernabé," one of the alleged members of the Grey Automobile Gang. *El Universal*, 5 February 1921, 1. Exhibition dates for the Pathé films are drawn from Amador and Ayala Blanco, *Cartelera cinematográfica 1912–1919*, 33.

99. Abel, "The Thrills of *Grande Peur*"; Serna, *Making Cinelandia*, 24–26.

100. "La modernización de nuestros ladrones," *Excélsior*, 26 October 1919, 15.

101. Jerónimo Coignard [pseud. Francisco Zamora], "El cine y la moralidad," *El Universal*, 1 September 1919, 3.

102. De los Reyes, *Cine y sociedad en México*, 1:256. See also Matute, "Salud, familia y moral social," 33–34; Serna, *Making Cinelandia*, 74–76.

103. Quoted in "La censura de las películas no es anticonstitucional," *El Universal*, 29 January 1920, 11.

104. The three serials were *The Exploits of Elaine* (Louis Gasnier and George B. Seitz, 1914), the *New Exploits of Elaine* (George B. Seitz, 1915), and the *Romance of Elaine* (George B. Seitz, 1916).

105. Nemo [pseud.], "La cinematografía en Estados Unidos," *Don Quijote*, 28 May 1919, n.p.

106. Amador and Ayala Blanco, *Cartelera cinematográfica*, 54; *El Nacional*, 26 August 1916, 6; *El Universal*, 1 March 1917, 1; *El Universal*, 4 January 1918, 8.

107. Serna, *Making Cinelandia*, 109; advertisement for International Pictures, *Excélsior*, 8 January 1920, 8.

108. Bean, "Technologies of Early Stardom and the Extraordinary Body."

109. Don Manolito [pseud.], "Cines: Arte americano," *Arte y Sport*, 27 March 1920, 11.

110. Nemo [pseud.], "La cinematografía en Estados Unidos," *Don Quijote*, 28 May 1919, n.p.

111. Altman, "A Semantic/Syntactic Approach to Film Genre."

112. Hipólito Seijas [pseud. Rafael Pérez Taylor], "Por la pantalla: La hija del circo," *El Universal*, 16 March 1917, reprinted in González Casanova, *Por la pantalla*, 167.

113. Hipólito Seijas [pseud. Rafael Pérez Taylor], "La garra de hierro," *El Universal*, 23 March 1917, reprinted in González Casanova, *Por la pantalla*, 179.

114. Hipólito Seijas [pseud. Rafael Pérez Taylor], "Los vampiros," *El Universal*, 26 May 1917, reprinted in González Casanova, *Por la pantalla*, 232–33. Serna, *Making Cinelandia*, 25.

115. Marco-Aurelio Galindo, "Los estrenos cinematográficos: La mujer y el cadáver," *El Universal Ilustrado*, 15 September 1921, 1–2.

116. The sole example I have encountered is a Spanish-language novelization of *Los misterios de Nueva York* published as a folletín in the French-language newspaper *Le Courrier du Mexique et de l'Europe* after the film's first run had ended.

117. Nemo [pseud.], "La cinematografía en Estados Unidos," *Don Quijote*, 28 May 1919, n.p.

118. Martín Luis Guzmán (attributed), "Por el teatro del silencio: Frente a la pantalla," *El Universal*, 26 December 1920, 19. See also "Fósforo," "El cine y el folletín," *Frente*

a la Pantalla, 25 November 1915, reprinted in González Casanova, *El cine que vio Fósforo*, 136.

119. Martín Luis Guzmán (attributed), "Por el teatro del silencio: Frente a la pantalla," *El Universal*, 26 December 1920, 19.

120. Lázaro P. Feel [pseud. Rafael López], "Crónica semanal: La película policíaca," *Revista de Revistas*, 24 September 1916, 2.

121. Singer, *Melodrama and Modernity*, 59–101.

122. "En torno de un automóvil," *El Universal Ilustrado*, 10 January 1919, 6.

123. Quoted in de los Reyes, *Cine y sociedad en México*, 1:239.

124. De los Reyes, *Cine y sociedad en México*, 1:240.

125. Advertisement, *El Universal*, 30 January 1919, 1; Hipólito Seijas [pseud. Rafael Pérez Taylor], "Un lío cinematográfico," *El Universal*, 2 February 1919, reprinted in González Casanova, *Por la pantalla*, 338.

126. Advertisement, *El Universal*, 30 January 1919, 7.

127. Advertisement, *Excélsior*, 2 September 1919, 8.

128. Gabriel Ramírez, *El cine yucateco*, 59.

129. "La banda del automóvil," *Excélsior*, 2 September 1919, 7; *El Universal*, 2 September 1919, 6.

130. "Acusación por una Película de Cine," *Excélsior*, 5 December 1919, 7; "Teme que recojan la película," *El Universal*, 12 September 1919, 9.

131. Silvestre Bonnard [pseud. Carlos Noriega Hope], "El automóvil gris," *El Universal*, December 1919, 5.

132. J. L. del C. [pseud.], "El año cinematográfico," *Don Quijote*, 31 December 1919, n.p.

133. Silvestre Bonnard [pseud. Carlos Noriega Hope], "La banda del automóvil," *El Universal*, 11 September 1919, 7.

134. Advertisement, *Excélsior*, 15 January 1920, 8; Epifanio Soto Jr., "Crónica de Méjico," *Cine-Mundial*, February 1920, 252.

135. "La cinematografía en México," *Don Quijote*, 1 October 1919, n.p.

136. Piccato, *City of Suspects*, 185.

137. De los Reyes, *Cine y sociedad*, 1:183.

138. De los Reyes, *Cine y sociedad*, 1:248.

139. Piccato, *City of Suspects*, 178.

140. Serrano and del Moral, *Cuadernos de la Cineteca Nacional*, 28–29, 37–38. The original script is held in the Archivo General de la Nación.

141. Silvestre Bonnard [pseud. Carlos Noriega Hope], "El automóvil gris," *El Universal*, 13 December 1919, 5.

142. Schroeder-Rodríguez, "Latin American Silent Cinema," 50.

143. Schroeder-Rodríguez, "Latin American Silent Cinema," 50.

144. On urban reforms in Mexico City, see Piccato, *City of Suspects*, 17–21; Tenorio Trillo, "1910 Mexico City"; Tenenbaum, "Streetwise History." On criminal or illegitimate activity within circuits of modern traffic, see Whissel, *Picturing American Modernity*, 161–84, 206–14.

145. Ramírez Berg, "*El automóvil gris* and the Advent of Mexican Classicism," 4.

146. Epifanio Soto Jr., "Crónica de Méjico," *Cine-Mundial*, February 1920, 252.

147. "'La banda del automóvil' es un portento de fotografía," *El Heraldo de México*, 4 September 1919, 8.

148. This was a novel practice for local productions; the most successful locally produced film of the previous year, *Santa*, was filmed entirely with natural light in an improvised space in the Cinema Olimpia. José María Sánchez García, "Tres películas inolvidables," *Cinema Repórter*, 15 March 1952, 78.

149. "'La banda del automóvil' es un portento de fotografía," *El Heraldo de México*, 4 September 1919, 8.

150. On the electrification of Mexico City during the Porfiriato, see Briseño, *Candil de la calle, oscuridad de su casa*.

151. "'La banda del automóvil' será un suceso," *El Heraldo de México*, 10 September 1919, 9.

152. Mraz, *Photographing the Mexican Revolution*, 35.

153. Epifanio Soto Jr., "Crónica de Méjico," *Cine-Mundial*, November 1919, 897.

154. Advertisement, *Cine-Mundial*, January 1920, 61–62; "Los Sres. Camus, Vollrath y Carrasco en Nueva York," *Cine-Mundial*, January 1920, 156.

155. "Una casa de comercio iba a ser robada," *El Pueblo*, 7 September 1916, 1.

156. J. L. del C. [pseud.], "El año cinematográfico," *Don Quijote*, 31 December 1919, n.p.

157. De los Reyes, *Cine y sociedad en México*, 1:246–47.

158. *Excélsior*, 7 September 1919, sec. 2, 1.

159. *Don Quijote*, 31 December 1919, n.p.

160. Epifanio Soto Jr., "Crónica de Méjico," *Cine-Mundial*, November 1919, 897.

161. De los Reyes, *Cine y sociedad en México* 2:73–88.

162. Zeta [pseud. Francisco Zamora], "La figura de la semana: Alicia Olvera," *El Universal Ilustrado*, 30 December 1920, 14. Female readers were attributed with a particular taste for sensational true-crime narratives; for example, see Jack the Ripper [pseud.], "Los crímenes del día y sus efectos," *El Universal Ilustrado*, 30 October 1919, 22.

163. Piccato, *City of Suspects*, 103–32.

164. Piccato, "The Girl Who Killed a Senator," 128.

165. Cube Bonifant, "Crónicas cinematográficas: 'Redención' película mexicana en siete rollos," *El Demócrata*, 4 July 1924, 3.

166. "Hilda North: Estrella cinematográfica americana, grabará una película de Series en México," *Excélsior*, 10 November 1919, 8.

167. "Chucho el Roto en Película," *Don Quijote*, 19 November 1919, n.p.

168. See Serna, *Making Cinelandia*, 127–38; Hershfield, *Imagining la Chica Moderna*, 58–60.

169. De los Reyes, "Las películas denigrantes a México"; Serna, "'As a Mexican I Feel It's My Duty,'"; Vasey, *The World According to Hollywood*, 93–94, 170–76.

170. Advertisement, *Excélsior*, 14 October 1922, sec. 2, 6.

171. The paradigmatic example is *The Perils of Pauline* (Louis Gasnier and Donald Mackenzie, 1914).

172. This strategy was also customary in publicity surrounding U.S. serial queens. See advertisement, *Excélsior*, 15 October 1922, 6; advertisement, *El Universal*, 15 Octo-

ber 1922, 6; photographs, Archivo General de la Nación (Mexico), GD126, Propiedad Artística y Literaria, Caja 393, Expediente 2077, fs. 7.

173. Singer, *Melodrama and Modernity*, 208–9.

174. The secretary of war later funded another film, *Cuando la patria lo manda* (*When the Fatherland Calls*), based on the same events. See de los Reyes, *Cine y sociedad en México*, 2:92.

175. José María Sánchez García, "Comentarios adicionales: Lo que dice Ángel E. Álvarez," *Cinema Repórter*, 13 October 1954, 30.

176. De los Reyes, *Cine y sociedad en México*, 2:223. The film premiered on 14 October 1922 in ten theaters; its final day of exhibition was 17 October, when it was shown in only two theaters. Advertisement, *El Universal*, 14 October 1922, 6; advertisement, *El Universal*, October 17, 1922, 4.

177. Script, *Fanny o el robo de los veinte millones*, Archivo General de la Nación (Mexico), GD126, Propiedad Artística y Literaria, Caja 393, Expediente 2077, fs. 7, 7–8.

178. Military aviation played a pivotal role in *Alas abiertas* (*Wings Outspread*, Ernesto Vollrath and Luis Lezama, 1921).

179. Script, *Fanny o el robo de los veinte millones*, Archivo General de la Nación (Mexico), GD126, Propiedad Artística y Literaria, Caja 393, Expediente 2077, fs. 7, 3; Piccato, *City of Suspects*, 35.

180. Script, *Fanny o el robo de los veinte millones*, Archivo General de la Nación (Mexico), GD126, Propiedad Artística y Literaria, Caja 393, Expediente 2077, fs. 7, 4, 9–10.

181. Quoted in José María Sánchez García, "Comentarios adicionales: Lo que dice Eduardo Urriola," *Cinema Repórter*, 20 October 1954, 29–30.

182. Bean, "Technologies of Early Stardom and the Extraordinary Body," 12.

183. Script, *Fanny o el robo de los veinte millones*, Archivo General de la Nación (Mexico), GD126, Propiedad Artística y Literaria, Caja 393, Expediente 2077, fs. 7, 11–13.

184. Script, *Fanny o el robo de los veinte millones,* Archivo General de la Nación (Mexico), GD126, Propiedad Artística y Literaria, Caja 393, Expediente 2077, fs. 7, 11–13.

185. Epifanio Soto Jr., "La producción mejicana tan denigrante como la Yanqui," *Cine-Mundial*, December 1922, 688.

2. On Location

1. Silvestre Bonnard [pseud. Carlos Noriega Hope], "El héroe de la película," *El Universal*, 12 September 1920, 18. See also Silvestre Bonnard [pseud. Carlos Noriega Hope], "Fernando Elizondo e Italia Almirante Manzini," *El Universal*, 10 August 1920, 12.

2. Miquel, *Por las pantallas*, 74.

3. Silvestre Bonnard [pseud. Carlos Noriega Hope], "El héroe de la película," *El Universal*, 12 September 1920, 18.

4. Silvestre Bonnard [pseud. Carlos Noriega Hope], "El héroe de la película," *El Universal*, 12 September 1920, 18.

5. Altamirano's novel was completed in 1888, but published posthumously only in 1901. Advertisement, *El Universal*, 6 November 1920, 8.

6. Miquel, *Por las pantallas*, 128.

7. Miquel, *Por las pantallas*, 92–94. On film-related contests, see Serna, *Making Cinelandia*, 144–51.

8. On cultural nationalism in the postrevolutionary period, see Knight, "Popular Culture and the Revolutionary State in Mexico"; Vaughn and Lewis, *The Eagle and the Virgin*; Rick A. López, *Crafting Mexico*.

9. On representations of Mexico and ideologies of empire in sensational literature during the Mexican–American War, see Streeby, *American Sensations*, especially 93–97, 102–4, 112–38. On U.S. films about the Mexican Revolution, see Orellana, *La mirada circular*, revised and translated as *Filming Pancho*; de los Reyes, *Con Villa en México*.

10. On "denigrating films" and the 1922 boycott, see de los Reyes, "Las películas denigrantes a México"; Serna, "'As a Mexican I Feel It's My Duty,'"; Serna, *Making Cinelandia*, 154–79; Vasey, *The World According to Hollywood*, 93–94, 170–76.

11. Gunckel, *Mexico on Main Street*, 32; De los Reyes, *Cine y sociedad en México*, 2:230–34.

12. R[afael] Bermudez Z[atarain], "Notas cinematográficas," *El Universal*, 27 February 1921, 22.

13. Quoted in an interview with Silvestre Bonnard [pseud. Carlos Noriega Hope], "Siluetas de artistas cinematográficas," *El Universal*, 8 May 1921, section 4, 6.

14. Vollrath produced *La parcela* independently after ending his working relationship with Camus. See Epifanio Soto Jr., "Ernesto Vollrath: Primera figura del cine mejicano," *Cine-Mundial*, October 1922, 542.

15. De los Reyes, *Filmografía del cine mudo mexicano, 1920–1924*, 72, 111, 140, 166.

16. One reviewer noted that *El Zarco* was "inspired by" Altamirano's text rather than being an adaptation. David Wark [pseud.], "Por nuestras pantallas: La resonancia de la semana: 'El Zarco,'" *El Universal*, 14 November 1920, 22. *La parcela* was described as "taken from scenes of the novel by Mr. José López Portillo y Rojas." Blas Hernán, "Crónicas de cine: 'La parcela,'" *Revista de Revistas*, 25 February 1923, 38.

17. On landscape and location shooting in silent westerns, see Smith, *Shooting Cowboys and Indians*, 15, 38; Abel, *Americanizing the Movies and "Movie-Mad" Audiences*, 63. On landscape and expansionist ideology in early American film more broadly, see Bertellini, *Italy in Early American Cinema*, 95–133.

18. De los Reyes notes a decline from fourteen films in 1922, to ten in 1923, to five in 1924. De los Reyes, *Cine y sociedad en México*, 2:244.

19. On the use of films in public-health campaigns, see de los Reyes, *Cine y sociedad en México*, 3:415, 434–39; Serna, *Making Cinelandia*, 71–73; Agostoni, "Popular Health Education and Propaganda in Times of Peace and War," 56, 59.

20. De los Reyes, *Cine y sociedad en México*, 3:440–44.

21. De los Reyes attributes the film's commercial failure to the first factor, Esperanza Vázquez Bernal and William M. Drew to the second. See de los Reyes, *Cine y sociedad en México*, 3:443; Drew and Vázquez Bernal, *"El Puño de Hierro,"* 18.

22. De los Reyes, *Cine y sociedad en México*, 2:212–13.

23. Saragoza, "The Selling of Mexico."

24. Bertellini, *Italy in Early American Cinema.*

25. Monterde, "Carlos Noriega Hope y su obra literaria," 12–13.

26. On film-related contests, see Serna, *Making Cinelandia*, 103, 113–15, 148–50. On the India Bonita contest, see Rick A. López, *Crafting Mexico*, 29–64.

27. Rick A. López, *Crafting Mexico*, 30, 129–37.

28. Rick A. López, *Crafting Mexico*, 8.

29. Gunckel, *Mexico on Main Street*, 132.

30. Silvestre Bonnard [pseud. Carlos Noriega Hope], "La India Bonita en el teatro y en el cine," *El Universal Ilustrado*, 17 August 1921, 31.

31. Saragoza, "The Selling of Mexico," 99–101.

32. Dolores del Río's casting in the title role of *María Candelaria* (Emilio Fernández, 1944) is perhaps the best-known example.

33. "'En la hacienda': La próxima película nacional," *El Universal Ilustrado*, 19 January 1922, 29.

34. Saragoza, "The Selling of Mexico"; Berger, *The Development of Mexico's Tourism Industry*, 11–26.

35. De los Reyes, *Cine y sociedad en México*, 3:444–45.

36. De los Reyes, *Cine y sociedad en México*, 2:211, 215–16.

37. De los Reyes, *Cine y sociedad en México*, 2:219.

38. Gabara, *Errant Modernism*, 146, 168.

39. Miquel, *Por las pantallas*, 95.

40. Advertisement, *Film Daily*, 17 April 1920, 4.

41. Contreras Torres later traveled to Los Angeles for the filming of *El hombre sin patria*, boasting of the Hollywood stars he met during the process. Miguel Contreras Torres, "Cómo filmé una película en Los Angeles," *El Universal Ilustrado*, 17 August 1922, 34–35, 63.

42. Advertisement, *El Universal*, 30 January 1922, 6; advertisement, *El Universal*, 1 February 1922.

43. Quoted in de los Reyes, *Filmografía del cine mudo mexicano, 1920–1924*, 121.

44. Silvestre Bonnard [pseud. Carlos Noriega Hope], "Estrella de cine, ferrocarrilero y hombre de buena voluntad," *El Universal*, 11 July 1920, 18.

45. Roberto el Diablo [pseud. Roberto Núñez y Domínguez], "Crónicas de cine: El primer mexicano que filma en Nueva York," *Revista de Revistas*, 25 July 1920, 28.

46. Écran [pseud.], "La última odisea cinematográfica," *El Universal*, 8 August 1920, 9. The journalist uses the correct spelling of *desesperado* (desperate), incorrectly spelled as the English loanword *desperado*.

47. El Caballero Mordaz [pseud.], "De cómo 'El Zarco' causó alboroto en Tacuba," *El Universal*, 27 August 1920, 8.

48. El Caballero Mordaz [pseud.], "De cómo 'El Zarco' causó alboroto en Tacuba," *El Universal*, 27 August 1920, 8.

49. Noriega Hope recounted his trip in a series of newspaper articles and his book *El mundo de las sombras: El cine por dentro y por fuera* (*The World of Shadows: Cinema Inside and Out*).

50. Silvestre Bonnard [pseud. Carlos Noriega Hope], "Cómo se hizo una película de charros," *El Universal*, 7 November 1920, 22.

51. Roberto El Diablo [pseud. Roberto Jesús y Núñez], "La hermosa novela 'El Zarco' en película," *Revista de Revistas*, 24 October 1920.

52. El Caballero Mordaz [pseud.], "Un conquistador," *El Universal*, 12 September 1920, 6, emphasis in original.

53. Serna, "'We're Going Yankee,'" 175–80.

54. Quoted in Juan de Ega, "El alma de México en el cine," *El Universal Ilustrado*, 17 March 1921, 17.

55. Rick A. López, *Crafting Mexico*, 30–32, 53, 61–64.

56. Quoted in Juan de Ega, "El alma de México en el cine," *El Universal Ilustrado*, 17 March 1921, 17.

57. Quoted in Silvestre Bonnard [pseud. Carlos Noriega Hope], "Cómo se hizo una película de charros," *El Universal*, 7 November 1920, 22.

58. Quoted in Silvestre Bonnard [pseud. Carlos Noriega Hope], "En busca de las estrellas," *El Universal*, 6 February 1921, 20.

59. Nájera Ramírez, "Engendering Nationalism," 6.

60. Quoted in Juan de Ega, "El alma de México en el cine," *El Universal Ilustrado*, 17 March 1921, 17.

61. De los Reyes, *Filmografía del cine mudo mexicano, 1920–1924*, 112–13.

62. On the recognition of virtue in melodrama, see Brooks, *The Melodramatic Imagination*, 29–36.

63. "Un enorme escándalo en varias salas de cine," *El Universal*, 7 November 1920.

64. In an advertisement for *El caporal*, the company marketed itself as "the house of monumental serials." Advertisement, *El Universal*, 1 July 1921, 3. The company announced its decision to distribute *De raza azteca* in an advertisement in *El Universal*, 29 January 1922, 6.

65. Epifanio Soto Jr., "Yo prefiero las morenas, dice Miguel Contreras Torres," *Cine-Mundial*, November 1922, 604.

66. Silvestre Bonnard [pseud. Carlos Noriega Hope], "Cómo se hizo una película de charros," *El Universal*, 7 November 1920, 22. See also Bill Hart [pseud.], "Al margen de 'El Zarco,'" *El Universal*, 16 January 1921, 21.

67. Silvestre Bonnard [pseud. Carlos Noriega Hope], "Cómo se hizo una película de charros," *El Universal*, 7 November 1920, 22.

68. Cube Bonifant, "Por la hoja de plata: Permitan que les cuente algo," *El Universal Ilustrado*, 7 July 1921, 15.

69. "Fue un éxito el estreno de *El caporal*," *El Universal*, 3 July 1921, 6.

70. "Una gran película de tendencias nacionalistas," *El Universal*, 4 February 1922, 6.

71. De los Reyes, *Filmografía del cine mudo mexicano, 1920–1924*, 141–42.

72. Roberto El Diablo [pseud. Roberto Núñez y Domínguez], "Contreras Torres y su nueva película 'De raza azteca,'" *Revista de Revistas*, 18 December 1921, 42.

73. Epifanio Soto Jr., "Crónica de Mejico," *Cine-Mundial*, April 1922, 204.

74. "Un realismo hasta ahora no empleado en México distingue a la última producción de Contreras Torres," *El Universal*, 20 August 1922, 10.

75. Silvestre Bonnard [pseud. Carlos Noriega Hope], "El nacionalismo agresivo," *El Universal*, 15 October 1922, sec. 4, 5.

76. Epifanio Soto Jr., "La producción mexicana tan denigrante como la Yanqui," *Cine-Mundial*, December 1922, 667–68.

77. Silvestre Bonnard [pseud. Carlos Noriega Hope], "Las películas mexicanas de acción directa," *El Universal*, 10 December 1922, section 4, 6.

78. Serna, *Making Cinelandia*, 171, 173.

79. The footage was preserved in the office of William Mayer, García Moreno's business partner, and salvaged by Aurelio de los Reyes. De los Reyes, *Cine y sociedad en México*, 3:440.

80. Drew and Vázquez Bernal, "*El Puño de Hierro*," 13, 16.

81. De los Reyes, *Cine y sociedad en México*, 3:444.

82. Drew and Vázquez Bernal, "*El Puño de Hierro*," 18.

83. Wood, "Recuperar lo efímero," 131.

84. De los Reyes, *Cine y sociedad en México*, 3:440.

85. Drew and Vázquez Bernal, "*El Puño de Hierro*," 20.

86. Dávalos Orozco and Vázquez Bernal, *Carlos Villatoro*, 18.

87. Advertisement, *Alborada*, 16 January 1927, 2.

88. Drew and Vázquez Bernal, "*El Puño de Hierro*," 13.

89. Drew and Vázquez Bernal, "*El Puño de Hierro*," 11.

90. "Sección de Rotograbado," *El Dictamen*, 21 May 1927, n.p.

91. "Una película hecha por ferrocarrileros," *El Universal Ilustrado*, 24 February 1927, 15.

92. De los Reyes, *Cine y sociedad en México*, 3:444.

93. Kirby, *Parallel Tracks*, 5.

94. Gonzales, *The Mexican Revolution*, 69, 197.

95. Hoy, *A Social History of Mexico's Railroads*, xx.

96. Moore, *Forty Miles from the Sea*, 97–99.

97. See Waters, "Remapping Identities," 221–22.

98. See Whissel, *Picturing American Modernity*, especially 161–84, 206–14.

99. Hoy, *A Social History of Mexico's Railroads*, 112–20.

100. Schivelbusch, *The Railway Journey*, 31.

101. Advertisement, *El Universal*, 17 April 1927, 10; "La industria nacional y el cinematógrafo," *El Universal*, 13 April 1927, 4.

102. See Martin Lefebvre on the distinction between setting (a representation of place subordinated to its narrative function) and landscape as "space freed from eventhood." Lefebvre, "Between Setting and Landscape in the Cinema," 22.

103. Drew and Vázquez Bernal, "*El Puño de Hierro*," 13.

104. Kirby, *Parallel Tracks*, 107.
105. On melodrama's dialectic between "too late" and "in the nick of time," see Linda Williams, *Playing the Race Card*, 30–31; Linda Williams, "Melodrama Revised," 69–74.
106. Advertisement, *El Dictamen*, 10 February 1927, 12.
107. "Revista de espectáculos: Del estreno del 'Tren Fantasma' en Veracruz," *El Dictamen*, 15 February 1927, 8.
108. "Una película de factura veracruzana," *El Dictamen*, 2 June 1927, 8; de los Reyes, *Cine y sociedad en México*, 3:434–40. On postrevolutionary public-health campaigns, see Pierce, "Fighting Bacteria, the Bible, and the Bottle."
109. Drew and Vázquez Bernal, "*El Puño de Hierro*," 16. On the overlap between educational and exploitation film in the United States and exploitation's repurposing of existing clinical footage, see Schaefer, "Exploitation as Education."
110. Drew and Vázquez Bernal, "*El Puño de Hierro*," 16.
111. "Espectáculos: '*El puño de hierro*' y sus intérpretes," *El Dictamen*, 6 June 1927, 6.
112. Drew and Vázquez Bernal, "*El Puño de Hierro*," 18–19.

3. Reconstructing Crime in Rio de Janeiro and São Paulo, 1906–1913

1. Bretas, *Ordem na cidade*, 84–85.
2. *Correio da Manhã*, 12 November 1908, 10. The film was first exhibited on 3 August 1908. *Gazeta de Notícias*, 3 August 1908, 6. Melo Souza, *Imagens do passado*, 247.
3. Melo Souza, *Imagens do passado*, 17.
4. Melo Souza, *Imagens do passado*, 16.
5. Melo Souza, *Imagens do passado*, 87–104. See also Bernadet, *Historiografia clássica do cinema brasileiro*, 34–48. Works that propose the existence of a "bela época" of Brazilian cinema include Randal Johnson, *The Film Industry in Brazil*, 19–40; Salles Gomes, "Cinema."
6. Bernadet, *Filmografia do cinema brasileiro*, n.p. The films were also publicized, respectively, under the titles *1.400 contos* (the monetary amount of the theft) and *O crime de Paula Matos*, a reference to the location where the murder occurred.
7. Whissel, *Picturing American Modernity*, especially 161–84, 206–14.
8. Bernadet, *Historiografia clássica do cinema brasileiro*, 85–86.
9. Schwartz, *Spectacular Realities*.
10. Guimarães, "Imaginários do sensacionalismo," 109–10; Needell, *A Tropical Belle Époque*, 28–51.
11. Chaloub, *Trabalho, lar e botequim*, 19–20.
12. Franco, *Cruel Modernity*, 2.
13. Ministério da Agricultura, Indústria e Comércio, *Recenseamento do Brasil realizado em 1 de Setembro de 1920*, vol. IV, part IV, ix.
14. "Monstruoso crime," *Correio Paulistano*, 5 September 1908, 1.
15. "Civilização e policia," *Gazeta de Notícias*, 17 October 1906, 1.
16. On the U.S. case, see Spencer, *The Yellow Journalism*, 102–16.
17. National census figures, available on the website of the Instituto Brasileiro de Geografia e Estatística, http://www.censo2010.ibge.gov.br/sinopse/index.php?dados=6&uf=00.

18. Love, "Political Participation in Brazil," 9.
19. See Needell, *A Tropical Belle Époque*, 31–45; Hardoy, "Theory and Practice of Urban Planning in Europe."
20. Melo Souza, *Imagens do passado*, 116.
21. Meade, *"Civilizing" Rio*, 36.
22. Bretas, *Ordem na cidade*, 21.
23. Bretas, *Ordem na cidade*, 44, 49.
24. "Estranguladores do Rio," *Jornal do Brasil*, 16 October 1906, 3.
25. Santos, "Historical Roots of the 'Whitening' of Brasil," 61–63.
26. Marcos Luiz Bretas notes that a report by the police reformer Alfredo Pinto broke down crime statistics by nationality to demonstrate the dangers posed by foreigners. Bretas, *Ordem na cidade*, 69.
27. Bretas, *Ordem na cidade*, 19.
28. See Gunning, "Embarrassing Evidence," 53–59.
29. "Relatório de policia," *Boletim de Policia*, July 1908 (ano II, n. 3), 138. I have found only fragmentary information regarding the adoption of photographic identification by the authorities in Rio de Janeiro.
30. Bretas, *Ordem na cidade*, 134.
31. Melo Souza, *Imagens do passado*, 152.
32. Sekula, "The Body and the Archive," 7.
33. Meade, *"Civilizing" Rio*, 113–14.
34. Meade, *"Civilizing" Rio*, 3.
35. Schwartz, *Spectacular Realities*, 5.
36. For explorations of the relationship between film and the crônica, see Conde, *Consuming Visions*, 21–49; Süssekind, *Cinematograph of Words*, 22–30.
37. Do Rio, *A alma encantadora das ruas*, 9. See also do Rio, *Cinematógrafo*. Despite his Afro-Brazilian heritage and presumed homosexuality, João do Rio [pseud. Paulo Barreto] is usually considered an apologist for rather than a critic of Brazil's First Republic.
38. Valéria Guimarães comments on do Rio's crime reportage in "Imaginários do sensacionalismo," 98.
39. Do Rio, "Tabuletas," *Gazeta de Notícias*, 7 March 1907, reprinted in do Rio, *A alma encantadora das ruas*, 97–98.
40. Werneck Sodré, *Historia da imprensa no Brasil*, 304, 309.
41. Guimarães, "Imaginários do sensacionalismo," 100.
42. Werneck Sodré, *Historia da imprensa no Brasil*, 292–94, 313.
43. "Simples apresentação," *Revista da Semana*, 20 May 1900, 2.
44. Süssekind, *Cinematógraph of Words*, 21.
45. Do Rio, *Cinematógrafo*, x. These translations are my own; an alternate translation appears in Conde, *Consuming Visions*, 185–87.
46. Do Rio, *Cinematógrafo*, v.
47. Do Rio, *Cinematógrafo*, xi.
48. Do Rio, *Cinematógrafo*, v.

49. Toulmin and Loiperdinger, "Is It You?," 16.

50. Hansen, *Babel and Babylon*, 90–25.

51. Melo Souza, *Imagens do passado*, 143–46.

52. Binóculo [pseud. Figueiredo Pimentel], *Gazeta de Notícias*, 15 February 1908, 2; Binóculo [pseud. Figueiredo Pimentel], *Gazeta de Notícias*, 17 February 1908, 2.

53. Melo Souza, *Imagens do passado*, 152.

54. Needell, *A Tropical Belle Époque*, 167–71.

55. Do Rio, *A alma encantadora das ruas*, 174.

56. Do Rio, *A alma encantadora das ruas*, 174–75.

57. Do Rio, *Cinematógrafo*, 32.

58. See especially Horkheimer and Adorno, *Dialectic of Enlightenment*.

59. Guimarães, "Tensões e ambigüidades na crônica sensacionalista," 231.

60. "A quadrilha da morte," *Gazeta de Notícias*, 16 October 1906, 1.

61. On literary treatments of the illumination and electrification of Rio de Janeiro, see Beal, *Brazil Under Construction*, 23–54. On parallels between the screen and the shop window, see Friedberg, *Window Shopping*, 66–68.

62. Meyer, "Voláteis e versáteis."

63. Broca, *Românticos, pre-românticos, ultraromânticos*, 174–75.

64. Sevcenko, *Literatura como missão*, 201–34.

65. Barreto, *Recordações do escrivão Isaías Caminha*, 206.

66. Barreto, *Recordações do escrivão Isaías Caminha*, 198, 196.

67. Guimarães, "Tensões e ambigüidades na crônica sensacionalista," 237.

68. Meyer, *Folhetim*, 341–42.

69. Do Rio, *A alma encantadora das ruas*, 85; *Fon-Fon*, 4 January 4, 1908, n.p.

70. Barreto, *Recordações do escrivão Isaías Caminha*, 199.

71. Barreto, *Recordações do escrivão Isaías Caminha*, 201.

72. *Correio da Manhã*, 10 July 1913, 3.

73. "O Folhetim," *Gazeta de Notícias*, 5 April 1907, 1.

74. "Leitores de jornais," *Fon-Fon*, 8 June 1907, n.p., emphasis in original.

75. *Correio da Manhã*, 21 October 1906, 1–3.

76. "Crime monstruoso," *Gazeta de Notícias*, 13 September 1908, 1.

77. Melo Souza, *Imagens do passado*, 212; Pedro Lima, "Reminiscência para a Historia do Cinema Brasileiro: Antônio Leal Filmou as Primeiras Cenas," *O Jornal*, 12 May 1946, 32. "A Tragédia de S. Paulo," *Careta*, 19 September 1908, n.p.

78. Antônio Leal, manuscript document, Cinemateca Brasileira, Arquivo Pedro Lima, APL/PT I, 1.

79. "O Rio vai ter uma fabrica de 'fitas' cinematográficas," *A Noite*, 19 January 1916, 1.

80. Melo Souza, *Imagens do passado*, 291; Conde, *Consuming Visions*, 77–84.

81. "Palcos e salões," *Jornal do Brasil*, 4 November 1906, 8.

82. Azevedo, *Teatro a vapor*, 46.

83. Needell, *A Tropical Belle Époque*, 134–37.

84. Azevedo, *Teatro a vapor*, 50.

85. Azevedo, *Teatro a vapor*, 51.

86. "Palcos e salões," *Jornal do Brasil*, 5 November 1906, 4.

87. A play on the subject by José de Castro was advertised at the Teatro S. José but then postponed. *Jornal do Brasil*, 11 November 1906, 14. A one-act comedy entitled "Um crime na Rua da Carioca" was performed as a supplement to another play in the Teatro Lucinda. Advertisement, *Gazeta de Notícias*, 25 November 1906, 12; advertisement, *Gazeta de Notícias*, 10 January 1907, 6.

88. "A quadrilha da morte," *Gazeta de Notícias*, 1 November 1906, 1.

89. The film was shown between 12 and 19 November. Advertisement, *Gazeta de Notícias*, 9 November 1906, 6; advertisement, *Gazeta de Notícias*, 19 November 1906, 6.

90. Advertisement, *Gazeta de Notícias*, 9 July 1908, 6.

91. Melo Souza, *Imagens do passado*, 155. I have been unable to confirm this claim in press records from the period.

92. Binóculo [pseud. Figueiredo Pimentel], *Gazeta de Notícias*, 9 July 1908, 6.

93. Leal made the film for 4 contos, and the box-office take was 57 contos. (A conto is equivalent to one thousand mil-réis, the basic unit of currency in Brazil during the period.) Antônio Leal, "As grandes industrias: 'Films,'" *Gazeta de Notícias*, 19 December 1915, 2; Melo Souza, *Imagens do passado*, 247.

94. Advertisement, *Gazeta de Notícias*, 6 July 1908, 6; advertisement, *Gazeta de Notícias*, 10 July 1908, 6.

95. Advertisements, *Gazeta de Notícias*: 3 August 1908, 6; 17 August 1908, 6; 3 September 1908, 6; 13 September 1908, 6; 16 November 1908, 6; 18 November 1908, 6.

96. Advertisement, *Gazeta de Notícias*, 12 September 1908, 6.

97. Leite, *Fortaleza e a era do cinema*, 451.

98. Advertisement, *Gazeta de Notícias*, 4 August 1908, 6.

99. The tableaux list of the film is as follows: "1. The drama of the crime. 2. On the Avenida Central. 3. Embarking at Prainha. 4. Blacksmith's Isle. 5. The first strangling. 6. Searching for the stone [used to weight down Carluccio's body]. 7. Landing at São Cristóvão. 8. The robbery. 9. Second strangling. 10. Division of the jewels. 11. The capture. 12. The informant. 13. Arrest of the first bandit. 14. On the border of Jacarepaguá. 15. Arrest of the second [criminal]. 16. Two years later. 17. In prison." Advertisement, *Gazeta de Notícias*, 4 August 1908, 6.

100. "A Tragédia de S. Paulo," *Careta*, 19 September 1908, n.p.

101. Advertisement, *Gazeta de Notícias*, 12 September 1908, 6.

102. The version of the film made by Júlio Ferrez was shown from 2–5 October in the Cinema Pathé, and from 4–8 October in the Cinema Rio Branco. Advertisements, *Gazeta de Notícias*: 2 October 1908, 8; 4 October 1908, 12; 5 October 1908, 6; 8 October 1908, 6.

103. Melo Souza, *Imagens do passado*, 247.

104. The Iris-Theater showed *A mala sinistra*, likely the film by Leal, on 23 and 24 October. Advertisement, *O Estado de São Paulo*, 23 October 1908, 7; advertisement, *O Estado de São Paulo*, 24 October 1908, 7.

105. "Notícias diversas," *O Estado de São Paulo*, 24 September 1908, 4.

106. "Palcos e circos," *O Estado de São Paulo*, 2 December 1908, 3.

107. Advertisement, *O Estado de São Paulo*, 19 September 1908, 7.
108. "Palcos e circos," *O Estado de São Paulo*, 21 September 1908, 3; "Teatros e salões," *A Ronda*, 25 September 1908, n.p.
109. Melo Souza, "As imperfeições do crime da mala."
110. Melo Souza, *Imagens do passado*, 247.
111. Melo Souza, "As imperfeições do crime da mala," 110.
112. Melo Souza, "As imperfeições do crime da mala," 111.
113. Galvão, *Crônica do cinema paulistano*, 23.
114. Melo Souza, "As imperfeições do crime da mala," 112.
115. Quoted in Vicente Paula de Araújo, *A bela época do cinema brasileiro*, 270.
116. Melo Souza, "As imperfeições do crime da mala," 109.
117. Advertisement, *Gazeta de Notícias*, 13 October 1908, 6.
118. Yumibe, *Moving Color*, 7.
119. "A mala sinistra," *Correio da Manhã*, 15 October 1908, 2.
120. "Palcos e salões," *Jornal do Brasil*, 13 October 1908, 11.
121. Binóculo, [pseud. Figueiredo Pimentel], *Gazeta de Notícias*, 13 October 13, 3.
122. Binóculo, [pseud. Figueiredo Pimentel], *Gazeta de Notícias*, 14 October 1908, 3.
123. Advertisement, *Jornal do Brasil*, 11 October 1908, 20.
124. Advertisement, *Gazeta de Notícias*, 10 March 1908, 6.
125. Burch, *Life to Those Shadows*, 193.
126. Advertisement, *Gazeta de Notícias*, 5 March 1909, 6; advertisement, *Correio da Manhã*, 29 March 1909, 8.
127. *Gazeta de Notícias*, 3 March 1909, 2.
128. Antônio Leal, manuscript document, Cinemateca Brasileira, Arquivo Pedro Lima, APL-PT/1.
129. Advertisement, *Jornal do Brasil*, 5 March 1909, 6.
130. Maria Eugenia Celso, quoted in Besse, "Crimes of Passion," 653.
131. See Caulfield, *In Defense of Honor*. See also Fausto, *Crime e cotidiano*, 173–225.
132. Fonseca, *Crimes, criminosos e a criminalidade em São Paulo*, 136–37.
133. Advertisement, *Gazeta de Notícias*, 5 March 1909, 6.
134. "Espectáculos," *Gazeta de Notícias*, 5 March 1909, 1.
135. Advertisement, *Gazeta de Notícias*, 3 March 1909, 6; advertisement, *Gazeta de Notícias,* 17 March, 1909, 6; Bernadet, *Filmografia do cinema basileiro*, n.p.
136. Advertisement, *Gazeta de Notícias*, 29 March 1909, 6.
137. Conde, *Consuming Visions*, 153.
138. "Palcos e salões," *Jornal do Brasil*, 2 April 1909, 12.
139. Advertisement, *Jornal do Brasil*, 2 April 1909, 12.
140. Advertisement, *Jornal do Brasil*, 2 April 1909, 12.
141. Advertisement, *Jornal do Brasil*, 2 April 1909, 12.
142. The film was released in the Cinema Palace on 1 April, exhibited continuously for a week, and reprised for six days in early May. Advertisements, *Gazeta de Notícias*: 1 April 1909, 6; 7 April 1909, 6; 8 May 1909, 6; 11 May 1909, 6.
143. Melo Souza, *Imagens do passado*, 286.

144. This strategy was also evident in the case of the film *O crime dos Banhados* (*The Crime of Banhados,* Francisco Santos), a reconstruction of the brutal murder of a family produced in Pelotas in the state of Rio Grande do Sul in 1913.

145. According to newspapers, Candido Castro provided direction for *O caso dos caixotes* and actor Luiz Rocha for *Um crime sensacional. Correio da Manhã,* 11 September 1912, 14; "Da platéia," *A Noite,* 8 August 1913, 4. The first film was advertisted as measuring 1,200 meters with 220 tableaux, and the second as 1,500 meters with 300 tableaux.

146. Advertisement, *Correio da Manhã,* 1 September 1912, 16, emphasis in original. On the Bonnot gang and French crime films, see Abel, "The Thrills of *Grande Peur,*" 3–8.

147. Advertisement, *Correio da Manhã,* 11 September 1912, 14.

148. "A quadrilha vermelha," *A Noite,* 3 August 1912, 1.

149. The theater advertised a legal complaint made by Barata Ribeiro's lawyer. "Da platéia," *A Noite,* 24 September 1912, 4. The revue premiered on 26 September 1912; its 113th and final performance occurred on 3 November 1912. "Da platéia," *A Noite,* 27 September 1912, 2; advertisement, *A Noite,* 2 November 1912, 8.

150. Advertisement, *Correio da Manhã,* 11 September 1912, 14.

151. "Da platéia: O 'Film nacional,'" *A Noite,* 11 September 1912, 2.

152. Advertisement, *Correio da Manhã,* 1 September 1912, 16.

153. Advertisement, *Correio da Manhã,* 11 September 1912, 14.

154. According to advertisements in the *Correio da Manhã, O caso dos calxotes* was first shown on 11 September in the Cinema Odeon and Cinema Ideal. The film was shown at the Parque Fluminense on 16 and 17 September, and in the Cinema Edison and the Cinema Lapa on 25 September.

155. According to Jean-Claude Bernadet, *O caso dos calxotes* was exhibited in three different theaters for a total of five evenings in late September and early October, before being reprised in 1914 and 1918. *Um crime sensacional* had a more limited run: four total nights of exhibition in two theaters. Bernadet, *Filmografia do cinema brasileiro,* n.p.

156. Advertisement, *Correio da Manhã,* 7 August 1913, 14.

157. Cartoon, *A Noite,* 26 July 1913, 1.

158. These terms refer to elegant gowns and tuxedos, repsectively. "Da platéia," *A Noite,* 18 August 1913, 4. After attaining rather limited success in the Lírico, "O crime do jardineiro" was later reprised in a theater in the working-class neighborhood of Cascadura.

159. "Da platéia," *A Noite,* 18 August 1913, 4.

160. "Da platéia," *A Noite,* 8 August 1913, 4. A near-identical statement appears in the *Gazeta de Notícias,* 9 August 1913, 1.

161. "O crime da Rua Fluminense," *A Noite,* 8 July 1913, 1, 3.

162. "O crime de Paula Matos," *Gazeta de Notícias,* 11 July 1913, 1.

163. "Face a face, o bandido Augusto Henriques accusa o Sr. Joaquim Freire, irmão da vítima!," *Gazeta de Notícias,* 26 July 1913, 1.

164. Advertisement, *Gazeta de Notícias*, 15 August 1913; advertisement, *Correio da Manhã*, 19 August 1913, 14; advertisement, *Correio da Manhã*, 22 August 1913, 12.

165. Unidentified press clipping, Arquivo Geral da Cidade do Rio de Janeiro, Coleção Pedro Lima, C: Cx 15/15.

166. Advertisement, *Gazeta de Notícias*, 16 August 1913, 10. Press reports suggested that the financial demands made by Henriques's wife, who had moved to Portugal because of an illness, were the motive for the crime. However, references to the "demon woman" in advertisements for *Um crime sensacional* suggest a much more active role in inciting the violence.

167. Advertisement, *Gazeta de Notícias*, 15 August 1913, 10.

168. Advertisement, *Correio da Manhã*, 15 August 1913, 4.

169. Advertisement, *Gazeta de Notícias*, 15 August 1913, 10.

170. "A Central do Brasil," *Correio da Manhã*, 10 May 1913, 3; "A estrada da morte," *Correio da Manhã*, 29 May 1913, 3; "Na Central do Brasil," *Correio da Manhã*, 13 July 1913, 5.

171. "A 'Estrada da morte,'" *Correio da Manhã*, 29 May 1913, 3.

172. "A Central é inimiga de 'fitas!,'" *A Noite*, 31 July 1913, 2.

173. Advertisement, *Gazeta de Notícias*, 15 August 1913; advertisement, *Correio da Manhã*, 19 August 1913, 14; advertisement, *Correio da Manhã*, 22 August 1913, 12.

174. Bernadet, *Filmografia do cinema brasileiro*, n.p.

4. *The Serial Craze in Rio de Janeiro, 1915–1924*

1. "Sensação e mistério!," *Palcos e Telas*, 18 December 1919, n.p.

2. "Um caso estranho," *Palcos e Telas*, 1 January 1920, n.p.

3. *A Noite*, 25 October 1917, 1, 5.

4. Freire, "Carnaval, mistério e gangsters," 147–48.

5. Freire, "Carnaval, mistério e gangsters," 158–60.

6. The term is taken from Sommer, *Foundational Fictions*. The Italian immigrant Vittorio Capellaro was an especially prolific director of literary adaptations; he adapted *O guaraní* to the screen twice, once in 1916 and again in 1926, in collaboration with Paramount, and *Iracema* in 1919.

7. By 1922, Brazil constituted one of Hollywood's top five markets outside Europe, and was in third place by 1926. Thompson, *Exporting Entertainment*, 139.

8. Melo Souza gives the date for the opening of Fox's Brazilian branch as 1916 (*Imagens do passado*, 328); Thompson gives the date as 1915 (*Exporting Entertainment*, 72).

9. Freire, "Carnaval, mistério e gangsters," 142–43.

10. "Sensação e mistério!," *Palcos e Telas*, 18 December 1919, n.p.

11. See Angenot, *Le roman populaire*, 4–7; Singer, *Melodrama and Modernity*, 281–87.

12. Singer, *Melodrama and Modernity*, 263; see also 26.

13. Stamp, *Movie-Struck Girls*, 111.

14. Hayward, *Consuming Pleasures*, 2; see also 5–8.

15. Canjels, *Distributing Silent Film Serials*, xxi.

16. Altman, "A Semantic/Syntactic Approach to Film Genre."

17. Advertisement, *Correio da Manhã*, 17 April 1917, 10.

18. Sandberg, "Location, 'Location.'"

19. "'Le film du diable,' no Odeon," *A Noite*, 13 April 1917, 5.

20. J.H.C., "Brazil as a Film Producer," *Moving Picture World*, 19 September 1917, 1990.

21. Advertisement, *Correio da Manhã*, 12 April 1917, 12; advertisement, *Correio da Manhã*, 15 April 1917, 14.

22. J.H.C., "Brazil as a Film Producer," *Moving Picture World*, 19 September 1917, 1990.

23. For a fuller summary, see Freire, "O cinema no Rio de Janeiro."

24. J.H.C., "Brazil as a Film Producer," *Moving Picture World*, 19 September 1917, 1990.

25. "Um concurso interessante," *O Paiz*, 17 November 1916, 4.

26. "'Le film du diable' no Odeon," *A Noite*, 13 April 1917, 5.

27. "'Le film du diable,'" *A Época*, 1 April 1917, 4.

28. "Um importantissimo 'film' nacional: O 'Film du diable,'" *O Imparcial*, 19 March 1917, 4.

29. "Da platéia: A cinematografia nacional," *A Noite*, 1 April 1917, 5; J.H.C., "Brazil as a Film Producer," *Moving Picture World*, 19 September 1917, 1990.

30. Advertisement, *Correio da Manhã*, 19 April 1917, 12.

31. "Um film em beneficio dos orphãos da guerra," *Correio da Manhã*, 1 April 1917, 4; advertisement, *Correio da Manhã*, 17 April 1917, 10; advertisement, *Correio da Manhã*, 22 April 1917, 12.

32. Dall'Asta, "Italian Serial Films and 'International Popular Culture,'" 304.

33. Bretas, *Ordem na cidade*, 64.

34. Giddens, *The Consequences of Modernity*, 124–28; Stephen Kern, *The Culture of Time and Space*, 259–86.

35. Gunning, "Heard over the Phone," 195.

36. This may refer to either Cato the Elder or Cato the Younger, Roman statesmen who lived in the first century BCE and were known for their conservative stances on social mores.

37. "Os ladrões e o cinema," *Selecta*, 25 August 1915, n.p.

38. This story also appeared in a Porto Alegre magazine in 1919. Steyer, *Cinema, imfrensa e sociedade em Porto Alegre*, 241.

39. Elysio de Carvalho, "Os laboratórios do crime," *Selecta*, 8 September 1915, n.p.

40. Bean, "Technologies of Early Stardom and the Extraordinary Body," 12–13.

41. Gunning, "Heard over the Phone," 188, 195.

42. Advertisement, *A Noite*, 11 April 1916, 5.

43. Beginning to rise in 1909, injuries and deaths in automobile accidents peaked in 1913 at 927 and 65, respectively, falling somewhat in the latter half of the teens. Bretas, *Ordem na cidade*, 72–73. The number of private automobiles registered in Rio de Janeiro almost doubled between 1909 and 1913, increasing from 219 to 433, while the number of cars for hire leaped from 133 to 1,675 during the same period. "O automóvel no Rio," *Selecta*, 18 August, 1915, n.p.

44. "O que lêem as crianças no Brasil," *A Noite*, 2 May 1914, 4.

45. "De volta: O novo 'Fantômas,'" *A Noite*, 2 November 1915, 2.

46. "Em pleno mistério: Wu-Fang no Rio," *A Noite*, 21 July 1916, 1.

47. "Como nos Mistérios de Nova York," *A Noite*, 31 January 1918, 4.

48. Freire, *Carnaval, mistério e gangsters*, 143–44.

49. Advertisement, *Correio da Manhã*, 30 May 1913, 16; advertisement, *A Noite*, 16 November 1915, 5; advertisement, *A Noite*, 6 February 1916, 5.

50. Advertisement, *A Noite*, 17 September 1916, 5.

51. Advertisements in *A Noite* establish the following exhibition schedule: the second episode appeared on the program on 28 March, the third not until 25 April, the fourth on 12 May, the fifth on 18 June, the sixth on 25 July, the seventh on 14 September, the eighth and ninth on 21 September, and the final episode on 4 January 1917.

52. "O romance-cinema: 'Os mistérios de Nova York,'" *A Noite*, 8 March 1916, 1.

53. Advertisement, *A Noite*, 9 March 1916, 5.

54. Advertisement, *A Noite*, 11 April 1916, 5, emphasis added.

55. Canjels, *Distributing Silent Film Serials*, 41, 51–56.

56. For details on the publication of the tie-in in Mexico, see 268n116.

57. Lima, "Na década de 10, os fã lotavam o Íris e o Ideal," 38.

58. See Dahlquist, *Exporting Perilous Pauline*; Bao, "From Pearl White to White Rose Woo."

59. Advertisement, *A Noite*, 7 November 1916, 5.

60. Advertisement, *A Noite*, 17 November 1916, 5.

61. Quoted in Melo Souza, *Imagens do passado*, 330.

62. "Klaxon," *Klaxon* 1, May 1922, 3.

63. "O romance-cinema: 'Os mistérios de Nova York,'" *A Noite*, 8 March 1916, 1. Both *truc* and *ficelle* appear in French in the original. Translating literally to "string," *ficelle* can also refer to a trick or deception.

64. Advertisement, *A Noite*, 26 April 1916, 5; Freire, *Carnaval, mistério e gangsters*, 145.

65. Tsivian, "Between the Old and the New," 39.

66. Freire, *Carnaval, mistério e gangsters*, 148, 170.

67. "Film em séries," *Palcos e Telas*, 11 April 1918, n.p.

68. Elmina S. Hart [pseud.], "Sidney, o bandido," *Palcos e Telas*, 31 March 1921, n.p.

69. "Argumentos (Gênero Pearl White)," *Palcos e Telas*, 25 July 1918, n.p.

70. Singer, *Melodrama and Modernity*, 278.

71. *Palcos e Telas*, 13 June 1918, n.p.

72. *Palcos e Telas*, 13 June 1918, n.p.

73. Leal indicates that he left for Europe in 1914 and fought briefly in the First World War before returning to Brazil; however, he does not provide exact dates. Antônio Leal, manuscript document, Arquivo Pedro Lima, Cinemateca Brasileira, APL-PT/1.

74. Antônio Leal, "As grandes industrias: 'Films,'" *Gazeta de Notícias*, 19 December 1915, 2; "O Rio vai ter uma fabrica de 'fitas' cinematográficas," *A Noite*, 19 January 1916, 1.

75. Antônio Leal, manuscript document, Arquivo Pedro Lima, Cinemateca Brasileira, APL-PT/1. See also "Uma estrela no 'film' nacional," *A Noite*, 29 August 1916, 5.

76. "Os filmes nacionais: A 'Moreninha' no cinema," *A Noite*, 9 July 1916, 2.

77. Antonio Leal, manuscript document, Arquivo Pedro Lima, Cinemateca Brasileira, APL-PT /I.

78. "A 'Luciola' no cinema: Surge no Brasil a arte cinematográfica," *A Noite*, 14 September 1916, 4.

79. Advertisement, *A Noite*, 14 December 1916, 4.

80. Advertisement, *A Noite*, 14 December 1916, 4; advertisement, *A Noite*, 16 December 1916, 5.

81. Advertisement, *A Noite*, 8 December 1916, 2; advertisement, *A Noite*, 10 December 1916, 5.

82. "A industria do cinematógrafo no Brasil: Os dois filmes nacionais desta semana," *A Noite*, 16 December 1916, 2.

83. Freire, *Carnaval, mistério e gangsters*, 159–60.

84. Freire, *Carnaval, mistério e gangsters*, 154.

85. "Os mistérios do Rio de Janeiro," *O Imparcial*, 4 March 1917, 3.

86. *Os mistérios do Rio de Janeiro, ou os ladrões de Casaca*, an 1860 novel by Antonio Jeronymo Machado Braga, included the phrase in its title. An 1881 novel with this title by José Leão Rocha is mentioned in Jadaf, *Rodapé das misceláneas*, 32. On the "mysteries-of-the-city" genre in popular literature, see Denning, *Mechanic Accents*, 85–117.

87. "Novidade literaria sensacional: Os mistérios do Rio de Janeiro," *A Noite*, 27 February 1918, 6.

88. "Cinemas: Dois 'films' nacionais," *Correio da Manhã*, 26 October 1917, 5.

89. "Cinemas: Dois 'films' nacionais," *Correio da Manhã*, 26 October 1917, 5.

90. Advertisement, *Correio da Manhã*, 23 October 1917, 10.

91. "Cinemas: Dois 'films' nacionais," *Correio da Manhã*, 26 October 1917, 5.

92. Singer, "Serial Melodrama and Narrative *Gesellschaft*," 70.

93. Undated notes, Acervo Alex Viany, reference number a5gbi7.11. Available from http://www.alexviany.com.br.

94. Advertisement, *Correio da Manhã*, 15 June 1916, 13.

95. "Cinemas: Dois 'films' nacionais," *Correio da Manhã*, 26 October 1917, 5.

96. Schroeder-Rodríguez, "Latin American Silent Cinema," 36.

97. "Cinemas: Dois 'films' nacionais," *Correio da Manhã*, 26 October 1917, 5. Singer, *Melodrama and Modernity*, 209.

98. "Cinemas: Dois 'films' nacionais," *Correio da Manhã*, 26 October 1917, 5; advertisement, *A Noite*, 22 April 1917, 2; *A Noite*, 7 August 1917, 5.

99. "Cinemas: Dois 'films' nacionais," *Correio da Manhã*, 26 October 1917, 5.

100. "Cinemas: Dois 'films' nacionais," *Correio da Manhã*, 26 October 1917, 5.

101. "A quadrilha do esqueleto," *Jornal do Brasil*, 24 October 1917, 9.

102. Freire, *Carnaval, mistério e gángsters*, 165, emphasis in original.

103. "Os mistérios do Rio de Janeiro," *O Imparcial*, 4 March 1917, 3.

104. Advertisement, *Gazeta de Notícias*, October 29, 1917, 8.

105. "Cinemas: Dois 'films' nacionais," *Correio da Manhã*, 26 October 1917, 5; advertisement, *A Noite*, 23 October 1917, 5.

106. Advertisement, *A Noite*, 24 October 1917, 5.

107. Needell, *A Tropical Belle Époque*, 74–77.

108. Advertisement, *A Noite*, 24 October 1917, 5.

109. "Cinematografia nacional: O Rio vai ter seu primeiro filme característico," *A Noite*, 20 October 1917, 1.

110. "Cinematografia nacional: O Rio vai ter seu primeiro filme característico," *A Noite*, 20 October 1917, 1.

111. Advertisement, *A Noite*, 24 October 1917, 5.

112. "Cinematografia nacional: O Rio vai ter seu primeiro filme característico," *A Noite*, 20 October 1917, 1.

113. Advertisement, *A Noite*, 24 October 1917, 5.

114. "Cinematografia nacional: O Rio vai ter seu primeiro filme característico," *A Noite*, 20 October 1917, 1.

115. "Cinematografia nacional: O Rio vai ter seu primeiro filme característico," *A Noite*, 20 October 1917, 1.

116. See Porto Rocha and Carvalho, *A era das demolições*.

117. Freire, *Carnaval, mistério e gangsters*, 165.

118. Advertisement, *Correio da Manhã*, 12 April 1917, 12.

119. Advertisement, *Correio da Manhã*, 28 October 1917, 12.

120. "Cinemas: Dois 'films' nacionais," *Correio da Manhã*, 26 October 1917, 5.

121. *A Noite*, 26 October 1917, 5.

122. On 30 and 31 October, *A quadrilha do esqueleto* was shown in the Mattoso and Haddock Lobo cinemas; on 1 November, it was exhibited in the Modelo, and on 3 and 4 November, in the Cinema Rio Branco in the nearby city of Petrópolis. *A Noite*, 30 October 1917, 2; *A Noite*, 2 November 1917, 2. Beginning on 4 January, the film was shown in São Paulo, exhibited for a single day each in the Central, the Coliseu, the Rio Branco, the Royal, the Brasil, and the São Paulo, only failing to appear on a marquee on the sixth and tenth of the month. It was then shown at the Guarani in Santos on the twelfth, returning to the state's capital to be shown in the América and the Mafalda for a single day at the end of the month, and returning to the Éden and the Mafalda in February. Bernadet, *Filmografia do cinema brasileiro 1900–1935*, n.p.

123. The film was shown in the São Pedro cinema on 6 and 7 April and in the América on the ninth and twelfth of the same month. Bernadet, *Filmografia do cinema brasileiro*, n.p.

124. A comedy and a drama by Medeiros Albuquerque, both produced by the production company, were exhibited later that year. Advertisement, *A Noite*, 9 December 1917, 5.

125. Tibiriçá went on to produce a number of sensationalistic features in the 1920s, including the 1926 *Vício e beleza* (*Vice and Beauty*), which focused on cocaine abuse, and the 1928 *O crime da mala* (*The Crime of the Trunk*), discussed in the conclusion.

126. Galvão, *Crônica do cinema paulistano*, 304.

127. Galvão, *Crônica do cinema paulistano*, 304.

128. *Selecta*, 31 January 1925, n.p.

129. "O cinema no Brasil: Telo-objetiva," *Selecta*, 24 August 1927, n.p.

130. "O cinema no Brasil: Antonia Denegri admira o cinema, por que ele tem uma infinidade de sensações!," *Selecta*, 3 January 1925, n.p.

131. Bean, "Technologies of Early Stardom and the Extraordinary Body," 18, 32.

132. The plot details are drawn from "Filmagem brasileira," *Para Todos* . . . , 8 November 1924, n.p.

133. "O cinema no Brasil," *Selecta*, 26 April 1924, n.p.

134. "O cinema no Brasil," *Selecta*, 22 November 1924, n.p.

135. I discuss the nomadic film director's career in chapter 5 in this volume.

136. I thank Luciana Corrêa de Araújo for bringing this to my attention.

137. Steyer, *Cinema, imprensa e sociedade em Porto Alegre*, 86–87.

138. Details about the publication of these serialized novels are drawn from *A Ordem*, 26 October 1917, 2; *A Ordem*, 30 November 1917, 4. *O enigma da máscara* was advertised (inaccurately) as the "first cinematographic novel in the world," making it unlikely that *Os mistérios de Nova York* was exhibited with a tie-in. *Jornal do Recife*, 20 August 1917, 6.

139. *Moderno-Jornal*, 31 May 1918, 2.

5. Regional Modernities

1. "Cinematográficas," *Selecta*, 25 October 1924, n.p.

2. Sérgio Loreto of Pernambuco viewed locally produced films privately. "O cinema no Brasil," *Selecta*, 16 December 1925, n.p.; "A opinião do nossos leitores," *Selecta*, 24 March 1926, n.p. Antonio Carlos of Minas Gerais visited the set of *Sangue mineiro*; *Selecta*, 26 June 1929, 16; he also screened *Entre as montanhas de Minas* in the governor's palace, according to *Correio Mineiro* (Belo Horizonte), 30 August 1928. Unpaginated press clipping, Coleção Pedro Lima, Arquivo Geral da Cidade do Rio de Janeiro. On the involvement of the two governors in filmmaking activities, see Corrêa de Araújo, "Melodrama e vida moderna," 121; Salles Gomes, *Humberto Mauro, Cataguases, Cinearte*, 254–55, 385.

3. Cunha Filho, *A utopia provinciana*, 218.

4. See Jung, "Local Views"; Toulmin, Popple, and Russell, *The Lost World of Mitchell and Kenyon;* Toulmin and Loiperdinger, "Is It You?"

5. Martin L. Johnson, "The Places You'll Know," 35.

6. "Onde será a Los Angeles do Brasil?," *Selecta*, 19 July 1924, n.p.; "Hollywood em miniatura," *Diário de Notícias* (Porto Alegre), 19 February 1928, 16.

7. On regional literary movements, see Bomeny, *Guardiães da razão*; Pontes de Azevedo, *Modernismo e regionalismo*.

8. Salles Gomes, *Humberto Mauro, Cataguases, Cinearte*, 299. Salles Gomes bases his estimate on figures published in *Para Todos* . . . , in turn drawn from municipal censorship files.

9. Galvão, "Cinema brasileiro," 33.

10. See especially Cunha Filho, *A utopia provinciana*; Schvarzman, *Humberto Mauro e as imagens do Brasil*.

11. Ana M. López, "Early Cinema and Modernity in Latin America," 49.
12. Pedro Lima describes the Iris movie theater, an early venue for the exhibition of serials, as "very 'chic.'" Lima, "Na década de 10, os fã lotavam o Íris e o Ideal," 38.
13. Bean, "Technologies of Early Stardom and the Extraordinary Body," 12.
14. Lefebvre, "Between Setting and Landscape in the Cinema," 23–29.
15. On travelogues and their mobilization of a nonclassical gaze, see Peterson, *Education in the School of Dreams.*
16. Lefebvre, "Between Setting and Landscape in the Cinema," 48.
17. See Salles Gomes, *Humberto Mauro, Cataguases, Cinearte,* 308–13; Shaw and Dennison, *Brazilian National Cinema,* 118–19; Xavier, *Sétima arte,* 179–81.
18. Rodrigues, *O Brasil na década de 1920,* 66.
19. Altman, "A Semantic/Syntactic Approach to Film Genre."
20. Luciana Corrêa de Araújo notes that films produced in Pernambuco deviate from this narrative pattern, in that they associate urban space with modernity and rural space with authoritarian violence. Corrêa de Araújo, "Tensões, idealizações e *ambiguidades,*" 21–22.
21. Cunha Filho, *A utopia provinciana,* 101.
22. Rodrigues, *O Brasil na década de 1920,* 22.
23. Leff, "Economic Development in Brazil." In *Coffee and Transformation in São Paulo, Brazil,* Maurício A. Font questions the degree of power held by large plantation owners during the First Republic, noting the growing importance of small landholders and the dissatisfaction of traditional elites in the years leading up to the Revolution of 1930.
24. Albuquerque Jr., *The Invention of the Brazilian Northeast,* 15.
25. Albuquerque Jr., *The Invention of the Brazilian Northeast,* 24–25.
26. Cunha Filho, *A utopia provinciana,* especially 159–68.
27. Lobato, *Cidades mortas,* 3.
28. Salles Gomes, *Humberto Mauro, Cataguases, Cinearte,* 10–11.
29. On the expansion of coffee farming and the role of independent producers in older areas of cultivation, see Font, *Coffee and Transformation in São Paulo, Brazil,* 14–15, 23–29; on exaggerated accounts of decline, see Woodward, "Cornelismo in Theory and Practice," 112.
30. Bomeny, *Guardiães da razão,* 50–56.
31. "Condor Film," *Diário do Povo* (Campinas), 16 October 1924, 1.
32. See Salles Gomes, *Humberto Mauro, Cataguases, Cinearte,* 295–354; Xavier, *Sétima arte,* 167–97.
33. Pedro Lima, "Cinema brasileiro: Um film sobre o Brasil," *Cinearte,* 22 August 1928, 7.
34. Askari, "An Afterlife for Junk Prints," 99.
35. José Franco, "A estrela morta," *A Pilhéria,* no. 256, 21 August 1926, n.p.
36. "Cinematográficas," *Selecta,* 9 August 1924, n.p.
37. "A propósito do comércio cinematográfico," *Cinearte,* 27 October 1926, 3.
38. Operador [pseud.], "Linhas atravessadas," *Para Todos . . . ,* 20 October 1923, 24.

39. Operador [pseud.], "Linhas atravessadas," *Para Todos* . . . , 20 October 1923, 24.
40. Operador No. 2 [pseud.], "Os altos e baixos da cinematografia," *Para Todos* . . . , 3 July 1920, n.p.
41. Letter from Paulo Kunhardt, "A página dos nossos leitores," *Para Todos* . . . , 6 August 1921, n.p.
42. "Crônica," *Cinearte*, 7 March 1928, 3.
43. "Crônica," *Cinearte*, 15 August 1928, 3.
44. "Cinemas e cinematografistas," *Cinearte*, 14 April 1926, 28.
45. "Cinemas e teatros," *Para Todos* . . . , 25 October 1919, n.p.
46. "Questionário," *Para Todos* . . . , 13 November 1920, n.p.
47. Letter from Roma [pseud.], "A página dos nossos leitores," *Para Todos* . . . , 25 September 1920, n.p.
48. "Crônica," *Para Todos* . . . , 9 June 1923, n.p. The Avenida Central was renamed the Avenida Rio Branco in 1912.
49. Cyclone Smith [pseud. Mario Mendonça], "A página dos nossos leitores: O Cinema em Recife," *Para Todos* . . . , 20 December 1924, n.p. Luciana Corrêa de Araújo notes identifies the reader as Mário Mendonça, who provided information about the film scene in Recife to *Para Todos* . . . and *Cinearte* for a number of years. Corrêa de Araújo, "O cinema silencioso pernambucano segundo as revistas cariocas," 236.
50. Cinema Pathé ledger, Colecção Família Ferrez, Arquivo Nacional, reference number FF-FMF6.1.0.9.
51. Ernani Vieira, "Cinematográficas . . . ," *Para Todos* . . . , 19 March 1921, n.p.
52. White had previously been the subject of another poem by a film fan in Salvador in the northeastern state of Bahia. "Cinematográficas . . . ," *Para Todos* . . . , 8 January 1921, n.p.
53. "Questionário," *Para Todos* . . . , 20 October 1923, 49.
54. *Para Todos* . . . , 14 June 1924, n.p.
55. The other two films mentioned are impossible to identify definitively, since both *The Count of Monte Cristo* and *Robinson Crusoe* were adapted to the screen multiple times during the teens and twenties in France and the United States.
56. Chapters of *The Three Musketeers* were shown in July and September 1923, suggesting that its exhibition was drawn out and irregular. "Teatros e salões," *Gazeta de Campinas*, 18 July 1923, 2; "Teatros e salões," *Gazeta de Campinas*, 25 July 1923, 1; "Teatros e salões," *Gazeta de Campinas*, 26 September 1923, 1.
57. *Diário de Notícias*, 6 May 1928, 7. The film's exhibition was advertised 31 May 1928, 11.
58. J.G., "As Lutas no cinema: Os Artistas lutam a valer," *Selecta*, 2 May 1928, n.p.
59. Smith, *Shooting Cowboys and Indians*, 187–88, 193.
60. Letter from Gil Berto [pseud.], "A página dos nossos leitores," *Para Todos* . . . , 13 January 1923, n.p.
61. Unidentified reader, "A página dos nossos leitores," *Para Todos* . . . , 14 November 1925, 7.
62. Letter from Nivea Delorme, "A página dos nossos leitores," *Para Todos* . . . , 24 March 1923, n.p.

63. Press sheet, "O vale dos martírios." Cinemateca Brasileira, reference number 1747.

64. "Notícias do cinema brasileiro: 'O vale dos martírios,'" *Correio da Manhã*, 3 February 1927, 12.

65. Pedro Lima, "Filmagem brasileira," *Cinearte*, 2 February 1927, 4; "O melhor film brasileiro de 1927," *Cinearte*, 25 April 1928, 4.

66. Quoted in Souza, "O cinema em Campinas," 20–21.

67. Fragments of the film are included in the 1973 film *Um drama caipira dedicado a Caio Scheiby* (*A Backwoods Drama Dedicated to Caio Scheiby*), directed by Carlos Roberto de Souza.

68. "'João da Mata,'" *Para Todos* . . . , 17 November 1923, 43.

69. These plot details are drawn from a program from the Rink and Colyseu movie theaters. Arquivo Geral da Cidade do Rio de Janeiro, Coleção Pedro Lima, J Cx. 1/2.

70. "'João da Mata,'" *Para Todos* . . . , 17 November 1923, 43.

71. Quoted in Mendes, *Efémerides Campineiras*, 139.

72. In addition to its four or five screenings in Campinas between 8 and 20 October, *João da Mata* was shown in Rio in a program with an installment of the imported serial *The Mysteries of Paris*; in the city of São Paulo; in several towns in the interior of the state; and in one town in Minas Gerais. Souza, "O cinema em Campinas," 54–60.

73. Stigger, "*Amor que redime*," 43–45.

74. Souza, "O Cinema em Campinas," 72–73, 88.

75. *Sofrer para gozar* program, Coleção Pedro Lima, Arquivo Geral da Cidade do Rio de Janeiro, CP/PL/S:CX 1/7.

76. The summary was published both in *Para Todos* . . . , 25 April 1925, 54, and in *Selecta*, 18 April 1925, n.p.

77. *Sofrer para gozar* program, Coleção Pedro Lima, Arquivo Geral da Cidade do Rio de Janeiro, CP/PL/S:CX 1/7.

78. Souza, "O cinema em Campinas," 90.

79. "Teatros e cinemas," *Diário do Povo*, 27 December 1923, 2.

80. Letter from Diogo de Mariz, "A opinião dos nossos leitores," *Selecta*, 17 March 1926, 5.

81. I use the term "misplaced" in the sense developed by Roberto Schwarz in *Misplaced Ideas*, 19–31.

82. Letter from Pedrinho [pseud.] of Amparo, São Paulo, "A opinião dos nossos leitores," *Selecta*, 17 March 1926, 5.

83. Quoted in Pedro Lima, "Como ingressei no cinema," *Selecta*, 8 November 1924, n.p.

84. Bicalho, "The Art of Seduction," 31.

85. Quoted in Pedro Lima, "Como ingressei no cinema," *Selecta*, 8 November 1924, n.p.

86. Letter from Angelo Thomaz Russo to Pedro Lima, Campinas, April 27, 1927, Cinemateca Brasileira, Arquivo Pedro Lima, APL-C/143.

87. Cunha Filho, *A utopia provinciana*, 26–27.

88. Cunha Filho, *A utopia provinciana*, 48.

89. Albuquerque Jr., *The Invention of the Brazilian Northeast*, 27.

90. Luciana Corrêa de Araújo, "Melodrama e vida moderna," 120.

91. Lucilla Ribeiro Bernadet, interview with Gentil Roiz, quoted in Ribeiro Bernadet, "O cinema em Pernambuco," 92.

92. Letter from an unidentified reader, "A página dos nossos leitores," *Para Todos . . .* , 14 November 1925, 7.

93. Pedro Lima, "A filmagem em Recife," *Selecta*, 18 April 1925, n.p.

94. Ribeiro Bernadet, "O cinema em Pernambuco," 47.

95. Letter from Guido Mondin, quoted in Antonio Jesus Pfeil, "Eduardo Abelim: Um primitivo do cinema gaúcho," *Correio do Povo* (Porto Alegre), 31 March 1974, 22.

96. *A Tela*, 15 September 1927. Unpaginated press clipping, Arquivo Pedro Lima, Cinemateca Brasileira, APL-G32-301.

97. *Diário de Notícias*, 4 March 1927, quoted in Antonio Jesus Pfeil, " 'Um drama nos pampas': Cinema gaúcho em tempo de 'western,' " *Correio do Povo*, 21 April 1974, 25.

98. Jota Soares, *Diário de Pernambuco*, 4 August 1963, reprinted in Soares, *Relembrando o cinema pernambucano*, 62.

99. See Singer, *Melodrama and Modernity*, 208–9.

100. Jota Soares, "Voltando a detalhar *Retribuição*," *Diário de Pernambuco*, 28 July 1963, reprinted in Soares, *Relembrando o cinema pernambucano*, 61.

101. See Gunning, "A Tale of Two Prologues."

102. The cinematographer's birth name was Manoel Chagas. Manuscript document, Arquivo Pedro Lima, Cinemateca Brasileira, APL-R/98.

103. For example, commenting on the film *Braza dormida*, the journalist Mucio Leão notes that the hero "failed to lose his habit of looking into the lens" throughout the film. Mucio Leão, "Tudo pelo amor do meu Brasil," *Jornal do Brasil*, 23 March 1929, 5. Similarly, a reviewer of the film *Revelação* complains that one of the villains "makes love to the camera." Ben Hur [pseud.], *O Libertador*, undated press clipping, Coleção Pedro Lima, Arquivo Geral da Cidade do Rio de Janeiro.

104. Unidentified press clipping, Coleção Pedro Lima, Arquivo Geral da Cidade do Rio de Janeiro.

105. *Jornal do Comércio*, 17 March 1925, 3.

106. Singer, *Melodrama and Modernity*, 208–9.

107. Didino, *O Cangaço no cinema brasileiro*, 38.

108. Ribeiro Bernadet, *O cinema em Pernambuco*, 87.

109. The film's director, Gentil Roiz, later made a promotional film for a patent medicine, which showed the treatment transforming a beggar afflicted with syphilis into a dignified young man who marries a schoolteacher. Cunha Filho, *A utopia provinciana*, 38, 134.

110. Ribeiro Bernadet, *O cinema em Pernambuco*, 87.

111. Shelley Stamp discusses how marriage, deferred throughout several installments, provided a semblance of narrative closure to serials. Stamp, *Movie-Struck Girls*, 128–32.

112. Samuel Campello, "Fitas de cinema," *Diário de Pernambuco*, 22 March 1925, 4.

113. Humberto Mauro's 1928 *Braza dormida* ends in a very similar fashion, with the couple setting off on their honeymoon in an open car.

114. Ribeiro Bernadet, *O cinema em Pernambuco*, 87–88; Hansen, "The Mass Production of the Senses," 71.

115. Letter from Izidoro Junior of Recife, "A opinião dos nossos leitores," *Selecta*, 17 March 1926, 5.

116. Carl Bennett, "Progressive Silent Film List," http://www.silentera.com/PSFL //companies/M/index.html.

117. Jota Soares, "Contribuição do interior do estado," *Diário de Pernambuco*, 17 March 1963, reprinted in Soares, *Relembrando o cinema pernambucano*, 41.

118. Salles Gomes, *Humberto Mauro, Cataguases, Cinearte*, 95–100.

119. Salles Gomes, *Humberto Mauro, Cataguases, Cinearte*, 133–34.

120. "Tesouro perdido," *O Combate* (São Paulo), 17 January 1928, unpaginated press clipping, Coleção Pedro Lima, Arquivo Geral da Cidade do Rio de Janeiro.

121. Schvarzman, *Humberto Mauro e as imagens do Brasil*, 40.

122. *O Cataguazes*, 6 March 1927, unpaginated press clipping, Coleção Pedro Lima, Arquivo Geral da Cidade do Rio de Janeiro.

123. "'O tesouro perdido' está no Rio," *Correio da Manhã*, 20 March 1927, 13.

124. "'Tesouro perdido,'" *Diário da Noite* (São Paulo), 18 February 1928, unpaginated press clipping, Coleção Pedro Lima, Arquivo Geral da Cidade do Rio de Janeiro.

125. "O melhor film brasileiro de 1927," *Cinearte*, 25 April 1928, 4.

126. Salles Gomes, *Humberto Mauro, Cataguases, Cinearte*, especially 123–26, 169–76, 367–77; Schvarzman, *Humberto Mauro e as imagens do Brasil*, 31–45.

127. "'Senhorita Agora Mesmo,'" *Cinearte*, 14 September 1927, 6.

128. Luciana Corrêa de Araújo, "Os seriados norte-americanos," 171.

129. Advertisement, *Diário de Noticias*, 14 April 1929, 10.

130. *A Tela*, 30 April 1928, unpaginated press clipping, Coleção Pedro Lima, Arquivo Geral da Cidade do Rio de Janeiro.

131. "Aurora-Film," *A Província* (Recife), 10 October 1926, 1.

132. Luciana Corrêa de Araújo, "Melodrama e vida moderna," 117.

133. Schvarzman, *Humberto Mauro e as imagens do Brasil*, 48.

134. Gomes, *Pioneiros do cinema em Minas Gerais*, 129.

135. "Entre as montanhas de Belo Horizonte," *Diário da Manhã* (Belo Horizonte), 25 January 1928, 1, press clipping, Coleção Pedro Lima, Arquivo Geral da Cidade do Rio de Janeiro.

136. "'Entre as montanhas de Minas': O Primeiro 'film' de aventuras executado em Belo Horizonte," *Correio Mineiro*, 26 August 1928, unpaginated press clipping, Coleção Pedro Lima, Arquivo Geral da Cidade do Rio de Janeiro.

137. "Cinematografia mineira: 'Entre as montanhas de Minas,'" *O Estado de Minas* (Belo Horizonte), 26 August 1928, unpaginated press clipping, Coleção Pedro Lima, Arquivo Geral da Cidade do Rio de Janeiro.

138. "'Entre as montanhas de Minas,'" *O Estado de Minas*, 30 August 1928, unpaginated press clipping, Coleção Pedro Lima, Arquivo Geral da Cidade do Rio de Janeiro.

139. "Cinematografia mineira: 'Entre as montanhas de Minas,'" *O Estado de Minas*, 26 August 1928, unpaginated press clipping, Coleção Pedro Lima, Arquivo Geral da Cidade do Rio de Janeiro.

140. "'Entre as montanhas de Minas' será a primeira pelicula da Bellorizonte Film," *O Jornal*, 10 August 1928, unpaginated press clipping, Coleção Pedro Lima, Arquivo Geral da Cidade do Rio de Janeiro. "Cinematografia mineira: 'Entre as montanhas de Minas,'" *O Estado de Minas*, 26 August 1928, unpaginated press clipping, Coleção Pedro Lima, Arquivo Geral da Cidade do Rio de Janeiro.

141. Pedro Lima, "Cinema brasileiro," *Cinearte*, 15 August 1928, 6.

142. The film's cinematographer, Rodrigo Octavio Arantes, had to call on two more-experienced cameramen working in Belo Horizonte, Igino Bonfioli and José Silva, in order to capture the sequence in which Hugo flees in his automobile. Gomes, *Pioneiros do cinema em Mina Gerais*, 59, 132.

143. "'Entre as montanhas de Minas' será a primeira pelicula da Bellorizonte Film," *O Jornal* (Rio de Janeiro), 10 August 1928, unpaginated press clipping, Coleção Pedro Lima, Arquivo Geral da Cidade do Rio de Janeiro.

144. The summary describes it as a "model establishment, where the greatest harmony between employees and overseers reigns." "'Entre as montanhas de Minas' será a primeira pelicula da Bellorizonte Film," *O Jornal* (Rio de Janeiro), 10 August 1928, unpaginated press clipping, Coleção Pedro Lima, Arquivo Geral da Cidade do Rio de Janeiro.

145. "'Entre as montanhas de Minas' será a primeira pelicula da Bellorizonte Film," *O Jornal*, 10 August 1928, unpaginated press clipping, Coleção Pedro Lima, Arquivo Geral da Cidade do Rio de Janeiro.

146. Pedro Lima, "Cinema brasileiro," *Cinearte*, 15 August 1928, 6.

147. "'Entre as montanhas de Minas' será a primeira pelicula da Bellorizonte Film," *O Jornal*, 10 August 1928, unpaginated press clipping, Coleção Pedro Lima, Arquivo Geral da Cidade do Rio de Janeiro.

148. Letter, J. H. Penna to Pedro Lima, 30 January 1930, Arquivo Pedro Lima, Cinemateca Brasileira, APL-C/331; Gomes, *Pioneiros do cinema em Minas Gerais*, 133.

149. Souza, "O cinema em Campinas," 294.

150. "'Mocidade louca,'" *Cinearte*, 7 September 1927, 6.

151. Unidentified press clipping, Coleção Pedro Lima, Arquivo Geral da Cidade do Rio de Janeiro.

152. Singer, *Melodrama and Modernity*, 151.

153. "'Mocidade louca,'" *Cinearte*, 7 September 1927, 6.

154. Souza, "O cinema em Campinas," 308.

155. "'Mocidade louca,'" *Cinearte*, 7 September 1927, 36.

156. "Teatros e cinemas—'Mocidade louca,'" *Diário do Povo*, 14 August 1927, 6.

157. Pedro Lima, "Filmagem brasileira," *Cinearte*, 7 September 1927, 4. Visual effects are also used in a scene in which the hero and heroine appeared dancing on the spinning disc of a record player, representing the heroine's daydream.

158. A. Till, *Gazeta de Campinas*, 19 July 1927, unpaginated press clipping, Coleção Pedro Lima, Arquivo Geral da Cidade do Rio de Janeiro.

159. A. Till, *Gazeta de Campinas*, 19 July 1927, unpaginated press clipping, Coleção Pedro Lima, Arquivo Geral da Cidade do Rio de Janeiro.

Conclusion

1. "Novo crime da mala," *Correio Paulistano*, 10 October 1928, 8.

2. Letter from Antonio Tibiriçá to Pedro Lima, Montevideo, 6 April 1927, Cinemateca Brasileira, Arquivo Pedro Lima, APL-C/136; letter from Antonio Tibiriçá to Pedro Lima, Montevideo, 18 May 1927, Cinemateca Brasileira, Arquivo Pedro Lima, APL-C/147; advertisement, *La Película* (Buenos Aires), 9 February 1928, unpaginated press clipping, Coleção Pedro Lima, Arquivo Geral da Cidade do Rio de Janeiro.

3. Undated letter, Coleção Pedro Lima, Arquivo Geral da Cidade do Rio de Janeiro, C:Cx 15/15.

4. For a nuanced reading of the work of Fernández that emphasizes the constitutive tensions of the nationalist projects associated with his work, see Tierney, *Emilio Fernández*.

5. Shaw and Dennison, *Brazilian National Cinema*, 73–76.

6. Desmond Arias and Goldstein, "Violent Pluralism," 4–5.

7. Denyer Willis, *The Killing Consensus*, 5.

8. Caldeira, *City of Walls*, 19–20.

9. Robb Larkins, *The Spectacular Favela*, 5.

10. Robb Larkins, *The Spectacular Favela*, 13.

11. Bentes, "The *Sertão* and the *Favela* in Contemporary Brazilian Film," 124–25.

12. Laura Podalsky, *The Politics of Affect and Emotion in Contemporary Latin American Cinema*, 8.

13. Piccato, "Murders of *Nota Roja*," 196–97.

14. Piccato, "Murders of *Nota Roja*," 198.

15. Hallin, "*La Nota Roja*."

16. William Booth, "Mexico's Crime Wave Has Left about 25,000 Missing, Government Documents Show," Americas, *Washington Post*, 29 November 2012, https://www.washingtonpost.com/world/the_americas/mexicos-crime-wave-has-left-up-to-25000-missing-government-documents-show/2012/11/29/7ca4ee44-3a6a-11e2-9258-ac7c78d5c680_story.html.

17. The figure refers to weapons whose origin could be traced. Mary Beth Sheridan, "Mexico's Calderón Tells Congress He Needs U.S. Help in Fighting Drug Wars," Nation, *Washington Post*, 21 May 2010, http://www.washingtonpost.com/wp-dyn/content/article/2010/05/20/AR2010052002911.html; U.S. Department of State, "Mérida Initiative," http://www.state.gov/j/inl/merida/.

18. Knight, "Narco Violence and the Modern State in Mexico," 126–27.
19. Eiss, "The Narco-media," 80.
20. Ed Vulliamy, "Ciudad Juárez Is All Our Futures," Mexico: Opinion, *Guardian*, 20 June 2011, http://www.theguardian.com/commentisfree/2011/jun/20/war -capitalism-mexico-drug-cartels.
21. See Ávalos, "The Naco in Mexican Film."
22. Amaya, "Authorship and the State," 506.
23. Amaya, "Authorship and the State," 516.
24. Herlinghaus, *Violence without Guilt*, 36.
25. Zavala, "Imagining the U.S.-Mexico Drug War," 342, 349.
26. Eiss, "The Narco-media," 79, 83.
27. Dana Priest, "Censor or Die: The Death of Mexican News in the Age of Drug Cartels," Investigations, *Washington Post*, 11 December 2015, https://www.washingtonpost .com/investigations/censor-or-die-the-death-of-mexican-news-in-the-age-of-drug -cartels/2015/12/09/23acf3ae-8a26-11e5-9a07-453018f9a0ec_story.html.
28. Campbell, "Narco-Propaganda in the Mexican 'Drug War,'" 60–77; Womer and Bunker, "Sureños Gangs and Mexican Cartel Use of Social Networking Sites"; Monroy Hernández et al., "The New War Correspondents."
29. Eiss, "The Narco-media," 90.
30. Eiss, "The Narco-media," 90.
31. Kirk Semple and Elizabeth Malkin, "Panel Assails How Mexico Handled Case," World: Americas, *New York Times*, 25 April 2016, http://www.nytimes.com/2016 /04/25/world/americas/inquiry-challenges-mexicos-account-of-how-43-students -vanished.html.

BIBLIOGRAPHY

Archival Sources
BRAZIL
Arquivo Geral da Cidade do Rio de Janeiro - Coleção Pedro Lima
Arquivo Nacional (Rio de Janeiro) - Coleção Família Ferrez
Biblioteca Nacional (Rio de Janeiro)
Cinemateca Brasileira (São Paulo) - Arquivo Pedro Lima
Fundação Joaquim Nabuco (Recife)
Museu da Imagem e do Som (Rio de Janeiro) - Coleção Jurandyr Noronha

MEXICO
Archivo General de la Nación (Mexico City) - Propiedad Literaria y Artística
Biblioteca Miguel Lerdo de Tejada (Mexico City)
Biblioteca Nacional (Mexico City)
Cineteca Nacional (Mexico City)
Filmoteca de la Universidad Nacional Autónoma de México (Mexico City)
Hemeroteca Nacional (Mexico City)

Periodicals
BRAZIL
Boletim de Policia (Rio de Janeiro, RJ)
Careta (Rio de Janeiro, RJ)
A Cena Muda (Rio de Janeiro, RJ)
Cinearte (Rio de Janeiro, RJ)
Correio da Manhã (Rio de Janeiro, RJ)
Correio do Povo (Porto Alegre, RS)
Correio Paulistano (São Paulo, SP)
Diário de Noticias (Porto Alegre, RS)
Diário de Pernambuco (Recife, PE)
Diário do Povo (Campinas, SP)

O Estado de São Paulo (São Paulo, SP)
Fon-Fon (Rio de Janeiro, RJ)
Gazeta de Campinas (Campinas, SP)
Gazeta de Notícias (Rio de Janeiro, RJ)
O Imparcial (Rio de Janeiro, RJ)
O Jornal (Rio de Janeiro, RJ)
Jornal do Brasil (Rio de Janeiro, RJ)
Jornal do Comércio (Recife, PE)
Jornal do Recife (Recife, PE)
Klaxon (São Paulo, SP)
Moderno-Jornal (Recife, PE)
A Noite (Rio de Janeiro, RJ)
A Ordem (Recife, PE)
Palcos e Telas (Rio de Janeiro, RJ)
Para Todos . . . (Rio de Janeiro, RJ)
A Pilhéria (Recife, PE)
A Província (Recife, PE)
A Ronda (São Paulo, SP)
Selecta (Rio de Janeiro, RJ)
A Tela (Porto Alegre, RS)
Verde (Cataguases, MG)

MEXICO
Alborada (Orizaba, VE)
Arte y Sport (Mexico City, DF)
Cinema Repórter (Mexico City, DF)
El Correo Español (Mexico City, DF)
Le Courrier du Méxique et de l'Europe (Mexico City, DF)
El Demócrata (Mexico City, DF)
El Dictamen (Veracruz Llave, VE)
Don Quijote (Mexico City, DF)
Excélsior (Mexico City, DF)
Gaceta de Policia (Mexico City, DF)
El Heraldo de México (Mexico City, DF)
El Imparcial (Mexico City, DF)
El Nacional (Mexico City, DF)
El Pueblo (Mexico City, DF)
Revista de Revistas (Mexico City, DF)
El Tiempo (Mexico City, DF)
El Universal (Mexico City, DF)
El Universal Ilustrado (Mexico City, DF)

UNITED STATES
Cine-Mundial (New York, NY)
Moving Picture World (New York, NY)

Secondary Sources

Abel, Richard. *Americanizing the Movies and "Movie-Mad" Audiences, 1910–1914*. Berkeley: University of California Press, 2006.

———. *Menus for Movieland: Newspapers and the Emergence of American Film Culture, 1913–1916*. Oakland: University of California Press, 2015.

———. "The Thrills of *Grande Peur*: Crime Series and Serials in the Belle Époque." *Velvet Light Trap* 37, no. 3 (spring 1996): 3–9.

Agostoni, Claudia. "Popular Health Education and Propaganda in Times of Peace and War in Mexico City, 1890s–1920s." *American Journal of Public Health* 96, no. 1 (2006): 52–61.

Albuquerque, Durval Muniz de, Jr. *The Invention of the Brazilian Northeast*. Foreword by James N. Green. Translated by Jerry Dennis Metz. Durham: Duke University Press, 2014.

Altman, Rick. "A Semantic/Syntactic Approach to Film Genre." *Cinema Journal* 23, no. 3 (1984): 6–18.

Amador, María Luisa, and Jorge Ayala Blanco. *Cartelera cinematográfica 1912–1919*. Mexico City: Universidad Nacional Autónoma de México, 2009.

Amaya, Hector. "Authorship and the State: Narcocorridos in Mexico and the New Aesthetics of Nation." In *A Companion to Media Authorship*, ed. Jonathan Gray and Derek Johnson, 506–24. Malden, MA: Wiley-Blackwell, 2013.

Anderson, Benedict. *Imagined Communities: Reflections on the Origins and Spread of Nationalism*. New York: Verso, 1983.

Andrew, Dudley. "An Atlas of World Cinema." In *Remapping World Cinema: Identity, Culture, and Politics in Film*, ed. Stephanie Dennison and Song Hwee Lim, 19–29. London: Wallflower, 2006.

Angenot, Marc. *Le roman populaire: Recherches en paralittérature*. Montréal: Les Presses de l'Université de Quebec, 1975.

Araújo, Luciana Corrêa de. "O cinema silencioso pernambucano segundo as revistas cariocas." *Estudos SOCINE de Cinema* IV (São Paulo: Nojesa Edições, 2005): 236–42.

———. "Melodrama e vida moderna: O Recife dos anos 20 em *A filha do advogado*." *Cadernos da pos-graduação da UNICAMP* 3 (2006): 113–28.

———. "Os seriados norte-americanos e o cinema brasileiro dos anos 1920." *Contracampo* 24, no. 1 (2012): 159–77.

———. "Tensões, idealizações e ambigüidades: As relações entre campo e cidade no cinema em Pernambuco nos anos 1920s." *Imagofagia* 8 (2013): 1–24.

Araújo, Vicente Paula de. *A bela época do cinema brasileiro*. São Paulo: Editora Perspectiva, 1976.

Askari, Kaveh. "An Afterlife for Junk Prints: Serials and Other 'Classics' in Late-1920s Tehran." In *Silent Cinema and the Politics of Space*, ed. Jennifer M. Bean, Anupama Kapse, and Laura Horak, 99–120. Bloomington: Indiana University Press, 2014.

Ávalos, Adán. "The Naco in Mexican Film: *La banda del carro rojo*, Border Cinema, and Migrant Audiences." In *Latsploitation, Exploitation Cinemas, and Latin America*, ed. Victoria Ruétalo and Dolores Tierney, 185–200. New York: Routledge, 2011.

Azevedo, Artur. *Teatro a vapor*. Edited by Gerald Moser. São Paulo: Editora Cultrix, 1977.

Bao, Weihong. *Fiery Cinema: The Emergence of an Affective Medium in China, 1915–1945*. Minneapolis: University of Minnesota Press, 2015.

———. "From Pearl White to White Rose Woo: Tracing the Vernacular Body of Nüxia in Chinese Silent Cinema, 1927–1931." *Camera Obscura* 20, no. 3 (2005): 193–231.

Barreto, Afonso Henriques de Lima. *Recordações do escrivão Isaías Caminha*. Rio de Janeiro: Editora Mérito, 1949.

Barros Lémez, Álvaro. *Vidas de papel: El folletín en el siglo XIX*. Montevideo: Monte Sexto, 1992.

Barthes, Roland. "The Reality Effect." In *The Rustle of Language*. Translated by Richard Howard, 76–82. Berkeley: University of California Press, 1989.

Bartra, Armando. "The Seduction of the Innocents: The First Tumultuous Moments of Mass Literacy in Postrevolutionary Mexico." In *Everyday Forms of State Formation: Revolution and the Negotiation of Rule in Modern Mexico*, ed. Gilbert M. Joseph and Daniel Nugent, 301–25. Durham: Duke University Press, 1994.

Beal, Sophia. *Brazil Under Construction: Fiction and Public Works*. New York: Palgrave Macmillan, 2013.

Bean, Jennifer M. "Technologies of Early Stardom and the Extraordinary Body." *Camera Obscura* 16, no. 3 (2001): 8–57.

Bentes, Ivana. "The *Sertão* and the *Favela* in Contemporary Brazilian Film." In *New Brazilian Cinema*, ed. Lúcia Nagib, 121–38. London: I. B. Tauris, 2003.

Berger, Dina. *The Development of Mexico's Tourism Industry: Pyramids by Day, Martinis by Night*. New York: Palgrave Macmillan, 2006.

Bernadet, Jean-Claude. *Filmografia do cinema brasileiro, 1900–1935: Jornal O Estado de São Paulo*. São Paulo: Secretaria da Cultura, 1979.

———. *Historiografia clássica do cinema brasileiro*. São Paulo: Annablume Editora, 1995.

Bertellini, Giorgio. *Italy in Early American Cinema: Race, Landscape, and the Picturesque*. Bloomington: Indiana University Press, 2010.

Berumen, Miguel Ángel, and Claudia Canales, eds. *México: Fotografía y Revolución*. Mexico City: Fundación Televisa, 2009.

Besse, Susan K. "Crimes of Passion: The Campaign against Wife-Killing in Brazil, 1910–1940." *Journal of Social History* 22, no. 4 (1989): 653–66.

Bicalho, Maria Fernanda Baptista. "The Art of Seduction: Representation of Women in Brazilian Silent Cinema." *Luso-Brazilian Review* 30, no. 1 (1993): 21–33.

Bomeny, Helena. *Guardiães da razão: Modernistas mineiros*. Rio de Janeiro: Editora Universidade Federal do Rio de Janeiro, 1994.

Bordwell, David, Janet Staiger and Kristin Thompson. *The Classical Hollywood Cinema: Film Style and Mode of Production to 1960*. New York: Columbia University Press, 1985.

Borge, Jason, ed. *Avances de Hollywood: Crítica cinematográfica en América Latina, 1915–1945*. Buenos Aires: Beatriz Viterbo Editora, 2005.

———. *Latin American Writers and the Rise of Hollywood Cinema*. New York: Routledge, 2008.

Bretas, Marcos Luiz. *Ordem na cidade: O exercício cotidiano da autoridade policial no Rio de Janeiro, 1907–1930*. Rio de Janeiro: Rocco, 1997.

Briseño, Lillian. *Candil de la calle, oscuridad de su casa: La iluminación en la Ciudad de México durante el Porfiriato*. Mexico City: Miguel Ángel Porrúa, 2008.

Broca, Brito. *Românticos, pre-românticos, ultraromânticos*. São Paulo: Polis, 1979.

Brooks, Peter. *The Melodramatic Imagination: Balzac, Henry James, Melodrama, and the Mode of Excess*. New Haven: Yale University Press, 1976.

Bruno, Giuliana. *Streetwalking on a Ruined Map: Cultural Theory and the City Films of Elvira Notari*. Princeton: Princeton University Press, 1993.

Buffington, Robert M. *Criminal and Citizen in Modern Mexico*. Lincoln: University of Nebraska Press, 2000.

———. *A Sentimental Education for the Working Man: The Mexico City Penny Press, 1900–1910*. Durham: Duke University Press, 2015.

Bunker, Steven B. *Creating Mexican Consumer Culture in the Age of Porfirio Díaz*. Albuquerque: University of New Mexico Press, 2012.

Burch, Nöel. *Life to Those Shadows*. Translated and edited by Ben Brewster. Berkeley: University of California Press, 1990.

Caldeira, Teresa Pires do Rio. *City of Walls: Crime, Segregation, and Citizenship in São Paulo*. Berkeley: University of California Press, 2000.

Campbell, Howard. "Narco-Propaganda in the Mexican 'Drug War': An Anthropological Perspective." *Latin American Perspectives* 41, no. 2 (2014): 60–77.

Canjels, Rudmer. *Distributing Silent Film Serials: Local Practices, Changing Forms, Cultural Transformation*. New York: Routledge, 2011.

Castillo Troncoso, Alberto del. "El surgimiento del reportaje policíaco en México: Los inicios de un nuevo lenguaje gráfico (1888–1910)." *Cuicuilco* 5, no. 13 (1998): 163–94.

Caulfield, Sueann. *In Defense of Honor: Sexual Morality, Modernity, and Nation in Early-Twentieth-Century Brazil*. Durham: Duke University Press, 2000.

Chaloub, Sidney. *Trabalho, lar e botequim: O cotidiano dos trabalhadores no Rio de Janeiro da belle époque*. São Paulo: Editora Brasilense, 1986.

Combs, C. Scott. *Deathwatch: American Film, Technology, and the End of Life*. New York: Columbia University Press, 2014.

Conde, Maite. *Consuming Visions: Cinema, Writing, and Modernity in Rio de Janeiro*. Charlottesville: University of Virginia Press, 2012.

Crary, Jonathan. *Techniques of the Observer: On Vision and Modernity in the Nineteenth Century*. Cambridge: Massachusetts Institute of Technology Press, 1990.

Cuarterolo, Andrea. *De la foto al fotograma: Relaciones entre cine y fotografía en la Argentina (1840–1933)*. Montevideo: Centro de Fotografía Ediciones, 2013.

Cunha Filho, Paulo Carneiro da. *A utopia provinciana: Recife, cinema, melancolia*. Editora Universitária Universidade Federal de Pernambuco, 2010.

Dahlquist, Marina, ed. *Exporting Perilous Pauline: Pearl White and the Serial Film Craze*. Urbana: University of Illinois Press, 2013.

Dall'Asta, Monica. "Italian Serial Films and 'International Popular Culture.'" Translated by Giorgio Bertellini. *Film History* 12, no. 3 (2000): 300–307.

Dávalos Orozco, Federico, and Esperanza Vázquez Bernal. *Carlos Villatoro: Pasajes en la vida de un hombre del cine*. Mexico City: Universidad Nacional Autónoma de México, 1999.

Debord, Guy. *Society of the Spectacle*. Detroit: Black and Red, 1983.

Debroise, Olivier. *Mexican Suite: A History of Photography in Mexico*. Translated and revised by Stella de Sá Rego. Austin: University of Texas Press, 2001.

Delgadillo, Willivaldo, et al. *La mirada desenterrada: Juárez y El Paso vistos por el cine (1896–1916)*. Ciudad Juárez: Cuadro X Cuadro, 2000.

de los Reyes, Aurelio. *Cine y sociedad en México, 1896–1930, vol. I: Vivir de sueños, 1896–1920*. Mexico City: Universidad Nacional Autónoma de México, 1983.

———. *Cine y sociedad en México, 1896–1930, vol. II: Bajo el cielo de México, 1920–1924*. Mexico City: Universidad Nacional Autónoma de México, 1993.

———. *Cine y sociedad en México 1896–1930, vol. III: Sucedió en Jalisco o los Cristeros*. Mexico City: Universidad Nacional Autónoma de México, 2013.

———. *Con Villa en México: Testimonios sobre camarógrafos norteamericanos en la Revolución*. Mexico City: Universidad Nacional Autónoma de México, 1985.

———. *Filmografía del cine mudo mexicano, 1896–1920*. Mexico City: Filmoteca de la Universidad Nacional Autónoma de México, 1986.

———. *Filmografía del cine mudo mexicano, 1920–1924*. Mexico City: Filmoteca de la Universidad Nacional Autónoma de México, 1994.

———. "Gabriel Veyre y Fernand Bon Bernard, representantes de los Hermanos Lumière en México." *Anales del Instituto de Investigaciones Estéticas* 67 (1995): 119–37.

———. "Las películas denigrantes a México." In *México/Estados Unidos: Encuentros y desencuentros en el cine*, ed. Ignacio Durán, Iván Trujillo, and Mónica Verea, 23–35. Mexico City: Instituto Mexicano de Cinematografía, 1996.

———. "The Silent Cinema." In *Mexican Cinema*, ed. Paulo Antonio Paranaguá, trans. Ana M. López, 63–78. London: British Film Institute, 1995.

Denning, Michael. *Mechanic Accents: Dime Novels and Working-Class Culture in America*. Rev. edn. New York: Verso, 1998.

Denyer Willis, Graham. *The Killing Consensus: Police, Organized Crime, and the Regulation of Life and Death in Urban Brazil*. Oakland: University of California Press, 2015.

Desmond Arias, Enrique, and Daniel M. Goldstein. "Violent Pluralism: Understanding the New Democracies of Latin America." In *Violent Democracies in Latin*

America, ed. Enrique Desmond Arias and Daniel M. Goldstein, 1–34. Durham: Duke University Press, 2010.

Didino, Marcelo. *O Cangaço no cinema brasileiro*. São Paulo: Editora Annablume, 2010.

Doane, Mary Ann. *The Emergence of Cinematic Time: Modernity, Contingency, the Archive*. Cambridge: Harvard University Press, 2001.

do Rio, João [Paulo Barreto]. *A alma encantadora das ruas*. Rio de Janeiro: H. Garnier, 1910.

———. *Cinematógrafo: Crônicas cariocas*. Porto: Livraria Chardron, 1909.

Drew, William M., and Esperanza Vázquez Bernal. "*El Puño de Hierro*: A Mexican Silent Film Classic." *Journal of Film Preservation* 10, no. 66 (2003): 10–22.

Eiss, Paul K. "The Narco-media: A Reader's Guide." *Latin American Perspectives* 195, no. 4 (2014): 78–98.

Fabio Sánchez, Fernando. "Vistas de modernidad y guerra: el documental antes y después de la Revolución, 1896–1917." In Fernando Fabio Sánchez and Gerardo García Muñoz, eds. *La luz y la guerra: El cine de la Revolución Mexicana*, 101–67. Mexico City: Consejo Nacional para la Cultura y las Artes, 2010.

Fausto, Boris. *Crime e cotidiano: A criminalidade em São Paulo, 1880–1924*. São Paulo: Editora Brasiliense, 1984.

Ferreras, Juan Ignacio. *La novela por entregas 1840–1900: Concentración obrera y economía editorial*. Madrid: Taurus, 1972.

Field, Allyson Nadia. *Uplift Cinema: The Emergence of African American Film and the Possibility of Black Modernity*. Durham: Duke University Press, 2015.

Fonseca, Guido. *Crimes, criminosos e a criminalidade em São Paulo (1870–1950)*. São Paulo: Editora Resenha Tributária, 1988.

Font, Maurício A. *Coffee and Transformation in São Paulo, Brazil*. Lanham, MD: Rowman and Littlefield, 2010.

Franco, Jean. *Cruel Modernity*. Durham: Duke University Press, 2013.

Freire, Rafael de Luna. "Carnaval, mistério e gangsters: O filme policial no Brasil (1915–1950)." PhD diss., Universidade Federal Fluminense, 2011.

———. "O cinema no Rio de Janeiro, 1914–1929." In *Nova história do cinema brasileiro*, ed. Fernão Ramos and Sheila Schvarzman. São Paulo: Serviço Social do Comércio. Forthcoming.

Friedberg, Anne. *Window Shopping: Cinema and the Postmodern*. Berkeley: University of California Press, 1994.

Fullerton, John. *Picturing Mexico: From the Camera Lucida to Film*. New Barnet, UK: John Libbey, 2014.

Gabara, Esther. *Errant Modernism: The Ethos of Photography in Mexico and Brazil*. Durham: Duke University Press, 2008.

Gallo, Rubén. *Mexican Modernity: The Avant-Garde and the Technological Revolution*. Cambridge: Massachusetts Institute of Technology Press, 2005.

Galvão, Maria Rita. "Cinema brasileiro: O período silencioso." In *Cinema Brasileiro*, ed. João Bénard da Costa and Maria José Horta Paletti, 15–77. Lisbon: Cinemateca Portuguesa, 1987.

———. *Crônica do cinema paulistano*. São Paulo: Ática, 1975.

García Canclini, Néstor. *Hybrid Cultures: Strategies for Entering and Leaving Modernity*. Translated by Christopher L. Chiappari and Silvia L. López. Minneapolis: University of Minnesota Press, 1995.

Garramuño, Florencia. *Primitive Modernities: Tango, Samba, and Nation*. Translated by Anna Kazumi Stahl. Stanford: Stanford University Press, 2011.

Garza, James Alex. *The Imagined Underworld: Sex, Crime and Vice in Porfirian Mexico City*. Lincoln: University of Nebraska Press, 2007.

Gaudreault, André, and Philippe Marion. "The Cinema as a Genealogy for the Model of Media." *Convergence* 8, no. 4 (2002): 12–18.

Gautreau, Marion. "La Revolución Mexicana a los ojos del mundo: Diferentes perspectivas en la prensa ilustrada." In *México: Fotografía y Revolución*, ed. Miguel Ángel Berumen and Claudia Canales, 119–28. Mexico City: Fundación Televisa, 2009.

Gerow, Aaron. *Visions of Japanese Modernity: Articulations of Cinema, Nation, and Spectatorship, 1895–1925*. Berkeley: University of California Press, 2010.

Giddens, Anthony. *The Consequences of Modernity*. Stanford: Stanford University Press, 1990.

Gledhill, Christine. "The Melodramatic Field: An Investigation." In *Home Is Where the Heart Is: Studies in Melodrama and the Woman's Film*, ed. Christine Gledhill, 5–39. London: British Film Institute, 1987.

Gomes, Paulo Augusto. *Pioneiros do cinema em Minas Gerais*. Belo Horizonte: Editora Crisálida, 2008.

Gonzaga, Alice. *Palácios e poeiras: 100 anos de cinemas no Rio de Janeiro*. Rio de Janeiro: Fundação Nacional de Artes, 1996.

Gonzales, Michael J. *The Mexican Revolution, 1910–1940*. Albuquerque: University of New Mexico Press, 2002.

González Casanova, Manuel, ed. *El cine que vio Fósforo: Alfonso Reyes y Martín Luis Guzmán*. Mexico City: Fondo de Cultura Económica, 2003.

———, ed. *Por la pantalla: Genesis de la crítica cinematográfica en México*. Mexico City: Universidad Nacional Autónoma de México, 2000.

Guimarães, Valéria. "Imaginários do sensacionalismo: Transferências culturais entre Brasil e França no início do século XX." *Letras* 23, no. 47 (2013): 97–123.

———. "Tensões e ambigüidades na crônica sensacionalista: O jornalismo no Rio de Janeiro e São Paulo no início do século XX." In *Nas tramas da ficção: História, Literatura e Leitura*, ed. Clóvis Gruner and Cláudio DeNipoti, 225–43. Cotia, Brazil: Editora Atliê, 2009.

Gumucio Dagron, Alfonso. *Historia del cine boliviano*. Mexico City: Filmoteca de la Universidad Nacional Autónoma de México, 1983.

Gunckel, Colin. *Mexico on Main Street: Transnational Film Culture in Los Angeles Before World War II*. New Brunswick, NJ: Rutgers University Press, 2015.

Gunning, Tom. "Before Documentary: Early Non-Fiction Films and the 'View' Aesthetic." In *Uncharted Territory: Essays on Early Non-fiction Film*, ed. Daan Hertogs and Nico de Klerk, 9–24. Amsterdam: Nederlands Filmmuseum, 1997.

————. "The Cinema of Attraction[s]: Early Film, Its Spectator, and the Avant-Garde." In *The Cinema of Attractions Reloaded*, ed. Wanda Strauven, 381–88. Amsterdam: Amsterdam University Press, 2006.

————. "Embarrassing Evidence: The Detective Camera and the Documentary Impulse." In *Collecting Visible Evidence*, ed. Jane M. Gaines and Michael Renov, 3–64. Minneapolis: University of Minnesota Press, 1999.

————. "Heard over the Phone: *The Lonely Villa* and the de Lorde Tradition of the Terrors of Technology." *Screen* 32, no. 2 (1991): 184–96.

————. "A Tale of Two Prologues: Actors and Roles, Detectives and Disguises in *Fantômas*, Film and Novel." *Velvet Light Trap* 37 (1996): 30–36.

Gutiérrez Ruvalcaba, Ignacio. "A Fresh Look at the Casasola Archive." *History of Photography* 20, no. 3 (1996): 191–95.

Guzmán, Martín Luis. *El águila y la serpiente*. Mexico City: Editorial Anahuác, 1941 [1928].

————. *The Eagle and the Serpent*. Translated by Harriet de Onís. New York: Doubleday, 1965.

Haber, Stephen. "Financial Markets and Industrial Development: A Comparative Study of Governmental Regulation, Financial Innovation, and Industrial Structure in Brazil and Mexico, 1840–1930." In *How Latin America Fell Behind: Essays on the Economic Histories of Mexico and Brazil, 1800–1914*, ed. Stephen Haber, 146–78. Stanford: Stanford University Press, 1997.

Hagedorn, Roger. "Technological and Economic Exploitation: The Serial as a Form of Narrative Presentation." *Wide Angle* 10, no. 4 (1988): 4–12.

Hallin, Daniel C. "*La Nota Roja*: Popular Journalism and the Transition to Democracy in Mexico." In *Tabloid Tales: Global Debates over Media Standards*, ed. Colin Sparks and John Tulloch, 267–84. Lanham, MD: Rowman and Littlefield, 2000.

Hansen, Miriam. *Babel and Babylon: Spectatorship in American Silent Film*. Cambridge: Harvard University Press, 1991.

————. "The Mass Production of the Senses: Classical Cinema as Vernacular Modernism." *Modernism/Modernity* 6, no. 2 (1999): 59–77.

Hardoy, Jorge E. "Theory and Practice of Urban Planning in Europe, 1850–1930: Its Transfer to Latin America." In *Rethinking the Latin American City*, ed. Richard E. Morse and Jorge E. Hardoy, 20–49. Baltimore: Johns Hopkins University Press, 1992.

Hayward, Jennifer. *Consuming Pleasures: Active Audiences and Serial Fictions from Dickens to Soap Opera*. Lexington: University of Kentucky Press, 1997.

Herlinghaus, Hermann. "La imaginación melodramática." In *Narraciones anacrónicas de la modernidad: Melodrama e intermedialidad en América Latina*, ed. Hermann Herlinghaus, 21–59. Santiago de Chile: Editorial Cuarto Propio, 2002.

————. *Violence without Guilt: Ethical Narratives from the Global South*. New York: Palgrave Macmillan, 2009.

Hershfield, Joanne. *Imagining la Chica Moderna: Women, Nation, and Visual Culture in Mexico, 1917–1936*. Durham: Duke University Press, 2008.

Hjort, Mette, and Scott MacKenzie. *Cinema and Nation*. New York: Routledge, 2000.

Holden, Robert H. *Armies without Nations: Public Violence and State Formation in Latin America, 1821–1960*. New York: Oxford University Press, 2004.

Horkheimer, Max, and Theodor W. Adorno. *Dialectic of Enlightenment*. New York: Continuum, 2002.

Hoy, Teresa van. *A Social History of Mexico's Railroads: Peons, Prisoners and Priests*. Lanham, MD: Rowman and Littlefield, 2008.

Instituto Nacional de Estadística, Geografía e Informática. *Estadísticas Históricas de México*. Mexico City: Instituto Nacional de Estadística, Geografía e Informática, 1986.

Jablonska, Aleksandra, and Juan Felipe Leal. *La Revolución Mexicana en el cine nacional: Filmografía 1911–1917*. Mexico City: Universidad Pedagógica Nacional, 1991.

Jadaf, Yasmin Nadil. *Rodapé das misceláneas: O folhetim nos Jornais de Mato Grosso, séculos XIX e XX*. Rio de Janeiro: 7 Letras, 2002.

Johnson, Martin L. "The Places You'll Know: From Self-Recognition to Place Recognition in the Local Film." *The Moving Image* 10, no. 1 (2010): 24–50.

Johnson, Randal. *The Film Industry in Brazil: Culture and the State*. Pittsburgh: University of Pittsburgh Press, 1987.

Jung, Uli. "Local Views: A Blind Spot in the Historiography of Early German Cinema." *Historical Journal of Radio, Film and Television* 22, no. 3 (2002): 253–73.

Kern, Stephen. *The Culture of Time and Space, 1880–1918*. Cambridge: Harvard University Press, 1983.

Kirby, Lynne. *Parallel Tracks: The Railroad and Silent Cinema*. Durham: Duke University Press, 1997.

Knight, Alan. "Narco Violence and the Modern State in Mexico." In *Violence, Coercion, and State-Making in Twentieth-Century Mexico: The Other Half of the Centaur*, ed. Wil Pansters, 115–34. Stanford: Stanford University Press, 2012.

———. "Popular Culture and the Revolutionary State in Mexico, 1910–1940." *Hispanic American Historical Review* 74, no. 3 (1994): 393–444.

Leal, Juan Felipe. *El documental nacional de la Revolución Mexicana: Filmografía 1910–1914*. Mexico City: Voyeur/Juan Pablos Editor, 2012.

Leal, Victor Nunes. *Coronelismo: The Municipality and Representative Government in Brazil*. Translated by June Henfry. New York: Cambridge University Press, 1977.

Lefebvre, Martin. "Between Setting and Landscape in the Cinema." In *Landscape and Film*, ed. Martin Lefebvre, 19–59. New York: Routledge, 2006.

Leff, Nathaniel H. "Economic Development in Brazil, 1822–1913." In *How Latin America Fell Behind: Essays on the Economic Histories of Mexico and Brazil, 1800–1914*, ed. Stephen Haber, 34–64. Stanford: Stanford University Press, 1997.

Leite, Ary Bezerra. *Fortaleza e a era do cinema*. Fortaleza: Secretaria de Cultura e Desporto do Ceará, 1995.

Lerner, Jesse. *El impacto de la modernidad: Fotografía criminalística en la Ciudad de México*. Mexico, D.F.: Conaculta, 2007.

Levy, David. "Re-constituted Newsreels, Re-enactments and the American Narrative Film." In *Cinema 1900/1906: An Analytical Study*, ed. Roger Holman, 243–60. Brussels: Fédération Internationale des Archives du Film, 1982.

Lima, Pedro. "Na década de 10, os fã lotavam o Íris e o Ideal." *Filme Cultura* 47 (1986): 38–39.

Lobato, José Bento Renato Monteiro. *Cidades mortas*. São Paulo: Monteiro Lobato, 1921 [1919].

Lomnitz, Claudio. *Death and the Idea of Mexico*. New York: Zone, 2008.

López, Ana M. "Calling for Intermediality: Latin American Mediascapes." *Cinema Journal* 54, no. 1 (2014): 135–41.

———. "Early Cinema and Modernity in Latin America." *Cinema Journal* 40, no. 1 (2000): 48–78.

López, Rick A. *Crafting Mexico: Intellectuals, Artisans, and the State after the Revolution*. Durham: Duke University Press, 2010.

Losada, Matt. "Allegories of Authenticity in Argentine Cinema of the 1910s." *Hispanic Review* 80, no. 3 (2012): 486–506.

Love, Joseph L. "Political Participation in Brazil, 1881–1969." *Luso-Brazilian Review* 7, no. 2 (1970): 3–24.

Ludmer, Josefina. *The Corpus Delicti: A Manual of Argentine Fictions*. Translated by Glen S. Close. Pittsburgh: University of Pittsburgh Press, 2004.

Luna, Andrés de. *La batalla y su sombra: La Revolución en el cine mexicano*. Xochimilco, Mexico: Universidad Autónoma Metropolitana, 1984.

Martín Barbero, Jesús. *De los medios a las mediaciones: Comunicación, cultura, hegemonía*. Barcelona: Ediciones G. Gili, 1987.

———. "Memory and Form in the Latin American Soap Opera." Translated by Marina Elias. In *To Be Continued: Soap Operas around the World*, ed. Robert C. Allen, 276–300. New York: Routledge, 1995.

Martínez Carril, Manuel. "*El pequeño héroe del Arroyo de Oro*." In *South American Cinema: A Critical Filmography, 1915–1994*, ed. Timothy Barnard and Peter Rist, 293–94. New York: Garland, 1996.

Martínez Pardo, Hernando. *Historia del cine colombiano*. Bogotá: Editorial América Latina, 1978.

Matabuena Peláez, Teresa. *Algunos usos y conceptos de la fotografía durante el Porfiriato*. Mexico City: Universidad Iberoamericana, 1991.

Matute, Álvaro. "Salud, familia y moral social (1917–1920)." *Históricas* 31 (1991): 25–34.

Mayer, Ruth. *Serial Fu Manchu: The Chinese Supervillain and the Spread of Yellow Peril Ideology*. Philadelphia: Temple University Press, 2014.

McCann, Bryan. *Hello, Hello Brazil: Popular Music in the Making of Modern Brazil*. Durham: Duke University Press, 2004.

Meade, Everard. "Modern Warfare Meets 'Mexico's Evil Tradition': Death, Memory, and Media During the Mexican Revolution." *InterCulture* 5, no. 2 (2008): 119–49.

Meade, Teresa A. *"Civilizing" Rio: Reform and Resistance in a Brazilian City, 1889–1930*. College Park: Pennsylvania State University Press, 1997.

Melo Souza, José Inácio de. *Imagens do passado: São Paulo e Rio de Janeiro nos primórdios do cinema*. São Paulo: Editora Senac, 2004.

———. "As imperfeições do crime da mala: Cine-gêneros e re-encenações no cinema dos primórdios." *Revista Universidade de São Paulo* 45 (2000): 106–12.

Mendes, José de Castro. *Efémerides Campineiras*. Campinas, Brazil: Editora Gráfica Palmeiras, 1963.

Meyer, Marlyse. *Folhetim: Uma história*. São Paulo: Companhia das Letras, 1996.

———. "Voláteis e versáteis: De variedades e folhetins se fez a crônica." In *A Crônica: O gênero, sua fixação e suas transformações no Brasil*, ed. Antonio Candido, 93–134. Campinas: Editora da Universidade Estadual de Campinas, 1992.

Ministério da Agricultura, Indústria e Comércio, *Recenseamento do Brasil realizado em 1 de Setembro de 1920*, vol. IV, part IV. Rio de Janeiro: Tipografia da Estadística, 1929.

Miquel, Ángel, "Las historias completas de la Revolución de Salvador Toscano." In *Fragmentos: Narración cinematográfica compilada y arreglada por Salvador Toscano, 1900–1930*, ed. Pablo Ortiz Monasterio, 23–37. Mexico City: Conaculta, 2010.

———. *Por las pantallas de la Ciudad de México: Periodistas del cine mudo*. Guadalajara: Universidad de Guadalajara, 1995.

———. *Salvador Toscano*. Guadalajara: Universidad de Guadalajara, 1997.

Monroy Hernández, Andres, et al. "The New War Correspondents: The Rise of Civic Media Curation in Urban Warfare." In *Proceedings of the 2013 Conference on Computer Supported Cooperative Work*, 1443–52. New York: Association for Computing Machinery, 2013.

Monsiváis, Carlos. *Los mil y un velorios: Crónica de la nota roja*. Mexico City: Conaculta, 1994.

Monterde, Francisco. "Carlos Noriega Hope y su obra literaria." In *Carlos Noriega Hope, 1896–1934*, ed. Francisco Monterde, 9–29. Mexico City: Instituto Nacional de Bellas Artes, 1959.

Moore, Rachel A. *Forty Miles from the Sea: Xalapa, the Public Sphere, and the Atlantic World in Nineteenth-Century Mexico*. Tucson: University of Arizona Press, 2011.

Mraz, John. *Photographing the Mexican Revolution: Commitments, Testimonies, Icons*. Austin: University of Texas Press, 2012.

Nájera Ramírez, Olga. "Engendering Nationalism: Identity, Discourse and the Mexican Charro." *Anthropological Quarterly* 67, no. 1 (1994): 1–14.

Navitski, Rielle. "Silent and Early Sound Cinema in Latin America: Local, National, and Transnational Perspectives." In *A Companion to Latin American Cinemas*, ed. Marvin D'Lugo, Ana M. López, and Laura Podalsky. New York: Routledge, forthcoming 2017.

Needell, Jeffrey D. *A Tropical Belle Époque: Elite Culture and Society in Turn-of-the-Century Rio de Janeiro*. Cambridge: Cambridge University Press, 1987.

Nieto, Jorge, and Diego Rojas. *Tiempos del Olympia*. Bogotá: Fundación Patriomonio Fílmico Colombiano, 1992.

Noriega Hope, Carlos. *El mundo de las sombras: El cine por dentro y por fuera*. Mexico City: Ediciones Andrés Botas e Hijo, 1920.

Orellana, Margarita de. *Filming Pancho: How Hollywood Shaped the Mexican Revolution*. Translated by John King. New York: Verso, 2009.

———. *La mirada circular: El cine norteamericano de la Revolución Mexicana, 1911–1917*. Mexico City: Editorial J. Ortiz, 1991.

Ortiz Gaitán, Julieta. *Imágenes del deseo: Arte y publicidad en la prensa ilustrada mexicana, 1894–1939*. Mexico City: Universidad Nacional Autónoma de México, 2003.

Ortiz Monasterio, Pablo, ed. *Fragmentos: Narración cinematográfica compilada y arreglada por Salvador Toscano, 1900–1930*. Mexico City: Conaculta, 2010.

Padilla Arroyo, Antonio. *De Belém a Lecumberri: Pensamiento social y penal en el México decimónico*. Mexico City: Archivo General de la Nación, 2001.

Paranaguá, Paulo Antonio. *Cinema na América Latina: Longe de Deus e perto de Hollywood*. Porto Alegre: L&PM Editores, 1984.

———. *Tradición y modernidad en el cine de América Latina*. Madrid: Fondo de Cultura Económica de España, 2003.

Pérez Montfort, Ricardo, ed. *Hábitos, normas y escándalo: Prensa, criminalidad y drogas durante el porfiriato tardío*. Mexico City: Plaza y Valdés Editores, 1997.

Peterson, Jennifer Lynn. *Education in the School of Dreams: Travelogues and Early Nonfiction Film*. Durham: Duke University Press, 2013.

Piccato, Pablo. *City of Suspects: Crime in Mexico City, 1900–1931*. Durham: Duke University Press, 2001.

———. "The Girl Who Killed a Senator: Femininity and the Public Sphere in Postrevolutionary Mexico." In *True Stories of Crime in Modern Mexico*, ed. Robert Buffington and Pablo Piccato, 128–53. Albuquerque: University of New Mexico Press, 2009.

———. "Murders of *Nota Roja*: Truth and Justice in Mexican Crime News." *Past and Present*, no. 223 (2014): 195–231.

———. "Public Sphere in Latin America: A Map of the Historiography." *Social History* 35, no. 2 (2010): 165–92.

Pick, Zuzana M. *Constructing the Image of the Mexican Revolution*. Austin: University of Texas Press, 2010.

Pierce, Gretchen. "Fighting Bacteria, the Bible, and the Bottle: Projects to Create New Men, Women, and Children." In *A Companion to Mexican History*, ed. William H. Beezley, 505–15. West Sussex: Wiley-Blackwell, 2011.

Podalsky, Laura. *The Politics of Affect and Emotion in Contemporary Latin American Cinema: Argentina, Brazil, Cuba, and Mexico*. New York: Palgrave Macmillan, 2011.

Pontes de Azevedo, Neroaldo. *Modernismo e regionalismo: Os anos 20 em Pernambuco*. João Pessoa: Secretaria de Educação e Cultura da Paraíba, 1984.

Porto Rocha, Oswaldo, and Lia Carvalho. *A era das demolições: Cidade do Rio de Janeiro, 1870–1920*. Rio de Janeiro: Prefeitura da Cidade do Rio de Janeiro, 1995.

Rama, Ángel. *The Lettered City*. Edited and translated by John Charles Chasteen. Durham: Duke University Press, 1996.

Ramírez, Gabriel. *El cine yucateco*. Mexico City: Filmoteca de la Universidad Nacional Autónoma de México, 1980.

Ramírez Berg, Charles. "*El automóvil gris* and the Advent of Mexican Classicism." In *Visible Nations: Latin American Film and Video*, ed. Chon Noriega, 3–32. Minneapolis: University of Minnesota Press, 2008.

Ribeiro Bernadet, Lucilla. "O Cinema em Pernambuco 1922–1931: Primera abordagem." Master's thesis, Escola de Comunicação e Artes, Universidade de São Paulo, 1970.

Rivera, Jorge B. *El folletín y la novela popular*. Buenos Aires: Centro Editor de América Latina, 1968.

Robb Larkins, Erika. *The Spectacular Favela: Violence in Modern Brazil*. Oakland: University of California Press, 2015.

Rodrigues, Marly. *O Brasil na década de 1920: Os anos que mudaram tudo*. São Paulo: Editora Ática, 1997.

Roniger, Luis. "Caciquismo and Coronelismo: Contextual Dimensions of Patron Brokerage in Mexico and Brazil." *Latin American Research Review* 22, no. 2 (1987): 71–99.

Salles Gomes, Paulo Emílio. "Cinema: A Trajectory within Underdevelopment." In *New Latin American Cinema, vol. 2: Studies of National Cinemas*, ed. Michael T. Martin, 263–71. Detroit: Wayne State University Press, 1997.

———. *Humberto Mauro, Cataguases, Cinearte*. São Paulo: Editora Perspectiva, 1974.

Sandberg, Mark B. "Location, 'Location': On the Plausibility of Place Substitution." In *Silent Cinema and the Politics of Space*, ed. Jennifer M. Bean, Anupama Kapse, and Laura Horak, 23–46. Bloomington: Indiana University Press, 2014.

Santoni, Pedro. "La policía de la Ciudad de México durante el Porfiriato: Los primeros años (1876–1884)." *Historia Mexicana* 33, no. 1 (1983): 97–129.

Santos, Sales Augusto dos. "Historical Roots of the 'Whitening' of Brazil." *Latin American Perspectives* 29, no. 1 (2002): 61–82.

Saragoza, Alex. "The Selling of Mexico: Tourism and the State, 1929–1952." In *Fragments of a Golden Age: The Politics of Culture in Mexico since 1940*, ed. Gilbert M. Joseph, Anne Rubenstein, and Eric Zolov, 91–115. Durham: Duke University Press, 2001.

Schaefer, Eric. "Exploitation as Education." In *Learning with the Lights Off: Educational Film in the United States*, ed. Devin Orgeron, Marsha Orgeron, and Dan Streible, 316–37. New York: Oxford University Press, 2012.

Schivelbusch, Wolfgang. *The Railway Journey: The Industrialization of Time and Space in the Nineteenth Century*. Berkeley: University of California Press, 1986.

Schroeder-Rodríguez, Paul A. "Latin American Silent Cinema: Triangulation and the Politics of Criollo Aesthetics." *Latin American Research Review* 43, no. 3 (2008): 33–57.

Schvarzman, Sheila. *Humberto Mauro e as imagens do Brasil*. São Paulo: Editora Universidade Estadual Paulista, 2003.

Schwartz, Vanessa. *Spectacular Realities: Early Mass Culture in Fin-de-Siècle Paris*. Berkeley: University of California Press, 1999.

Schwarz, Roberto. *Misplaced Ideas: Essays on Brazilian Culture*. New York: Verso, 1992.

Sekula, Allan J. "The Body and the Archive." *October* 39 (1986): 3–64.

Seltzer, Mark. *True Crime: Observations on Violence and Modernity*. New York: Routledge, 2007.

———. "Wound Culture: Trauma in the Pathological Public Sphere." *October* 80 (1997): 3–26.

Serna, Laura Isabel. "'As a Mexican I Feel It's My Duty': Citizenship, Censorship, and the Campaign against Derogatory Films in Mexico, 1922–1930." *Americas* 63, no. 2 (2006): 225–44.

———. *Making Cinelandia: American Films and Mexican Film Culture before the Golden Age*. Durham: Duke University Press, 2014.

———. "Mexican Film Culture at the Edge of the Caribbean: Silent Cinema in Yucatán." *Film History*, forthcoming.

———. "*La venganza de Pancho Villa*: Resistance and Repetition." *Aztlán* 37, no. 2 (2012): 11–42.

———. "'We're Going Yankee': American Movies, Mexican Nationalism, Transnational Cinema, 1917–1935." PhD diss., Harvard University, 2006.

Serrano, Federico, and Fernando G. del Moral, eds. *Cuadernos de la cineteca nacional: El automóvil gris*. Mexico City: Cineteca Nacional, 1981.

Sevcenko, Nicolau. *Literatura como missão: Tensões sociais e criação cultural na Primeira República*. Rev. edn. São Paulo: Editora Schwarz, 2003.

Shaw, Lisa and Stephanie Dennison. *Brazilian National Cinema*. New York: Routledge, 2007.

Singer, Ben. *Melodrama and Modernity: Early Sensational Cinema in Its Contexts*. New York: Columbia University Press, 2001.

———. "Modernity, Hyperstimulus, and the Rise of Popular Sensationalism." In *Cinema and the Invention of Modern Life*, ed. Leo Charney and Vanessa R. Schwartz, 72–99. Berkeley: University of California Press, 1995.

———. "Serial Melodrama and Narrative *Gesellschaft*." *Velvet Light Trap* 37 (1996): 72–80.

Smith, Andrew Brodie. *Shooting Cowboys and Indians: Silent Western Films, American Culture, and the Birth of Hollywood*. Boulder: University Press of Colorado, 2003.

Soares, Jota. *Relembrando o cinema pernambucano: Dos Arquivos de Jota Soares*. Edited by Paulo C. Cunha Filho. Recife: Editora Massangana, 2006.

Sommer, Doris. *Foundational Fictions: The National Romances of Latin America*. Berkeley: University of California, 1993.

Souza, Carlos Roberto de. "O Cinema em Campinas nos anos 20, ou, uma Hollywood brasileira." Master's thesis, Escola de Comunicação e Artes, Universidade de São Paulo, 1979.

Spencer, David R. *The Yellow Journalism: The Press and America's Emergence as a World Power*. Evanston, IL: Northwestern University Press, 2007.

Stamp, Shelley. *Movie-Struck Girls: Women and Motion Picture Culture after the Nickelodeon*. Princeton: Princeton University Press, 2000.

Steyer, Fábio Augusto. *Cinema, imprensa e sociedade em Porto Alegre, 1896–1930*. Porto Alegre: Editora da Pontífica Universidade Católica do Rio Grande do Sul, 2001.

Stigger, Helena. "*Amor que redime*: Reconstituição do pioneirismo do cinema gaúcho." In *Cinema gaúcho: Diversidades e inovações*, ed. Cristiane Freitas Gutfreind and Carlos Gerbase, 39–64. Porto Alegre: Editora Sulina, 2009.

Streeby, Shelley. *American Sensations: Class, Empire, and the Production of Popular Culture*. Berkeley: University of California Press, 2002.

———. *Radical Sensations: World Movements, Violence, and Visual Culture*. Durham: Duke University Press, 2013.

Suárez, Juana. *Critical Essays on Colombian Cinema and Culture: Cinembargo Colombia*. Translated by Laura Chesak. New York: Palgrave Macmillan, 2012.

Suárez, Juana, and Ramiro Arbeláez. "*Garras de Oro (The Dawn of Justice: Alborada de Justicia)*: The Intriguing Orphan of Colombian Silent Films." Translated by Laura A. Chesak. *Moving Image* 9, no. 1 (2009): 54–82.

Süssekind, Flora. *Cinematograph of Words: Literature, Technique, and Modernization in Brazil*. Translated by Paulo Henriques Britto. Stanford: Stanford University Press, 1997.

Tenenbaum, Barbara. "Streetwise History: The Paseo de la Reforma and the Porfirian State, 1876–1910." In *Rituals of Rule, Rituals of Resistance: Public Celebrations and Popular Culture in Mexico*, ed. William H. Beezley, Cheryl English Martin, and William E. French, 127–50. Wilmington, DE: Scholarly Resources, 1994.

Tenorio Trillo, Mauricio. "1910 Mexico City: Space and Nation in the City of the Centenario." *Journal of Latin American Studies* 28, no. 1 (1996): 75–104.

Thompson, Kristin. *Exporting Entertainment: America in the World Film Market, 1907–1934*. London: British Film Institute, 1985.

Tierney, Dolores. *Emilio Fernández: Pictures in the Margins*. Manchester, UK: Manchester University Press, 2007.

Timoteo Álvarez, Jesús, and Ascensión Martínez Riaza. *Historia de la prensa hispanoamericana*. Madrid: Editorial Mapfre, 1992.

Torre Rendón, Judith de la. "Las imágenes fotográficas de la sociedad mexicana en la prensa gráfica del porfiriato." *Historia Mexicana* 48, no. 2 (1998): 343–73.

Toulmin, Vanessa, and Martin Loiperdinger. "Is It You?: Recognition, Representation and Response in Relation to the Local Film." *Film History* 17, no. 1 (2005): 7–18.

Toulmin, Vanessa, Simon Popple, and Patrick Russell. *The Lost World of Mitchell and Kenyon: Edwardian Britain on Film*. London: British Film Institute, 2004.

Toussaint Alcaraz, Florence. *Escenario de la prensa en el Porfiriato*. Mexico City: Fundación Manuel Buendía, 1989.

Tsivian, Yuri. "Between the Old and the New: Soviet Film Culture in 1918–24." *Griffithiana*, nos. 55–56 (1996): 14–63.

———. *Early Cinema in Russia and Its Cultural Reception*. Translated by Alan Bodger. New York: Routledge, 1994.

Tucker, Lara. "*Páginas libres*: Inclusion and Representation in Early Argentine Cinematic Practices." *Revista de Estudios Hispánicos* 49, no. 1 (2015): 121–45.

Tuñón, Julia. *Historia de un sueño: El Hollywood tapatío*. Guadalajara: Universidad de Guadalajara, 1986.

Vanderwood, Paul J. *Disorder and Progress: Bandits, Police, and Mexican Development*. Lincoln: University of Nebraska Press, 1981.

Vanderwood, Paul J., and Frank N. Samponaro. *Border Fury: A Picture Postcard Record of Mexico's Revolution and U.S. War Preparedness, 1910–1917*. Albuquerque: University of New Mexico Press, 1988.

Vasey, Ruth. *The World According to Hollywood, 1918–1939*. Madison: University of Wisconsin Press, 1997.

Vaughn, Mary Kay, and Stephen E. Lewis, eds. *The Eagle and the Virgin: Nation and Cultural Revolution in Mexico, 1920–1940*. Durham: Duke University Press, 2006.

Vega Alfaro, Eduardo de la, ed. *Microhistorias del cine en México*. Guadalajara: Universidad de Guadalajara, 2000.

Vitali, Valentina, and Paul Willemen, eds. *Theorising National Cinema*. London: British Film Institute, 2006.

Waters, Wendy. "Remapping Identities: Road Construction and Nation Building in Postrevolutionary Mexico." In *The Eagle and the Virgin: Nation and Cultural Revolution in Mexico, 1920–1940*, ed. Mary Kay Vaughn and Stephen E. Lewis, 221–42. Durham: Duke University Press, 2006.

Weber, Max. "Politics as a Vocation." In *The Vocation Lectures*, ed. David Owen and Tracy B. Strong, trans. Rodney Livingstone, 32–94. Indianapolis: Hackett, 2004.

Werneck Sodré, Nelson. *Historia da imprensa no Brasil*. Rio de Janeiro: Civilização Brasileira, 1966.

Whissel, Kristen. *Picturing American Modernity: Traffic, Technology, and the Silent Cinema*. Durham: Duke University Press, 2008.

Williams, Daryle. *Culture Wars in Brazil: The First Vargas Regime, 1930–1945*. Durham: Duke University Press, 2001.

Williams, Linda. "Melodrama Revised." In *Refiguring American Film Genres: History and Theory*, ed. Nick Browne, 42–88. Berkeley: University of California Press, 1998.

———. *Playing the Race Card: Melodramas of Black and White from Uncle Tom to O. J. Simpson*. Princeton: Princeton University Press, 2001.

Wiltenburg, Joy. "True Crime: The Origins of Modern Sensationalism." *American Historical Review* 109, no. 5 (2009): 1377–1404.

Womer, Sarah, and Robert J. Bunker. "Sureños Gangs and Mexican Cartel Use of Social Networking Sites." *Small Wars and Insurgencies* 21, no. 1 (2010): 81–94.

Wood, David M. J. "Recuperar lo efímero: Restauración del cine mudo en México." In *El patrimonio de los siglos XX y XXI*, ed. Louise Noelle, 125–57. Mexico City: Universidad Nacional Autónoma de México, 2011.

Woodward, James P. "Coronelismo in Theory and Practice: Evidence, Analysis, and Argument from São Paulo." *Luso-Brazilian Review* 42, no. 1 (2005): 99–117.

Xavier, Ismail. *Sétima arte: Um culto moderno*. São Paulo: Editora Perspectiva, 1978.

Yumibe, Joshua. *Moving Color: Early Film, Mass Culture, Modernism*. New Brunswick, NJ: Rutgers University Press, 2012.

Zavala, Oswaldo. "Imagining the U.S.-Mexico Drug War: The Critical Limits of Narconarratives." *Comparative Literature* 66, no. 3 (2014): 340–60.

Websites and Online Databases

Acervo Alex Viany, http://www.alexviany.com.br.

Biblioteca Digital das Artes do Espetáculo, Museu Lasar Segall. http://www
.bjksdigital.museusegall.org.br.

Filmografia Brasileira, Cinemateca Brasileira. http://www.cinemateca.gov.br.

Fototeca Nacional, Instituto de Antropología e Historia, México. http://fototeca.inah
.gob.mx/fototeca/.

Hemeroteca Digital Brasileira, Biblioteca Nacional, Brasil. http://bndigital.bn.br
/hemeroteca-digital/.

Hemeroteca Nacional Digital de México, Universidad Nacional Autónoma de México.
http://www.hndm.unam.mx/index.php/es.

Media History Digital Library. http://mediahistoryproject.org.

Readex, Latin American Newspapers Series 1 and 2, 1905–1922. http://www.readex
.com/content/latin-american-newspapers-series-1-and-2-1805-1922.

Silent Era website. http://www.silentera.com.

INDEX

Abelim, Eduardo, 227
Accursed Gem, The, 194–95
Acre (state), 213
Actuality film, 6–7, 22, 31–35, 68, 75, 110,
    132, 149–55, 162, 166, 263n91
Adventures of Peg O' the Ring, The, 59
Affect, 13, 16–17, 202, 255
Afro-Brazilians, 141, 236, 277n37
Aitaré da praia, 232
Alagoas, 215
Alas abiertas, 89–90, 271n178
Alencar: Cacilda, 220, 223–26; José de, 140,
    169, 185
Allá en el Rancho Grande, 119
Allain, Marcel, 177
Alma encantadora das ruas, A, 135–39
Alma gentil, 206–7, 224
Altamirano, Ignacio, 87, 100, 272n5, 272n16
Alva Brothers (Carlos, Eduardo,
    Guillermo, and Salvador), 38, 50, 265n27
Álvarez, Ángel E., 77–79
Alves, Amilcar, 203, 218
Amores perros, 255
Apotheosis (in early film), 22, 50–53, 82,
    134, 153–56, 263n92
Arouca, Eduardo, 26, 168
Asalto y toma de Ciudad Juárez, 50
Assassination, 88, 257; of José Canalejas,
    263n91; of Venustiano Carranza, 36; of
    Francisco I. Madero and José María Pino

Suárez, 39; of José Manuel Pando, 23;
    of Rafael Uribe Uribe, 22; of Emiliano
    Zapata, 32
Assis, Machado de, 140
Attack and Capture of Ciudad Juárez, 50
Audiovisual Law of 1994 (Brazil), 254
Auler, William, 147
Aurora-Film, 224–26, 231
Automobile Gang, The, 33, 36, 60–63,
    68–75, 82, 89, 94, 250
Automobiles: mobility, 15, 94, 78, 131,
    203; role in crime, 55–56, 69–70, 176;
    accidents, 172–73, 176, 192, 219, 234,
    241–43, 283n43; use in film, 67–69, 216,
    227–31, 235–43 293n142. *See also* Grey
    Automobile Gang
Automóvil gris, El, 1–2, 22–24, 31–36,
    55–77, 82, 94, 105–6, 250
Aviation, 15, 78–81, 95, 196–97, 206,
    271n178
Azevedo, Artur, 147–49
Azteca Films, 99

Bachelor's Wife, The, 197, 206
Banda del automóvil, La, 24, 33, 36, 60–63,
    68–75, 82, 89, 94, 250
Barata Ribeiro, João dos Santos, 161–62
Barbosa, Albertina, 157
Barreto: Lima, 141–42; Paulo, 135–39, 142,
    277n37

Fraternal Blood, 49, 51
Freire. Adolfo, 126, 160, 163
Fuoco: Carluccio, 123, 144, 151, 279n99;
    Paulino, 123
Fusilamiento de Jáuregui, El, 23–24

Gaboriau, Émile, 140
Gaceta de Policía, 42–46, 266n53
Galindo, Marco-Aurelio, 59
Gamio, Manuel, 92
García Moreno, Gabriel, 25, 90–91, 96,
    104–9, 115, 119, 251
Garras de oro: Alborada de justicia, 22–23
Gaucho Nobility, 3
Gaumont, 155, 177, 213, 216
Gazeta de Notícias, 11, 123, 128, 135–40, 145,
    149, 153, 157, 163–64
Gender: femininity in Brazil, 124–25, 142,
    148–49, 156–59, 166, 182, 231, 234–37,
    242–44; femininity in Mexico, 36–37,
    71–82, 92–93; masculinity in Brazil,
    203, 234–44; masculinity in Mexico, 75,
    87–89, 92, 97–100. See also fifi;
    melindrosa; pelona
Genio del mal, El, 23
Ghione, Emilio, 184
Ghost Train, The, 25, 90–91, 104–19, 251
Golden Claws: The Dawn of Justice, 22–23
Gonzaga, Adhemar, 199, 207–8, 234, 237,
    246
González Iñárritu, Alejandro, 254
González: Luz, 37, 73–76; Manuel, 260n30,
    265n25; Pablo, 32–33, 65
Gran noticia, La, 87, 94
Granda, Higinio, 65–68
Grandezas de Pernambuco, As, 226
Grey Automobile, The, 1–2, 22–24, 31–36,
    55–77, 82, 94, 105–6, 250
Grey Automobile Gang, 2, 31–35, 45–46,
    52–56, 61–66, 268n98
Guarani, O, 169, 282n6
Gunche, Ernesto, 3
Guzmán, Martín Luis, 19–20, 60, 263n93

Half and Half, 95
Hart, William S, 95–98, 183

Hazards of Helen, The, 181, 197
Hei de vencer, 196–97
Heli, 256
Henriques, Secundino Augusto, 160–64,
    282n166
Herança perdida, 232
Historia completa de la Revolución, 35–36
Holmes, Helen, 36, 77, 181
Holmes, Sherlock (character), 177
Hombre sin patria, El, 76, 90, 102–3, 273n31
Horne, Walter H., 48
House of Hate, The, 58, 62
Huerta, Victoriano, 10, 51, 260n31
Hygiene. See public health

Immigrants: involvement in filmmaking,
    123, 197, 238, 282n6; involvement in film
    exhibition, 21, 150; as perpetrators of
    crimes, 66, 157; as victims of crimes, 1,
    123–24, 247
Immigration: 3, 20–21, 25, 123–24, 129–32,
    150, 157, 166, 174, 204
Imparcial, El, 11, 40–41, 44–45, 48, 261n35
In a Sister's Defense, 227
In the Springtime of Life, 232
Independence: of Latin American nations,
    9–10, 21–23, 38, 233
Indigenismo, 92–93, 101, 169
Industrialization, 2–3, 6, 12–19, 31, 258; in
    Brazil, 11, 128, 139, 199, 203–4, 208, 224,
    234, 237–42, 252; in Mexico, 9, 55, 118
Intermediality, 7–8, 13, 17–18, 186, 251,
    260n26. See also literature: novelizations
    of films
International Pictures Co., 100
Iracema, 169, 282n6
Irma Vep, 73. See also Musidora
Iron Claw, The, 59, 115, 183, 189, 197
Iron Fist, The, 25, 90–91, 104–6, 115–19, 251
I Will Triumph, 196–97

Jalisco, 93–94
João da Mata, 203, 217–28, 232, 290n72
Johnson, Noble, 228
Jóia maldita, A, 194–95
Jones, Buck, 214, 227

Pulitzer, Joseph, 23
Puño de hierro, El, 25, 90–91, 104–6, 115–19, 251

Quadrilha do esqueleto, A, 26, 168–69, 174–77, 182, 185–86, 189–94
Quando elas querem, 197, 206, 224
Queen of the South (2011 television series), 256

Race, 20–21, 41, 66, 92–93, 98–99, 131, 249, 258, 263n84
Radionovelas, 18
Railroads, 12–15, 19, 64, 85, 90–96, 104–13, 118, 160–65, 204, 211, 219–20, 239–43
Ramos, José Manuel, 90, 96
Ranchera music, 3, 248
Raza cósmica, La, 92
Recife, 27, 197, 199–209, 213, 217, 224–32, 236
Reconstruction: of events in film, 1–2, 5–7, 14, 22–26, 31–37, 64, 75, 124–26, 134, 147–68, 247–50, 281n144; of events using photography, 44–46, 57, 264n8, 266n59; of events in illustrations, 34, 45, 144–46
Red Circle, The, 183, 197
Redención, 37, 75–76
Reenactment. *See* reconstruction
Reeve, Arthur B., 179
Regional cinemas, 5–8, 25–27, 90–91, 104–20, 199–209, 216–46, 250–52
Retribuição, 203, 224–31, 237
Revelação, 235, 291n103
Revezes, 203, 226–28, 232
Revista da Semana, 136
Revista de Revistas, 55, 78, 93
Revolt of the Vaccine, 10, 131–33, 142
Revolt of the Whip, 132–33
Revolución en Veracruz, 50, 53
Revolución zapatista, 50, 52
Revolution, Mexican, 1–5, 10, 24, 32–41, 47–56, 61, 65–68, 75, 82–92, 103–9
Revolution of 1930, 11, 201, 244, 288n23
Reyes, Alfonso, 19–20, 60

Reyes Spíndola, Rafael, 38–42
Ribeiro, Chagas, 203, 226
Ricci, Felipe, 106, 203, 224, 236
Richebourg, Émile, 20
Rio de Janeiro: city, 1, 6, 10–11, 20–21, 25–27, 123–99, 206–13, 237–39, 245, 251–54; state, 204, 244
Rio Grande do Sul, 197, 205, 220, 244, 281n144
Ríos, Manuel de los, 106, 117
Robinson Crusoe, 214, 289n55
Rocambole, 56, 141, 175, 184
Rocca, Eugenio, 123, 148–50
Roiz, Gentil, 203, 225, 291n109
Roland, Ruth, 36, 181, 183, 228
Ronda, A, 152–53
Roosevelt, Theodore, 23
Rosas, Enrique, 1, 31–35, 50–53, 57, 62, 65–69, 73, 94, 99, 106
Roumagnac, Carlos, 42–43
Rural areas, 39, 68, 92, 203–4, 211, 245; settings of films in, 2–3, 25, 89, 95, 99, 209, 217–18, 226, 232–38, 260n17

Sáenz de Sicilia, Gustavo, 93
Saldanha, Judith, 164
Samba, 3, 246–48
Sánchez Valenzuela, Elena, 93
Sánchez Valtierra, Manuel, 24, 36
Sangre hermana, 49, 51
Sangue de irmão, 232
Sangue mineiro, 205, 236–38, 245n2
Santa: film (1918), 270n148; film (1931), 119
Santos, 154, 161, 172, 193–94, 248
São Paulo: city, 124–29, 132–34, 151–66, 193–201, 206, 209–11, 219–20, 224, 247–49, 253; state, 172, 185, 199, 204–5, 244
Scarlet Runner, The, 62
Selecta, 27, 175, 195–99, 207, 210, 214–15, 221, 232, 252
Selecta Film, 224
Senhorita Agora Mesmo, 234–35
Señor de los cielos, El, 256
Sensational Crime, A, 26, 126, 142, 160, 162–65, 281n145, 281n155, 282n166